Revolution
in El Salvador

SECOND EDITION

Revolution in El Salvador

From Civil Strife to Civil Peace

Tommie Sue Montgomery

Introduction by Ignacio Martín-Baró
and Rodolfo Cardenal

WESTVIEW PRESS
Boulder • San Francisco • Oxford

Copyright © 1982, 1995 by Westview Press, Inc., except maps, which are © copyright 1994 by Georgia State University, Department of Geography, Cartography Research Laboratory

Published in 1995 in the United States of America by Westview Press, Inc., 5500 Central Avenue, Boulder, Colorado 80301-2877, and in the United Kingdom by Westview Press, 36 Lonsdale Road, Summertown, Oxford OX2 7EW

Library of Congress Cataloging-in-Publication Data
Montgomery, Tommie Sue.
Revolution in El Salvador : from civil strife to civil peace . / Tommie Sue
    Montgomery : introduction by Ignacio Martín Baró and Rodolfo
    Cardenal. — 2nd ed.
        p.   cm.
    Includes bibliographical references and index.
    ISBN 0-8133-0070-3. — ISBN 0-8133-0071-1 (pbk.)
    1. El Salvador—History—1979–1992.   2. Insurgency—El Salvador—
History.   I. Title.
F1488.3.M66   1995
972.8405'3—dc20   94-5237
                                                                                          CIP

Printed and bound in the United States of America

        The paper used in this publication meets the requirements
 (∞) of the American National Standard for Permanence of Paper
        for Printed Library Materials Z39.48-1984.

10   9   8   7   6   5   4   3   2   1

A todos los salvadoreños
que aman la paz,
que han luchado de una u otra forma
por ella
y que siempre han entendido que
la paz, sin justicia, no merece tal nombre

Contents

Tables and Illustrations

xi

Photos

Acknowledgments

When I sat down twelve years ago to acknowledge all those without whose help, support, and collaboration the first edition of this book would not have been possible, I thought the list a long one. It was. That list, however, was nothing compared to the one I compiled as I worked on this new edition. Many people have given of their time, knowledge, and energy; each one of them has been precious and indispensable. In particular, my thanks go, first,

To all those who were acknowledged in the first edition, many of whom have continued to be wonderful, reliable sources of information through the years;

To the hundreds of Salvadoreans from all walks of life and all political persuasions who have given generously of their time to help me learn about and understand the trauma and complexity of the changes through which their country has passed;

To a succession of U.S. ambassadors to El Salvador and assorted other U.S. officials who have been generous despite our disagreements.

Those in El Salvador whom I especially want to acknowledge—some of whom I could not even admit knowing in 1982—include

Ignacio Martín-Baró and Segundo Montes, who were colleagues, friends, and bottomless founts of information;

Ricardo Stein and Antonio Cañas, former directors of the University Center for Research and Documentation (CUDI) at the Universidad Centroamericana José Simeón Cañas (UCA), who are brilliant political analysts;

Monseñor Ricardo Urioste, the retired vicar general of the archdiocese of San Salvador, and María Julia Hernandez, director of the archdiocesan human rights office, Tutela Legal, whose kindness, insight, courage, and faith have been a constant inspiration;

Rubén and María Ester Zamora, who have shared their lives, their home, and their rich understanding of El Salvador for fourteen years;

Roberto Cañas, who under another name was the first Salvadorean revolutionary to take the time to help this *gringa* understand what it means to be a revolutionary;

Francisco Altschul, Juan José Martel, and Miguel Sáenz, who have spent more hours than any of us can count over thirteen years explaining, updating, and analyzing conditions;

Marisol Galindo, Norma Guevara, Ana Guadalupe Martínez, and María Marta Valladares (Nidia Díaz), who among many other women across the political spectrum have contributed to my understanding of women's conditions;

Mauricio Melendez of the COPREFA staff, who facilitated many interviews with army officers;

Colonel Carlos Rolando Herrarte, who continued to talk with me even after he knew we disagreed profoundly in our respective analyses of the Salvadorean reality.

Since September 1991, many U.N. officials have shared their knowledge and expertise; the persons most responsible for facilitating these contacts are Mario Zamorano, who until the end of 1992 was ONUSAL's public information officer; Michael Gucovsky, the deputy chief of mission from April 1993 to February 1994; and Henry Morris, the mission coordinator.

In the United States, Peter Kornbluh of the National Security Archive and Janet di Vicenzo, formerly of the Archive, were helpful in securing U.S. government documents that have been released under the Freedom of Information Act.

Librarians at the U.S. Army War College provided access to original interviews done for an oral-history project on the war in El Salvador.

Heather Foote and David Holiday, both formerly of the Washington Office on Latin America and now, respectively, of the Unitarian Universalist Service Committee and Americas Watch, have long supported my research in a variety of ways.

Some of the best journalists to report from El Salvador have shared their knowledge, insight, and, occasionally, contacts with me; they include Mauricio Burgos, Douglas Farah, Tom Gibb, Cindy Karp, Thomas Long, Mary Jo McConahay, Ivan Montecínos, Chris Norton, Sandra Smith, and Frank Smyth.

Colleagues who have been especially helpful and supportive include Bill Bollinger of the University of California–Los Angeles, Martin Diskin of the Massachusetts Institute of Technology, Dennis Gilbert of Hamilton College, Bill Stanley of the University of New Mexico, Mercedes de Uriarte of the University of Texas, and George Vickers of the Washington Office on Latin America.

Special thanks are due Jeff McMichael of Georgia State University's Geography Department for his patience and skill in preparing the maps and organizing the tables.

There are several former students who are responsible for helping this book come together:

Nicola Poser, currently a graduate student at the University of Massachusetts–Amherst, prepared the bibliography;

Teresa Beckham, currently a graduate student at the University of North Carolina, translated the introduction;

Katherine Robinson worked on an earlier translation of Martín-Baró's original introduction;

Joni Saxon, a graduate student at Georgia Southern University, accompanied me on one research trip to El Salvador and carried out library research in Atlanta;

Catherine Murphy collaborated on a collateral research project on women in politics in El Salvador, conducting several interviews that have been useful in this edition.

Thanks also to Carlos Gamba, for tolerating with good humor my periodic travels to El Salvador and for supporting many days in front of the computer with his culinary skills.

Some research for this edition was carried out with the aid of faculty summer research grants from Dickinson College and Agnes Scott College. Collateral research on Salvadorean refugees in Belize was done in 1991 under a Fulbright grant. Last-minute information in late 1993 and early 1994 was obtained during my research under a North-South Center grant.

Tommie Sue Montgomery

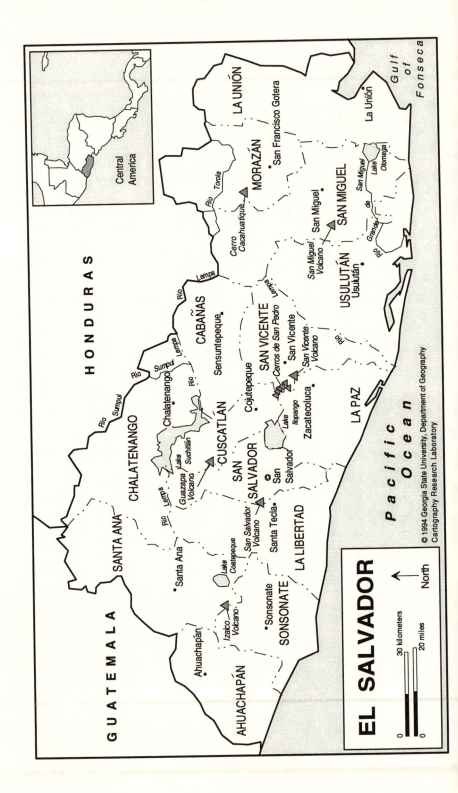

EL SALVADOR

Ignacio Martín-Baró and
Rodolfo Cardenal

Introduction—Fifteen Years Later: Peace at Last

On October 15, 1979, a coup d'etat executed by a group of young officers in the Salvadorean army put an end to a regime serving a social minority that had become increasingly dependent on the bloody repression of the masses and of any opposition group. As this work of Tommie Sue Montgomery well documents, those people, both civilian and military, who most committed themselves to this first renewal movement, saw themselves displaced from the government by those in power more accustomed to the subtleties of spy games. Therefore, the political project that the Christian Democratic Party of El Salvador embraced in 1980 was already compromised by the corrupt orders of the Armed Forces of El Salvador. Recognizing this fact, a group of Christian Democrats decided to break away from the project and from the party for political and even strictly ethical reasons.

When on June 1, 1989, almost ten years later, Alfredo Cristiani assumed the presidency of El Salvador, having triumphed in the elections as the candidate of the Nationalist Republican Alliance (ARENA), a cycle of Salvadorean history appeared to end. ARENA, a party of the extreme right, came into being as a political instrument to defend the interests of the Salvadorean economic elite during the unstable period after the 1979 coup. The party therefore had the clear objective of impeding any efforts to bring about serious social change. In 1982 ARENA scared the U.S. government with a partial victory in the Constituent Assembly elections and with the decision to place for election as president ARENA's founder and leader, former National Guard major Roberto D'Aubuisson—a man publicly recognized as the principal promoter

---

Ignacio Martín-Baró wrote a draft to introduce this book, titled "Ten Years Later: The War Continues," but he was unable to finish. The enemies of truth and light took his life violently, together with the lives of five other Jesuits, in the dawn of November 16, 1989. At the request of Tommie Sue Montgomery, I have taken the draft of Martín-Baró and have finished it, adding the last two years of negotiation and the signing of the peace treaty on January 16, 1992. For this reason I left his name and his ideas about the ten years of civil war. However, the war did not continue: "Fifteen Years Later: Peace at Last" seems to be arriving.   —Rodolfo Cardenal

1

of the death squads. It was the less than democratic diplomacy of General Vernon Walters that impeded that premature blow against U.S. interventionism in El Salvador and that placed Alvaro Magaña in the presidency. Similarly it was, at least partially, CIA money that won the election for José Napoleón Duarte in 1984 when the United States was again faced with the threat of D'Aubuisson. In 1988, however, conditions had changed, and with the resigned acquiescence of the U.S. Embassy, ARENA was able to recover for the bourgeoisie control of the Legislative Assembly that since 1985 had been in the hands of the Christian Democrats. ARENA's victory in the 1989 presidential elections completed the recovery of the state apparatus by the same social forces that had possessed it before 1979—but it was only for a short time because within two and a half years, they had to accept important changes in their political agenda.

It would be misleading, however, to think that everything returned to the status quo ante and that in El Salvador nothing substantial changed during the ten painful years between 1979 and 1989. ARENA's electoral victory did not completely return to the Salvadorean capitalist sector its previous control over the full apparatus of the state, much less its control over where and how people lived. It did return a divided state and a country in civil war. It suffices to look at the principal actors on the political battlefield of the country to understand that ARENA's triumph was not simply a restoration of the traditional Salvadorean regime—the reestablishment of the order of "the Fourteen Families."

ARENA did not have control over the Armed Forces, the U.S. government, or the forces of the Frente Farabundo Martí para la Liberación Nacional (FMLN). Above all, ARENA did not return to the Salvadorean oligarchy its control over the Armed Forces. The war permitted the Armed Forces significant institutional autonomy in economic power, which had been traditionally subordinated. Between 1980 and 1989, the army increased its size four times over, achieving financial development with interests of its own, including interests in competition with those of the bourgeoisie. As much as ARENA rose in power, it still had to negotiate with an army that was not disposed to lose some of its privileges or engage in politics that would generate problems with its new patron: the U.S. government.

The second actor that escaped the force of ARENA was the U.S. government. If, as Montgomery argues, the United States began to interfere significantly in the politics of the country only after 1960 with the coup d'etat against José María Lemus, after 1979 and the coup d'etat against General Carlos Humberto Romero, the interference turned into quasi-colonial domination. An examination of the period 1980–1992 clearly shows that "the embassy" constituted the principal force in the Salvadorean conflict: U.S. advice and financing defined the direction of the war from the government's side. U.S. aid (plus the remittance of thousands of Salvadoreans in the United States, which increased to several hundred thousand dollars annually) impeded the collapse of the Salvadorean economy. U.S. diplomacy promoted and managed internationally the cause of the Salvadorean government. Finally, negotiations to end the war were delayed or advanced according to the interests of U.S. foreign policy.

The third force over which, obviously, ARENA could not exercise control with its electoral triumphs was the FMLN. In a decade the FMLN accumulated military power made even more impressive in that it resisted the multimillion-dollar military aid of the United States, the giant development of the Armed Forces, the violent war between 1981 and 1983 (including a massive campaign of state and parastate terrorism), and a prolonged counterinsurgent war that unfolded between 1984 and 1991. It should be kept in mind that all of these developments took place in a country where the army could dispatch an air transport in twenty minutes to any corner of the national territory.

In addition to having limited control over the state apparatus when it attained power, ARENA encountered a country that was materially destroyed and socially polarized. The socioeconomic conditions of the majority of the Salvadorean populace are worse in 1993 than in 1979. If this situation of mass misery, caused by unjust and oppressive sociopolitical structures, was the fundamental cause of the conflict, the end of the war has given way to a new phase in the history of the country, one in which a new opportunity is presented to reconstruct the country in the intermediate and long term. The forces whose interests ARENA defends politically not only were principally responsible for the historical situation of injustice that caused the conflict, but over the years they also were the crucial actors in the development of the war. Through their systematic decapitalization and compulsive impoverishment of the country, in the opinion of some economists, they harmed the national economy more than the war itself. They also were responsible for these unjust conditions by their permanent politics of encouraging the war with their militaristic solution to the conflict and, worse, by their participation in the "dirty war" through the creation and financing of those paramilitary forces known as "death squads." They were responsible because, as Montgomery demonstrates, they actively participated in the socioeconomic and military policies developed during these years—first by aligning with the government and the assembly elected in 1982 but above all, by resisting and even opposing, against all reason, the socioeconomic and political changes without which the country could not be viable in the future.

In this sense, a book such as this constitutes a valuable historical record, particularly now that the armed conflict has ceased and some sectors are interested in having the origin and development of the war forgotten. With the return of ARENA to power there appeared a mystifying political discourse that was nothing but a variant of the discourse given by the Reagan administration. If for Ronald Reagan the Salvadorean war was the consequence of "communist aggression" executed from Cuba and Nicaragua, for ARENA the responsibility was attributed to the governmental reformism of the Christian Democrats, whose "communitarianism" had a simple cryptic variant: communist. In both cases, the fundamental causes of the armed conflict in El Salvador were ignored because they were assigned to forces considered "the enemies," and this focus allowed both the United States and the social groups that were backing ARENA to elude their historical responsibility.

It is evident that the Christian Democratic administration not only was inefficient, given that it did not achieve the purpose of peace and economic recovery that it initially proposed, but also that with the passage of the years, the administration was drowning in its own corruption. In good logic, however, the same and with greater reason could be said by ARENA about the Salvadorean Armed Forces: In spite of its disproportionate growth, in spite of the most specialized advisers and the best armaments to the point of saturation, in spite of consuming half of the national budget and an even greater part of international aid, and in spite of having free rein to develop a total war, including a massive "dirty war" campaign (state terrorism), and then a systematic counterinsurgency war afterward, the Armed Forces did not defeat the FMLN or weaken it significantly. This failure, recognized even by U.S. military analysts, was ignored in ARENA's official discourse, which directed all of its arsenal against the reformism of the Christian Democratic Party, demonizing it and blaming it for everything bad, to the point of talking about a lost decade: the 1980s.

This work of Tommie Sue Montgomery reviews the history that provides the reasons for the Salvadorean conflict—a history that Reagan ignored, that ARENA tries to forget, and that the mass media tend to omit as if events began the moment they began to report the problems. Given the "official story," fabricated in San Salvador or Washington, and given the events "without a story" of many journalistic reports, it is important to recall the roots of a civil war that, for its duration, turned into something familiar and unquestioned.

The need to keep the historical memory alive requires that this deplorable chapter written by the Reagan administration in its policy toward Central America—and more concretely toward El Salvador—not be closed without further consideration, especially when officials from this era freely declare that they were always in favor of peace. Reagan should not be made a scapegoat for prolonging the Salvadorean civil war (as some members of ARENA did at times), but it is undeniable that his administration must accept a large part of the responsibility. It was not in vain during these twelve years that the United States appropriated $6 billion for the Salvadorean conflict, nor was it in vain that the U.S. government became the new patron of the Salvadorean Armed Forces. The theoretical pretense was to "professionalize" the Salvadorean army and turn it into a pillar of democracy. The practical reality was to create an institution totally disproportionate to the size of the country, structurally opposed to any reform of its privileges and prerogatives, and convinced of its supremacy over other national institutions and, therefore, of its primacy over civilian power and even over the law itself. It could be said that the only Latin American institution that successive U.S. administrations truly trust is the army, although they later show great indignation for the Pinochets and the Noriegas—in great part U.S. creations—and the systematic political torture and death squads.

The brutal massacre of the six university Jesuits in the early hours of November 16, 1989, by an elite battalion trained by U.S. officials was one of the determining elements that changed the political orientation in Washington. This brutal murder appears to have opened the eyes of the architects of U.S. policy to the impossibility of professionalizing the Salvadorean army and of converting it into a pillar of democracy. It was then that they understood, in part due to the FMLN's general offensive that also occurred in November, the impossibility of winning the war with that army, the futility of establishing a democracy with the institution that most violated human rights, the complete failure of their foreign policy, and the fact that they had squandered billions of dollars. After November 1989, Washington began to look for a dignified way to disentangle itself from the chaotic situation that it helped create in one of its backyards.

As Montgomery well demonstrates, the Reagan administration had three objectives with its policy toward Central America: to depose the revolutionary government of Nicaragua, to establish a permanent military base in Honduras, and to defeat the Salvadorean FMLN militarily—all of which was done, of course, with the justification of promoting democracy in these countries. Five years after the Reagan decade, it is obvious from the blood and destruction, from the death and suffering that this militaristic policy scattered over Central America, that the policy was a failure.

This is not about mystifying the Salvadorean conflict as if it were merely a result of Latin culture, incompatible with a democratic order, or as if the United States did not have anything to do with its cause and development. Even though, according to the declarations of the late President Duarte, the interference of the embassy in the business of his government reached the point of wanting to choose ministers, Salvadorean history would be poorly understood with the elimination of the preponderant and powerful role of the U.S. government. Nothing is more disorienting, in this sense, than documents like those of the Kissinger commission that, by omission, seem completely to exempt the United States from any causal responsibility for the problems in the area. Historical memory is important not only so that present and future U.S. administrations do not continue committing the same or equivalent mistakes, but also so that they do not try to limit their analysis and responsibility to the moment in which a presidency begins. A bad diagnosis could only with difficulty lead to a good policy; the almost obsessive anticommunism of the Reagan administration resulted in a poor diagnosis of Central America's problems, and the consequent policy could only lead to the misfortune seen today.

In this manner the United States understood the situation after the FMLN's military offensive and the murder of the Jesuits. After that the United States looked for a means to disengage from the embarrassing situation in which it found itself in El Salvador. It is in this context that support for negotiations to the point of directly pressuring President Cristiani to overcome his and the army's resistance is understood. From this new U.S. determination, the negotiating process advanced rapidly and culminated in the signing of the peace accords in Chapultepec (Mexico) on January 16, 1992.

Not only the United States obtained benefits from the peace accords. ARENA was able to end the war in exchange for losing political space. Although it conceded the need for change with some hesitation, ARENA accepted both the failure of repression as a means of suppressing social conflict and the necessity for implementing reforms to modernize the state and society. At the same time, however, ARENA managed to maintain the capitalist economic model and its program of structural change. The FMLN politically unblocked the military stalemate at an international juncture that was unfavorable to the political possibilities of armed struggle. Instead, it accepted the capitalist economic order and existing state institutions to the point that political space was opened for it to act on and about these institutions. In the negotiations, the FMLN accepted much, almost too much, if we keep in mind the evolution of its positions concerning the economy and the state.

The Armed Forces, the third force that ARENA did not control, also came away from the negotiations with some benefits. First, the Armed Forces found a dignified out. Neither its existence nor certain economic privileges were questioned in exchange for reducing and purging the military. Second, a change in doctrine and subordination to civilian authority implied structural modifications for the army; nevertheless, the army continues to be a preponderant power. As long as the army exists, the possibility of using it as a destabilizing or counterrevolutionary force exists. This is a threat from which even the oldest Latin American democracies are not free.

The popular majority won an increase in political space; it incorporated into the culture a respect for human rights, an increase in representation, better general security, and benefits of the reconstruction plan in the old conflict zones. Still, members of the majority lost time and space for their historical project—a bitter result of the historical shortsightedness of their leaders who in 1979 bet on a radical exit that never appeared.

An objective evaluation of the advantages and disadvantages that the peace treaty afforded the different actors shows that all of them obtained important advantages just as all ceded important points. Whatever the case, the actor that lost the most was not the oligarchy but the popular majority, which could not make its historical agenda advance because it only won the power to promote that agenda in the future.

What is the significance of the peace accords after the failure of the socioeconomic model from before 1979 and after almost twelve years of civil war? What perspectives does it open for the future? The accords offer a good diagnosis of the political and social situation in El Salvador because they also try to respond to its most urgent problems. The greater part of the accords is dedicated to one of the fundamental elements of the diagnosis: the demilitarization of society, which is treated with extreme care and detail. The Armed Forces no longer will enjoy absolute power over civilian society and the law but rather will be dominated by the civilian sector. Together with demilitarization, a new concept of public security has been imposed, expressed in the elimination of the security forces, all of the paramilitary groups, and the office of military intelligence—all instruments of repression and a dirty war for decades. These groups are being replaced by a new police force (the National Civilian Police), whose fundamental characteristic will be to enforce human rights and political pluralism. These two basic elements of the peace accords, both of which support the new era that El Salvador has begun, are complemented by two other accords, also very important: the human rights accord, which guarantees the end of individual and group summary executions and torture; and the constitutional reform accord, which has substantially modified the judicial and electoral systems.

If the peace accords are fulfilled, the militarization that has characterized El Salvador for more than a decade will give way to democratization; effective participation of all political and social forces respecting differing ideas, ideologies, and creeds will be possible. To accomplish this, the country must learn to argue, to abandon dogmatism and sectarianism, and to respect differences. This has not been the practice, but without these changes it will not be possible to reach the consensus necessary for democratization.

In these new circumstances, the political presence of the FMLN will contribute to the transformation of the political scene and political battles. The FMLN has the capacity to do it because its ranks include many committed to continue working for social justice inside a democratic context. By late 1992 the FMLN was reported to have basic party structures in 230 municipalities and all fourteen of the country's departments. As a result, it is possible that the great political decisions increasingly will appear in the fight for survival of the masses, who live in the urban centers and in the sparsely populated rural zones most affected by the history of poverty. The government will find itself obligated to defend its programs with political instruments because the most powerful instrument of its past domination, the political and ideological support of the army, is gone.

In this manner the popular majority, which tends to be marginalized, now has the challenge of beginning to participate in directing the nation's destiny, forcing both the traditional political parties and the government to face popular demands directly and clearly. Keeping the army concentrated in its barracks opens space that can be used to express the demands of the popular majority. The first is a necessary condition for the second. It is in this manner, then, that the accords announce great political changes, so many that some speak of the birth of a new nation; others, more skeptical, still doubt the viability of the process after so many disappointments. Still, the peace accords include sufficient guarantees to ensure their fulfillment.

The first guarantee is the ability the opposition now has to supervise the government through the Peace Consolidation Commission (COPAZ). The second guarantee comes from the international community, which has not been disposed to permit any noncompliance with the accords. The commitment of the United States, the most determinant exogenous factor, has been clear. The enemies of before have turned into political voices with whom the future of the country can be discussed. Meanwhile, the friends of the dirty war of yesterday, the extreme military and political right, have changed into the new terrorists in the era of peace, as they were personally told by U.S. Secretary of State James Baker in El Salvador the day after the signing of the accords.

The mission of the United Nations in El Salvador is another fundamental guarantee to ensure compliance with the accords. This presence has three elements. First, the U.N. has responsibility for supervising respect for human rights. Second, it guarantees compliance with the stages agreed upon for arriving at the definitive end of the war and the complete integration of the

FMLN into the nation's political life. Third, it is responsible for observing and verifying the 1994 elections.

Last but not least, there is the guarantee of the organized people themselves, who monitor implementation of the accords to ensure full compliance. In 1992 one could anticipate that the 1994 election campaign would not be like those of the past, merely propaganda, but rather an arena where diverse political forces and distinct ideologies would participate freely and openly, generating not only political openness but also the possibility for people to vote for the party that best matched their aspirations.

The risks and difficulties of peace do not lie as much in the possibility of noncompliance with the peace accords as in the limited agreements on the other great Salvadorean problem: the unjust economic and social structure. Together with militarization of the society, this is the most vital theme for the immediate future in El Salvador because herein lies the fundamental root of the conflict now ended. Coordinating economic policy among the various social sectors cannot happen without opening to question and reformulation the prevailing economic model, with all its macroeconomic achievements and the social contradictions it has generated. The great challenge, which still has no adequate solution, is how to alleviate the scandalous level of present poverty with a program of structural adjustment. The first concern in the economic area is reconstruction, which is treated generically and vaguely in the peace accords; the concept implies that the present government has the capacity to impose its plan, but there is no guarantee that the plan will be the best for the nation. Nonetheless, it requires a certain consensus between the FMLN and the government because although the government has the financial advantage, the FMLN has the productive advantage. Still, only the pressure of donors and the popularly organized sectors will be able to guarantee these minimal agreements.

There also exists the danger of reducing the construction of the new country to its material aspects, forgetting that it is necessary to solidly establish new ethical principles. The first of these is the truth that is owed to the country. The false speakers of reconciliation have appeared, inviting the people to forget the past—the massive and systematic violations of human rights of tens of thousands of Salvadoreans. They proposed a general amnesty, understood as "forgive and forget," which is to say, an amnesty that would directly benefit the military personnel responsible for these violations. They even had the effrontery to ask that the Salvadorean people forget the best that they have: their dead *compañeros* and their martyrs. Reconciliation will never be reached through extending impunity because it can only be the fruit of truth and justice.

The first difficulties in the implementation process of the peace accords appeared in the most conflictive aspects of the national reality. Almost all of these difficulties came from the extreme political and military right, which Baker called "terrorist." This powerful group was intransigent and now, faced with the inevitable, has looked for ways to derail the peace accords, including political assassinations in late 1993. The most resistant sector of this group is tied to agricultural exports and deplores the end of militarism because, historically, it was the instrument the oligarchy used to avoid economic development and social and political transformation. The peace accords did not question the capitalistic system or the democratic state but rather oligarchical capitalism and its corresponding militarized state. The accords provide a great opportunity to defeat the oligarchy and its political and economic models and put an end to the militarism that has permitted its dominance for decades and has impeded the economic and political development of El Salvador. The oligarchical model is obsolete, and those who persist in trying to maintain it go against history.

The historical distrust that exists in El Salvador will only be overcome if the progressive capitalist sector has the political capacity to ally itself with other social forces instead of merely conceding some social and labor improvements to defeat those extreme oligarchical sectors. In this sense discussion of the neoliberal model is secondary, given the historic challenge that this alliance between progressive capitalism and other social forces represents to end oligarchical predominance over the productive apparatus and the state. The leadership of the FMLN understands this; in his speech at the ceremony marking the beginning of the cease-fire on February 1, 1992, Commander Joaquin Villalobos said, "We believe in the right to legitimate enrichment, based on the effort of work; we believe in individual liberty, but we do believe that without social sensibilities, riches instead of being a motor of development converts itself into a creator of conflict. We do not believe in the monopoly of riches and political power," he continued. "The problem is not that rich people exist, but rather that there are so few of them and that the majority of Salvadorans are extremely poor."

At first glance, the alliance between the progressive capitalist sector and the social movement could appear strange and even contradictory. On closer examination, it can be seen that things are not as contradictory as they appear. In the peace accords there is an implicit pact between progressive capitalism, supported by the United States and the international financial community, and the project of the FMLN. For both, the oligarchical agenda lacks future; therefore, both accept reforms (such as in agriculture) but not the loss of power. The alliance is possible because it has real foundations grounded in certain common interests, and it is necessary in order to take down the repressive apparatus that has sustained the hegemony of the oligarchy.

Surprisingly, the government of President Cristiani showed signs of not having political clarity about the possibilities of this process. His promise to modernize the state, the economy, and the society vacillated, when it was not contradictory. His government found itself trapped between the majority in ARENA who opted for a hard-line posture without a vision for the future and the small sector inclined to commit to the country's modernization.

El Salvador is finally moving toward a more economically and socially modern society. This movement, however, is a process; the fundamental key is that the participants work to continue advancing the process because each firm step makes it more irreversible. This book, with its detailed discussion and analysis of the significant actors, not only explains how El Salvador came to this juncture but also demonstrates why the failure of this process would be a calamity of historic proportions for all Salvadorans.

Prologue: Recollections and Reflections— Fifteen Years in El Salvador

Christmas Eve 1983: In Jucuarán, near the Pacific Ocean in southeastern El Salvador, the guerrillas of the Farabundo Martí Front for National Liberation (FMLN) are throwing a party for the townspeople. There are music and dancing before the midnight Mass that will be celebrated in the parish church by Father Rogelio Ponseele, a Belgian priest who has spent many years in the country, the last three of them in the mountains. A guerrilla approaches a North American journalist and hands her a slip of paper.

"Do you know this book? Can you get me a copy?"

The journalist stares at the piece of paper and bursts out laughing. "I have the book and I know the author," she says. On the paper is written:

"Tommie Sue Montgomery"

"Revolution in El Salvador"

"242 pages"

Two weeks later I arrived in El Salvador. As I walked into the hotel, the journalist, whom I will call Marie, happened to be in the lobby. She greeted me, then pulled me out of earshot.

"Did you bring any copies of your book with you? Can you spare one?" She related the events of Christmas Eve.

"What are you doing next Tuesday? I'm going back down there. Can you go? If so, I can deliver both the book and the author."

The next Tuesday, however, found me before daybreak on my way not to guerrilla territory but to San Miguel, located two and a half hours east of the capital (see Map P.1). Thanks to serendipity, which often provides rich and unexpected research opportunities in El Salvador, I had piggybacked onto two journalists' request for an interview with Colonel Domingo Monterrosa, commander of the Third Brigade and widely regarded as the Salvadorean army's most capable field commander. Monterrosa would die later that year in a helicopter crash caused by a bomb planted by the FMLN. But on Monday morning the journalists and I found ourselves by chance seated together in front of Lieutenant Colonel Ricardo Cienfuegos,[1] director of COPREFA, the

11

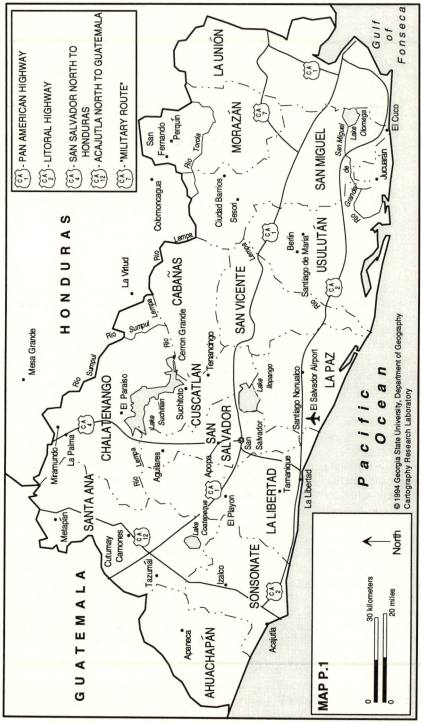

MAP P.1 Highways and place names of El Salvador

Colonel Domingo Monterrosa,
commander of the Third Brigade,
San *Miguel, 1983–1984.*

army press office; they wanted an interview with Monterrosa, Cienfuegos assumed we were together, so he picked up the phone, called the colonel, and arranged an interview for all three of us in less than a minute. I decided that the guerrillas could wait a few hours. Tuesday morning Monterrosa ushered us into his office promptly at 9:00 A.M. and said he could give us fifteen minutes. Monterrosa was bright, articulate, and concise. He said more in twenty minutes than many interviewees say in two hours.

The day had only begun, however. The two journalists returned to the capital to file their stories, while I waited for Marie at an open-air restaurant frequented by U.S. military advisers assigned to the Third Brigade. An hour and a half and one flat tire later Marie arrived. After a forty-five-minute ride, we turned down an all-weather road and a kilometer later ran into a guerrilla roadblock. Marie parked, walked over to the *muchachos* (boys), introduced herself, and said she was expected. I recognized one of the guerrillas; he had been part of the FMLN roadblock on the way to San Miguel early that morning. Marie explained my presence ... and we waited. The radioman, who looked to be no more than eighteen, communicated frequently with a base camp somewhere.

A short time later, a young man dressed in blue shirt and pants and a silver hard hat walked up. For a time he sat across the road from the pickup truck the rebels had "liberated" (their word) that morning from ANDA, the government water works agency. Then he walked over to the pickup and, after a few minutes of conversation, broke out a large bag of tiny pills and began pouring them into a clear plastic bag, which he handed over to the guerrillas. After the young man returned to sit under his tree, I walked over to ask him what the pills were and why he had given them to the FMLN. He was a health promoter working for the Ministry of Health out of San Salvador, and the pills were antimalarial.

"Don't you have to account for them?" I asked.

"It's just a matter of bookkeeping."

"But why give them to the guerrillas?"

"Look," he explained patiently, "the pills are for the people, and I know if I give them to the guerrillas they will get to the people."

"But aren't you afraid you'll get caught?" I persisted.

He shrugged his shoulders and chuckled. "No. Everybody does it."

This encounter, like many others over the course of a decade, raised the issue of hidden support for the FMLN. All such examples suggested a level of popular support for the revolutionary movement that was unseen and unreported. But my reflection was interrupted by the guerrillas signaling to us that permission to enter the zone had been received. A bone-jarring, two-hour ride later we entered the town of Jucuarán, which the Salvadorean army had abandoned without warning the previous September. A local official, with whom I talked on condition of anonymity and who was not an FMLN partisan, asserted that "on no level is there cooperation between civil officials and the guerrillas. ... I ... have nothing to do with them, nor they with me." He said that after the FMLN returned there was a meeting between the civilians and guerrillas in the town hall during which the FMLN told them "they hadn't come to interrupt [their] work."

"There is no fear of the guerrillas, " the official added. Before the army left, he said, there was a corporal who had raped and killed several girls and women, but everyone was too afraid to say anything. "Now," he said, "we can sleep without fear at night." Their "biggest danger," he continued, was when Jucuarán citizens went to Usulután. Families with sons in the Sixth Brigade would go to visit them, and "when the army sees they are from Jucuarán, they are taken, beaten, and detained. What we want," he concluded, "is that if the army has any doubt about someone living here, that they investigate first, before capturing and beating people."[2]

Marie and I slept on sheetless cots in the local health clinic, which looked as if it had not seen a doctor, nurse, or patient in five years. Nosing around I found packages of Noriday birth control pills all of which had long since expired, the oldest in October 1975 and the most recent in November 1977. I wondered how recently they had been given to women. There were also fliers promoting vasectomies.

Early Wednesday morning a courier took my book and disappeared. In the following hours I interviewed Father Rogelio Ponseele[3] and talked to the guerrilla who had greeted us on the highway the day before and was later

FMLN Comandante Pedro (David Pereira Rivera) gives instructions to one of his combatants, Zambel Villalta, southeastern El Salvador, January 1984. In 1994 Pereira was elected to the Legislative Assembly from Sonsonate.

driving the ANDA pickup. I discovered that two constituent groups of the FMLN were operating in the area: the Revolutionary Army of the People (ERP) and the Armed Forces of Liberation (FAL). Members of both groups had been at the roadblock Tuesday morning and on the road to Jucuarán that afternoon, an indication of growing unity in the FMLN. The driver, an eighteen-year-old named "Zambel," was a friendly sort from the FAL who suggested I might like to talk to the FAL commander as well as the ERP commander whom I expected to see. Zambel, however, wanted something in return: my tape recorder. We struck a deal: If he could produce Comandante Pedro, he could have my tape recorder. I did not think Zambel would deliver.[4]

Shortly thereafter three guerrillas who had driven us into Jucuarán appeared in a jeep. Marie had departed for San Salvador; I climbed into the jeep along with the men, all armed, courtesy of the U.S. government, with M-16s. Another bone-jarring hour later the road ended and we continued on foot. Fifteen minutes later my escort and I walked into a guerrilla camp.

In early 1984, FMLN forces could be found in concentrations of a few dozen to several hundred guerrillas. As the Salvadorean air force increased aerial bombings in 1983 and 1984, these concentrations became untenable, and units were broken down into self-sufficient platoons of fifteen or fewer combatants. The camp in Jucuarán was not only base for the elite Rafael Arce Zablah battalion (BRAZ) but also a guerrilla training camp. At the time of my visit, there were twenty-five trainees, including five women. When I arrived

Comandantes Balta
(Juan Ramón
Medrano) and
Filomena (Janeth
Samour Hasbun) wait
for a Cessna 0-2
"push-pull" airplane
to leave the valley in
which their guerrilla
camp was located.

they were marching four abreast and six deep up and down a soccer field, counting all the way. The training officer later explained that most recruits were illiterate; counting while marching taught them numbers as well as order and discipline.

Two hours after I arrived, five new recruits walked into camp with their guide. In an interview later that evening, the five men told me they had walked for three days from *haciendas* in the Department of San Miguel that had become cooperatives during the 1980 agrarian reform. In 1980–1981, they said, their situation improved because the government was providing technical and credit assistance. After 1982, however (when the right-wing ARENA party captured control of the Constituent Assembly and proceeded to gut the agrarian reform), their economic situation deteriorated to the point that they were earning less than they had before the reform. They also charged that the army and National Guard came every month to demand a "security payment," and the younger men said that they avoided recruitment into the army "by leaving the house whenever the army came to round us up." A twenty-year-old named Dubla said that soldiers had killed his mother and three aunts two years earlier, that his father was "already a collaborator," and that he expected his nineteen-year-old sister to arrive in camp soon. German, at forty-four the "old man" of the group, spoke for them all when he explained why they had decided to join the FMLN: "We decided to fight because we like what [the FMLN] is doing; we saw that this organization is seeking the liberation of the people."[5]

Early the next morning I received a handwritten note from Comandante Filomena (Janeth Samour Hasbun, the political officer) telling me the hour of my interview.[6] Before that, however, I made my way down to the creek to wash out some shirts. There I found two women washing breakfast dishes: heavy plastic plates from the U.S. Agency for International Development. No one could explain how at least fifteen AID plates had gotten to a guerrilla camp in southeastern El Salvador.

Two days after talking with Colonel Monterrosa, I was seated under an open-sided, thatched-roof chapel interviewing Juan Ramón Medrano, known as Comandante Balta, and Comandante Filomena. Balta was then the FMLN's commander in chief of the southeastern front—roughly one-sixth of the country. Suddenly we heard the drone of an airplane. A "push-pull," a search plane that carries up to fourteen rockets, appeared at the opposite end of the long valley. Balta and Filomena got up and quickly moved toward a creek about fifty meters away, while I scrambled to grab cameras, tape recorders, and notebooks. For the next twenty minutes a couple dozen guerrillas stood in a creek running down the mountainside waiting for the plane to go away; I sat on a large rock under a bush on the creek's edge because, they informed me, my white shirt could be seen at some distance from the air. As I listened to the plane fire four rockets about eight kilometers away, I thought about all the things I had seen and learned in El Salvador. It was like seeing one's life pass before one's eyes. I controlled my growing terror by taking photographs— and by promising myself that I would never again bring white shirts to El Salvador.

Two hours later I was on my way back to Jucuarán—walking all the way. To my eternal mortification, while I paused and panted every ten steps, my guerrilla guide took the fifty-degree incline that marked the first quarter mile as if he were taking a stroll on a country lane. An hour that seemed like ten later, I staggered into Jucuarán, desperate for a bath. Of course, there was no running water. The transformer that had supplied electricity to the town and power to the water pumps had been shot up in a firefight months earlier. An FMLN offer to repair or replace it had been declined by city officials out of fear of army retaliation. Fifty cents, however, bought a huge jug of water— enough to wash body and hair. An hour later my chauffeurs and I bounced out of Jucuarán in a cloud of dust. (Cleanliness aside, I needed to freshen up to avoid looking as if I had just spent several days in the mountains because I did not want to be stopped and questioned by the army and run the risk of having my notes, tapes, and film confiscated.)

When we arrived at the Río Grande de San Miguel (Big River of San Miguel), at least two dozen guerrillas from the ERP and FAL were relaxing, talking to each other or to civilians. There was Zambel, wearing the biggest grin I had ever seen. "Good-bye, tape recorder," I thought. Comandante Pedro, he informed me, would be there shortly. And the tape recorder? he inquired. "Why do you want it?" it finally occurred to me to ask. "Well, I like to write poetry and compose songs, and I don't have a way to record the songs."

Comandante Pedro (David Pereira Rivera) was the commander of all the FAL forces in the southeastern front.[7] This meant he ranked right under Balta. Not bad for three days' work, I thought: an army commander, three guerrilla commanders, five recruits, and the best-known priest in eastern El Salvador. Pedro and I talked for over an hour; then it was time to return to San Salvador. The FMLN had long since blown up the bridge over the river to keep army convoys out, so a raft with a rope and pulley system provided the final crossing out of the zone. The buses I had been told would come from Usulután never arrived. Finally, two Mexican journalists showed up, waiting for permission to go into the zone. One of them, an acquaintance, understood my desperate need to be back in the capital before dark for security reasons and agreed to drive me to Usulután. From there a taxi took me to the local airport—a grass strip—where twin-engine Cessnas provided service several times a day to and from the capital.

The plane arrived, discharged its passengers, began to load the next group—and then I discovered I would be the first person on the *next* flight, an hour later. There were soldiers standing around, and even as I chatted and joked with them I was increasingly nervous that an officer would appear and begin asking questions. My cover story was that I had been visiting people in the city of Usulután, but one educated look at me would reveal I had not seen a city in days. Then suddenly a well-dressed man of perhaps sixty offered me his seat. I accepted with genuine and profuse gratitude, even as I realized that he could be a cotton grower, a member of the oligarchy, and if he had any idea where I had been he might have arranged to make me crawl back to San Salvador. On the other hand, he might have been an FMLN collaborator who had correctly perceived the situation.

FROM ENEMIES TO *PAISANOS:* 1992

Until late 1991 the kind of experience described in the preceding section was the norm in war-torn El Salvador. Indeed, twelve students from Agnes Scott College and I had a parallel experience in January 1989 when we met with another colonel, Roberto Tejada, in Usulután, then with an FMLN commander, Enrique, barely twenty-five kilometers to the southeast and twenty-four hours later. On December 31, 1991, however, after twenty months of negotiations, the government of El Salvador and the FMLN reached a peace agreement, and the unthinkable became possible: All sectors of Salvadorean society were able and often willing to sit together and publicly discuss their respective points of view.

One such encounter occurred in September 1992 at the Latin American Studies Association congress in Los Angeles.[8] One of the plenary sessions focused on El Salvador between the cease-fire, which occurred the previous February 1, and the 1994 elections for a new president and all members of the

Legislative Assembly and mayors. There have been many panels and plenaries on El Salvador since 1980, but this plenary was unique: For the first time, representatives of the government, the army (Armed Forces of El Salvador, hereafter Armed Forces), the FMLN, a coalition of opposition parties, the Democratic Convergence (Convergencia Democratica), and a representative of the United Nations Observer Mission (ONUSAL) accepted invitations to participate.

There were two defining moments during the plenary. The first came near the beginning, when Colonel Carlos Rolando Herrarte, then commander of the Second Brigade in the western city of Santa Ana, delivered his prepared remarks.[9] Colonel Herrarte had been invited because in several private conversations over a year, he had been open, moderate, and clearly willing to accept the political and military changes that were coming. The first paragraph of his speech, however, was filled with cold war rhetoric about "terrorists" and "fighting communism." A pall settled over the audience. Two speakers later, Roberto Cañas, who was the FMLN's spokesman during the peace negotiations in 1991, took the podium and gently suggested that the time had come to change the language Salvadoreans use to talk with and about each other.

The second and, in symbolic terms, more significant moment came at the end. Colonel Herrarte responded affirmatively to a question concerning whether the Armed Forces would respect an electoral outcome that brought the FMLN to the presidency and control of the government. "The Armed Forces," he said, "are committed to upholding the constitutional order, and if the FMLN wins a free and fair election we will respect that." Then he turned to Roberto Cañas, who was seated on his right. Pointing to Cañas, Herrarte said, "And I hope that the next minister of defense will give me a job!" In that moment, as Cañas and everyone else roared with laughter, it was possible to see, not just imagine, the process of reconciliation taking place after eleven years of civil war.

ON DOING RESEARCH DURING
(AND AFTER) A WAR

If anyone had suggested when I first arrived in El Salvador in early November 1979 that on two different occasions, five years apart, I would interview a government army commander and a guerrilla army commander within forty-eight hours of each other, I would have thought them mad. It would have required an even greater stretch of imagination to envision a plenary with representatives of the army and the FMLN seated next to each other. In 1979 not only did I not know any revolutionaries, but the commanders of the five political-military organizations that would, a year later, create the FMLN were virtually inaccessible. In the fall of 1979 attending a press conference that the popular organizations held with some regularity in the law school auditorium at the national university (the University of El Salvador) was a major event. My first time, barely two weeks after arriving in the country, I was escorted by a university student whose name I had been given by mutual friends before leaving the United States. To say that I went with some trepidation would not be an overstatement.

In late 1979 there were only a handful of guerrillas in isolated base camps in the mountains of northern and eastern El Salvador. The action was in the cities, where five mass (popular) organizations, created during the 1970s, were staging frequent street demonstrations, occupying government ministries and embassies, and organizing every possible sector of Salvadorean society, from labor unions to teachers and students, from slum dwellers to white-collar professionals. With a few initial contacts and a great deal of luck, by the time I left El Salvador in late March 1980, I had been able to interview a large number of people involved in the mass movement as well as individuals from all other sectors of Salvadorean society.

After leaving El Salvador just four days before the assassination of Archbishop Romero, my expectations of returning for follow-up research in the next six months were dashed when friends with good connections in El Salvador advised me that my name was "on a list." As a result, I did not return for over two years. Additional interviews and information were collected in Washington, D.C., Mexico, and Managua. Since May 1982, however, I have made over thirty trips to El Salvador, and each trip has expanded the range of people across the political spectrum with whom I have been privileged to talk.

REFLECTIONS

There are obvious and not-so-obvious lessons from the "war stories" I have related—and from other experiences that considerations of space preclude recounting. One lesson is a willingness to talk to everyone. Information comes from unexpected places at unexpected times. For example, soldiers out of their officers' presence admitted they were forcibly recruited, were underage, and did not know what they were doing in the army. A businessman, off the record, asserted that resolution of the war must include the FMLN; another insisted, also off the record, that the "terrorists" and their followers must be physically eliminated. A taxi driver recounted his own war stories from taking journalists to the countryside and provided information not otherwise available on the newest areas in which the FMLN was operating.

Another lesson is that doing research in a country as politically polarized as El Salvador then was requires a strong stomach and an ability to keep one's face expressionless. These skills were useful when interviewing an oligarch in 1980 who presented an elaborate and coldly rational justification for the existing system (peasants are incapable of self-government) and asserted that the battle against international communism was being fought in El Salvador so it would not have to be fought in the United States. The skills were even more useful when visiting clandestine cemeteries where one encountered four new bodies or piles of human bones picked clean by vultures or when visiting the men's and women's prisons.

Another lesson is humility—humility in the face of extraordinary suffering, perseverance, strength, and determination, all rolled up into one grandmother who lost fourteen members of her family to the death squads or army; humility in the face of people who are not members of revolutionary organizations but who put their lives on the line every day because their belief in social justice makes them suspect in the eyes of the powerful; humility about one's own predictive abilities, when the "two or five years" until the Salvadorean government would be overthrown that I foresaw when writing the first edition stretches into eleven and ends with peace negotiations.

Still, the fundamental analysis of the first edition has withstood the test of time. In summer 1988, U.S. ambassador to El Salvador Edwin Corr said that if he had been writing the first edition in 1982, he would have written the same thing. But, he continued, things had changed since then, and he hoped the new edition would reflect those changes. Things did change after 1982. Politically, El Salvador moved from a civilian-military junta to an elected civilian president. Militarily, the Armed Forces expanded from 11,000 to 56,000 men—and the FMLN extended its operations to all fourteen provinces of the country. Economically, the country regressed to levels of the early 1970s by almost any measure. Meanwhile, the United States, which began by offering military assistance to the new junta in October 1979, was supporting the Salvadorean government and military at the rate of $1 million to $1.5 million per day a decade later.

During this period the justification for this intervention shifted from stopping the spread of communism to shoring up democracy. In 1982 I argued that the hand of the Soviet Union neither created nor manipulated every revolutionary process and that there was no evidence it was doing so in El Salvador. In fact, there is considerable evidence that it did not. I felt in 1982 that a revolution in El Salvador would make Nicaragua look like a picnic, that it would be very bloody, that the human cost would be enormous. As the war ended eleven years later, that assessment was more correct than I ever expected.

Throughout the years, I preferred a path to peaceful social change instead of the violence that dominated the headlines between 1979 and the beginning of 1992. But it is clear that violence was not introduced in El Salvador by the revolutionaries. Violence has been the most pervasive characteristic of Salvadorean history—from the easily identifiable repression of government forces and vigilantes in the pay of large landowners to the more subtle violence of malnutrition, high infant mortality, illiteracy, and housing more fit for chickens than human beings. During the 1980s, by all these measures (leaving aside the war) violence increased dramatically. In 1980 there were 200 *tugurios* (shantytowns) in San Salvador; in 1993 there were over 400 and they had grown in size as well as numbers.

In 1979 I arrived in El Salvador objective and neutral in the sense of feeling personally detached from what was happening there. I left with my objectivity intact, but my neutrality was buried with the bodies of those who had been gunned down, without provocation, by government forces on January 22, 1980. I am thankful my preferred path—"that the people of El Salvador determine their own future, that that future not be imposed on them either by a tiny minority of the Salvadorean population, the army, or by the government of the United States"—has been realized in the peace accords.

When I wrote in the first edition of this book that "my objective conclusion is that the present government in El Salvador will be overthrown ... despite the Reagan administration's best efforts," I underestimated that administration's determination to prevent the overthrow or collapse of the Salvadorean government and army. But I also wrote that "no lasting, viable political solution is possible in El Salvador without the participation of the Democratic Revolutionary Front and the Farabundo Martí Front for National Liberation. The remaining question is how much more blood will be spilled before the government of the United States accepts that basic fact."[10]

The answer is eleven years and almost 80,000 dead.

On December 29, 1991, the Bush administration sent six senior officials to the United Nations in New York, where the latest round in twenty months of peace talks between the Salvadorean government and the FMLN had been under way for two weeks. Progress was being achieved by centimeters because Salvadorean president Alfredo Cristiani, under great pressure from the extreme right, had remained in San Salvador. Ultimately, pressure from U.N. secretary general Javier Pérez de Cuéllar, several European and Latin American countries, and, not least, the United States brought him to New York on December 28. U.S. officials met with Cristiani and Defense Minister General René Emilio Ponce the next day. The negotiators went into round-the-clock talks, and minutes before midnight on New Year's Eve, the guerrillas and the government signed the final accord.

The process leading to that moment is a story of tenacity, perseverance, courage, and faith. It is also a story of how the people of El Salvador have learned (and are are still learning) to take control of their lives and their social and political institutions. It is a story about change, from the individual to the societal level. It is a testament to Otto von Bismarck's century-plus-old maxim: "Politics is the art of the possible."

1

The Roots of Revolution, 1524–1960

*Cuando la historia no se puede escribir con la pluma, hay que escríbirla con el fusil.**
　　　　　　　　　　　　　　　　　　　　—Augustín Farabundo Martí

THE BOTTOM LINE

In 1993, El Salvador had over 5 million people crammed into a territory the size of Massachusetts. Thus it had the highest population density in all of Latin America (256.8/square kilometer) (see Table 1.1). Salvadoreans are privileged to live in one of the most breathtakingly beautiful countries in the Western Hemisphere: Except for a narrow strip along the Pacific Coast, it is a land of undulating mountain ranges punctuated by a string of mostly extinct volcanoes that begins in Mexico and runs through most of the isthmus. It is a land that has produced incredible wealth since the Spanish conquest in the mid-1520s but in which 65 percent of the people (80 percent in rural areas) still live in abject poverty.

The dimensions of that poverty can be grasped by considering the following: In 1986, as in 1980, 51 percent of the rural population had no land, whereas in 1961 the landless had been 11.8 percent. At the other end of the economic scale, in 1971, 3.3 percent of all landowners (3,624) held 56 percent of the arable land; in 1987, 2.9 percent of the landowners (7,190) held 46 percent of the land.[1]

The effects in human terms of this inequality can be measured by comparing the income distribution to the minimum amount needed to maintain even the most basic life-style. According to official sources, a family of six in 1975 needed a monthly income of US$59 in order to provide life's basic necessities. But a Planning Ministry survey in 1976–1977 revealed that 12.4 percent of all families earned $40 per month or less; another 29 percent earned between $40 and $80; and 21 percent earned between $80 and $120. Furthermore, about 60 percent of rural families did not earn enough ($44) to provide

---

*When history can no longer be written with the pen, it must be written with the rifle.

23

TABLE 1.1   El Salvador: Basic Demographic Data

Land size (square kilometers)	20,935
Population (1993)	5.4 million
Population density (1991 per square kilometer)	256.8
Average annual rate of growth (1970–1980)	4.2%
(1982–1991)	1.6%
Percent urban (1979)	40.2
(1988)	48.2
Percent literate (1984)	66.9
Urban (1979)	82
Rural (1979)	47
Landless	34
Female	59
Male	65.5
Birthrate per 1,000 inhabitants (1978)	39.7
(1980–1985)	38.0
(1990)	32.9
Mortality rate per 1,000 inhabitants (1978)	6.9
(1980–1985)	10.8
(1990)	7.7
Infant mortality per 1,000 live births (1977)	59.5
(1980–1985)	77.0
(1990)	52.9
Years of life expectancy at birth (1979)	62.2
(1980–1985)	57.1
(1990)	66

Sources: Inter-American Development Bank; Dirección General de Estadística y Censos, El Salvador; *World Development Report, 1993.*

even a minimum diet.[2] Another measure: In 1969, a World Bank report found that the bottom 40 percent of the population earned 11.2 percent of total personal income. By 1985, this percentage had been reduced to 10.9 pecent. Meanwhile, the richest 10 percent of the population earned 36.4 percent of all income, whereas the poorest 70 percent earned 34 percent of the total. For 946,590 families in 1985, the average monthly income was $126, but the cost of living for basic needs (food, housing, clothes, health, and transportation) was $241. Rural families were far worse off than their urban cousins: Ninety-six percent versus 80 percent, respectively, did not earn enough to cover basic needs. Meanwhile, for the richest 5 percent (47,330 families), the average monthly income was $610; for the richest 1 percent (9,466 families), $1,078.[3]

The results are unequivocal: In the last decade of the twentieth century, El Salvador has the lowest per capita calorie intake of any Latin American country; 77 of every 1,000 infants die; half the houses consist of one room for families that average 5.6 members; 73 percent of the children suffer from malnutrition, and—in the countryside—63 percent of the people have no sanitary facilities, 55 percent no access to potable water, and 62 percent no electricity.[4]

These facts of Salvadorean life, although current, are not new. They are the result of developments that can be traced to the colonial period and were consolidated after independence—developments that in the last third of the twentieth century contributed to massive political unrest and eleven years of civil war. It is to the post-Columbian era that we first turn our attention before a more complete discussion of contemporary social, political, and economic realities is possible.

HISTORICAL PATTERNS

The history of El Salvador can be understood in terms of an interlocking and interacting series of phenomena that took shape during three hundred years of Spanish colonial rule and continued after independence. These phenomena may be summarized as follows:

1. An economic cycle of booms and depressions that replayed itself as variations on a theme several times between the sixteenth and nineteenth centuries
2. Dependence on a monocrop economy as the key to wealth, a focus that led to dependence on outside markets
3. Exploitation of the labor supply, first the Indians and later the peasants
4. Concentration of the land in the hands of an ever-decreasing number of proprietors
5. Extreme concentration of wealth in few hands, coupled with the utter deprivation of the overwhelming majority of the population
6. A laissez-faire economic philosophy and an absolute belief in the sanctity of private property
7. A classical liberal notion of the purpose of government—to maintain order
8. Periodic rebellion by exploited segments of the population against perceived injustices

These phenomena produced two persistent patterns: (1) The distribution of resources was unequal from the beginning, and the effects were cumulative as population pressures exacerbated inequities in the extreme; (2) there was always conflict between communal lands and private property, and the latter regularly gained at the expense of the former.

CONQUEST AND SETTLEMENT

First sighted by the Spanish in 1522, the land called Cuzcatlán repelled the first wave of would-be settlers two years later. The Pipil Indians, the dominant group among the Náhua, who had emigrated from Mexico centuries before, sent Hernán Cortés's captain, Pedro de Alvarado, scurrying back to Guatemala in less than a month. It took the Spaniards four years to establish a permanent settlement and another eleven to establish sufficient control over the indigenous population to consider them "subjects of the royal service." The social and political system that the Spanish disrupted and ultimately destroyed was a "military democracy organized by tribe, with common owner-ship of the land."[5] Pipil society was a class society that practiced monogamy and included the institution of slavery. In Cuzcatlán, however, people were enslaved as a result of war or civil wrong, and slavery was not hereditary.

The "Keys to Wealth"

The earliest colonists in Cuzcatlán, like their countrymen in Mexico and Peru, were driven by a desire for instant wealth that could be sent back to Spain as a nest egg (after giving the crown its share) to await the master's re-turn. Others soon came to stay, but in contrast to the Aztec and Inca empires, there was little gold or silver in Cuzcatlán—although the *conquistadores* pro-ceeded to extract what there was through the laborious method of panning, an endeavor they continued for approximately thirty years using conscripted in-digenous labor. Meanwhile, cattle and sheep were introduced, and the culti-vation of cereals for local consumption by the colonists began. With few natu-ral resources to exploit, the search for a "key to wealth" began.[6] This search was the first step in a cycle that would play itself out in the following manner:

- Discovery of a new crop
- Rapid development of the crop
- Period of great prosperity from the export of the crop
- Dramatic decline or stagnation
- Economic depression during which a frantic search for a replacement ensued
- Discovery of a new crop and the beginning of another cycle

Cacao. Although balsam trees were discovered along the Pacific Coast of Izalcos (now Sonsonate) and became an important export crop for the Audiencia between 1560 and 1600, it was cacao that provided the first key to wealth in El Salvador. The cacao plantations were owned and operated by the Indians, but they were soon forced to deal only with Spanish or *mestizo* export-ers. This arrangement evolved rather quickly into the *encomienda* (royal grant of authority over a defined area and persons living in it but not of the land it-self) system, and within twenty years the export of cacao came to be domi-nated by three *encomenderos*. As the popularity of cacao in Europe grew, prices rose. The first massive fortunes for the *encomenderos*, their progeny, and be-tween 100 and 200 creole and *mestizo* merchants who benefited from the spill-over were assured.

The plantations, which were located largely in the southwest, remained in indigenous hands, but the growing demand for cacao brought a corre-sponding need for more labor. However, the indigenous inhabitants, suscep-tible to imported disease, were dying in droves. Many migrated from the highlands to the coast but could not adapt to the climatic change. Meanwhile, the Spaniards began enslaving other Indians and shipping them to Panama and Peru. As the indigenous population declined, the colonists began import-ing slaves from Africa. By 1550 there was a large African population in El Salvador. The primary source of exploitation in this period, however, came from the system of tribute, a carryover from the Aztec system and a legalized form of extortion. Tribute was extracted from indigenous households or levied on property (primarily on cacao plantations), which kept many theoretically wealthy Indian growers in virtual poverty.

The first economic cycle peaked in the 1570s and had all the earmarks of a monoculture boom. Then the population decline, coupled with a halt in the importation of slaves, produced a crisis for the indigenous growers, who were unable to meet production demands and therefore to pay the required tribute. This situation produced a ripple effect that became a tidal wave. Smaller *encomiendas* began reverting to the crown; the larger ones consolidated their power. By 1600 the boom was over and economic decline had set in. Depression hit with full force in 1610 and continued for half a century; it produced the first extended economic crisis in Central America.

Indigo. The decimation of the indigenous population had three effects. It destroyed the traditional forms of tribal organization, spurred the development or reformation of indigenous villages, and created a Spanish-speaking peasantry for an emerging agrarian society. The decline of cacao set off a protracted search for a replacement crop, a new emphasis on cattle breeding and the cultivation of maize, and a consequent deemphasis of the cities.

The quest for a substitute export crop centered for a time on cochineal, a scarlet dye produced by the wingless female cochineal insect. But the Central American dye was never able to compete with that of Oaxaca, Mexico, and it waned as an export crop in the 1620s.[7] Another dye, however, fared much better. Indigo (*añil*), a deep blue dye, became the second key to wealth. Unlike cacao, which was labor-intensive, indigo required little attention. Fields could be "weeded" by cattle, which ignored the indigo plants. By 1600 indigo had replaced cacao as the chief export, but it was another century before the boom arrived. When it did, it lasted for 150 years.[8]

Enduring Patterns

The development of a monocrop economy, in which the cycles of development and decline were similar and only the crop changed, had significant consequences for El Salvador's later history:

1. The decline of cacao and the extended economic depression that followed created a need for the colonials quickly to find a means of survival. This led to development of the *hacienda* system; the *haciendas* were not unlike plantations in the antebellum South in that they were largely self-sufficient.

2. The development of *haciendas* led, in turn, to the creation of new relationships between landowners and indigenous folk or peasants that could, for the most part, be characterized as feudal. These new relationships were established primarily through debt peonage, a means of permanently binding the Indians to a *hacienda*, usually by tricking them into a debt they could not repay. These people came to be known as *colonos*, or serfs, living on the *hacienda* and depending on the landowner for their very existence. Another dependent relationship was *aparcería*, or sharecropping, in which the peasants gave either

part of the harvest from their small plots or worked several days a week for the *patrono*.

3. The expansion of *haciendas* with each succeeding depression also had the effect of concentrating land in a declining number of hands. Most of this expansion was accomplished through usurpation of communal or *ejidal* lands without compensation to the former owners.

4. These same landowners also exercised firm control over the political life of the colony by the late eighteenth century. This pattern of economic and political control would continue for 150 years.

5. The pattern of land concentration led to vast underemployment and unemployment among the peasantry, particularly during the indigo and coffee cycles, because both crops were labor-intensive for only three months; a vast work force had to remain idle the rest of the year.

6. The emphasis on a monocrop economy produced from the 1500s onward a need to import foodstuffs, including basic grains. The landowners and small middle class could afford to pay for the imported goods, but the peasantry could not.

7. During the colonial period, the usurpation of land led to periodic indigenous revolts that grew in size and number after independence. This unrest required the creation of local, then state "security forces" that from the beginning were in the pay of the landowners and always at their beck and call.

8. As land became increasingly concentrated in fewer hands, the ethnic composition of the country also rapidly changed. At the beginning of the seventeenth century, the country was about 85 percent indigenous, 10 percent *mestizo*, and 5 percent white. To this were added 4,000–5,000 African slaves. That the country was well on its way to becoming a *mestizo* nation was evident by 1780; that it had become one was clear thirty years later. By the twentieth century the slaves, who were freed in 1823, had been assimilated and officially ceased to exist as a separate racial group.[9]

THE NATIONAL PERIOD

Independence. Eduardo Colindres observed that in Central America independence was not a struggle but a "process."[10] The period between 1811 and 1821 was characterized by popular demonstrations in support of independence. In 1814 one demonstration was led by San Salvador's mayor, who organized and armed his people with what by 1980 would be called "popular arms"—rocks, machetes, and the like. In the 1820s a newly independent Mexico, looking to assert its hegemony over the region, invaded El Salvador twice and twice was driven out. In July 1823 the Federal Republic of Central America was created by the five former Central American colonies, and a year later Manuel José Arce, a Salvadorean, was elected its first president. The experiment lasted for fifteen years, then broke apart in the wake of a liberal-conservative struggle[11] exacerbated by regional economic woes—the beginning of the end of the indigo cycle.

The First Peasant Revolt. By 1821 one-third of the total land was concentrated into 400 *haciendas*, most of which were devoted to indigo cultivation.

The historical mentality of the landowners was a single-minded desire to maximize earnings. This attitude was rooted in an understandable fear of being financially ruined by an economic depression. The view that what was good for the landowners was good for the country took hold, and until they perceived the need for the development of infrastructure (railroads, roads, water lines) that coffee would require, "national development" was not part of their vocabulary.

This situation produced growing economic inequities that were exacerbated by mounting class and ethnic antagonisms. Tribute was abolished by Spain's parliament in 1811, but collection of it continued in El Salvador until 1814 when a priest told the Indians of Los Nonualcos, southeast of San Salvador, that tribute had been abolished and that the continuing collection was illegal. The enraged populace descended on the mayor and threatened his life if they did not get a refund. The Indians were driven off, but their rage festered. Meanwhile, incursions on communal lands became more frequent as the protection of the crown was withdrawn following independence. Insult was added to injury when the government imposed taxes on indigo harvests.[12]

These conditions provoked a major revolt in 1832 in the area of Los Nonualcos. Led by the *cacique* Anastacio Aquino, 3,000 peasants battled government troops for a year—until Aquino was captured, shot, and decapitated. His head was displayed publicly as a warning to other potential rebels. It would be a hundred years before Salvadorean peasants again attempted to overthrow the system.

The Era of El Grano de Oro

By the middle of the nineteenth century, the demand for indigo on the world market was in dramatic decline. This was due largely to the Civil War in the United States, which not only reduced that market but created shipping problems as a result of the Union's naval blockade, and to the development in Germany of a synthetic dye.

Well before these events occurred, however, enterprising Salvadoreans had discovered an extremely lucrative substitute: coffee. The rich lava soils of central and western El Salvador were especially appropriate for coffee bushes, which generally grow at elevations above 760 meters. It appears, however, that much of the early investment in coffee was not made by the indigo planters. The late Segundo Montes, a sociologist at the Jesuit Central American University (UCA) in San Salvador, researched archives at the Library of the Indies in Seville and found little overlap in the family names of indigo and coffee growers. By comparing original records of indigo farmers and nineteenth-century Salvadorean records, he challenged earlier scholarship that argued for continuity between the two groups. Montes offered two explanations for his finding that are not mutually exclusive: First, indigo growers lost so much money in the independence and early national period that they did not have the capital to invest in coffee, a plant that requires three years to begin producing. According to this theory, they were replaced by recent immigrants who arrived with the necessary financing. Second, the new immigrants married the daughters of the indigo oligarchy. "Many immigrants," Montes said in a July 1988 interview, "came as technicians or exporters of coffee. [They] had money, the [daughters] had a name."[13]

The development of coffee, the third key to wealth, contributed greatly to El Salvador's economic strength and stability, at least on a national level. But in order to facilitate the transition from indigo to coffee, the Salvadorean government decreed in 1856 that if two-thirds of the communal lands were not planted in coffee, the lands would revert to the state (Map 1.1). Many indigenous communities made a serious effort to comply with the decree, and tens of thousands of coffee plants were set out. That was not enough: An 1881 law mandated that all communal property be subdivided among the owners or become the property of the state. The next year all communal lands were abolished by decree, which deemed them "contrary to the political and social principles on which the Republic was established"—that is, the unfettered right of private property. In accordance with this decree, the indigenous peoples were evicted from their ancestral lands, often violently. Although five uprisings occurred in the coffee-growing areas between 1872 and 1898, within a few years the best land was concentrated in the hands of the "Fourteen Families." In the latter part of the century, most presidents were not only generals but also major coffee growers: Dueñas, Regalado, Escalón, Figueroa, and Meléndez. A century later these names identified many members of the economically dominant oligarchy.

The Liberal Basis of the State. The political and social principles on which the republic was founded were those of liberalism. There were differences in emphasis between those who stressed economic themes of the liberal creed and those who stressed political themes like free speech. All agreed, however, on the basic policies that would shape the Salvadorean nation: encouragement of coffee production, construction of railroads to the ports, elimination of communal lands, laws against vagrancy that permitted the state to force peasants to work for *hacendados* at low wages, and repression of rural unrest. The 1886 constitution guaranteed that these policies would be pursued without obstacle; it established a secular state, decentralized state authority by allowing for the popular election of municipal authorities, and confirmed the inviolability of private property.

The Instruments of Control. The task of dealing with recalcitrant peasants who periodically rebelled against their *patronos* was, for much of the nineteenth century, left in the hands of those selfsame *patronos* who employed private armies. Elements of these would become the Rural Police and the Mounted Police, created by decrees in 1884 and 1889, respectively, in the western coffee-growing departments. An 1895 decree extended these two forces over the entire country, and the Rural Police eventually became the National Police. In 1912, the National Guard was created and trained by officers from Spain. Its founder, President Manuel Henríquez Aragón, designed it for the countryside, intending to eliminate the *hacendados'* private armies and their excesses. But Henríquez was assassinated by landowners, and within a few years the National Guard had gained a reputation for being the "most cruel,

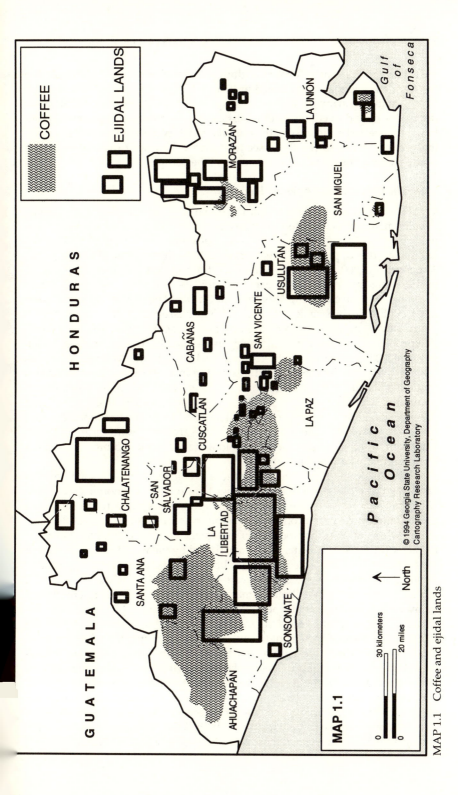

MAP 1.1   Coffee and ejidal lands

Map legend:

COFFEE

EJIDAL LANDS

GUATEMALA

HONDURAS

Gulf of Fonseca

Pacific Ocean

SANTA ANA

CHALATENANGO

AHUACHAPÁN

SAN SALVADOR

CUSCATLÁN

CABAÑAS

SONSONATE

LA LIBERTAD

SAN VICENTE

LA PAZ

USULUTÁN

SAN MIGUEL

MORAZÁN

LA UNIÓN

© 1994 Georgia State University, Department of Geography
Cartography Research Laboratory

MAP 1.1

0   30 kilometers
0   20 miles

North

most barbaric" security force.[14] A third security force, the Treasury Police (Policía de Hacienda), was created in 1936.

A national army began to take shape in the late 1850s because El Salvador in this period lived in fear of invasion from Guatemala. The army's attention was directed to defense of the national territory, and the task of maintaining order was left to the three security forces. Not until the late twentieth century would the army be used to control the people.

The Effects of Land Tenure Patterns

The positive contributions of the booming coffee market in traditional development terms included the construction of roads and of a railroad network between San Salvador, Santa Ana, Sonsonate, and the port of Acajutla. The social costs of progress, however, included a literacy rate of no more than 30 percent in 1900; high levels of malnutrition; and an extremely high rate of births outside marriage. By the early 1920s, 59 percent of the births in El Salvador were "natural children,"[15] as compared with 49 percent in Guatemala and 24 percent in Costa Rica. Rural family life was disrupted as thousands of people, mostly men, were forced to take up a nomadic existence in search of work. The problem of alcoholism could be measured in liquor consumption, which produced 25 percent of public revenue in 1918. Miguel Mármol, who was born in 1905, vividly remembered this period in a 1981 interview. Mármol, a shoemaker, said "It was difficult to live. … The basic foods of the Salvadorean population were very scarce. … Many *campesinos* as such disappeared, and the production of … beans, corn, rice, fruit, and vegetables stopped because the lands passed into the hands of the coffee growers. Many of these [peasants] went to Honduras or Guatemala looking for work and built the United Fruit Company banana plantations."[16]

The oligarchy tended to blame these problems on the personal failings of the working class and peasants rather than on socioeconomic conditions. Nonetheless, studies of the time held the economic system responsible and pointed not only to the problem of malnutrition but also to the fact that sorghum, which was used as fodder in Guatemala, was a principal food grain in El Salvador. These problems were exacerbated by the world financial crisis of 1914–1922, which combined to reduce both the capital available—especially to small and medium-sized producers—and the value of the *fincas* (small farms). In this economic climate small farmers could not secure credit, and many were forced out of business. Waiting to pick up the pieces were the *hacendados*, whose wealth, access to capital, and credit were intact. During the 1920s coffee became increasingly central to the economic life of the country. Production of "the golden grain" expanded rapidly; other crops and industries stagnated. This stimulus, coupled with growing business acumen and sophistication, brought the national economy out of the depression and into a boom. Coffee averaged between 75 and 80 percent of all exports between 1900 and 1922, then soared to 92 percent during the remainder of the 1920s. Similarly, land use increased dramatically. In 1919, 70,000 hectares were planted in coffee; by 1932 the figure had increased 34 percent, to 106,000 hectares.[17]

Miguel Mármol, 1981. He died June 24, 1993, in San Salvador, at the age of 87.

Meanwhile, living conditions of the average Salvadorean deteriorated. In a devastating commentary on the conditions of the time, El Salvador's most eloquent social critic, Alberto Masferrer, declared:

> The conquest of territory by the coffee industry is alarming. It has already occupied the high lands and is now descending to the valleys, displacing maize, rice, and beans. It is extended like the *conquistador,* spreading hunger and misery, reducing the former proprietors to the worst conditions—woe to those who sell! Although it is possible to prove mathematically that these changes make the country richer, in fact they mean death. It is true that the costs of importing maize are small in relation to the benefits of the export of coffee, but do they give the imported grain to the poor? Or do they make them pay for it? Is the income of the *campesino,* who has lost his land, adequate to provide maize, rice, beans, clothes, medicine, doctors, etc.? So, what good does it do to make money from the sale of coffee when it leaves so many people in misery?[18]

The attitude of the *hacendados* was expressed in a letter to *Patria,* which Masferrer edited: "Why must one be bothered with planting maize ... when one can plant coffee with little effort or risk? The idle lands around the volcanoes must be utilized. If the owners of these lands do not want to make use of them, they must sell them to those who would make them productive."[19] Many insisted that the peasants were being treated fairly—to which Masferrer replied: "Actually, there is no misery in El Salvador: The people go barefoot because they enjoy going without shoes, caressed by the fresh air; the laundry woman who earns four *colones* a week can save one-fourth of her earnings; and the child who comes to school without breakfast is convinced of the virtue of fasting."[20]

It was clear by the late 1920s that only one small sector was reaping the profits from *el grano de oro*. This situation was of concern to some, such as Masferrer, who warned that "as long as justice is not the same for everyone, none of us is safe."[21] A more prescient observation was tossed off by James Hill, an immigrant *hacendado* in Santa Ana: "Bolshevism? It is the tempest. The working people have meetings on Sundays and become excited. They say: 'We dig the holes for the trees, clean out the weeds, pick the trees, harvest the coffee. Who, then, earns the money? We earn it!' ... Yes, there will be problems one of these days."[22]

REVOLT

The "problems" that Hill anticipated in 1927 exploded five years later—the result of the social and economic conditions described previously, an increasingly militant labor union movement, and a flirtation with authentic electoral democracy that ended in a coup d'etat.[23]

The Rise of Working-Class Organizations

Labor organizations in El Salvador grew rapidly after the formation of the Central American Congress of Workers, which met in San Salvador in 1911. These early organizations tended to be oriented toward mutual assistance and savings among the membership. Emphasis was placed on education, temperance, and charitable work; there were regular disavowals of political sectarianism.[24] The growing maturity of the movement was evident at a national meeting in June 1918. More than 200 union delegates gathered for the purpose of organizing the Great Confederation of Workers of El Salvador (COES). The significance of the gathering was reflected in demands from nervous oligarchs that the government post troops near the meeting hall in order to quell any disturbance that might result from the proceedings. The workers, however, conducted their business with order and decorum.[25]

Soon, however, radical union organizers from Guatemala and Mexico began having some success among workers and students. These new unions did not affiliate with COES and, being consciously political, began to change the largely mutualist character of the Salvadorean union movement.[26] This influence expanded during the 1920s and produced an increasingly militant movement. Miguel Mármol, who would later be one of the founding members of the Salvadorean Communist Party, said that during this period "there were reformists, anarchists, anarchist-syndicalists, and us—the communists."[27]

The year 1929 brought the onset of the Great Depression—and a resulting plunge in coffee prices. The depression exacerbated social tensions, and the increasing militancy of the labor union movement, in the form of demonstrations and strikes, inflamed the situation. These events, however, occurred during the first presidential administration in El Salvador's history committed to allowing all political organizations to participate in the political life of the country. In this atmosphere, the Communist Party of El Salvador (PCS), the country's first revolutionary organization, was founded.

A Taste of Democracy

President Pío Romero Bosque, who had been handpicked by his conservative predecessor on the assumption that he would follow orders, insisted that there not be an "official" candidate (from the oligarchy) for the presidential election of 1930. The result was the election of Arturo Araujo, a wealthy landowner who had addressed the second national COES congress in 1919; who paid his employees double the going wages; who had the endorsement of Masferrer; who, in short, had become known as a friend of the working class and peasantry.

Araujo's candidacy had aroused expectations among the poor and fears among the establishment including the military, whose members he had courted by naming General Maximiliano Hernández Martínez his vice-presidential running mate. No traitor to his class, Araujo was not prepared to honor some of the more extravagant campaign promises his labor supporters had made in his name. Still, the oligarchy, which had been deeply suspicious of the free election, refused to lend its support to the new administration by accepting ministerial appointments, thereby denying its expertise to the government at one of the most critical points in the country's history.

The social, political, and economic situation deteriorated from the day Araujo was inaugurated. Denied the oligarchy's support and beset by increasing social unrest, Araujo was unable to deal with the crisis. On December 2, 1931, a coup d'etat (*golpe*) led by a handful of young officers toppled the nine-month-old regime; the president went into exile; and the military named his constitutional successor, Vice-President General Martínez, to succeed him. The United States, citing the 1923 Treaty of Washington, which had created guidelines for the recognition of new governments established under extraconstitutional circumstances, suspended diplomatic relations. Salvadoreans viewed this as another form of imperialism. Relations were not restored until Franklin Roosevelt became president in 1933. Thus began the longest unbroken record of military rule in Latin American history.[28]

El Negro

The role that Anastacio Aquino had played in 1832 was assumed by Augustín Farabundo Martí a hundred years later. No *cacique*, Martí was the son of a *mestizo hacendado* who had attended the national university long enough to become well read in positivist, utopian socialist, and Marxist-Leninist ideas. Expelled from the country in 1920 by President Jorge Meléndez for radical activities, Martí, who acquired the nickname "El Negro" because of his dark complexion, spent the early years of the decade traveling in Central America and the United States. In 1925 Martí returned to El Salvador where he worked for the Regional Federation of Salvadorean Workers—until he was exiled by then-president Alfonso Quiñonez. Martí, however, slipped back into the capital and picked up where he had left off. When President Romero Bosque had him jailed, Martí went on a hunger strike. The General Association of Salvadorean University Students (AGEUS), which had been founded in 1927, supported him, and Romero Bosque finally had him released. Martí then left El Salvador and a few months later joined Augusto César Sandino, who was fighting U.S. forces in Nicaragua. In 1929 Martí accompanied Sandino into exile in Mexico but, Martí later wrote, Sandino "would not embrace my communist program. His banner was only that of national independence ... not social revolution."[29] Martí returned to El Salvador in May 1930 and immediately plunged back into political work.

Agitation and Repression. Romero Bosque was willing to live with unions and political parties as long as they did not threaten his main support—the oligarchy. However, when he discovered that 80,000 *campesinos* had been organized, he issued a decree banning demonstrations, rallies, and leftist propaganda. The decree was ignored; the government arrested, fined, or jailed several hundred *campesinos* in Sonsonate for signing a petition against the decree. This led to the Campaign for the Liberation of Political Prisoners, which produced more repression and another decree banning all peasant or worker demonstrations. Between mid-November 1930 and late February 1931, about twelve hundred people were jailed for various radical activities.[30] One of those was Farabundo Martí. Romero Bosque decided to expel him once again, so Martí was put aboard a steamer in La Libertad and spent most of the next two months at sea. Finally, El Negro jumped ship in Corinto, Nicaragua, and made his way back to El Salvador, arriving in the capital on February 20—after Araujo's election.

Insurrection and Massacre. The following months were filled with organizing and propagandizing among university students and peasants in the central and western part of the country. Demonstrations and strikes were suppressed with increasing brutality. Legislation in March giving the security forces greater authority to deal with the unrest led to raids on leftist headquarters and mail searches for subversive material. Martí was again jailed for receiving a large quantity of Marxist literature that had been sent from New York. He began a hunger strike that lasted twenty-six days and led to his release. He was carried from the hospital, where he had been taken from jail, on the shoulders of his supporters. For the next several months Martí kept a relatively low profile as the political situation deteriorated and the demonstration-repression cycle escalated. Leftists greeted the coup on December 2 with cautious optimism, but their hopes were dashed when the legislative and municipal elections in early January 1932 were once again characterized by fraud. In the western part of the country, where the Marxists were strong, elections were suspended. In other towns the PCS claimed victory, but the government refused to certify the elections.

Martí, other radical leaders, and the PCS concluded that the Martínez regime had no intention of letting them participate or hold office through legal means; they then set the date for the insurrection. The plan called for simultaneous uprisings in several towns and army barracks on January 22, but the authorities learned of the plan several days in advance. Farabundo Martí was captured on January 18, along with two student supporters. Then communications broke down when other rebel leaders attempted to call off the revolt. The result was an unorganized, uncoordinated uprising that met with a swift and brutal response. Anyone in Indian dress or anyone running from the security forces was fair game. When the carnage was over, 30,000 people were dead. Less than 10 percent of those had participated in the uprising. Martí and the two students were tried by military tribunal and shot. The military consolidated its hold on the government, and there was no more pretense of popular political participation. *Campesino* unions were outlawed, and all political organizations were prohibited. The oligarchy achieved the social peace it wanted and considered necessary to rebuild a shattered economy.

The significance of these events in the history of El Salvador was captured by Jorge Arias Gómez:

> December 2, 1931, marks an era in the political life of the nation which has continued for almost 40 years. On that date, the oligarchy ceased to govern directly. If before the coup d'etat the political idea that only civilians must serve as president had triumphed and been consolidated, afterwards the opposite idea was pursued. If before, forces of the oligarchy were thrown into the struggle for power, organizing more or less successful parties and electoral movements; exciting the masses; afterward the entire oligarchy withdrew from the political game in order to leave it to military tyranny. ... In a few words, political power passed, on December 2, 1931, into the hands of the army. That was transformed, in practice, into the great elector and into a type of political party permanently in arms.[31]

A DIVISION OF LABOR

In 1980, Orlando de Sola, a Salvadorean oligarch, summed up the relationship between oligarchy and military after 1931. "We have traditionally bought the military's guns," he said, "and have paid them to pull the trigger."[32] The cyclical pattern of economic development that evolved in the colonial period had its counterpart in El Salvador's political life after 1932. Whereas the first pattern had served to consolidate economic power in the oligarchy, the second pattern served to perpetuate political power in the hands of the army. Meanwhile, the economic situation continued unchanged, and what reforms did occur in no way affected the sources and distribution of wealth or control of the national economy.

Political Cycles

The political cycle, although its pattern varied more than the economic cycle, contained the following elements:

- Consolidation of power by the new regime
- Growing intolerance of dissent and increasing repression
- Reaction from two quarters: the public and a progressive faction within the army officer corps, culminating ultimately in a

- Coup d'etat, led by progressive officers, that when successful led to
- Promulgation of various reforms
- Reemergence within the army of the most conservative faction, and
- Consolidation of that power once more

Between December 1931 and January 1980, El Salvador was convulsed six times by events that generally conformed to this pattern. Not all of these elements were fully played out in each cycle, particularly those of short duration: 1960–1961 and 1972. In 1979 reemergence of the most conservative faction began even before the coup.

Constants

Throughout these cycles, there were certain constants. The first was establishment of the official party. Created by Martínez and named in its first incarnation "Pro-Patria" (for the homeland), the official party was not a traditional political party. Salvadorean political scientist and political leader Rubén Zamora noted that although it occasionally fulfilled some of a party's traditional functions, in fact its real purpose was to be an instrument of social control. Zamora argued that before 1932 the oligarchy controlled the people through two mechanisms: through the security forces that operated as personal instruments of repression and, more subtly, through *compadrazgo*, a social institution that created familylike ties between *patrono* and *campesino*. After 1932 "the mechanisms of *compadrazgo* gradually passed to the state."[33] Indeed, Pro-Patria did not have a life of its own but functioned as the personal instrument of Martínez, who kept the peasants in line during the 1930s through a highly personalistic style of rule.[34]

The second constant in Salvadorean life was the use of repression to maintain order when persuasion failed. The security forces continued to serve at the beck and call of the oligarchy and were particularly effective in the countryside. Both security forces and army units were used in the cities whenever demonstrations by university students or labor unions threatened domestic tranquillity. Over the years techniques of repression became more sophisticated, as many leftist leaders would learn firsthand in the 1960s and 1970s.

Third, in each political cycle a time came when the government, feeling itself under siege, would with increasing frequency and vigor label all dissent "subversive" and the work of "communists." These were also the favorite labels of the oligarchy for anyone in El Salvador who advocated any social or economic change that would, in any measure, adversely affect its economic interests. These labels were applied to army officers, members of centrist political factions, church leaders, labor unions, and openly leftist mass organizations.

Fourth, each cycle brought some measure of social and economic reform, although it was never enough either to deal adequately with El Salvador's growing numbers of poor people or to tamper with the economic status quo.

Fifth, throughout the decades following the assumption of power by the military, two goals remained paramount: to protect the interests of the oligarchy and to preserve the institution of the Armed Forces. By 1980, however, the first goal was sacrificed to the second. Although civilians participated in each coup and staffed government ministries, the dominant elements within the army remained unwilling to give up control of the state. They were reinforced in that position by two other institutions: the *tanda* system and corruption.

A *tanda* is a graduating class at the Salvadorean military academy. In the 1930s *tandas* began to develop a strong sense of cohesiveness. During thirty-year careers, officers made alliances with their counterparts in *tandas* just ahead of or behind them in preparing to take political power and to share the benefits that were available through a thoroughly institutionalized system of corruption (see Chapters 2 and 7).

The First Cycle: 1932–1944

Martínez moved quickly and decisively to consolidate his power. After order was restored following the insurrection of January 1931, the government developed four means of keeping the population in line. It effected an administrative reorganization throughout the country that centralized decisionmaking and all public works and services. Second, Martínez further consolidated this control by replacing civilians with military officers at the local and national levels.[35] Third, labor unions, which had flourished during the Romero Bosque and Araujo presidencies, were officially discouraged on the grounds that they were subversive. Last, all peasant organizations were banned, as was the Communist Party. Indian *cofradías* (fraternal societies) were similarly accused and suffered a corresponding decline.[36] Virtually all political opposition disappeared for several years. The significant exception to this came from within the Armed Forces itself. Five times between 1934 and 1939, individuals or groups within the army attempted to overthrow Martínez. As Miguel Mármol put it, "Martínez was a one-man dictatorship, not an army dictatorship. [He] never governed with the monolithic support of the army."[37]

Economic Concerns. Dependence on a single crop continued. Government policy after the 1932 uprising was directed to protecting the interests of the coffee growers. Laws designed to discourage mechanization were drafted, and investment was encouraged only in industries that did not threaten artisan production, such as shoemaking. There was fear that industrialization would destroy such crafts and revive the alliance between peasants and workers that had led to the 1932 insurrection.[38] Not until after World War II was there any significant diversification of export crops.

In the financial area, a general moratorium on debts was decreed, and it was stipulated that debtors should not be prosecuted. In 1934 the Central Reserve Bank was created. The Coffee Growers' Association provided 36.5 percent of its capitalization; the two existing banks, owned by members of the oligarchy, held 27 percent; and the balance was retained by private stockholders. The creation of the Central Bank ensured that the coffee growers' interests would be protected by guaranteeing that their land would not be foreclosed and that sufficient capital would be available for the further development of coffee production.[39] A year after the Central Bank was founded, the government created the Banco Hipotecario, or national mortgage bank. Ostensibly, its purpose was to make mortgages more easily obtainable for small farmers and businesspeople, but it soon became yet another financial instrument by which the oligarchy extended its economic tentacles. The economic policies of the Martínez government included nationalization of all public utility companies and assertion of the right of eminent domain over municipal power companies.

Ultimately these policies, which in no way helped small entrepreneurs either recover from the depression or establish new businesses, bred discontent among the Salvadorean bourgeoisie. At the same time, conditions in the countryside were turning El Salvador into an urban nation; by 1935 more than one-third of the population lived in cities.[40] This migration created growing pressures for jobs and services that the government was ill-prepared—or ill-disposed—to alleviate. It was also unable to control political dissension in the cities, as the National Guard did so effectively in the countryside.

Foreign Policy. Martínez and other senior officers were attracted by the fascist governments of Germany and Italy. This attraction grew out of the failure of the liberal governments of Romero and Araujo, the communist involvement in the 1932 insurrection, and the resulting belief that what the country needed was a more elitist government. By 1936 army officers had begun training in Germany and Italy. During 1938 Italy sent El Salvador planes with spare parts, tanks, and tractors capable of being converted into armored cars—in exchange for $200,000 worth of coffee. In the same year a German colonel became director of the Military Academy. In 1940 Martínez decreed it a crime to express support for the Allies. Officers openly sympathetic to the Axis powers could be found in major government and military positions until late 1941.[41]

This sympathy for the Axis was not universally shared. When Italy declared war in June 1940, 300 Black Shirts marched in downtown San Salvador. They were greeted with jeers, a response that was rapidly repressed by the police. Ultimately, Martínez was forced to abandon his flirtation with Germany and Italy. Declining trade with the Axis for both military and domestic goods produced a 20 percent unemployment rate by late 1940. Opposition to Martínez's policy grew within the army, and in October Martínez abruptly reversed his foreign policy. In a public statement he condemned totalitarianism on the Continent and praised the Allies.[42]

Meanwhile, the United States had already indicated its willingness to become El Salvador's primary arms supplier. In June 1940, when the minister of defense asked U.S. military attaché Col. J. B. Pate for 35,000 rifles, Pate assured him that the means would be found "to help our exceptionally loyal friends in this matter."[43]

Sources of Dissension. Martínez's romance with the Axis was one reason for unhappiness within the army. The primary cause, however, was the perception that power, privilege, and opportunity were concentrated in an ever-smaller clique. The best positions were held by Martínez's cronies, and there

A remnant of Nazi influence: Salvadorean soldiers salute the High Command during ceremonies marking the National Day of the Soldier, May 7. Photo by Corinne Dufka, reprinted with permission.

was no policy of advancement that permitted other officers to aspire to better conditions. Younger officers in particular came to view the dictatorship as an obstacle to their personal ambitions.

The End of the Regime. In January 1944 a Constitutional Assembly was convened, ostensibly to amend the constitution so that German property could be expropriated. The hidden agenda, however, was to change the succession laws in order to permit Hernández Martínez a fourth term as president. This was the last straw for disenchanted army officers and increasingly restive members of the bourgeoisie. On April 2 an attempted coup was staged by army and air force officers. Martínez, with the support of the National Guard and National Police, survived the revolt at a cost of at least 200 lives. Martínez then turned his vengeance on the conspirators. Ten officers and thirty-three others were executed. Martial law was imposed throughout the country.

The retribution exacted by the regime was too much for the people. Students at the University of El Salvador struck in protest. They were quickly joined by high school students, clerks, and professionals. By the end of April the general strike had brought San Salvador to a standstill.[44] On May 8 Hernández Martínez announced his resignation.[45] The next day, with the general strike still in progress, the nation learned that its new provisional president was General Andrés Ignacio Menéndez.

Menéndez quickly named a cabinet that included representatives from the several political factions that had emerged since 1941. Freedom of the press was reinstated; a general amnesty was declared for all political prisoners and exiles; and Martínez's hated secret police was abolished. Menéndez appeared bent on opening up the political process.

The Second Cycle: 1944–1948

In the following weeks civilians became ever more vocal in their demands for free elections, for the removal of Martínez appointees, and for guarantees of fundamental civil liberties. Political parties were created or emerged from clandestine activity, precipitating a period of political ferment that had not been experienced since the 1931 presidential election. Presidential elections were scheduled for January 1945. The most prominent candidate was Arturo Romero, a young doctor who had been a civilian leader of the April revolt. Romero and his supporters were frankly committed to the restoration of civilian government and to sweeping economic and social reforms. With this commitment they were riding the crest of the antimilitarism that swept the country between May and October 1944.[46]

The power of the progressive forces was not consolidated, however. Their public demonstrations and lively campaigning convinced the conservatives that El Salvador was not yet ready for civilian rule. So, on October 21, 1944, a coup d'etat was led by the director of the National Police, Martínez ally Colonel Osmín Aguirre y Salinas. He met no resistance from the army. Arturo Romero went into exile in Costa Rica. Those remaining from the presidential campaign were a minor right-wing candidate and the official candidate, General Salvador Castaneda Castro, who had replaced Menéndez as provisional president immediately after the coup. The outcome was predictable.[47]

Four Years of Stagnation. On becoming president in March 1945, Castaneda was willing to permit some of the political organizations created in the ferment of 1944 to continue. He issued a general political amnesty, opened the borders, and undertook a reorganization of the government and army. But he was not inclined to carry forward the modest economic and social reforms Martínez had implemented. Castaneda's politics of stagnation were challenged in September when another general strike closed businesses, transportation, and newspapers in San Salvador. The masses and progressives within the middle class had seen an opportunity in the internecine military fights to force economic and social changes, but the president responded by instituting a variety of toothless reforms as a sop to the liberals. Then he began limiting their freedom in order to pacify the conservatives among his colleagues. After June 1945 the country operated almost continually under a state of siege.

Castaneda dramatically reduced the number of junior-grade officers and shipped a large number out of the country for training or service as diplomatic attachés between 1945 and 1948. (In an institution that eschewed punishment for lawbreakers and other young officers viewed as overly ambitious, "golden exile" quickly became an honored method of ridding the army of undesirables.) Castaneda thus created short-term relief but a long-term disaster for himself. Those sent abroad were among the remaining progressives in the Salvadorean army, and they returned as the 1948 presidential campaign began. The time they had spent out of the country served only to exacerbate a growing split within the officer corps.

The Noncampaign. The Castaneda administration bred nothing if not malaise among Salvadoreans. As the presidential campaign opened, there were no civilian candidates and little discussion of issues. What finally rattled the army and the people was the selection of an official candidate by the National Union Party (PUN), successor to Martínez's Pro-Patria. General Mauro Espinola Castro was a close ally of Castaneda but was understood to be a coward; he had reportedly deserted his position during the 1931 coup and had hidden during the April 1944 revolt. At sixty-five he was allegedly living with a woman of twenty and was known to be drinking heavily.

The political opposition finally had something to inspire it. News sheets appeared charging that the Ministry of Defense had become a political campaign headquarters, that military and government vehicles were being used for campaigning, and that the opposition was being denied access to radio but the PUN had unlimited broadcast time.[48] Unfortunately, the opposition's candidates, who included Aguirre y Salinas, were little better. As Espinola began losing support, fliers and posters appeared demanding Castaneda's continuation in office. When Espinola showed no sign of taking the hint, Castaneda moved to rescind the ban on reelection.

The National Assembly met on December 13 to call for the formation of a new constitutional assembly that would permit Castaneda to succeed himself. The next day fighting broke out in San Salvador between National Police loyal to the president and rebels in El Zapote barracks next to the Casa Presidencial. Castaneda sought refuge in the National Police headquarters, but soon after his arrival *golpistas* (military participants in a coup) took control of the building and devoted the remainder of the day to convincing a stubborn president that his career was at an end.[49]

The Third Cycle: 1948–1960

The nation was stunned. The identity of the *golpistas* was a mystery. Government ministers and the National Assembly president adjourned to the U.S. Embassy to try to learn their identity. The embassy shared their ignorance. When the Revolutionary Council announced itself later that day, there were three military officers and two civilians. In its initial statements the council broke with the past. It ended the state of siege, declared an amnesty, and announced the restoration of political rights. The council proclaimed its determination to initiate needed economic and social reforms. It also affirmed its determination to remove the army from politics and to make that institution a defender of the constitution.[50] In spite of Castaneda's unpopularity, Salvadoreans were underwhelmed. They had heard it all before.

Undeterred by popular apathy, the Revolutionary Council acted quickly. The council abrogated the constitution and reserved all legislative and executive powers to itself. It called for a freely elected constitutional assembly. It moved against former government officials and seventeen civilians whom it accused of malfeasance and corruption. Within two months of the coup, the council issued the "Law of Honesty," an ex post facto anticorruption law. The council created a momentum in its first weeks that demonstrated its commitment to both institutional and social change. Yet while this momentum was building, the old games once again began within the army. Less than a month after the coup, one of its leaders resigned from the council and took himself into exile in Honduras. Major Oscar Osorio, another council member, quickly emerged as the new strongman. In February 1949 the council granted itself a substantial pay raise. Young officers who had supported the coup were promoted. The defense budget was increased significantly.

As in 1944, there were two groups among the rebels. One recognized that some moderate reforms had to come in order to preserve peace, stability, and the institution of the army. The second group was committed to reform for its own sake. Both groups undoubtedly felt pressured by developments in Guatemala, where a 1944 revolt had succeeded and a progressive government, supported by the army, was making significant social and economic reforms. Those among the middle class who supported both the 1944 and 1948 movements did so out of essentially personal motives; they wanted to modernize and diversify the national economy, agriculture, and the system of national credit. They also wanted the government to facilitate the development of some industry. Meanwhile, all the economic and social problems described earlier worsened. According to an ecologist of the time (long before "ecology" became popular),

> There is an old saying, relished with patriotic fervor by the Salvadorians, that in their country "no one dies of hunger." They have accepted this national boast for so many decades that they do not realize it is fundamentally hunger from which most of them do die, that their only abundance is on the verbal level. ... Within the cultivable area is included a high proportion of ... land [that] can be safely farmed only by agricultural techniques far beyond the grasp (in 1948) of 90 percent of Salvadorians. In country districts, their illiteracy rate often approaches 100 percent.
>
> They have neither coal nor petroleum. Their hydroelectric developments are not adequate. ... "At maximum output during the rainy season, the available plant is sufficient to supply only minimum requirements, allowing no room for industrial expansion. At the restricted level of dry season capacity, maximum output is sufficient to meet only 60 percent of minimum needs." For cooking and industrial processes, Salvadorians are forced to depend almost entirely on firewood [but] their forests have been all but extirpated. [See Map 1.2] The average diet of the Salvadorian is estimated at fifteen hundred calories a day. ... In all the Western Hemisphere, only Haiti is in a more miserable situation than El Salvador.[51]

The Presidential Campaign. Nine months after the coup a new election law was decreed. All political parties based on religion, sex, class, foreign financial support, or communist affiliation were banned.[52] Decrees established an autonomous Central Election Council (CCE), which was charged with collecting

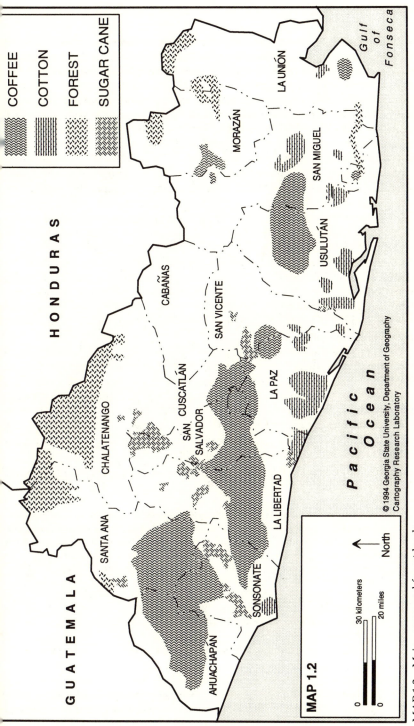

MAP 1.2 Major crops and forest lands

and counting the votes, and instituted women's suffrage and the secret ballot Oscar Osorio resigned from the Revolutionary Council to form the newest official party, the Revolutionary Party of Democratic Unification (PRUD); he became its candidate for the presidency. In the face of only nominal opposition from an old colleague who ran under the banner of the progressive Renovating Action Party (PAR), Osorio won with 60 percent of the vote. The PRUD captured a decisive majority in the Constitutional Assembly. In September 1950 Osorio was inaugurated, and the Assembly issued a new constitution under which the army acquired a new name, the Armed Forces of El Salvador, and had its strength set at 3,000 men. Neither the number nor the name, however, included the security forces, which retained their separate identities under the Ministry of Defense.

Reform and Economic Change. Once inaugurated, Osorio wasted no time before embarking on a series of public works and programs intended to encourage industry and trade, increase production, and diversify agriculture. Housing construction, health care, and sanitation projects were initiated. Labor unions were legalized in 1951, although demands for agricultural unions were ignored. A year later collective bargaining was instituted under government regulation. When the oligarchy began complaining about the reforms, the government reminded it of the "communist threat" in Guatemala. The grumbling died away.[53]

The economic model embraced by the Osorio regime and economic elite was "developmentalist" in encouraging growth and modernization of the industrial sector and diversification of agriculture. The government embarked on a road-building program and constructed the November 5 Dam on the Lempa River, which boosted energy output dramatically while cutting the cost of electricity by 25 percent. It also built the Puente de Oro (Bridge of Gold, so named because of its high cost), an 800-meter span across the Lempa on the Litoral Highway in south-central El Salvador.

By 1955 José María Lemus, who was handpicked by Osorio to succeed him, was praising the 1948 "revolution":

> The dispossessed classes have progressed in cultural and spiritual respects that concern the value of work and the enjoyment of human treatment regulated by law. And there has not been present, in the course of this great experience, the explosions of angry capitalists or the dangerous condition of mass discontent. The Revolution has constructed modern school buildings, raised educational standards in the most remote regions, sought a solution to the problem of urban housing by providing facilities for the proletariat and middle class, and has organized Rural Communities through which the problems of housing, work, and production in some zones have been resolved.[54]

This glowing assessment ignored what Alastair White recognized fifteen years later, that the Osorio and Lemus administrations,

> in attempting or appearing to effect a general expansion and improvement through industrial development ... tended to achieve only an expansion of job

opportunities for a new salaried middle class, and in attempting or appearing to introduce modern government provision for social development ... tended to create a relatively privileged sector within the working class, those with access to such innovations as social security, collective wage bargaining through the legal unions, and the government urban housing and rural land settlement schemes. These benefited a very small percentage of the poor, but could be represented demagogically as a social revolution being carried out by the government.[55]

Nothing was done that upset the oligarchy's control over the economy. The process of industrialization, which had been officially discouraged in the 1930s, found new life in the late 1940s and early 1950s. This was due not only to a regime change but also to increased coffee production and skyrocketing prices.[56] The oligarchy had to do something with its profits. Thus the traditional alliance between military and oligarchy acquired a new dimension, and others, including the existing (if minuscule) industrial sector and technocrats, were brought into the process.

Much of the new capital went to "import substitution," and industries were developed through joint-venture capital of the oligarchy and multinational corporations. This industrial expansion created an internal contradiction: The import-substitution model implicitly assumed an expanding domestic consumer market to absorb the goods that were being produced. But the linchpin of the oligarchy-state alliance was an understanding that El Salvador's first key to wealth, the land, was untouchable. Thus the possibility of developing through agrarian reform a class of small farmers who would become sufficiently affluent to acquire purchasing power was negated. Furthermore, El Salvador continued to be a net food importer. As prices rose, the problems of the poor, which Masferrer had condemned in the 1920s, were exacerbated rather than reduced.

In the long run neither industrialization nor agricultural diversification created new sources of employment. In fact, the number of jobs available, relative to working-age population, declined. Two examples illustrate the problem. In the industrial sector, prior to the arrival in the 1950s of the ADOC shoe factory, which was jointly owned by six oligarchic families, there were several thousand shoemakers and assistants in El Salvador. ADOC created several hundred industrial jobs, but it put most of the shoemakers out of business. In the agricultural sector, cotton production expanded from 9,800 hectares in 1942 to 19,030 hectares in 1951; by 1960 it increased to more than 43,000 hectares and five years later tripled to 122,300 hectares. This expansion took place at the expense of forests, cattle ranching, and subsistence farming and of both tenants and squatters. From the perspective of the growers, however, the return was well worth the price: By 1964 cotton accounted for 24 percent of El Salvador's total exports.[57] Meanwhile, thousands of tenant farmers were pushed off land that had previously provided them with subsistence crops.[58] The effect was noted by William Durham in his study of the ecological origins of the 1969 war between El Salvador and Honduras: "From a balance of payments point of view the country as a whole is better off with land in export

crops. But the problem is … that most Salvadoreans do not derive much benefit from export production."[59]

National Politics Under Osorio. The Revolutionary Council's promise tc
remove the army from politics soon proved empty. The PRUD emerged as a
political actor in its own right in 1952 when the CCE lost its autonomy and
came under PRUD control for the National Assembly elections. In that year
and in 1954, the regime so restricted the activities of opposition parties in the
election campaign that they withdrew their candidates. Osorio's justification
for this renewed interference was that an open campaign would permit communism to flourish in El Salvador.[60] The increasing radicalization of the Guatemalan government was a source of major concern to military and oligarchy
alike, and there was agreement between them that radical elements in El Salvador should be given no opportunity to gain a toehold in the country's political life.

By middecade army officers once again held a large number of government posts, including a majority of the departmental governorships and key
offices in new institutes that had been established to develop and carry out
various reforms. When Osorio announced that his chosen successor was a civilian, a large delegation of officers immediately informed the president that
although civilian participation in the government was acceptable, a civilian
president was not.[61] Osorio then chose Lieutenant Colonel José María Lemus.

The opposition waged a lackluster campaign; issues were all but ignored and party platforms were monotonously alike. Still, the government
and the PRUD did not take any chances. The National Guard repeatedly disrupted rallies and meetings of the opposition. Two months before the March
election, the opposition formed two coalitions in an effort to create a meaningful contest, but the CCE disqualified three of the five opposition candidates.
On election day the army was very much in evidence, and army officers
thought to be loyal to anyone other than Lemus were detained. To no one's
surprise, Lemus won.[62]

The Lemus Regime. The heavy-handed tactics and fraud perpetrated by
the government and the PRUD in the 1954 and 1955 elections created tensions
both within the Armed Forces and between civilian and military sectors.
Meanwhile, economic pressures were growing in the form of rising production costs and falling yields and prices. When Lemus spoke on the eleventh
anniversary of the "revolution" in December 1959, he could do no better than
rail against the communist threat. The crowd booed and jeered.[63]

The 1950s provided sufficient political latitude to permit the development of several center-to-left-leaning organizations. As demands for reform
increased, however, the regime grew more defensive. Increased repression
produced more opposition.[64] In an act of desperation, Lemus attempted to
rally popular support by announcing in July 1960 a sweeping program of social and economic reforms. Three weeks later the government trucked 20,000
peasants into the capital for an anticommunist rally. Archbishop Luís Chávez
y González concluded the rally with a mass. The following day students held
a rally of their own in the Plaza Libertad in downtown San Salvador. They
praised the Cuban Revolution, attacked government repression, and strongly

criticized the church for getting involved in politics. Security forces rounded up and incarcerated demonstrators. Lemus closed the national university, provoking even greater demonstrations. In September one student was killed and several persons (including the rector of the University of El Salvador) were arrested in a confrontation with police. Newspapers that had long supported the government broke with it over the growing repression.[65]

Coup d'Etat. In that same month Osorista officers and civilians began conspiring to overthrow Lemus. The revolt on October 25 was quick and bloodless. The new six-man junta included three civilians. The October coup marked both change and continuity in the political cycles that had begun in 1932. It represented a continuation of the pattern described earlier. But it also brought an important change: the introduction of the United States as a significant actor in Salvadorean politics. Unlike in 1932, when U.S. offers of assistance in the wake of the peasant insurrection were rebuffed, after 1960 the United States slowly increased its influence over the course of events in El Salvador.

As discussed in the next chapter, the United States did not play an important role in all the acts that were to follow. At times its presence was crucial in determining the course of events; at times it was absent from the stage when its presence might have prevented incipient tragedy; at times it initiated or encouraged action but then stepped back into the wings. It is clear, however, that after 1960 the United States was an actor with which the Salvadoreans—and at times other Central Americans—had to deal.

2

Challenges to Power, 1960–1980

... And the United States'
President's more
my country's President
than my country's President is,
the one who
like I say
right now is
named Colonel Fidel
Sánchez Hernández.

—Roque Dalton, "O.A.S."

To all appearances, by 1960 the oligarchy and the Armed Forces had institutionalized their relationship and solidified their respective places in El Salvador. The new decade, however, introduced a number of fresh actors on the political stage; some of them would eventually disappear, others would play a growing role, and one would walk on and off the stage, sometimes in a supporting role, other times as the protagonist. All, in one way or another, would affect the future course of events in El Salvador. The first group included other Central American countries and some small political parties that played significant roles in the 1960s before fading from the scene; the second group included other parties that played an increasingly important role into the 1970s and even—in some cases—the 1980s.

The third actor was the United States, which created the story line and wrote the draft for its future role (twenty years later) during the 1960s. The rationale was anticommunism; the plot included the Alliance for Progress and counterinsurgency; the action swung between encouragement for democracy and a willingness to leave the military-oligarchy power structure in place. At times, as during the tenure of Ambassador Murat Williams, the North Americans were diplomatic; sometimes they were aggressive, as in the successful effort to end the 1969 war with Honduras; sometimes they had a profound effect on the course of events by refusing to act, as in the 1972 elections. But regardless of its chosen role at a given moment, the United States was a new and permanent actor on the Salvadorean political stage after 1960.

REFORM, TO A POINT: 1960–1972

The junta that assumed office after the October coup dissolved the National Assembly and the Supreme Court. Like its predecessors, the junta lifted the state of siege, opened the borders to political exiles, and released Lemus's political prisoners into the arms of a waiting and jubilant crowd. According to junta member Fabio Castillo, "the Governmental Junta attempted to create a democratic climate and elaborated political and social guidelines which stressed development of a [completely open] electoral process and an educational program with the objectives of suppressing illiteracy and raising the educational level of the population."[1]

Visits by the members of the junta to the various army barracks to introduce themselves revealed the concerns of the officers. Would transfers occur without approval of the officers affected? Would the army continue its preeminent role in the national life? How would the regime deal with increasingly vocal communist and leftist groups?[2]

The presence of Castillo on the junta did nothing to assuage the officers' concerns. A professor of pharmacology at the national university, Castillo was an unabashed supporter of the Cuban Revolution. The appointment of a largely civilian cabinet caused further worry as the growing public clamor for change intensified. When the junta announced its intent to hold truly free elections and to permit the participation of all political groups, consternation moved the officers to action.

Three months to the night after the ouster of Lemus, officers in the San Carlos barracks commandeered the country's communications system and announced a revolt. Two members of the junta fled to Guatemala; the others, including Castillo, were arrested. It was all over within twelve hours, whereupon the successful rebels gathered at San Carlos and selected Colonel Julio Adalberto Rivera to head a new junta. Rivera asserted that the character of the revolt was anticommunist and anti-Cuba.[3]

The Role of the United States

The October coup had occurred just days before the U.S. presidential election in which John F. Kennedy defeated Richard Nixon. Thus it was a lame-duck Eisenhower administration that decided to withhold diplomatic recognition of the civilian-military junta.

Fabio Castillo, in testimony before the U.S. Congress in 1976, recounted his experiences with the U.S. chargé d'affaires who, Castillo charged, intervened openly. On one occasion the chargé, accompanied by oligarch Ricardo Quiñonez, visited Castillo and told him that "the U.S. Embassy did not agree with the holding of a free election and added that the Embassy would agree to a 'free election' held with two candidates previously approved by them." Castillo rejected the proposal, whereupon "Quiñonez, unable to control his anger, turned to the chargé and said: 'You see, they are Communists, we have to go ahead.'"

Two weeks later the chargé approached Castillo, who was also minister of education, at a diplomatic reception and tried again. "I guess you don't really want to go ahead with those plans to teach the people how to read and to educate them as you have previously announced." Castillo responded that "that was the explicit wish of the people of El Salvador who had been left in great ignorance and poverty." The chargé, who by this time was, according to Castillo, quite angry, replied, "Don't you know that educated people will ask for bread?" Castillo answered, "What's wrong with hungry people wanting bread and work?"

Castillo charged that from that time on "members of the U.S. Military Mission openly intensified their invitation to conspiracy and rebellion." He further asserted that "members of the U.S. Military Mission were at the San Carlos Headquarters on the day of the coup." Castillo affirmed that he "was able to see them there at 1:30 p.m." when he talked with Colonel Rivera.[4] The Kennedy administration, in office less than a week, immediately recognized the Rivera government. Murat Williams, who had been a young political officer in El Salvador during the 1948 coup, returned a few days after the 1961 countercoup as Kennedy's new ambassador.

The Rivera Era

On January 25, 1961, El Salvador had yet another government. The Civilian-Military Directorate, composed of Rivera, another colonel, and three civilians, was created. Two of the civilians resigned in April, partly in opposition to proposed reforms, partly because they were figureheads. In September Rivera resigned from the junta and joined with conservative Christian Democrats who had recently formed the latest incarnation of the official party, the National Conciliation Party (PCN).[5]

The two remaining members of the directorate set the election of a constitutional assembly for December 17. Only the PCN and five minor conservative parties were allowed to participate. To no one's surprise, the PCN garnered an overwhelming victory. A month later the Constitutional Assembly revised the 1950 constitution, gave itself the status of a national assembly, and scheduled a presidential election for April. The PCN nominated Rivera. AGEUS, the university student organization, provided Rivera's only competition: a donkey.[6]

If Rivera's regime was not to go the way of Lemus's, he would have to do something different. Encouraged by the United States through its ambassador, Murat Williams,[7] and to the dismay of the oligarchy, President Rivera opened the electoral process to opposition parties. He established proportional representation in the National Assembly, thus guaranteeing the opposition representation commensurate with its electoral strength. According to Williams, Rivera and Fabio Castillo were former schoolmates and "great friends." Rivera, Williams said, "in effect carried out the reforms that Castillo would have done."[8]

Williams's efforts were not universally praised. Soon after arriving in El Salvador he said he wanted to meet Castillo. Told by the political counselor that he "couldn't do it because your predecessor told us to have nothing to do with those people," Williams picked up the phone, called the national university to which Castillo had returned, and invited him to dinner at the ambassador's residence. Through this and similar activities, Williams soon alienated the oligarchy. Word spread north, and he was cautioned by then U.S. ambassador in Mexico Thomas Mann who told him, "Murat, you're making a big mistake in El Salvador not cooperating with the oligarchs. They have the power." After Lyndon Johnson became president in November 1963, Mann was named assistant secretary of state for inter-American affairs. Williams was recalled as ambassador in 1964.[9]

The Christian Democratic Party. After the Cuban Revolution the United States cast about for an alternative to right-wing military dictatorship and left-wing revolution in Latin America. The program developed under the rubric of the Alliance for Progress had three dimensions: political, economic, and military. The military dimension focused on "counterinsurgency"; the economic dimension emphasized a capitalist development model; the political focus emphasized a "third way" between the Scylla of leftist revolution and the Charybdis of right-wing military dictatorship. Christian Democrats offered the third way—a "revolution in liberty"—through social and economic reforms via the preferred model.[10] Thus the United States was only too happy to encourage the fledgling Christian Democratic Party (PDC) in El Salvador during the 1960s. Some U.S. officials envisioned a process of democratization that would culminate in a peaceful transition from military to civilian rule. U.S. hopes and Rivera's strategy coincided from 1962 to 1968, an alignment that led to gains by the opposition in the National Assembly and in mayoral and local elections as the decade progressed.

The PDC incorporated three distinct ideological positions from its founding. All came from Catholic thought, but one was reactionary and the other two were progressive. The reactionary faction split off and formed the PCN. Of the remaining two, one was inspired by the most progressive social doctrine of the Catholic Church and programmatically shared much in common with the international social democratic movement. The other, although it supported social and economic change, was conditioned in its thinking by a strong dose of anticommunism. The roots of future dissension and division were firmly planted when, early in the party's existence, the man who emerged as its principal theoretician, Roberto Lara Velado, came out of the first group, whereas the man who would become its dominant public figure, José Napoleón Duarte, belonged to the latter.[11]

From a small electoral showing in the 1964 municipal and National Assembly elections, the PDC eclipsed other opposition parties and by 1968 was challenging the PCN for control of the Assembly (see Table 2.1).

ORDEN. The military side of U.S. policy sought to forestall second Cubas through improved state security forces. This objective was spelled out in the March 1963 Declaration of San José, issued at the end of a meeting of the Central American presidents. "Communism is the chief obstacle to economic development" in Central America, asserted President Kennedy, who had chaired the meeting. In a 1967 staff memo Byron Engle, director of AID's Public Safety Program, wrote that the United States was "developing within the civil security forces ... an investigative capability for detecting criminal and/

TABLE 2.1   Christian Democratic Party Electoral Results in Municipal and National Assembly Elections, 1964–1976 (based on official government figures)

	1964	1966	1968	1970	1972	1974	1976[a]
Seats in National Assembly (of 52)	14[b]	15	19[c]	16[d]	0	15	0
Mayors	37[e]	83[e]	78[f]	8[e]	17[e]	17[e]	0
Percent popular vote	26	31	42[g]	27	57	NA[h]	—

[a]In 1976 the experiment in democracy was over. The opposition abstained for the first time since 1962 in protest against the manipulation of the electoral process by the PCN and government.

[b]The PAR also won six seats.

[c]Other opposition parties also gained six seats.

[d]Other opposition parties also won two seats.

[e]Including San Salvador.

[f]Including San Salvador, Santa Ana, and San Miwel, the three largest cities.

[g]Sixty percent in San Salvador.

[h]The government never published the election returns. According to Stephen Webre (in *José Napoleón Duarte and the Christian Democratic Party in Salvadoran Politics 1960–1972*), "An independent student of Salvadoran politics calculated that the UNO would have come out of a fair race with a majority in the Legislative Assembly" (Baton Rouge: Louisiana State University Press, 1979; p. 187).

Sources: Stephen Webre, *José Napoleón Duarte and the Christian Democratic Party in Salvadoran Politics 1960–1972* (Baton Rouge: Louisiana State University Press, 1979), pp. 81, 98, 102, 136, 147, 187; Rubén Zamora, "Seguro de vida o despojo? Análisis político de la transformación agraria" [Life insurance or plunder? Political analysis of the agrarian transformation] *ECA* 31, no. 335-336 (Sept.-Oct. 1976): 514, 517.

or subversive individuals and organizations and neutralizing their activities."[12] The U.S. set up agencies in each of the Central American countries and helped create a regional communications network that enabled each country to trade information on "subversives" traveling among them.

The United States became active in El Salvador in 1963. General José Alberto "Chele" Medrano, a senior officer in the National Guard and the Armed Forces High Command, was chosen to oversee developments. According to Medrano,

> ORDEN [Organización Democrática Nacional—"order" in Spanish] "grew out of the State Department, the CIA, and the Green Berets during the time of Kennedy. We created these specialized agencies to fight the plans and actions of international communism. We organized ORDEN, ANSESAL (Salvadorean National Security Agency), and counterinsurgency courses, and we bought special arms—G3 automatic rifles—to detain the communist movement. We were preparing the team to stop communism."[13]

Medrano organized a complex, multitiered paramilitary and intelligence network extending from the Casa Presidencial (the executive offices of the president) to the most remote villages. ORDEN was its rural arm and was intended, according to Medrano, to "indoctrinate the peasants regarding the advantages of the democratic system and the disadvantages of the communist system." In 1963 a Green Beret colonel, Arthur Simons, who was commander of the Eighth Special Forces Group in Panama, sent Medrano a team of ten counterinsurgency trainers. In discussions among themselves, "the idea occurred to [them] to catechize the people. [They] talked about how [they] had to indoctrinate the people, because he who has the population wins the war." In Medrano's view, "The army can easily annihilate guerrillas in the urban zone, but the peasants are tough. They can walk at night, see in the dark, see among the trees. We couldn't let them be deceived by the guerrillas." People so identified were considered "communists" and reported to ORDEN, which passed the information on to ANSESAL. There "we would study it and pass it on to the president, who would take appropriate action."[14]

"Appropriate action" usually meant murder, and sometimes the assassinations were carried out by ORDEN. Other times the army, National Guard, or a death squad known as Mano Blanca (White Hand) did them. Raul Castro, who followed Murat Williams as ambassador to El Salvador in 1964, asserted that Mano Blanca "was an offshoot of ORDEN, and the same people in ORDEN were to some extent the same people in the Mano Blanca. Even today, some of the same people are in the Death Squads. That was the origin."[15]

The Green Berets helped Medrano develop the structure and ideology of ORDEN, then trained a team of Salvadorean officers who included Nicolás Carranza and Domingo Monterrosa, two names that would figure prominently in the 1980s. Roberto D'Aubuisson, another Medrano protégé, would become the best known of all. Meanwhile, the officers trained civilian ORDEN leaders who then established local chapters.[16] ORDEN functioned as a quasi-legal entity until the October 1979 coup, after which it was formally abolished but continued to operate in another guise. Estimates on membership ranged from 50,000 to 150,000, with 100,000 card-carrying members the most commonly accepted figure. Many men, however, joined as a means of self-protection. If they were stopped for any reason by the security forces and could produce an ORDEN card, they were assured that nothing would happen to them. Without it, they were at the mercy of their captors. Knowledgeable Salvadoreans estimated that only 5 to 10 percent of ORDEN members actually functioned as vigilantes and *orejas* (literally "ears"—informers) for the government.†*

Economic Reforms Under Rivera

By some indicators, President Rivera succeeded not only in reversing the economic decline El Salvador endured during the late 1950s but also in setting the country on an economic course that created boom conditions. For example, the annual rate of growth of value added in the industrial sector between 1962 and 1967 was as much as 11.7 percent. In fact, the conditions that

---

* The symbol "†" throughout this book indicates privileged interviews (with informants who must remain anonymous).

produced the boom and bust under Osorio and Lemus remained unchanged. The substitute for agrarian reform was the economic integration of Central America. The reasoning, at least in El Salvador and Guatemala, the two most developed countries in the area, was that the unrestricted flow of capital, people, and goods throughout the isthmus would create additional markets for industrial products, new opportunities for investment, and a means of relieving the growing population pressure. Supported by the United Nations Economic Commission for Latin America (CEPAL) the idea of integration was at first opposed by the United States because CEPAL had suggested a limited and strongly regulated role for foreign investment as well as an emphasis on planned and balanced development and the elimination of competition and duplication of industries. These plans had to be dropped before the United States came around in the late 1950s.[17]

The result was the creation in 1961 of the Central American Common Market. CACM's impact was soon apparent. Intraregional trade increased 32 percent each year between 1962 and 1968, and the increase averaged 26 percent between 1960 and 1972. The nature of the goods being traded changed from unprocessed agricultural products to nondurable consumer goods.[18] In El Salvador, furthermore, the nature of industry had shifted by this time from import substitution to industry for export—that is, the assembly or packing of imported components.[19] For companies like Texas Instruments and Maidenform, this technique significantly increased their profit margin because item 807 of the U.S. Tariff Code required that duty be paid only on the "value added" to the product, that is, the cost of labor. At salaries averaging $4.00 per day, these companies' imports from El Salvador began growing: By 1975 their value was $12 million; four years later it had more than doubled, to $25.9 million.[20]

The Effects of Industrialization. The economic reforms of the early 1960s began attracting both domestic and foreign investment. The Alliance for Progress helped create the boom-time aura through the allocation of funds for housing, school construction, health facilities, and water and sewage projects. The army began providing workers for various public construction projects, and although the tactic demonstrated that the army was "working for the people," it also deprived civilians of hundreds of jobs in a country where the unemployment rate ranged between 30 and 57 percent.[21]

Industrial expansion occurred without commensurate growth in the level of employment because factories brought in the most modern machinery, which required few workers. Furthermore, the government provided no incentives for labor-intensive industry. On the contrary, the stated objective of the 1965–1969 development plan to promote "the use of modern equipment and methods" was officially encouraged by at least two means: the tariff-free importation of capital equipment and the provision by the Salvadorean Institute for Industrial Development of low-interest loans for the purchase of machinery.[22]

In industry, as in agriculture, the oligarchy's primary interest was the profit margin. According to two independent Salvadorean economic analysts, Salvadorean investors were in the habit of earning a 25 to 40 percent rate of re-

Brickmaker near San Salvador. In this labor-intensive work, the man carries a quantity of clay from a large pile about twenty-five meters away, dumps it in the frame, smooths it down with the level resting on the water pail, removes the frame, places it in the next space, and begins again. The bricks behind him are dry.

turn on investment, as compared with an expectation in the United States and Europe of 10 to 12 percent. Because they had investment alternatives both within and outside the country, this was a realistic goal. Cuban-born Peter Dumas, who at the time was part-owner and general manager of the Sheraton Hotel in the capital, said he came to El Salvador with the attitude that on a $1 million investment he would lose 5 percent the first year and 2 percent the second and make 3 percent the third and 12 percent thereafter. But Salvadoreans, he said, "thought I was crazy. They wanted a 100 percent return the first year." He added that by 1980 most Salvadorean businessmen were willing to accept a return of three or four points over the going interest rate—but by then investment had plummeted, a casualty of the growing political unrest.

Changes in Agriculture. A minimum-wage law for agricultural workers in May 1965 theoretically was to bring a new, higher standard of living for Salvadorean peasants. Its effect, however, was to create many thousands more landless and underemployed or unemployed people. As we saw in Chapter 1, from colonial times *colonos* and *aparceros* had formed an integral part of the *hacienda* system. In 1965, however, the government decided it was time to abolish that vestige of feudalism. As David Browning noted, provision of food and a *milpa* (small plot of land) for each worker was "officially discouraged and the colono or *aparcero* [was] expected to become a laborer whose sole connection with the property that he worked on [was] the wage paid to him by the

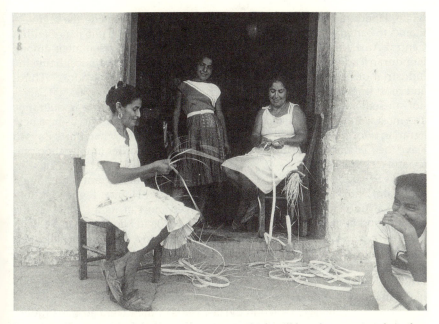

Women in Tejutepeque, Cabañas, make *trenzas,* which will later be sewn into hats that campesinos wear. The women are paid the equivalent of twenty-five cents per two-meter *trenza,* each one of which takes four to six hours to make.

owner." The effect was dramatic. The 1971 census recorded a decline during the preceding decade in the number of *colonos* from 55,769 to 17,019. At the same time the number of landless *campesinos* increased from 30,451 (11.8 percent of all rural Salvadoreans) in 1961 to 112,108 (29.1 percent) ten years later. By 1975 the figure had climbed again, to 166,922 landless people (40.9 percent).[23]

Origins of the "Soccer War"

A second reason for the dramatic increase in landless peasants was the 100-hour war between El Salvador and Honduras in 1969, which left several thousand dead and at least 100,000 Salvadoreans homeless. Dubbed the "Soccer War" by foreign journalists because it followed a series of bitterly contested games between the two countries during the qualifying rounds for the 1969 World Cup, the miniwar was in fact the result of at least three other, far more profound issues.[24]

First, the two countries were at odds over their border—a dispute that extended all the way back to independence. Second, they were at odds over the effect of CACM on their respective economies. El Salvador saw its balance of trade within the isthmus increase markedly as it began producing industrial goods for export; Honduras watched its balance of trade decline. Meanwhile, Honduras enjoyed a favorable balance of trade outside the region—thanks to bananas, lumber, and meat—but suffered a great imbalance within Central America. This state of affairs caused increasing resentment among Honduran leaders as they realized their country was, in effect, subsidizing the industrial development of its neighbors, in particular El Salvador.[25] Third, and most important, was the presence in Honduras of at least 300,000 Salvadorean settlers. Many of these people were second-generation immigrants, and most were successful small farmers. In April 1969 Honduras, using a new agrarian reform law, notified Salvadorean farmers that they had thirty days to leave their land. In June Honduras reversed its open-border immigration policy and closed its border.

El Salvador responded by closing its border to immigrants and filing a complaint with the Inter-American Commission on Human Rights. On July 14, El Salvador invaded Honduras, destroyed most of its air force on the ground, and advanced far enough to cut the roads to Nicaragua and Guatemala. Five days later the war ended, thanks in part to a cease-fire arranged by the Organization of American States, but due largely to U.S. pressure on the Salvadorean government in the form of threatened economic sanctions. Within El Salvador the war was enormously popular and served to take people's minds off the country's growing economic problems.

Those problems emerged in the last years of the Rivera administration. World market prices for coffee dropped; disease and drought severely affected the cotton crop; sugarcane surpluses increased as world demand plummeted. Private investment declined as budget and international payment deficits mounted. The government was forced to curtail many public works projects and social welfare programs. Unemployment grew. These conditions bred popular unrest as the unemployed took to the streets for the first time since 1959 to demand relief.

The 1967 Presidential Election

It was in this context that President Rivera dictated to the PCN national convention his choice of General Fidel Sánchez Hernández as successor. Although the PDC offered a candidate, the only opponent who received any attention from Sánchez was the PAR candidate, Fabio Castillo. Castillo had become rector of the University of El Salvador in 1963. During his four-year tenure, he significantly upgraded the quality of education, expanded enrollment, and began providing scholarships for needy students. Sánchez Hernández set the tone of the campaign by declaring that the people had a choice between communism and liberty.[26]

The Catholic Church jumped into the fray with a condemnation of the PAR by the bishop of San Vicente, Monseñor Pedro Aparicio.[27] Aparicio also threatened to excommunicate parishioners who had the temerity to ally themselves with the PAR. Finally, the Episcopal Conference issued a declaration two weeks before the election reminding the flock of the church's blanket condemnation of communism.[28] The outcome of the election was at once predictable and surprising: predictable because Sánchez Hernández won; surprising because the PAR garnered 14.4 percent of the national vote, the Christian Democrats ran second with 21.6 percent, and the PCN led with 54.4 percent. In the Department of San Salvador, however, the PAR led the PDC 29 percent to 25 percent; the PCN gained only a plurality, 41 percent.[29]

The Man on Donkey-Back

The economic woes that Sánchez Hernández inherited grew worse. Labor unions joined the protests, and many teachers and workers went on strike. The president responded by naming a colonel as minister of labor and charging that the unrest was communist-inspired.[30] Meanwhile, the army began demanding a larger budget and new equipment and began receiving counterinsurgency training that had been offered by the United States in the mid-1960s. The growing political unrest in El Salvador and the restiveness in the army, coupled with the intraregional economic issues, provided Sánchez with all the excuses he needed to invade Honduras on July 14, 1969.

The Benefits and Costs of War. In the short term, Sánchez succeeded in distracting his country's people from their economic woes. The most famous picture to come out of the four-day battle was that of the president astride a donkey at the Salvadorean-Honduran border. In the long run, however, Sánchez Hernández's little war only exacerbated the deteriorating economic conditions within the country. The war itself was expensive: About $20 million—or one-fifth of El Salvador's annual budget—was expended in those four days.[31]

The Honduran market, which in 1968 had taken $23 million in Salvadorean goods, vanished. El Salvador's route via the Pan American Highway to Nicaragua and Costa Rica, its other CACM trading partners, was closed for a time. The Common Market itself was a shambles. El Salvador suddenly found itself with tens of thousands of new landless and jobless citizens inside its boundaries.

Agrarian Reform. Sánchez Hernández, who prided himself on being a moderate, decided to capitalize on his popularity by initiating a series of mild reforms, the most significant of which was to be a "democratic program of agrarian reform."[32] The president argued that this reform had long been needed and was made even more necessary by the recent influx from Honduras. Enrique Alvarez Córdova, one of the more progressive members of the oligarchy, was minister of agriculture.[33] Alvarez was among those who most strongly influenced the proposed reform.

The National Assembly, operating with a coalition of opposition and progressive PCN members, and with both government and PDC agrarian reform bills on its agenda, called a National Agrarian Reform Congress. Composed of delegates from all sectors of Salvadorean society, the congress met in San Salvador in January 1970. During the first session the entire private sector walked out after losing a roll-call vote on the question of whether the congress should pass resolutions and make recommendations. The private sector opposed this, arguing that agrarian reform was a technical, not a political, issue and that there was therefore no sense surveying national opinion on the question—the very point of the congress.

The delegates then went far beyond anyone's expectations by identify ing the concentration of land in few hands as the major barrier to full employ ment and development of national resources and by concluding that, unde these circumstances, it was "not only a right of the state but a duty" to insti tute "massive expropriation in favor of the common good."[34] The delegate also tackled another taboo—the long-proscribed *campesino* unions—and ar gued that the only way agrarian reform would work was to ensure the partici pation of the projected beneficiaries, the peasants. The delegates argued tha the only way to achieve this was for the government to restrain the *hacendado* and their minions within the Armed Forces while defending the right of the *campesinos* to organize.[35]

The 1970 National Elections

Two months after the Agrarian Reform Congress, national elections re duced the opposition's seats in the National Assembly from almost half t barely a third. As shown in Table 2.1, the Christian Democrats and other pro gressive opposition parties had come within two seats of a majority in the As sembly in the 1968 elections. The PDC also controlled mayoralties in El Salva dor's three largest cities. After the war, however, the PDC and othe opposition parties lost seven seats, and the PCN swept seventy of the seventy eight mayoralties that the PDC had held during the previous four years. N more was heard about agrarian reform until the mid-1970s. The decline in th electoral fortunes of the opposition was, in a sense, temporary. The economi problems described earlier persisted in spite of a short-lived surge in coffe prices resulting from a blight in Brazil in 1969–1970. Meanwhile, the opposi tion parties decided to form a coalition for the 1972 presidential elections.

THE CRITICAL ELECTION OF 1972

Stephen Webre, in his study of the Christian Democratic Party in Salva dorean politics, observed that "the real question facing El Salvador in 1968 was not whether the opposition would continue to make gains, but what the PCN would do when the electoral solution became absolutely incompatibl with its survival as the dominant party."[36] The answer to that question cam with the 1972 presidential election.

The Opposition Comes Together. In the late 1960s two other oppositior parties were formed. One was the Revolutionary National Movement (MNR) which affiliated with the Socialist International. Its secretary general was a lawyer, Guillermo Manuel Ungo, whose father had been one of the founders of the PDC a decade before. The other party was the Nationalist Democrati Union (UDN), which described itself as the "noncommunist" left but wa strongly influenced by the proscribed Salvadorean Communist Party.[37]

In September 1971 the PDC, MNR, and UDN announced their intentior of forming a permanent coalition, the National Opposition Union (UNO), no just for purposes of the coming election but of working together on a continu ng basis. "We have a common goal," they stated in their joint manifesto, "capable of transcending the problem of differences of ideology and strategy; we desire a positive change in the existing structures of political and economic power which have demonstrated their injustice and have had a clearly retrogressive effect on our development."[38] The PDC had long opposed coalitions, but by 1971 it recognized that the greatest problem facing the opposition was its disunity. In addition, the PDC, as the largest of the three parties, negotiated with the other two from a position of strength.

The Campaign. To no one's surprise, José Napoleón Duarte, who had served for several years as mayor of San Salvador and was far and away the most popular opposition figure in the country, was chosen to lead the UNO ticket. Duarte asked for and got Ungo as his vice-presidential running mate. UNO's platform was modest: "We do not promise to create a paradise overnight. We merely intend to start the country down a different road from that which it has followed for so long and which has brought it to such grave and overwhelming difficulties."[39]

As in the past, President Sánchez Hernández dictated his choice of successor to the PCN and the army: his presidential chief of staff, Colonel Arturo Armando Molina. Two other candidates, both to the political right of Molina, graced the ballot. One, José Antonio Rodríguez Porth, was the candidate of those oligarchs who had diversified their holdings into industry and commerce. The other, General José Alberto Medrano, was the choice of the landed oligarchy. By then Medrano was a hero of the Soccer War and former director of the National Guard. The year before, Medrano had been arrested for killing a policeman on the general's own doorstep. The policeman had been sent to arrest him for complicity in an attempted coup. Medrano pleaded self-defense and a jury acquitted him.

Attention focused on Molina and Duarte, both of whom mounted vigorous national campaigns. As the campaign heated up, Duarte and Ungo became the objects of ad hominem attacks intended to call their honesty and competence into question and to portray them as communists or at least fellow travelers. Despite the polemics, there was only one direct physical attack. Duarte's campaign caravan was fired on by unidentified assailants in eastern El Salvador in late December 1971; the driver of the lead car was killed. President Sánchez condemned the killing and ordered an investigation, but nothing came of it.

Mayoral and Assembly elections were scheduled for March, after the presidential election. The PCN did not fear losing the presidency, but it did fear losing its majority in the National Assembly. To avoid such an outcome, the CCE disqualified on technicalities UNO Assembly slates in the six largest departments in the country—including San Salvador, where UNO strength was greatest. Thus, before the balloting for president, the PCN had ensured that there was no way the UNO could win a majority in the Assembly.

February 20, 1972. The cancellation of the UNO slates, the bitter campaign rhetoric, and the murder of the UNO driver merely set the stage for

election day. Turnout was heavy, and as the returns began coming in from the
rural departments, Molina took a commanding lead. Then the tide turned
Duarte carried San Salvador, home to 30 percent of the nation's voters, two to
one. The government immediately prohibited further announcement of re
turns. Finally, almost twenty-four hours after the polls closed, the CCE an
nounced that Molina had won by a margin of 22,000 votes. UNO had a differ
ent count. Its figures, taken directly from election boards around the country
showed Duarte 9,500 votes ahead.[40] Molina agreed to a recount. Duarte and
Ungo announced they would ask the CCE to nullify the votes and schedule a
new election. Because Rodríguez Porth and Medrano had garnered 100,000
votes between them, neither Molina nor Duarte had an absolute majority. The
constitutional procedure in such an event was to throw the election into the
National Assembly, which hastily convened on February 25 and elected
Molina president.

   March 12, 1972. Duarte and the UNO then called on voters in the Depart
ment of San Salvador to deface their ballots in the Assembly elections. Under
Salvadorean law, marred ballots were counted as null votes, and if they ex
ceeded the number of valid votes, the election theoretically was nullified. Al
most 75,000 voters heeded the UNO's call, a clear majority of the 144,101 votes
cast. The UNO asked the departmental electoral board to nullify the election
and on March 23 it did. The CCE promptly overturned that decision.

Coup d'Etat

   Shortly after midnight on March 25, the San Carlos and El Zapote bar
racks in the capital revolted. Led by Colonel Benjamin Mejía, the rebel
quickly gained control of San Salvador and captured President Sánchez
Hernández and his daughter. With San Salvador secure, Mejía went on na
tional radio and announced "the triumph of the military youth." His an
nouncement was premature. Although he had the solid support of the army in
San Salvador, the air force and all the security forces remained loyal to the
government. Even as Mejía was speaking, the air force began bombing the
city. The National Guard converged on the capital from all points, and the ini
tially bloodless coup became a bloody fight for San Salvador. Duarte, at
Mejía's request, issued an appeal by radio for listeners to support the rebels.[41]

   As rebel positions crumbled, Duarte sought refuge in the home of the
Venezuelan Embassy's first secretary. After Sánchez Hernández regained his
office, soldiers found Duarte and carted him off. The Christian Democratic
government of Venezuela threatened to break diplomatic relations if Duarte
was not freed. The Salvadorean government's announcement of plans to
shoot all *golpistas* brought concerted protest from the diplomatic corps
Sánchez Hernández agreed to ship the plotters into exile. Duarte took up resi
dence in Venezuela, and Molina was duly inaugurated.[42]

   As Stephen Webre observed in a masterpiece of understatement, the log
ical flaw of the electoral solution of the 1960s was that it "encouraged an active
opposition but, by definition, forbade that opposition to come to power."[4]
The army had been willing to lose some of its support from the most reaction

ary elements of the oligarchy, as symbolized in the candidacies of Rodríguez Porth and Medrano, but it was not willing to give up one iota of real political power.

Corruption as an Instrument of the Status Quo

"It is a notorious and public fact," wrote retired Salvadorean army lieutenant colonel Mariano Castro Morán, "that corruption has come to pervade all levels of public administration. ... The continuation in government of the regime's functionaries is not only because of political ambition but because they try to continue enriching themselves. ... It is the survival imperative of a mafia encrusted with power." Castro Morán cited several examples of corruption, including that resulting from the construction of the new airport and superhighway connecting it and San Salvador in the late 1970s. But, he suggested, "the most eloquent [indictment] is the silence and failure to investigate [cases of corruption] by the authorities."[44]

It is impossible to understand the relationship between the oligarchy and the military after 1932 without understanding the institutional system of corruption that guaranteed that key army officers would become and remain loyal not to the interests of the whole country but to their benefactors and their institution. Peter Dumas, of the San Salvador Sheraton Hotel, asserted during an interview that the private sector was "more corrupt" than the army. He explained that as long as officers were in the barracks there was no opportunity for them to become corrupt.[45] When they assumed positions in state-owned companies such as ANTEL (the telecommunications company), however, opportunities for corruption abounded. Dumas described how the system might work for him: An officer would be invited to dinner at the hotel, to return and bring his family, and to use hotel facilities (gratis, of course) for a birthday party or similar event; there would follow an invitation to spend the weekend at the manager's beach house. Later the officer would be offered the opportunity to buy 10 percent of a business with guarantees that if he needed a loan one would be available at attractive interest rates, courtesy of a bank owned by members of the oligarchy. This, Dumas concluded, was only one example of how a "very elastic system" of corruption worked.

Members of the army provided further confirmation of the system. A lieutenant colonel suggested that low salaries "led directly to corruption," then added that military personnel "were poorly paid intentionally—in order to make them ripe for corruption." In January 1980, those salaries ranged from $1,120 for a colonel to $600 for a lieutenant. A sergeant's salary was $200, a corporal's $100, and a soldier's $80; also included were uniforms, meals, and bed. René Guerra y Guerra, who was a senior official of ANTEL in the late 1970s, related how a cabinet member approached him at a funeral and offered $80,000 to help a certain supplying company win a bid from ANTEL. Guerra declined the offer, but later a company official offered him $40,000 more, telling him that the country was close to collapse and the money could be a "colchón" (literally, a mattress, a cushion) for him. Again, Guerra said, he refused. He concluded by noting that "corruption has been a tool of the oligarchy [which has] yielded economic profits to the oligarchy—ultra right—and political profits to the far left."[46]

REACTION AND REPRESSION

Alastair White observed in his 1973 study of El Salvador that the years after 1932 were characterized by an erratic oscillation between "concession and repression" with little effort to maintain a balance between the two. White noted that on the one hand, Araujo in 1931 and Menéndez in 1944 fell after making too many concessions to popular demands; on the other hand, Martínez in 1944, Castaneda in 1948, Lemus in 1960, and Sánchez Hernández in 1972 all went too far in the opposite direction.[47]

After the aborted coup and the inauguration of Molina, it appeared for a brief time that the balance had been restored. But 1972 proved to be a watershed. The army-dominated government had increasingly infuriated most of the oligarchy by its modest reform efforts, and it had alienated many workers, peasants, and youth by the inadequacy of those reforms and by the blatant fraud that paraded as an election.

Molina, his legitimacy weakened by the attempted coup, searched desperately for a means to reinforce his authority. He found it, as so many of his predecessors had, in "anticommunism" and "law and order." The scapegoat for his campaign became the University of El Salvador (UES), a target of increasingly frequent right-wing attacks. Charging that the UES "had fallen into the hands of the Communists," Molina induced the National Assembly in July to issue a decree ending the university's autonomy[48] and ordered its campuses in San Salvador, Santa Ana, and San Miguel occupied by security forces. Many professors, students, and administrators were arrested; foreigners among them were expelled; and a good number of Salvadoreans were exiled. The university was reopened in September 1973 under government control and with a government-appointed rector.[49]

Molina scored points among Salvadorean conservatives, who viewed the university (not without reason) as a hotbed of revolution. But the repressive character of this action undoubtedly contributed to the increasing radicalization of thousands of young Salvadoreans and provided one more reason for them to believe that meaningful social, political, and economic change was impossible under the existing regime.

And Now ... Miss Universe

In the midst of these developments, El Salvador won the privilege of hosting the 1975 Miss Universe pageant. Apart from the perceived prestige associated with the event, Salvadorean government and business leaders saw in it an opportunity for worldwide publicity that would promote a nascent tourist industry. Thousands of other Salvadoreans saw it differently. They saw a set of warped priorities that led the government to spend about $30 million on the pageant in the face of massive social needs.[50] So it was that UES students in Santa Ana demonstrated in protest; the demonstration was forcibly disbanded by the National Guard. At that, more than 2,000 UES students in San Salvador marched in solidarity from the university to the Plaza Libertad downtown. They suddenly found themselves surrounded by units of the National Guard with all avenues of escape cut off. The troops—without provocation, according to eyewitnesses—opened fire on the demonstrators, leaving at least thirty-seven dead and several dozen more "disappeared."[51]

This massacre occurred at a time of increasing violence at both ends of the political spectrum. On one side, revolutionary organizations created at the beginning of the decade were kidnapping members of the oligarchy with increasing regularity and holding them for enormous ransoms. On the other, security forces were engaging in official repression, such as the massacre in the hamlet of La Cayetana in November 1974. Peasants there had been engaged for some time in a land dispute with a neighboring *hacendado*. The National Guard and National Police, accompanied by members of ORDEN, surrounded the town and opened fire. Six farmers were killed; thirteen "disappeared"; twenty-five were arrested.[52]

In August 1975 an extremist organization, the FALANGE (Anticommunist Wars of Elimination Liberation Armed Forces), made its debut with a public commitment to exterminate all communists and their sympathizers in El Salvador. The FALANGE would be joined by several other groups[53] in the following years, all of which had four things in common: They were all connected with certain army officers; their membership consisted of off-duty National Guardsmen and National Police, supplemented by ORDEN members, occasional mercenaries, and right-wing members of the oligarchy; they all received money from various members of the oligarchy; and they all carried the generic name "death squad."[54]

Electoral Fraud Redux

The mayoral and Assembly elections in 1974 were marked by even more blatant manipulation than had been evident two years earlier. The CCE never published official returns, but the government announced that the UNO had won fifteen seats in the Assembly and that the PCN controlled thirty-six. In 1976 UNO nominated no candidates, refusing to dignify what it was certain would be another electoral farce. Thus, for the first time in fourteen years, the opposition deliberately abstained.

Agrarian Reform ... Again

On the heels of the 1976 election, Molina and the National Assembly decreed a modest agrarian transformation ("reform" was a word they avoided) and nationalized almost 61,000 hectares in the departments of Usulután and San Miguel. Most of this transformation zone was either cow pastures or planted in cotton, and the aim was to divide it among 12,000 *campesino* families. The decree followed a 1974 law that permitted, under certain conditions, the forced rental or even expropriation of fallow or insufficiently exploited land and a 1975 law that created the Salvadorean Institute of Agrarian Transformation (ISTA).

TABLE 2.2   Economic Groups and Number of Businesses by Economic Sector, 1974
(businesses as percent of total in parentheses)

	Coffee-Growing Oligarchy		Non-Coffee-Growing Oligarchy		Other Businesspersons		Total Businesses
Agriculture	65	(86.5)	10	(2.6)	27	(10.9)	102
Mining	—	—	2	(1.2)	49	(8.2)	6
Construction	49	(55.1)	36	(32.1)	91	(2.8)	124
Industry	156	(72.7)	98	(15.9)	16	(11.4)	415
Commerce	185	(53.3)	92	(28.5)	199	(18.2)	476
Transportation	9	(8.7)	10	(28.6)	40	(62.7)	59
Services	82	(72.9)	32	(10.2)	130	(16.9)	244
Total	546	(66.0)	280	(18.7)	600	(15.3)	1,426

Source: David Mena, Universidad Centroamericana José Simeón Cañas, 1980.

The first two laws had raised howls of protest from the oligarchy, whose attempt to have them struck down in court failed. The creation of the transformation zone led the oligarchy, through its various interest groups such as the National Association of Private Enterprise (ANEP), to launch a massive opposition campaign. As in the past, ANEP insisted it was "not against agrarian transformation" but charged that this particular project (like all others before it) was precipitous; that it had been rushed through without sufficient forethought or consultation; and that the planners were "divorced from national realities."[55]

The oligarchy did not stop with *campos pagados* (paid political advertisements). Minister of Defense Carlos Humberto Romero had already been chosen by Molina as his successor with the understanding that Romero would support the agrarian reform. But Romero had other loyalties: He went to Molina and threatened him with a coup d'etat if the agrarian reform went forward.† Molina, seeing the proverbial handwriting, met with members of the oligarchy and arranged a "compromise" that effectively emasculated the program.[56]

INDUSTRIAL GROWTH DURING THE 1970s

While the oligarchy was winning its political battles, it was also continuing to expand its economic interests. We saw earlier that industrialization resulted from an alliance between the oligarchy and the military and incorporated other elements in Salvadorean economic life. The primacy of the coffee-growing families in the industrial sector and their alliance with foreign investment are important factors because they confirm the concentration of wealth and economic control in the country.

Table 2.2 reveals the extent to which coffee-growing families controlled the industrial life of El Salvador. They had invested a total of $278 million by 1974, more than 50 percent of it in industry.[57] Meanwhile, non-coffee-growing members of the oligarchy had $79 million invested, nonmembers of the oli-

TABLE 2.3   Distribution of Foreign Capital by Country and Economic Group, 1974
(millions of dollars; as percent of total in parentheses)

	Coffee-Growing Oligarchy		Non-Coffee-Growing Oligarchy		Others		Total
United States	$9.2	(80.7)	$1.0	(8.7)	$1.21	(10.6)	$11.4
Panama	8.37	(76.0)	0.7	(6.4)	1.91	(17.4)	11.0
Canada	15.38	(88.4)	—	—	2.01	(41.6)	17.4
Japan	10.89	(93.9)	0.15	(1.3)	0.6	(5.2)	11.6
Europe	8.06	(66.1)	2.31	(18.9)	1.81	(14.8)	12.2
Latin America	1.79	(94.2)	0.04	(2.1)	0.099	(5.2)	1.9
Central America	0.8	(34.7)	0.02	(0.8)	1.5	(65.0)	2.3
Others	—	—	0.014	(100.0)	—	—	0.014
Total	$54.5	(80.3)	$4.2	(6.3)	$8.1	(13.4)	$66.8

Source: David Mena, Universidad Centroamericana José Simeón Cañas, 1980.

garchy $64.27 million. Table 2.3 demonstrates the extent of the alliance between foreign investment and the coffee-growing members of the oligarchy. Only one group of foreign investors—other Central Americans—invested their money in any significant amount outside this group.

In El Salvador the U.S. economic presence was strong. Although in the context of Latin America, U.S. investment was minuscule (less than 1 percent of total U.S. investment in the hemisphere), within El Salvador the impact was powerfully felt. That investment climbed from $19.4 million in 1950, of which about 25 percent was invested in industry, principally in textiles, pharmaceuticals, chemicals, petroleum, paper products, and food, to $42.8 million in 1975. Gross U.S. investment for 1974 was $9.2 million, of which 56 percent was invested in industry. One must also keep in mind that most "Panamanian" investors were subsidiaries of U.S. concerns; hence total U.S. investment was considerably larger than the $9.2 million figure. (Fully 63 percent of all foreign investment in 1974 was in industry, with services in second place at 27.6 percent.)[58]

The concentration of wealth may be viewed in another way. An examination of the distribution of capital invested by Salvadoreans in nonagricultural corporations (see Table 2.4) shows that 5.2 percent of all owners (the last three categories in Table 2.4) controlled $2.25 billion or 57 percent of all corporate capital in 1980. Meanwhile, 77 percent of the proprietors held only 18 percent of the corporate investments. From another perspective, Manuel Sevilla of the UCA defined the oligarchy as 114 (not fourteen!) family groups (1,309 individuals) whose nonagricultural investments in 1,716 corporations exceeded 1 million colones in 1984 ($400,000) and whose capital holdings totaled $1.71 billion. The top twenty family groups, listed in Table 2.5, controled $1.106 billion, or 64.7 percent of the total; the top fourteen controlled $939 million, or 55 percent. The concentration of wealth within the Salvadorean economic elite was such that although oligarchy families controlled only a slight majority (57 percent) of the 3,000 corporations that filed tax forms in 1979, they controlled 84.5 percent of the capital investment.[59]

TABLE 2.4   Distribution of Capital Invested by Salvadoreans
in the National Economy, 1980

Amount of capital held (in dollars)	Owners		Capital	
	Number	Percent	Amount (in millions of dollars)	Percent
Under $20,000–80,000	26,251	77.27	10.56	18
$80,000–200,000	4,161	12.25	24.76	13
$200,000–400,000	1,800	5.3	502.40	12
$400,000–2 million	1,517	4.5	1,196.44	30
$2-4 million	160	0.5	426.88	11
Over $4 million	76	0.2	625.00	16
Total	33,965	100	3,986.04	100

Source: Manuel Sevilla, "Visión global sobre la concentración económica en El Salvador" (Overview of the concentration of wealth in El Salvador), Boletín de Ciencias Económicos y Sociales, May-June 1984, p. 177.

Effects of Investment Patterns

One important effect of the investment pattern was that industrial investments became concentrated in the urban zones, a factor that did not alleviate the growing underemployment in the countryside and exacerbated the population problem in the cities (especially the capital) as people migrated looking for work. Table 2.6 illustrates this rural-urban shift between 1950 and 1980. The total percentage of people employed in agriculture dropped from 65 to 43 percent in thirty years. Meanwhile, industrial employment increased only from 15.5 to 19.4 percent; employment in services made up the difference. The table also reveals the changing patterns of employment for men and women. Perhaps the most interesting statistic is that although the number of women in industry increased, their percentage in industrial jobs declined. In short, the number of persons employed by the industrial sector remained tiny relative to the pool of available labor. Still, urban unemployment in San Salvador in 1974 was 14 percent, a figure that did not decline in succeeding years and grew rapidly in the 1980s.

The distribution of capital, not surprisingly, is reflected in the distribution of income. As shown in Table 2.7, 42 percent of all Salvadorean families earned $80 per month or less in 1976–1977; 6 percent of families earned $400 per month or more. For the poorest, given inflation, $960 per year is not significantly more than the $618 urban families were earning in 1950 and is only $256 more than a family of six needed in 1975 to provide life's basic necessities. The concentration of wealth, income, and the primary means of production had profoundly negative effects in the social, economic, and political spheres. Beyond the mere concentration of wealth and capital, the Salvadorean economy was unable to sustain internal growth, and the oligarchy did not take advantage of opportunities for expansion that derived from more diverse integration in the international economy. Economic decisions were made on the basis of a small group of people, not in terms of social needs or national interest. Other costs were lack of efficiency in the use of primary resources and chronic underutilization of the work force, capital, and land.[60] The most seri-

TABLE 2.5   Family Group Ownership of and Investment in Nonagricultural Businesses in El Salvador, 1979

Family Group	Number of Businesses	Total Capital
Regalado	135	$176,073,840
Meza Ayau	104	95,584,464
Freund	47	90,924,772
Hill (Arguello, Llach)	86	85,536,160
Alvarez	95	66,908,400
Salaverría	85	64,693,040
De Sola	69	58,000,000
Simán	52	54,092,320
Guirola	52	49,016,800
González Guerrero	49	47,431,920
Liebes	41	40,751,120
Ortiz Mancia	33	37,624,000
Quiñonez	45	36,560,000
Sol Millet	26	35,820,160
Wright	61	33,390,116
Dueñas	44	32,056,400
Palomo	29	29,392,720
García Prieto	46	29,200,000
Baldochi-Dueñas	22	29,076,400
Guttfreund	27	14,159,920
Hasbun-Handal	6	4,620,720
Cristiani-Burkard	8	2,416,000
Magaña	4	1,374,400
Vidri Miró	4	433,660

Note: The original list cites 114 family groups, which include 1,309 individuals with declared capital investments totaling one million colones ($400,000) or more. This table includes the top twenty family groups, by size of total investments, three other family groups whose names appear in this study, and the family group with the smallest total investment.

Source: Ministry of the Treasury, Statistics on Capital Holdings, San Salvador, 1980, cited in Manuel Sevilla, "Visión global sobre la concentración económica en El Salvador," Boletín de Ciencias Económicos y Sociales, May–June 1984, pp. 188–189.

ous cost, of course, was growing social and political unrest, which led to civil war by 1980.

The 1977 Election—and After

The UNO decided to enter the political fray once again in 1977. With Duarte still in exile, the coalition turned to a retired colonel, Ernesto Claramount, to head its ticket and chose the former PDC mayor of San Salvador, José Antonio Morales Erlich, as his running mate. Of this election Mariano Castro Morán wrote "In [San Salvador] there was a massive turnout. Some irregularities were noted that led people to expect a normal electoral fraud. Disquieting news arrived from the countryside. ... Voting was im-

TABLE 2.6   Sectorial Distribution of the Labor Force in Agriculture, Industry, and Services, by Decade and Sex, 1950–1980 (in thousands)

	Total			Males			Females		
	Agri-culture	Industry	Services	Agri-culture	Industry	Services	Agri-culture	Industry	Services
1950	447	106	131	434	78	61	14	28	78
Percent	65.4	15.5	19.2	75.7	13.6	10.7	12.4	24.9	62.8
1960	517	145	179	506	109	84	10	35	96
Percent	61.5	17.2	21.4	72.4	15.7	12	7.3	25	67.7
1970	662	170	350	650	126	166	13	44	184
Percent	56	14.4	29.6	69	13.4	17.6	5.2	18.4	76.5
1980	685	308	594	665	236	291	20	72	303
Percent	43.2	19.4	37.5	55.8	19.8	24.4	5	18.2	76.8

Source: Inter-American Development Bank, Economic and Social Progress in Latin America, 1987 Report (Washington, D.C.: IDB, 1988), pp. 98, 104.

peded from early morning when the ballot boxes were found stuffed with ballots marked for the official party. ... Violence was used the length and breadth of the country to prevent voting, to stuff ballot boxes, and to alter votes. There was a blatant assault on the ballot boxes to stuff them for the PCN.[61]

UNO poll watchers were arrested or physically removed from numerous polling places. Still, in many locations where UNO observers remained, Claramount led by a significant margin.[62] As the UNO denounced the stolen election, Claramount, Morales Erlich, and at least 15,000 supporters gathered in the Plaza Libertad, where the colonel announced his readiness to "remain in the plaza as long as the people want me to." Three days later the crowd had grown to 50,000, and talk of a general strike was in the air. On the night of February 27–28, the National Police moved in armored cars and opened fire. At least four dozen people were killed as Claramount and 1,500 supporters fled into El Rosario Church, which fronts the plaza. Claramount was persuaded by friends to go into exile. As he departed El Salvador, he issued a warning: "This is not the end," he said. "It is only the beginning."[63]

The Romero Regime

The violence in the Plaza Libertad set the stage for the next two and a half years. Between July 1, 1977, and October 15, 1979, El Salvador was buffeted by a rising spiral of mass demonstrations and protests, government repression, left-wing kidnappings, occupations of public buildings, labor strikes, and death-squad murders.

The new Carter administration immediately served notice that human rights would be a major criterion for determining whether or not a government would receive military assistance. It then sent mixed signals to El Salvador. On one hand, it reduced the number of U.S. Military Group personnel (trainers) to six by June 1977 as an expression of "dissatisfaction over lack of progress on the Richardson case."[64] Ronald J. Richardson was a young U.S.

TABLE 2.7 Distribution of Monthly Family Income in El Salvador, 1976–1977

Income Categories (dollars)	Total Income (dollars)	Percent of Total	Number of Families	Percent of Total	Average Income per Family (dollars)
40	2,621,402	2.3	97,046	12.4	27
40–80	13,431,278	12.0	288,711	29.4	59
80–120	16,086,080	14.4	164,263	21.1	98
120–240	28,762,948	25.8	176,805	22.7	163
240–400	19,174,067	17.2	64,229	8.2	299
400 up	31,599,999	28.3	48,711	6.2	649
Total	111,675,744	100.0	779,765	100.0	143

Source: Ministry of Planning, "Distribution del ingreso y gasto por deciles de hogares, 1976–77" [Distribution of income and expenditures by deciles of households], January 1980, tables 1–4.

African American who disappeared while in the custody of the National Guard in late 1976. On the other hand, President Carter replaced Ambassador Ignacio Lozano, a Ford appointee who had been sharply critical of the Salvadorean government's human rights performance, with Frank Devine, a career diplomat whose major qualification for the job was twenty-eight years in the foreign service. Devine's view of Carter's human rights policy is reflected in his memoirs: "[Human rights] was an appropriate emphasis ... [but] there is ... a difference between doing this in one's own country and asserting the right or duty to impose our human rights standards upon other countries, which may or may not be ready for them."[65]

Devine believed that "President Romero recognized that human rights had become a serious issue. ... [H]e terminated the state of siege ... took some positive steps, and made certain public commitments that gave rise to at least momentary hope that human rights might be better respected under the new administration."[66] What Romero did, in fact, was to have the National Assembly promulgate the Law for the Defense and Guarantee of the Public Order, which gave the military virtual carte blanche to pick up anyone it remotely suspected of being subversive in word or deed.[67] As a result, the number of disappeared doubled, and political assassinations increased ten times.[68]

Finally, the sixth cycle began on October 15, 1979, with a coup d'etat. An old Salvadorean saying, *Cuando no hay balazos, el golpe es malo* (When there are no bullets, the coup d'etat is worthless), in one sense portended the outcome of the second coup of October. In another sense, however, the coup dramatically altered the course of Salvadorean history.

PRELUDES TO A COUP

The origins of and planning for the coup were unique in Salvadorean history: For the first time, there was civilian involvement from the beginning, and as the plot developed over a period of five months, civilians were increasingly involved in preparations for a postcoup government. The idea itself grew out of the frustration of two brothers, Lieutenant Colonel René Guerra y Guerra and his businessman brother, Rodrigo. Both had been educated in the United States and shared a concern about economic injustice and political dictatorship. After failing in March and April to rally enough support to force Romero's resignation, and as the repression grew, they began talking between themselves then slowly with others whom they believed shared their concerns.[69]

By August there were three critical developments. First, on May 2 members of the Popular Revolutionary Bloc (BPR), the largest of El Salvador's popular organizations, occupied the Metropolitan Cathedral in downtown San Salvador and three embassies to demand the release of five imprisoned leaders, including their secretary general, Facundo Guardado. A week later the people in the cathedral were joined by several hundred demonstrators in the street outside. Suddenly the National Police opened fire; when the shooting ended twenty-five minutes later, twenty-two people lay dead. The government's claim that the BPR had instigated the massacre by firing machine guns from the cathedral towers was refuted by foreign journalists and other eyewitnesses.[70]

Second, the Sandinista National Liberation Front (FSLN) and a popular insurrection succeeded on July 17 in driving Anastasio Somoza out of Nicaragua, thus ending a forty-seven-year dynasty. Third, with Somoza's departure the National Guard, which had been the dictator's personal army, collapsed.[71] The dissolution of the Nicaraguan National Guard, many of whose members fled through El Salvador, had a profound effect on many Salvadorean officers. They saw men who had lost homes, money, and country. They looked at the growing strength of the popular organizations and guerrillas. They saw the same fate that befell the Nicaraguans befalling them before long. The Nicaraguan Revolution, more than any other single event, galvanized the feeling within the Young Military that the time for change had come.

Another event, which had no direct bearing on the coup but had great significance for later political developments, also occurred in May. President Romero invited leading members of the oligarchy to a meeting at the Casa Presidencial where they heard a lecture on the organization of the revolutionary movement. According to Orlando de Sola, who was present, the aide giving the lecture said, "You better take care of yourselves because we cannot do it."[72] De Sola left, furious. "It was an abdication!" he later told Laurie Becklund of the *Los Angeles Times*. "It was like he told us to abandon ship. For the first time, I thought, we're in deep trouble. We're no longer in complete control. ... They were telling us to arm ourselves." Becklund wrote that de Sola "became one of a ... few dozen businessmen, mostly coffee, cane and cotton growers, who would form the heart of what more moderate businessmen called the extreme right."[73] This event was important because, first, it produced the first crack in the army-oligarchy coalition that had endured for forty-seven years and that would rupture completely before another forty-seven weeks had passed. Second, it pushed the most reactionary members of the oligarchy, together with like-minded members (and former members) of the military, to create their own death squads and, eventually, a political party. Despite the Guerra brothers' care and good intentions, at least one officer, Colonel Jaime Abdul Gutiérrez, who did not share their economic and political views got wind of the plot and sent two emissaries to plead with Archbishop Romero for Gutiérrez's inclusion in the coup.[74] Romero counseled the Guerras to include him, reasoning that it would be easier to keep an eye on him; the effect, however, was to introduce the fox into the chicken coop. Indeed, Romero later advised the coup plotters to exclude Gutiérrez and Colonel José Guillermo García from the new government. García was at the time commander of a small garrison in San Vicente, sixty-four kilometers east of San Salvador.

While the military was planning for the coup, civilians were looking ahead to the problems of governance. Throughout the summer a group of civilians coordinated by Rodrigo Guerra worked on the Proclamation of the Armed Forces (Proclama de la Fuerza Armada), which they would issue immediately after the coup. These discussions focused on the country's problems and the necessary reforms. In June, the Guerras hinted at the possibility of a coup d'etat to U.S. Ambassador Frank Devine, who indicated that this was a serious matter but that he was not disposed to oppose it. The Salvadoreans remained in sporadic contact with the embassy through the months of planning, but the United States was never involved in any way in the planning or execution of the coup.[75]

THE BEGINNING OF THE END: 1979–1980

Soon after garrisons began to fall around the country on Monday morning, October 15, Colonel Gutiérrez, in the name of the Coordinating Committee, called President Romero and the High Command and ordered them to leave the country by 3:00 P.M. After some stalling, Romero and company were on their way to Guatemala by 5:00.

Commitment and Betrayal

Despite the months of planning and the socioeconomic commitments of the *golpistas*, their objectives were derailed in the days before and immediately after the coup occurred; Gutiérrez and his cohorts thwarted them. First Gutiérrez arranged René Guerra's removal as one of the two military members of the junta by calling a meeting of the Young Military (as the conspirators came to be known) to which Guerra and his followers were not invited. Gutiérrez argued that as a lieutenant colonel, Guerra was too junior in rank for such an important position; Gutiérrez was elected in his stead. Second, hours after General Romero departed the country, Gutiérrez, without consultation with or authorization from his colleagues, called Colonel José Guillermo García in San Vicente and offered him the post of minister of defense. Third, García invited Colonel Nicolás Carranza, who was on the CIA payroll at $90,000 a year, to be vice-minister of defense.[76] In short, before the coup was twenty-four hours old, the most reactionary remnants of the officer corps had reasserted control over the Armed Forces. These were men who, whatever their commitment to the reforms pledged in the Proclama, believed that it was necessary to deal first with the "subversion" and later address the socioeconomic problems of the country. The other military member, Colonel Adolfo Majano, was firmly committed to the Proclama but lacked the will to assert any control over his right-wing colleagues.

Three examples illustrate the difficulties. First, on the night of October 15, García's first act as defense minister was unilaterally to send the army to attack units of the Revolutionary Army of the People (ERP) that were occupying two working-class suburbs of San Salvador; he then informed Gutiérrez and Majano. René Guerra was notified; he called the military members of the junta and told them García had to be stopped. They agreed but did nothing.[77] Second, on October 17 the Young Military met to discuss the Proclama and argued that the reforms should be implemented as peacefully as possible. García and Carranza argued for restructuring the army and postponing the reforms; Gutiérrez supported the two men. Majano, according to an officer present, talked of nothing but "changes, changes, changes."† Thus, by the end of the first week, the Young Military recognized that a new division existed within the army between the High Command (with Gutiérrez) on one side and the bulk of the officer corps (with Majano) on the other.

Third, the junta's decision to eliminate ANSESAL, the intelligence agency that had run ORDEN and had been responsible for fingering "subversives" who subsequently turned up dead (or did not turn up at all), was derailed by Gutiérrez and ANSESAL's deputy director, Major Roberto D'Aubuisson. Days after the coup, they agreed to remove the ANSESAL files, which contained photos and personal histories of suspected "subversives," from the Casa Presidencial to army headquarters to put them beyond the reach of civilian officials. D'Aubuisson made copies for himself, then made diabolical use of them in early 1980.[78] He reorganized ANSESAL under the army chief of staff's office; it acquired a new name, the National Intelligence Agency (ANI) and expanded responsibilities and, like its predecessor, had close links with the CIA.[79] Before the end of the year, however, D'Aubuisson resigned from the army and with other like-minded colleagues began to develop a right-wing political-military structure patterned on the Communist Party model but in support of the Armed Forces and their quasi-fascist political ideology.[80]

Years later, from exile, Adolfo Majano acknowledged the naïveté; the Young Military, he said, thought that "the right was going to go running without firing a shot. They were wrong. The right put up an organized battle. ... They began to create clandestine groups like the White Warriors Union. ... They began to create a network of their people inside the armed forces. But they were outside the armed forces too, and that was very important."[81] The most obvious and vocal manifestation of this new right-wing organization appeared in December in a series of marches for "Peace and Work" sponsored by the Nationalist Feminine League.

The fact that two of the most thoughtful and progressive civilians in El Salvador had been invited onto the junta could not offset these problems. Román Mayorga Quiroz, rector of the Central American University in San Salvador and author of a book[82] in which he argued for a number of social and economic reforms in El Salvador with which the officers were in accord, conditioned his acceptance on a cleanup of the military, on meaningful socioeconomic change, and on a second junta member from the Popular Forum, a progressive, ad hoc group of civilians. The following day Guillermo Manuel Ungo was selected by the Forum to be its man on the junta. The third member, Mario Andino, a businessman, was selected by Majano and Gutiérrez after they consulted the business community. Together these men put together a cabinet that was widely regarded as the most progressive in Salvadorean history.

Public Reaction. Reaction to the coup ranged from shock on the part of the Salvadorean oligarchy to outrage on the part of the popular organizations. The oligarchy's silence, however, lasted as long as it took for its members to realize that the junta was serious about the proposed reforms and that the army apparently had every intention of supporting them. Then, as before, anguished protests and increasing attacks on the reform proposals began. The responses of the revolutionary organizations were more complex. None believed, with some reason given past history, that the army was serious about the Proclama. Yet there were indications that the various organizations had adopted a wait-and-see attitude. The Popular Forces of Liberation (FPL), for example, publicly opposed the junta; but one of its clandestine members, a university professor of philosophy named Salvador Samayoa, was named minister of education. The ERP attempt to spark an insurrection on October 15 failed largely because people were willing to give the new government a chance.

The junta immediately created a special human rights commission to investigate the whereabouts of political prisoners. Those who were alive were freed in the general amnesty, but many others had simply "disappeared";[83] the commission's failure to account for these provoked criticism that the new government was covering up the sins of its predecessor.[84] The most serious result was that repression increased. More people died in the first three weeks after the coup than had died in any equivalent period during the Romero regime.[85] The junta's failure to bring the security forces under control provoked harsh criticism both from the popular organizations and the Catholic Church.

The Role of the United States, Redux. President Jimmy Carter's administration publicly breathed a sigh of relief that President Romero was gone. In the next breath it offered renewed economic and military assistance to the Revolutionary Junta of Government. In the following weeks, U.S. policy began operating on two levels. Officially that policy was to support human rights and to encourage social, political, and economic changes enumerated in the Proclama. At the same time, U.S. actions in fact produced very different results from those the embassy claimed to want.

First, having made an issue of human rights from early 1977 until October 15, 1979, the United States thereafter fell silent in the face of an escalating number of massacres and assassinations at the hands of the Salvadorean security forces and "men in civilian clothes." Officially, according to embassy officers, the human rights policy continued in force but was being pursued through quieter channels. Second, growing agitation from the left—in the form of demonstrations and the occupation of embassies, factories, farms, and various security forces' barracks around the country—led to encouragement of a law-and-order line within the Armed Forces.

One must understand that U.S. officials had a liberal-democratic definition of "law and order," which assumed a functioning legal system and a well-trained, relatively well-educated police force that was not serving during off-duty hours as paid assassins or vigilantes for the rich. As none of these preconditions obtained in El Salvador, "law and order" translated into repression. Officials denied this; rather, they argued that the "terrorist" activities of the left provoked harsh tactics and that when the left was brought under control these tactics would no longer be necessary. They also expressed the hope that with the resumption of military aid, which in fall 1979 included troop training, the Salvadorean Armed Forces could be made more efficient and less barbaric in their crowd-control methods.[86]

Third, the embassy, particularly its senior officials, actively supported the business community. Ambassador Devine acknowledged that he "went to bat" for the private enterprise sector because he felt it had "been done an injustice" by the government after October 15.[87] U.S. officials failed to understand that pushing a law-and-order line on the one hand and supporting private enterprise on the other played directly into the hands of the most conservative sectors of Salvadorean society.

The Government Resigns

By late December the civilians on the junta and their colleagues in the cabinet had had enough of repression and military intransigence on reforms. They delivered an ultimatum demanding a halt to the growing repression; the Young Military, however, deliberated for three days before rejecting the demand saying the military could not be involved in a political question. The crisis broke on December 26 when García appeared, uninvited and accompanied by the High Command, at a cabinet meeting. According to a government official present at that meeting, a "screaming match" ensued during which García told the ministers they were going too far with their proposed reforms. The ministers responded by telling the officers that the reforms were none of their business. To military men accustomed to ruling, that was heresy. Many in the cabinet felt they should resign that day. Instead, they took their case to the Young Military, but that group declined to intervene.[88]

As the year ended, Archbishop Romero's effort to mediate failed. So, on January 3, Guillermo Manuel Ungo, Román Mayorga, the entire cabinet (minus García and Carranza), and all heads of state-owned companies resigned. One day later, Mario Andino also left the junta.[89]

Illusion and Reality

The coup of October appeared to alter radically the roles that each of the major actors on the Salvadorean political stage had been playing. It seemed that the oligarchy, for the first time, had been shoved into the wings. The army had seemingly cast itself in a role different from its traditional part as the oligarchy's handmaiden. From now on, it proclaimed, it would be the servant of the people. Within three months, however, it was clear that the more things changed, the more they stayed the same. Each of these actors began following its own two-track policy. The most right-wing sector of the oligarchy began to develop its own political-military organization that was at first exclusively clandestine but that would eventually lead to creation of a political party. The army's two-track policy was reform with repression. The Janus-headed policy of the United States was to promote a "transition to democracy" through reforms and elections while pursuing a military policy of "low-intensity conflict" designed to defeat the left.

Before we examine these policies and how they developed after the resignation of the government of the first junta, it is necessary to examine the roles of two other actors. As we have seen, until 1960 the army and the oligarchy largely had the stage to themselves. Then the United States made its appearance as an important actor. During all this time, the Catholic Church had been silently supportive by its inaction, although it occasionally sallied forth to warn the faithful against the dangers of communism. In the late 1960s, however, the church began to speak out on issues of social justice and human rights. Its increasingly pointed attacks on governmental repression, coupled with its concerted efforts at evangelization through the development of Christian Base Communities (CEBs), not only made it an object of persecution by 1970 but also led (unintentionally) to its participation in the founding of the first mass-based popular organization in 1974. In the next two chapters we will examine these two actors that joined the oligarchy, military, and United States on the stage of Salvadorean political life.

3

The Church

*Si me matan, resucitaré en el pueblo salvadoreño.**

—Oscar Arnulfo Romero

When the National Assembly convened the Agrarian Reform Congress in January 1970, governmental, nongovernmental, labor, and business groups were invited to participate. Among the nongovernmental groups that accepted was the Roman Catholic Church. Archbishop Luís Chávez y González handpicked a progressive group of priests and laity to represent the church, and Father José Inocencio Alas, a young diocesan priest from the parish of Suchitoto, forty-eight kilometers northeast of the capital, was chosen to present the church's position on the issue. It was a position so strongly in support of agrarian reform that it created a very "strong commotion," according to Monseñor Arturo Rivera Damas, then auxiliary bishop of San Salvador. Hours after Alas made his presentation, he was abducted by men in civilian clothes in front of the National Palace. Eyewitnesses immediately called the Arzobispado (archdiocesan offices). Rivera Damas, on receiving the news, got in his car and went to see the president of the National Assembly. Rivera announced that he was going to the Ministry of Defense and would stay there until Alas was produced.

When Rivera told Minister of Defense Fidel Torres that he was going to sit in his office until Alas appeared, Torres "blanched," then picked up the phone. After each of several calls Torres reported the same response: "We don't have him." Rivera reminded Torres that in the history of El Salvador there were frequently situations like this, and the response was always the same: *"No lo tenemos."* Rivera was soon joined by Monseñor Ricardo Urioste, who declared he would stay with Rivera. Torres attempted to strike a bargain: He would notify them of Alas's whereabouts at 9:00 P.M. (it was then 5:30 P.M.), but the priests would have to leave. Torres promised that Alas would not be killed. Rivera and Urioste, unimpressed, did not move. Two hours later Torres satisfactorily assured Rivera and Urioste that Alas was alive and

---

If they kill me, I will be resurrected in the Salvadorean people.

81

would be released unharmed. The two prelates departed. Meanwhile, the radio station of the archdiocese, YSAX, had begun broadcasting the news of Alas's abduction. It stayed on the air all night relaying the news and calling on priests and parishes to pray for Alas. Years later, Rivera Damas said that "in those days we only asked people to pray; we did not know how to denounce."

Alas was beaten, drugged, and left naked on the edge of a cliff in the mountains south of San Salvador. When Monseñor Urioste subsequently asked Alas if he had been thinking about being rescued, Alas replied, "No, I was thinking about the resurrection."[1]

This incident represented several "firsts" for the Salvadorean church. It was the first time the church had participated in a political event like the congress and the first time it had taken a policy position on the issue of agrarian reform. Alas's abduction was the first direct attack by government agents on the church, and it marked the beginning of a history of random and systematic persecution directed at both clergy and laity. Finally, Minister of Defense Torres's experience of having a cleric sit in and make demands was the first such confrontation in Salvadorean history. In short, the Agrarian Reform Congress marked a turning point, both in church-state relations and in the church's role as a political actor in El Salvador.

During the next two decades the Salvadorean church would pass through several periods, which can be summarized as follows:

- 1968–1977: This stage brought emphasis on evangelization and pastoral work through the development of Christian Base Communities.
- February 1977–March 1980: This period marked Oscar Arnulfo Romero's tenure as archbishop, during which the pastoral work of earlier years continued but attention was increasingly focused on Romero and his denunciations of poverty and injustice. Also during this time violent attacks against the church increased rapidly and culminated in the assassination of Romero.
- March 1980–March 1983: Apostolic administrator Arturo Rivera Damas assumed a lower profile and pursued three principal objectives: to rejuvenate the church's pastoral work that had been destroyed by repression, including the murder of priests, nuns, and lay leaders; to promote dialogue between the government and the guerrillas; and to heal profound divisions among the Salvadorean bishops.
- March 1983–1988: Pope John Paul II visited El Salvador; Rivera Damas was named archbishop; the pope publicly honored Romero, then called for dialogue as the only road to peace. These two themes had a dual impact: The latter opened new opportunities for Rivera and his peacemaking efforts; the former released pent-up popular desires to honor the slain archbishop. In administration, new dioceses were created and new bishops named, moves that diluted the weight of the conservatives in the Episcopal Conference. The Lutheran, Baptist, and Episcopal churches in El Salvador became in-

creasingly involved in issues of social justice, which led to significant growth. Pentecostal sects, which had long been present, received some support from the government and also experienced rapid growth.

- 1988–1993: The Catholic and Protestant churches joined in an ecumenical effort to create a national debate on peace and the future of the country. This was an important source of pressure on all parties to the conflict. The Catholic and Lutheran churches were included as observers on commissions set up by the peace process. The Pentecostal churches continued their rapid growth.

This chapter deals with events surrounding the church through the end of March 1980. Chapter 5 includes a discussion of the 1980–1982 period; Chapter 6 covers events after the visit of Pope John Paul II in March 1983. Later chapters present discussion of the Protestant churches in El Salvador and their growing role.

VATICAN II AND MEDELLÍN

The events of January 1970 marked a turning point, not a beginning. The beginning can be dated from the Second Vatican Council (Vatican II), which convened in 1962 under Pope John XXIII and closed three years later under Pope Paul VI. Prior to Vatican II, national churches in Latin America presented a uniformly traditional religious image, accompanied by sharply conservative social and political attitudes. Virtually everywhere, including El Salvador, the church was allied with wealth and power.

Vatican II created an environment in which this state of affairs began to change. The council, strongly influenced by Pope John XXIII's social encyclicals, especially *Pacem in Terris*, stated in its closing document *Gaudium et Spes* two new principles that would have particular impact in Latin America. They asserted that the church is in and of the world, with concerns well beyond the purely spiritual. They also emphasized that the church is a community of equals by baptism. The prelates refused to condemn communism per se, instead joining criticism of certain of its practices with an equally strong critique of capitalism's abuses.[2]

Three years after the end of Vatican II, bishops from all over Latin America gathered in Medellín, Colombia, for the Second Episcopal Conference (CELAM II). Penny Lernoux correctly noted that Medellín was "one of the major political events of the century: it shattered the centuries-old alliance of Church, military, and the rich elites."[3] At Medellín the bishops called upon the church "to defend the rights of the oppressed"; to promote grassroots organizations; "to denounce the unjust action of world powers that works against self-determination of weaker nations"; in short, to make a "preferential option for the poor."[4]

The primary means of accomplishing these ends was the development of Christian Base Communities (CEBs). It can be argued that these communities have been the most revolutionary development in the Latin American church because, for the first time in history, the masses of the people began participating in and taking responsibility for important aspects of their own lives and for each other; they were no longer merely observers at a ritual conducted for their benefit by a resident or visiting priest. This form of participation, however, has had social consequences. With a growing frequency that disturbs traditionalists, CEB members have moved beyond purely religious concerns to political issues. Nowhere in Latin America has this been more true or had more profound consequences than in El Salvador.

Thus when one speaks of the "Salvadorean church," one must specify whether the reference is to the hierarchy (the bishops) or to what came by 1980 to be known as the *iglesia popular* (popular church)—that is, the tens of thousands of people, most of them poor, who came to believe that "liberation" is not only something one achieves at death but also something that, with God's blessing, one can struggle for and possibly achieve during one's lifetime.

POLITICAL DIVISIONS WITHIN THE CATHOLIC CHURCH

The reaction in the Latin American church to the conciliar and Medellín documents is usually described as falling into one of two categories, whether the reference is to the "historical" church versus the "institutional" church or to the "prophetic" church versus the "sacramental" church. The former term of each pair refers to the local church when it existed as small communities of believers without any bureaucratic superstructure; the latter refers to the institutional church with its bureaucratic interests that often have little to do with the fundamental values of Christianity, especially as they are interpreted by liberation theology. Whatever the labels, Medellín initiated a dynamic process of reflection that encouraged Catholics (as well as Protestants) throughout the continent to rethink their faith. Most important, the emphasis on identifying the church with the poor led to the assumption of a more prophetic attitude toward politics and society.[5] This has been expressed in a theology of liberation that has interpreted the gospel as demanding that Christians be a force actively working to liberate the great majority of the people from poverty and oppression. By the mid-1970s the theology of liberation had become the "common coin of discourse"[6] among progressive Christians.

Division Within the Hierarchy

In El Salvador, as elsewhere in Latin America, two strains of liberation theology developed. Whereas four of the six members of the Salvadorean hierarchy adhered to an institutional, sacramentalist view of the church's role in society,[7] the remaining two prelates, both in the archdiocese of San Salvador (and Archbishop Oscar Romero before his death), promoted the positions of Vatican II and Medellín from the beginning. (Until January 1987, the archdiocese encompassed four departments, 40 percent of the population, and 57 percent of the priests and religious [brothers and nuns] in the country.)

Archbishop Romero suggested that the key to this division within the church was stated at the Third Conference of Latin American Bishops (CELAM III) in Puebla, Mexico, during January 1979:

In Latin America not all members of the church have converted to the poor. I believe that the path to unity lies in a "preferential option for the poor." If bishops, priests, and laity took this option—we found Jesus Christ among the poor and there was no problem—but the thing is, we do not believe much in that. ... The pope in Puebla called attention to the divisions within the Church: an institutional church and a charismatic one that arises from the people. I always preach respect for the institution, to the hierarchy, but I say, "don't say the 'real church' if we only save the institution."[8]

Two Interpretations of Liberation Theology

Romero reflected one strain of liberation theology; about 30 percent of the younger priests represented the other. As Father Benito Tovar put it in an interview, they "use the analysis of Marxism because it is objective and scientific. But we are not Marxists. We are not able to understand Marx as a religion because we are Christians."

Within the archdiocese a clear pastoral line was laid down by Archbishops Chávez and Romero: Priests were to be guided by church doctrine issuing from Rome and CELAM; clergy could (indeed, were obliged to) "accompany" their people, but they could not take a political stance. During the early 1970s this pastoral line held little difficulty for even the most committed priests, but as the political situation deteriorated toward the end of the decade, disagreement developed between Romero and the younger priests. The position of the latter, in the words of one during a monthly priests' meeting with Romero in December 1979 was, "You cannot have a pastoral line without having a political option. You [Romero] have got a political option, and we do too."† In the view of these priests, their archbishop's option was to support the junta, a charge that was unfair if understandable. To them, a logical extension of the defense of the people's right to organize was support of the organizations they had created. And because many members and leaders of these organizations came out of the parishes' Christian Base Communities, there was yet another reason to support the organizations and the option for change that they represented. This division within the archdiocese, although heated at times, never produced an open split like that in the hierarchy. Within the archdiocese, both sides of the liberation-theology debate took great care not to create a situation in which reconciliation would be difficult or impossible.

In the discussion that follows, the "church" refers to that group of bishops, clergy, religious, and laity who followed Medellín and Puebla in committing themselves to a "preferential option for the poor."[9] It is this part of the church that became a major political actor in El Salvador during the 1970s.[10]

THE BEGINNINGS OF CHURCH ACTIVISM

With Vatican II and Medellín as doctrinal guides and support, Archbishop Chávez began immediately to encourage adherence to and development of new pastoral approaches. Such episcopal encouragement was confined largely to the archdiocese. In other dioceses the bishops continued to behave as though Vatican II and Medellín had never occurred. This unwillingness to move with the times would have profound consequences. For the moment, however, it is sufficient to note that the archdiocese became the locus of ferment within the Salvadorean church and that its impact and influence reached into every corner of the country.[11]

Archbishop Chávez, according to Arturo Rivera Damas, was very "anxious to put into practice the social doctrines that came out of the Council and to have them diffused and practiced." On August 6, 1966, the archbishop issued a pastoral letter, "The Responsibility of the Laity in the Ordering of Temporal Life," that put some distance between the church and the military government, "which saw in it support for the Christian Democrats ... and criticism of capitalism."[12] The letter also occasioned something close to a rupture with members of the oligarchy, who not only disliked the perceived attack on capitalism but also recognized the social and political danger of such grassroots activism. To a group of people used to having things their own way, the specter of politicized masses was disturbing, to say the least.

The ferment that began with this pastoral letter received an official impetus with the decision to hold a "pastoral week" in July 1970; it was convoked by agreement of the Salvadorean Episcopal Conference (CEDES). Only the three bishops of the archdiocese participated, and the remainder of the hierarchy subsequently denounced the final document. The flap was the first open rift within CEDES; it would not be the last. The dissident bishops found the conclusions too extreme and motivated "by youthful fervor." One of the points that bothered the prelates most was "the denunciation of their connivance with the Salvadorean oligarchic minority, which oppressed the great majority of *campesinos* and workers." These bishops were also disturbed by the "necessity to promote lay pastoral agents as an indispensable means to bring the Gospel to the *campesino* masses." CEDES took the final document and diluted the first part, which contained an analysis of the structural injustice and institutionalized violence in El Salvador. In the second part, a theological reflection on these data, the bishops "emphasized the vertical (person-God) dimension while reducing to almost nothing the horizontal (person-person) dimension." But all CEDES changed was wording. "In practice, the final conclusions were not touched."[13]

Christian Base Communities

An explosion of pastoral activity throughout the archdiocese and elsewhere led within a few years to the establishment of hundreds of Christian Base Communities. The work was spearheaded by a nun, a priest, and two prelates in the Arzobispado who provided the necessary coordination and support for priests and religious working in parishes from the Guatemalan border (on the west) to the Gulf of Fonseca (on the east). CEBs were the means by which church doctrine developed during Vatican II could be implemented: to bring the laity into the life of the church, to teach that the Christian community is a community of equals before God in which all have obligations to each other and responsibilities to share. CEBs are small groups, usually no more than twenty or thirty within a parish, who meet regularly for Bible study. An initial course is led by the priest or religious working with the CEB, but the group is encouraged to develop its own leadership—a necessary step in a country like El Salvador where the ratio of priests to parishioners was 1:10,000 during the 1970s.[14]

The people soon elect their catechists (lay teachers) and "delegates of the Word" (lay preachers). The catechists assume responsibility for one specific area, such as baptism, catechism, or marriage preparation classes. They receive additional training, but their responsibility is to lead the community in weekly worship services. Catechists and delegates are selected not only for their leadership qualities but also for their moral rectitude and their Christian commitment. There is a strong tradition against electing someone who is inclined to be overbearing or authoritarian. Willingness to be of service to the community is crucial.

In sum, CEBs have an impact in four ways. First, they provide a means of bringing people together—an organization, which for the poor of El Salvador was unique, particularly for *campesinos* who had been denied the right to organize since the 1932 insurrection. Second, the election and development of catechists and delegates of the Word mean the emergence of grassroots leadership. Third, the CEBs provide experience in participatory democracy; all decisions are made collectively, not imposed by priests or nuns. For the first time people are involved in making decisions that affect their lives. Fourth, the CEBs are the primary medium by which the message of liberation theology is delivered. Through Bible study, as well as homilies and priest-parishioner dialogues during the Mass, people begin "doing theology"—interpreting the biblical message in the context of their own lives and experiences.[15]

The impact of this new pastoral approach is reflected in an anecdote related by Charles Clements, a U.S. doctor who in 1982–1983 provided medical care to civilians in the Guazapa front, an area under guerrilla control. Clements told of peasants who said how proud they were when Father José Alas, who went to Suchitoto in December 1968 and began developing CEBs, asked their opinions on various questions because "no one except another *campesino* had ever asked [their] view on anything."[16]

The Training of Lay Leaders. Between 1970 and 1976 seven centers were established in El Salvador for the training of catechists and delegates. Over the course of the decade approximately 15,000 leaders were trained. According to Walter Guerra, a Salvadorean priest who spearheaded the development of these centers, the content of the courses emphasized "an integral formation" and spanned topics from Bible study and liturgy to agriculture, cooperativism, leadership, and health. This broad training, Guerra said, was necessary because "the catechist, among us, is a man who not only works as a religious person but assumes leadership that is also social, including, at times, political in our rural communities."[17]

Guerra noted that a 1978 survey of the catechists and their work in the diocese of Santa Ana found that they "really made a great contribution" to their communities. After as little as three or four months, Guerra found in his visits that "the people were changing; communities were engaging in dia logue to resolve their problems (which had never happened before); and there was religious renewal as well."

Reflection on The Word. The process of study and selection of leaders is closely bound up with the content of the courses in which the people are in volved. The message is a radical break with the past: that it is not God's wil that the people be poor; that, before God, they are equal to the *hacendado* down the road; that they have a basic human right to organize in order to begin tak ing control of their lives; and that throughout human history God has been a God of justice who has always acted on behalf of the poor and oppressed.

Once peasants recover from the shock of hearing these words, amazing things begin to happen that those in power inevitably call "subversive." Said Maryknoll Sister Joan Petrik, who worked with *campesinos* in the mountains above La Libertad, El Salvador, for seven years: "When I first arrived in Tamanique, every time a child died the family would say, 'It's the will of God. But after the people became involved in the Christian communities, that atti tude began to change. And after a year or so I no longer heard people in the communities saying that. After a while they began to say, 'The system caused this.'" Sister Joan also observed that, after a time, one could walk into a village where CEBs had been established and identify the people who were members of the communities simply by the way they carried themselves. "They walk upright, their heads held high, with self-confidence," she noted. The other peasants would shuffle along with their heads bowed.[18]

Zacamil. These experiences were repeated in urban areas. In the parish of Zacamil, a poor neighborhood on the north side of San Salvador, a team o Belgian missionary priests began working in 1970. One of those priests, Pablo Galdámez (a pseudonym), who was forced into exile in 1980, recounted the experience of that community in terms of the steps a man must take on the way to ordination as a Catholic priest: porter (opening doors); exorcist (driv ing out demons); lector (reading); acolyte (one who accompanies); deacon (serving); and priest (offering sacrifice). "We did all of this in our communi ties," he wrote in his memoir of the parish, "priests and people alike. (It didn' matter what our official status was; we were all becoming 'priests in life' in those years.)"[19]

He described the development process: "Our communities began by calling people to congregate, inviting them to come together. The invitees multiplied and became doorkeepers themselves. ... The first demon that had to be driven out ... was demon booze." Chico was an alcoholic who belonged to ORDEN and tried to hang himself one night. His wife summoned the neighbors who cut him down, then tied him up for several days until he was sober. Then they took him to Alcoholics Anonymous. Chico, in time, "became a community doorkeeper." The people saw that "evil spirits could be driven out!"

The process continued: "Then we started being lectors." A worker begar meeting with fellow workers. A young married couple offered their home fo meetings. In a neighboring slum a young university student began a CEE there. And so on. Later there emerged "an order of acolytes" who made it pos sible for people to attend CEB meetings. Some babysat; others helped members finish work so they could all come; others carried chairs to very poor homes so meetings could be held there. Being a deacon meant "finding ways that would keep [the people] faithful to their new commitment." Helping alcoholics was one way. Marriage encounters were another. "People were discovering the feeling of love and ... started [looking] at their union with new eyes." The result was that couples who had lived together for many years began deciding to get married in the church: "Those first weddings were unforgettable fiestas. The whole community was there, including the couples' children. For [them] it was an honor to be there to hear their mom and dad promise mutual love. ... Those fiestas were also the sign of God's fidelity, a sign of God's commitment to the poor. ... That was really a sacrament."[20]

The community of Zacamil moved beyond these activities. "We knew Berta's little boy needed an egg and a piece of meat everyday if he was to get well. ... [And] there were lots of Bertas. So we investigated the problem ... and organized the first Caritas program in our communities to provide nutritional assistance to children and mothers-to-be."[21] Later, vendors in the La Placita market came to Galdámez and asked him to celebrate a mass in honor of the market's patron saint. As it happened, the vendors were being victimized by loan sharks: "They borrow a little money in the evening. Then the next morning they buy fruit or vegetables. At noon, along comes the moneylender for the interest—20 percent." On a 100-colon loan, the vendors were required to repay 20 colones per day (half of it interest) for ten days: 100 percent interest in the end.

During the mass, Galdámez

> opened a dialogue with them—on their love for one another, on the big problems they had—and soon we were talking about the biggest thing that bound them together: no money to send the kids to school, to take them to the hospital, or even to feed them three meals a day.
>   And up came the subject of the moneylenders. Some of the women expressed gratitude for their services. ... Others were silent. Then, timidly, somebody said they only made things worse. There was a moment of confusion. Majestic on his makeshift pedestal, the Sacred Heart of Jesus presided over their decisive moment of "conscientization" when the poor had the floor, when the poor could speak out. Then one of the women shouted out, "The interest sure is high!" Others seconded her, then quickly covered their faces with their shawls, reciting prayers, as if asking forgiveness for their rebelliousness. That was when the moneylender left in a huff.[22]

The next day the market women met with the community of Zacamil to start a new cooperative. The two new moneylenders were women from the community who went every day and kept careful accounts.

Aguilares and Rutilio Grande

The examples from Zacamil are dramatic, but nowhere did the development of CEBs have a faster or more profound impact than in the small town of Aguilares, thirty-five kilometers north of San Salvador. There, in September

1972, Father Rutilio Grande and three fellow Jesuits arrived to take up pastoral duties. What happened in Aguilares in the succeeding four and a half years was replayed in many locales throughout El Salvador, sometimes with equally dramatic results.

Grande and his fellow priests divided Aguilares into ten mission zones and the surrounding countryside into fifteen other zones. They talked with residents in each zone about the best place to locate the mission center, then visited families to learn about individual and community problems. In short, they conducted a socioeconomic, religious, and cultural survey of the parish.

Later, in each mission center, they conducted evangelizing sessions with children, then adults; the purpose was to give the people a basic outline by which they could continue celebrating the Word of God on their own. In this way the priests were able to begin a process of "self-evangelization," of building a community, and of selection by the community of catechists and delegates of the Word. These lay leaders then received weekly training and instruction from the priests.

Between September 1973 and June 1974, the priests and lay leaders[23] established ten urban and twenty-seven rural CEBs and trained 326 catechists and delegates for such responsibilities as prebaptismal instruction (37); catechists (38); youth work (18); musical groups (72); founding and encouraging new CEBs (58, of whom 17 moved on to continue the work in other communities); and assisting in various courses (29).[24]

It cannot be emphasized too strongly that the work of Grande and his associates was consciously, deliberately, and exclusively pastoral, never political. At the same time, the content of their evangelizing message, although always drawn from the Bible and the social doctrine of the church, was profoundly radicalizing in a political as well as a religious sense.

Beginning with the assertion that God was "not in the clouds, lying in a hammock" and was not detached from and uncaring about his creation, the priests sought to convey to their parishioners the notion of a God of justice and love who acts on the side of the poor and oppressed. From the Exodus story (Exod. 3) through the Old Testament, God is portrayed as one who cares passionately about his people, especially the poor, and wreaks his vengeance on the rich and powerful who became and remain that way through the exploitation of others.

This message continues in the New Testament with the proclamation of the "good news" in Luke 4: "The Spirit of the Lord is upon me, because he has chosen me to bring good news to the poor. … To proclaim liberty to the captives and recovery of sight to the blind, to set free the oppressed."[25]

Jesus' "preferential option for the poor," the message ran, did not mean that he hated the rich. On the contrary, he had many wealthy friends. In this sense, Grande continued, Jesus was the "liberator" of all people, poor and rich alike. This liberation results in a totally integrated human being, a person transfigured (converted) so that all aspects of one's life—family, business, pleasure—are a unified whole. Such liberation, Grande preached, would free the oppressed *and* their oppressors.

It does not require much imagination to understand the impact of such a message on *campesinos* for whom the biblical message until this time had been "accept your lot here on earth because your real reward will come in the here-after." The *campesinos* lost little time relating the gospel message to their own "situation of misery and injustice. They began to emerge from their *conciencia mágica* realizing that the will of God was not to maintain things as they were. They became self-confident, lost their bashfulness and insecurity; they discovered that they could speak and they could think."[26]

The results were electric. On May 24, 1973, eight months after the arrival of the priests in Aguilares, 1,600 workers in the La Cabaña sugar mill struck on payday for six hours because they did not receive an orally promised salary increase. The strike was peaceful and ended when management granted a partial raise. The strike was not organized by the parish, but many of the workers were members of the CEBs, and some of the leaders were delegates of the Word. This involvement produced in Grande a tension he would live with for the rest of his life. "He saw clearly that his mission was to evangelize and not political organization, but at the same time he understood that conscientization in a situation of injustice and oppression would necessarily lead to organization."[27] The tension was exacerbated by the Christian Federation of Salvadorean Campesinos (FECCAS), an organization founded in 1964 in the wake of the Christian Democratic Party. Its purpose was to defend the rights of the *campesinos,* and it had established a base in Aguilares prior to the arrival of Grande. FECCAS quite naturally found a receptive audience among the people in the CEBs, and it participated in the strike at La Cabaña. In 1973 and 1974, FECCAS expanded rapidly throughout the country, independently of what was happening in the parish of Aguilares. Nevertheless, Rutilio Grande was considered by the government and the oligarchy to be responsible for everything from the strike at La Cabaña and subsequent similar actions elsewhere to the growth of FECCAS.

By mid-1975 the priests of Aguilares were being called "subversives" by a *grupo fantasma* (literally, phantom group),[28] the Conservative Religious Front. By Christmas, President Molina was making public statements against what he termed "liberationist clerics." In the meantime, Father Rafael Barahona, a diocesan priest from San Vicente, was taken into custody and transported to National Guard headquarters in San Salvador. There he was severely beaten as his assailants "used profanity to insult me as a priest. One of them struck me and said mockingly: 'I am excommunicated, I am excommunicated.'"[29] Barahona's bishop, Monseñor Pedro Aparicio, obliged not only the soldier but all the other government officials responsible for Barahona's incarceration. "The torturer who clamored for excommunication now has it," a furious bishop wrote the national government. In one of his rare defenses of the pastoral work of his priests, Aparicio inquired if "the Constitution of El Salvador has two interpretations, one for the authorities and the other for the people? We would like a response, if it would not annoy you, Honorable Authorities, so as not to teach our students a mistaken lesson."

La Universidad Centroamericana
José Simeón Cañas

While the church at the parish level was beginning to resocialize the people from a religious perspective, a new national university was founded in

1966 with the intention of teaching the children of the ruling class about the social and economic reality in which a majority of their fellow citizens lived, creating a sense of responsibility for changing this reality, and giving them the education necessary to do so. That, at least, was the intent of the Jesuits who formed the intellectual and administrative backbone of the Central American University (UCA). Their benefactors, the self-same oligarchy, had different objectives. They did not want their children to attend and be corrupted by the University of El Salvador, which was perceived as a hotbed of Marxism and revolution. The oligarchs wanted for their children a good, conservative, Catholic education that would prepare them to continue in their fathers' footsteps.[30]

The Salvadorean oligarchy contributed heavily to the construction of the new campus on the southwest side of the capital and thus felt a strong sense of proprietorship. But in 1970, at the time of the Agrarian Reform Congress, the UCA's Superior Council issued the first in a series of manifestos concerning various issues confronting the country. In this document the Jesuits in effect told the oligarchy that UCA was not its university and proceeded to take a strong position in favor of agrarian reform.

The UCA's vice-rector at the time was Luís de Sebastián, an economist; he said that when the university began to speak out through its manifestos, some sources of funding dried up. He added that although UCA's "political line" was not clear in 1970, by 1975, when security forces fired point-blank at a student demonstration, killing at least thirty-seven, the university's political position of opposition to the government and its policies had become unambiguous.

By the mid-1970s the Department of Theology practiced this commitment in a different way. It began offering night courses to lay leaders in CEBs "to help our people [serve] in mature faith and realistic hope." Almost 150 members from the parish of Zacamil attended classes twice a week. These people, in the words of Pablo Galdámez, "became the theologians of the people, with their Bible under one arm and their newspaper under the other."[31]

Political Effects of Church Activism

President Molina's decree of a limited agrarian reform in March 1976 received strong support from the church and UCA.[32] When the vituperative opposition of affected economic interests forced Molina hastily to withdraw his proposal, UCA published an editorial, "A sus ordenes, mi capital,"[33] in its journal, Estudios Centroamericanos. The university's reward for its efforts was a bomb at the administration building—the first of six that year—for which right-wing groups took responsibility.

In this period the right began looking for scapegoats on which to blame Molina's lapse and found one in the church, which, they decided, was "inciting the people to revolt." To appease the oligarchy, Molina and Minister of Defense Humberto Romero arrested five priests and expelled eighteen others, including two Jesuits from UCA. The climate was such that by May 1977 fliers urging Salvadoreans to "Be a Patriot! Kill a Priest!" were circulating in the capital. By then two priests had been assassinated, one of them Rutilio Grande as he drove with two parishioners from Aguilares to El Paisnal to celebrate Mass on the afternoon of March 12, 1977. The three Jesuits who had been working with Grande were expelled.[34]

The murders of Grande and of Father Alfonso Navarro a month later came in the midst of a wave of persecution the like of which the Latin American church has rarely experienced. Between February 21 and May 14, 1977, ten priests were exiled; eight were expelled, five of them tortured beforehand; two were arrested; one was beaten; and Rafael Barahona was again detained and tortured.

Barahona's incarceration occurred the day before Oscar Romero was installed as archbishop of San Salvador, succeeding the aged Chávez. The day after his installation, Romero went to the Casa Presidencial and requested the release of his priest. President Molina's response was: "I will release Barahona but you cannot ask us to treat them [priests] any differently until they go back to their basic business, which is religion. These priests of yours," Molina continued, "have become politicians, and I hold you responsible for their behavior." Romero looked Molina straight in the eye. "With all due respect, Mr. President," the archbishop said, "we take our orders from someone higher."[35]

OSCAR ARNULFO ROMERO
BECOMES ARCHBISHOP

The selection of Monseñor Oscar Romero, bishop of Santiago de María, as archbishop of San Salvador was greeted with widespread dismay throughout the archdiocese. The old archbishop, priests, religious, and laity had hoped that Arturo Rivera Damas, the auxiliary bishop since 1960, would be chosen. But Rivera had too many enemies going back to the mid-1960s, when the oligarchy had accused him (erroneously) of ghosting Archbishop Chávez's pastoral letters. Then he had incensed the government when he confronted Minister of Defense Torres over the abduction of Father Alas in 1970. In the meantime he had strongly supported the pastoral line of the archdiocese and had spoken out forcefully against official repression. So when the papal nuncio, being of a mind similar to that of the oligarchy and the government, asked the powerful whom they preferred, their choice was Romero. Romero, who was born in San Miguel, three hours to the east of the capital, had spent most of his priestly life in the eastern section of the country. He was considered quiet and noncontroversial. His detractors considered him an ally of the oligarchy and were extremely worried that he would halt or even try to reverse the process of evangelization that had been developed during the previous eight years.

A month before Romero's installation, Rivera Damas was in Rome, where he was informed why he had been passed over. "We don't want anyone who is going to oppose the government," a cardinal with some responsibility in the selection process told him.†

Ignacio Ellacuria, S.J., rector of the Universidad Centroamericana José Simeón Cañas (UCA) in San Salvador, responds to a question during a press conference after mass on March 9, 1980. To his right is Segundo Montes, S.J., director of Social Sciences and the Human Rights Institute at the UCA; to his left, Archbishop Oscar Arnulfo Romero.

Romero's "Transformation"

As we have seen, Romero stunned everyone by wasting no time declaring where he stood. But it was the assassination of Grande only three weeks after his installation that turned Romero into an unflinching prophet of the church. In an interview three months before his death, Romero described his process of "transformation":

> I have always tried to be faithful to my vocation, my priesthood. My fidelity to the Church's orientations (and to those encyclicals and council documents that asked for a larger service to the people) has always been the rule of my priesthood. The poor people didn't take me by surprise; I have always felt a preference for the poor, the humble, and believe that the trajectory of my priestly life has been like one facet. I wasn't aggressive against the powerful classes when the government was, perhaps, a little diplomatic, and I still have some friends among the very powerful, but many have been lost.
>
> There were times when the old archbishop, Monseñor Chávez, was suffering the expulsion of priests and couldn't make himself understood with the government; they wouldn't pay attention to him. I felt we should defend this position; the following month after my arrival Father Rutilio Grande was killed, which also reinforced my decision because Father Rutilio, before his death, was with me by my side in a priests' meeting, the first one I had.
>
> I asked them to help me carry on with the responsibility; there was much enthusiasm from the clergy to help me and I felt that I would not be alone taking

care of the situation but that I could count on all of them. That union with the clergy vanquished all our fears. They had the idea that I was conservative, that I would maintain relations with the government, with the rich, and that I would ignore the people's problems, the repression, the poverty. I found here many committed clergy and communities that thought a lot about the situation in the country. Some of them feared I would stop everything and asked what I was thinking of doing. My response was that they should continue and that we should try to understand each other well, and to work in a promotion of the Church's work as Vatican II and Medellín had asked us to do. Father Grande's death and the death of other priests after his impelled me to take an energetic attitude before the government. I remember that because of Father Grande's death I made a statement that I would not attend any official acts until this situation [who had killed Grande] was clarified. I was very strongly criticized, especially by diplomats. A rupture was produced, not by me with the government but the government itself because of its attitude.

I support all of the priests in the communities. We have managed to combine well the pastoral mission of the Church, preference for the poor, to be clearly on the side of the repressed, and from there to clamor for the liberation of the people.[36]

Romero understood well why this commitment would cause him and other priests to be labeled subversives; the moment anyone raised the issue of defense of the poor in El Salvador, he remarked shortly before the inauguration of President Romero, "you call the whole thing into question. That is why they have no other recourse than to call us subversives—that is what we are." Archbishop Romero declined to attend the inauguration of President Romero on July 1, 1977, reasoning that it was preferable to risk exacerbating hostilities than to appear and thereby bless a system characterized by fraud, corruption, and repression.[37]

During Oscar Romero's three years and one month as archbishop, the role of the church in the political life of the country expanded with each succeeding crisis. At the same time, under ever-increasing difficulties brought about by waves of persecution against priests, religious, and CEB members, the church itself was growing and was having a greater and greater impact on the life of average Salvadoreans—which is to say, the poor. Although CEBs multiplied, the focus increasingly was on the diminutive archbishop of San Salvador, both within and outside the country.

"The Voice of Those Who Have No Voice"

Romero's message reached into almost every corner of the country (as well as Guatemala, Honduras, and Nicaragua) via the archdiocesan radio station, YSAX. Within a short time, the 8:00 Mass on Sunday morning became the single most listened-to program in the nation. In second place were YSAX's commentaries, written by as many as twenty different people whose identities were a carefully guarded secret.[38] In third place was Romero's weekly interview. All these programs were broadcast three times in order to reach the largest possible audience.

Romero's Sunday morning Mass provided many lessons, but for the social scientist perhaps the most striking aspect was that it had become a means
of socialization. Although it rarely lasted less than two hours, hundreds came
and sat on hard wooden pews for the duration—or were glued to their radios.
Philip Land, a U.S. priest, related that having been advised not to attend the
mass because the people were too restive and one could never tell what might
happen, he wandered into San Salvador's central market, where he found that
almost every stall had a radio—and every radio was tuned to YSAX.[39] It was a
common practice in villages, when no priest was present, to gather in the
church and turn on the radio. In some villages the mass was broadcast over
the ubiquitous loudspeaker system in the plaza.

All of these people were waiting for "Monseñor's" homily, which generally ran an hour and a half. Each sermon had an invariable pattern: He began
with a theological exposition—always with three points—on the scriptural
readings of the day. Then he would relate the scripture to the reality of life in
El Salvador. This was followed by church announcements, then a recitation of
the events of the week just ended, including a reading of every documented
case of persons who had been killed, assaulted, or tortured (regardless of per-
petrator) or who had disappeared. The Salvadorean reality meant that the list
of attacks at the hands of the government's security forces and right-wing terrorist groups was many times longer than the list of those by left-wing guerrillas.[40] When an event warranted it, such as the coup of October 15 or the promulgation of the agrarian reform, Romero would conclude with a "pastoral
position" on the question.

These homilies, then, were not only religious instruction for the people
but were oral newspapers as well. As such they were a potent force in El Salvador from 1977 onward. Just how potent can be measured by the fact that the
YSAX transmitter or antenna was bombed ten times in three years—twice in
January and February 1980. It should be added that the archdiocesan newspaper, *Orientación,* was also the recipient of several bombs after Romero became
archbishop. In spite of or perhaps because of the attacks, circulation almost tripled in the first half of 1977 and had surpassed 12,000 copies per week by
early 1980.[41]

THE COST OF COMMITMENT

We have seen that the church in El Salvador, against opposition from its
own ranks and the larger society, became a powerful advocate of political and
economic change in Salvadorean society. Its increasingly vocal opposition to
and condemnation of official repression and the refusal of the government to
implement desperately needed reforms; its unequivocal support of the right
of the people to organize themselves to demand better wages and working
and living conditions; and its criticism of the oligarchy for its political intransigence and complicity in repression—all brought down on the church the
wrath of the government and oligarchy alike. The fact that Archbishop
Romero also condemned terrorist activities of the left was ignored by the
right.

In the parish of Zacamil the first persecutions "came from men of the church, from priests, all acting very piously. ... For the first time questions came up about certain 'traffickers in the faith.' A letter arrived from the Ministry of the Interior ordering the priests to report there. They had been denounced as subversives and charged with trying to get the "students and peasants to rise up against the government. ... In fact, we weren't even working with students or peasants at that time. ... The denunciation had been signed by four priests belonging to ... ORDEN."[42]

The church has paid an immense price for its effort to be faithful. Rutilio Grande is usually counted as the first assassinated priest, but Father Nicolás Rodríguez was abducted by the National Guard on January 2, 1972. His dismembered body was found several days later. In a 1980 interview Arturo Rivera Damas said that the church at the time accepted the government's explanation that Rodríguez's death was the work of unknown assailants because "we couldn't believe that they could kill a priest." Between March 1977 and June 1981 ten more priests and a seminarian within a month of ordination were assassinated. At least sixty priests were expelled or forced into exile. Some of these, along with many others who did not leave, were picked up and beaten or tortured. The Jesuits' house in San Salvador was sprayed with bullets and bombed on three occasions.

Nuns were not spared. In January 1980 two Mexican nuns working in the parish of Arcatao, Chalatenango, were recalled by their superior after they were taken and held in the local National Guard barracks for several hours. Only when Archbishop Romero demanded their release were they brought into San Salvador and given into his custody. In June a Salvadorean nun was attacked with a machete and sustained severe cuts on her face and neck.[43] On December 2 Maryknoll Sisters Maura Clark and Ita Ford, Ursuline Sister Dorothy Kazel, and lay missioner Jean Donovan were raped and murdered by the National Guard.[44]

The assassination of Archbishop Romero during a mass on March 24, 1980,[45] was the most heinous of the attacks on the church to that time. His death silenced the most forceful voice for justice in El Salvador. But if those responsible for his murder thought they would silence the church by silencing "the voice of those who have no voice," they were mistaken. They did not understand what Oscar Romero knew very well: "I am not the Church," he would say. "The hierarchy is not the Church; the Church is the people."

The church's advocacy of social justice operated at three levels: some of the bishops, the UCA, and the parish. The first two levels have received the most attention in and outside El Salvador, but it was at the parish level that the transformation of the church was the most profound and had the greatest impact on political developments within the country.

THE CHURCH AND
THE POPULAR ORGANIZATIONS

As discussed previously in the example of Aguilares, many people, once they shed their *conciencia mágica*, moved quickly to political action by joining or supporting an existing *campesino* organization. It is less well known that the church, at the parish level, spawned the mass popular organizations that in less than six years brought El Salvador to the brink of revolution. To understand the connection between the church and these organizations, we must review the experience of the parish of Suchitoto and its priests, José Inocencio (Chencho) Alas and his brother, Higinio.[46]

Chencho Alas arrived in Suchitoto in December 1968. Within two months several Christian Base Communities were functioning; thirty-two would be established in a short time. In February 1969 the priest began a two-month course in which the CEBs discussed biblical themes and the form of the CEBs. The objective of the course, according to Alas, was "to prepare the people, following Medellín, to succeed in constructing their own destiny." At the end of the course the CEBs elected nineteen *campesinos* as delegates of the Word. The delegates then received additional training and a course in public speaking.

While these courses were going on, the ubiquitous problem of land tenancy was coming to a head in Suchitoto. Miguel Angel Salaverría, Roberto Hill, and eight more of the country's wealthiest oligarchs created in 1969 the Parcialaciones Rurales de Desarrollo (Rural Subdivisions for Development), a private company whose stated objective was "to contribute to the agricultural development of the country through promoting private rural property, rationally exploited and efficiently administered, through a system of credits for the acquisition of land."[47] Between 1970 and 1975 the group purchased twenty-two properties totaling 12,403 *manzanas* (1 *manzana* = 0.7 hectare), subdivided them, and resold the parcels. Figures from the company indicate that the average purchase price per *manzana* was $195; that after additional costs for purchase, investment, improvements to the property, taxes, interest, and operating expenses, the cost per *manzana* increased to $351; that the average sale price per *manzana* was $440; and that the average size property was 9.1 *manzanas*. Hence the average parcel cost $4,000; a 20 percent down payment meant the purchaser had to have $800 earnest money—an amount far beyond the pocketbook of the average Salvadorean *campesino*. Loans were available at 12 percent, payable over eight years.[48]

According to José Alas, Roberto Hill purchased the Hacienda La Asunción near Suchitoto for $97 per *manzana*, subdivided it, and put it back on the market for $280 to $680 per *manzana*. This so outraged the *campesinos* that they mobilized the entire town, and 3,000 people demonstrated in front of the *hacienda* to demand lower prices for the land. Receiving no response, 400 *campesinos* then demonstrated in San Salvador—the first such demonstration (not staged by the government) since 1932.

As it happened, a monthly clerics' meeting was being held in the Arzobispado at the time of this demonstration, and Alas took advantage of the opportunity to ask his fellow priests and Archbishop Chávez to support the *campesinos'* cause. Alas recalled that Chávez, not having been confronted with such a request previously, "did not know exactly what to do. Yet he did not oppose the idea." The result, according to Alas, was a "very violent meeting because, for that era, it was very difficult for the clergy to accept such a task."

They believed that the work one must do in the countryside was evangelization, defined as administering the sacraments." In the end, Chávez and two other priests, Alfonso Navarro and Rutilio Sánchez, who were working in Suchitoto with Alas at the time, supported Alas and the *campesinos'* demand for a price of $200 per *manzana.*

The demonstration moved the National Assembly, where the opposition was just two votes shy of a majority, to pass a law obliging Hill to sell the land for $200 per *manzana.* Hill and the oligarchy were livid, but among the *campesinos* a "very positive atmosphere was created."

In April 1969 Alas began a weekly course for the delegates of the Word on justice and peace, a major theme of Medellín. These sessions, Alas said, always began with "the Celebration of the Word and communion." Out of this and succeeding courses grew a recognition of "the need to form an organization of the people to deal with the state." During the next five years Alas, who was joined by his brother Higinio in 1972, continued to hold courses for the CEBs, primarily on biblical themes. By 1973, however, they began systematically to study socialist and capitalist ideology. Alas said that earlier, explicitly political themes were occasionally addressed, as during the 1972 presidential election when they discussed agrarian reform, but there never had been a systematic study of these issues.

In October 1972 the government announced its intention to build a second dam, the Cerron Grande, on the River Lempa above Suchitoto, a project that would flood thousands of hectares. That, plus the blatantly fraudulent municipal and national elections in March 1974, served to convince the *campesinos* that they needed a more formal organization to press their demands on the national government. After those elections, *campesinos* and FUERSA, ANDES-21, and FECCAS held two meetings in Suchitoto to create a national organization. That organization, the United Popular Action Front (FAPU), was formally established in April 1974 during a meeting of José Alas, a group of *campesinos,* and representatives of the Unitary Union Federation of El Salvador (FUSS), the Salvador Allende University Front of Revolutionary Students (FUERSA), the National Association of Salvadorean Educators (ANDES-21), the PCS, and others in the Basilica of the Sacred Heart in San Salvador.[49]

Thus, for the first time in Latin American history, a popular mass organization came directly out of the evangelizing efforts of the Roman Catholic Church. As we shall see in the next chapter, although the umbilical cord tying the church and FAPU together was quickly cut, the influence of the church would continue to be strongly felt.

4

The Revolutionaries

I noted the small crucifix around his neck. I asked if he was religious.

"No, not anymore. ... Camilo, I was raised on the message of Father Alas and Father Grande. Though others said we would never bring change without guns, we thought it was possible. We demonstrated, we organized, and we said 'no' for the first time in our lives. You know what it brought. ... Alas was kidnapped ... and left for dead. Father Rutilio was machine gunned. My own father was cut to pieces.

"That man Gulliver, you know him? Gulliver went to a land where all the people were very small. When he stood up, he ripped apart the threads that they used to imprison him. Now we have stood up too. ... We know what we are fighting for."

—Commander Raul Hercules (Fidel Recinos)
to Dr. Charles Clements, Guazapa Front, 1982[1]

In the United States there is an image of the Latin American revolutionary: the bearded fanatic who takes to the mountains where, motivated by blind hatred, he carries out "terrorist" attacks against the existing regime. Or, as Eduardo Sancho (Fermán Cienfuegos), one of the top five FMLN commanders, once said, "[The Reagan administration] believe[s] that all revolutionaries are Stalinists, that we eat babies."[2] This caricature was slowly destroyed for all but the most extreme rightists during the twenty months of peace negotiations in 1990 and 1991. But it never bore much resemblance to the character of the revolutionary struggles in Central America or to the thousands of people who chose to commit their lives, their fortunes, and their sacred honor to the struggle for a different society and political order.

Observers often date the struggle to overthrow the civilian-military government in El Salvador from 1970, when the first of five political-military organizations (OP-Ms) was founded (see Table 4.1). As we have seen, however, El Salvador has a long history of struggle against political and economic injustice that, for four hundred years, was unshaped by any political ideology. The resistance of the Pipil Indians in the 1520s, the Indian-Ladino uprising in 1832, and the revolts against land usurpation by the oligarchy in the late nineteenth century were all reactions to real and perceived wrongs committed by the powerful. Not until 1932 did the struggle acquire overtones of a political ideology—the Marxism-Leninism of the Communist Party of El Salvador (PCS). Even then the PCS, whose leadership was exclusively Salvadorean, only provided a means of organizing and a vision of a new society; it did not create the conditions that led to revolt.

101

TABLE 4.1   The Farabundo Martí Front for National Liberation (FMLN)

Political-Military Organization	Popular Organization[a]	Armed Forces
Popular Forces of Liberation (Fuerzas Populares de Liberación, FPL-1970)	Popular Revolutionary Bloc (Bloque Popular Revolucionario, BPR-1975)	Popular Forces of Liberation (Fuerzas Populares de Liberación, FPL-1970)
National Resistance (Resistencia Nacional, RN-1975)	United Popular Action Front (Frente de Acción Popular Unificada, FAPU-1974)	Armed Forces of National Resistance (Fuerzas Armadas de Resistencia Nacional, FARN-1975)
Party of the Salvadorean Revolution (Partido de la Revolución Salvadorena, PRS-1977)	28th of February Popular Leagues (Ligas Populares 28 de Febrero, LP-28-1978)	Revolutionary Army of the People (Ejército Revolucionario del Pueblo, ERP-1972)
Communist Party of El Salvador (Partido Comunista de El Salvador, PCS-1930)	Nationalist Democratic Union (Unión Democrática Nacionalista, UDN-1967)	Armed Forces of Liberation (Fuerzas Armadas de Liberación, FAL-1979)
Revolutionary Party of Central American Workers (Partido Revolucionario de los Trabajadores Centroamericanos, PRTC-1976)	Popular Liberation Movement (Movimiento de Liberación Popular, MLP-1979)	Revolutionary Party of Central American Workers (Partido Revolucionario de los Trabajadores Centroamericanos, PRTC-1976)

Note: Years cited are dates of founding.
[a]The popular organizations ceased to exist by late 1980.

Thus one can say that, historically, the necessary conditions for revolution in El Salvador have been economic oppression and political repression. The sufficient conditions, however, have varied. In 1832 the sufficient conditions were forced conscription and onerous taxes on indigo. In 1932 the sufficient condition became a stolen election. By the late 1960s and early 1970s there was once again electoral fraud at the end of a decade of increasing political competition. There was also one other, new element: the church.

Like the church, the Salvadorean revolutionary movement has passed through a series of phases since 1970:

- *1970–March 1980: Mass struggle.* Emphasis on building mass-based organizations and political education. Small guerrilla units are created.
- *March 1980–January 1981: Transition.* Evolutionary period dating from the assassination of Monseñor Romero. Increased repression. Mass organizations dismantled. Organizing emphasis shifted from urban to rural. Resources redirected to building a revolutionary army.

- *January 1981–1984: Armed struggle.* Emphasis on military expansion and training. Large concentrations of as many as 1,000 guerrillas each in the countryside. Political work focused on organizing *campesinos* in zones under FMLN control. Virtually no political work in the cities.
- *1984–1988: Armed and political struggle.* Breakdown of guerrilla forces into small, self-sufficient units as a result of U.S.-supplied air war and need to expand political base. Political work in rural and urban areas, occasioned by the electoral process creating "political space" closed for previous four years.
- *1989–1991: Negotiating struggle.* Continued geographic expansion. Wide-ranging analysis of the situation led to audacious proposal for popular participation in elections. War brought to the capital with attacks on military targets for the first time. Serious peace talks began.
- *1992–1994: Transition to political struggle.* The revolutionary movement becomes a legal political party and participates in the 1994 elections.

This chapter examines the years between 1970 and late 1981.

THE POLITICAL-MILITARY ORGANIZATIONS

After 1932 the PCS was outlawed and its members were subjected in the ensuing decades to severe repression. Yet, as the party noted in a declaration on the fiftieth anniversary of the 1932 uprising, "In spite of everything, [it] was the only revolutionary organization capable of resistance during decades of repressive assaults by various governments that linked the cruel chain of reactionary dictatorship."[3]

Its leaders were often jailed and tortured. One, Salvador Cayetano Carpio, wrote of his experiences in the jails of the "reformist" government of Oscar Osorio.[4] In the 1960s, Cayetano Carpio became secretary general of the PCS, and when a debate arose over whether the moment had once again come for armed struggle, Carpio led the faction within the party that believed the time was ripe. He explained in a February 1980 interview what happened:

> After a long process of ideological struggle within the traditional organizations [political parties] it became evident that they ... denied the possibility and necessity of the Salvadorean people undertaking the process of revolutionary armed struggle. ... By the end of 1969 it was very clear that El Salvador, its people, needed an overall strategy in which all methods of struggle could be used and combined in dialectical fashion.[5]

The PCS itself acknowledged in a January 1982 declaration that "tendencies appeared that, evaluating the [1932] insurrection only on the basis of its results, renounced the armed struggle thereby giving birth to and perpetuating reformist positions."[6] Carpio called the "tendencies" "a stubborn majority" who "blocked the advance towards the political-military strategy that the people needed for moving towards new stages of struggle," without whom "no need would have arisen to create ... the Popular Forces of Liberation [FPL]."[7] Carpio resigned from the PCS, went underground with a small group of comrades, and began building the first of the political-military organizations, the FPL.

It is no accident that "political-military organization" was the self-description of El Salvador's revolutionary organizations, for they were, from their inception, more than armed bands. Each had a clear political line to which it held tenaciously. By the late 1970s that tenacity was impeding the process of unity that they all recognized would be necessary if they were ever to achieve victory.

In 1972 a second political-military organization was founded. The Revolutionary Army of People (ERP) also came out of the PCS, but its composition was broader: Juventud Comunista (Young Communists), youth from the Christian Democratic Party, and elements from the radicalized sector of the Salvadorean bourgeoisie. In contrast to the youth of most ERP members, Carpio was fifty at the time of his resignation from the party.

Both the FPL and the ERP had a strongly militaristic conception of the revolutionary struggle. As Carpio put it in his interview, "The armed struggle would be the main thread running through the people's revolutionary fervor and would become in the process the basic element for the destruction of the counterrevolutionary forces." Although the FPL did recognize the need for a "political-military strategy," the political aspect would, for several years, be treated as less important than the military. The ERP embraced the *foco* (nucleus) theory, a Latin American term that refers to a small group of committed, armed revolutionaries who do not need a mass movement in order to triumph.

The leadership of these and subsequent organizations came, to some extent, out of the church. Carpio studied for a time in El Salvador's Conciliar Seminary. Many among the ERP leadership were Christian radicals of the 1960s. A large number within the National Resistance (RN), an ERP faction, were Protestants, and at least two were Baptist ministers.

Within the ERP two tendencies were present from the beginning. One, as suggested previously, emphasized military means. The other tendency, the National Resistance, believed that political as well as military action was necessary. The members of the RN quietly worked with the *campesinos* of Suchitoto in 1973–1974, particularly as the Cerron Grande dam project got under way. Without the knowledge of Father José Alas, they encouraged the formation of FAPU in 1974.[8] So, although it is accurate to say that the first of the popular organizations came out of the church, it is also true that some members of the young political-military organizations were working toward the same end: the organization of the people.

The differences in political lines within the OP-Ms led directly to a split in the ERP. The RN faction that had helped spawn FAPU included Roque Dalton, El Salvador's leading contemporary poet. Dalton's insistence on the need for a political as well as a military line led to a collective decision by the hardliners (who included Joaquin Villalobos, by the 1980s considered the FMLN's most effective military commander) to charge him with treason, try him in absentia, find him guilty, and condemn him to death.[9]

Dalton's assassination in May 1975 split the ERP. The RN immediately created a revolutionary or vanguard party and named its armed branch the Armed Forces of National Resistance (FARN). FAPU, established the year before, became the mass organization. Thus the RN had, from its inception, a more formal structure than the other OP-Ms. Not until early 1978 did the ERP finally decide that an affiliated mass organization was necessary and spawn the 28th of February Popular Leagues (LP-28). Then, two years later the ERP and LP-28 created a revolutionary party, the Party of Salvadorean Revolution (PRS).

The fourth OP-M was the PCS, which during the 1960s chose to follow a reformist course in Salvadorean political life by participating in the electoral process through its legal front, the UDN. The rationale for doing so was not "to achieve power, but rather to rescue the working masses from the influence of the ... Christian Democrats [who] had won a great following among workers. ... For us elections were an instrument for placing our program at the center of political debate, and ... for raising the political consciousness of the masses of workers arriving from the countryside to work in the factories."[10] Following the February 28, 1977, massacre in the Plaza Libertad, however, the PCS changed its policy; it concluded, as the other OP-Ms had done years before, that the time had once again come for armed struggle.[11]

After the massacre it began to create militias that toward the end of 1979 became the Armed Forces of Liberation (FAL). While the UDN participated in the government of the first junta following the October coup, the PCS moved toward unity with other OP-Ms. During the last week in December 1979 the PCS formed a coordinating body with the RN and the FPL. A week after the government's resignation, the UDN joined with other mass organizations to form the Revolutionary Coordination of the Masses (CRM).

The fifth OP-M developed from a different conception of struggle. The Revolutionary Party of Central American Workers (PRTC) was created at the end of a founding congress on January 26, 1976. Many of its members were involved in the initial nuclei that became the ERP in 1972. Some members also came out of unions that were under PCS influence. The PRTC's conception of the struggle was regional, rooted in the history of Central America that recalled, among other events, the Central American Federation of the early nineteenth century; the Central American Workers' Confederation, which enjoyed a brief life in the 1920s; and the struggle of Augusto César Sandino in Nicaragua, which was joined by other Central Americans, including Farabundo Martí. Until late 1980 the PRTC remained a regional party; on October 29 of that year, however, the national units of the party separated, although they maintained ties with each other.[12]

THE POPULAR ORGANIZATIONS

The founding of FAPU and other popular organizations had antecedents in organizations such as FECCAS, founded in the early 1960s, whose strength was in Aguilares, Chalatenango, and San Vicente. The government, worried about the increasing agitation in the countryside caused by peasants demanding their rights, had created the paramilitary ORDEN[13] and, in 1966, the Salvadorean Communal Union (UCS). Founded with the assistance of the American Institute for Free Labor Development (AIFLD), the UCS, whose membership by 1980 was estimated at 120,000, was seen by the government and the U.S. Embassy as a vehicle for co-opting a significant number of peasants into the system through the creation of a privileged class among the *campesinos.* The object was to head off any "radical" or "communist" agitation in the countryside. The UCS functioned as intended for more than a decade. In mid-1980, however, after several UCS leaders had been killed by security forces and one UCS cooperative had been invaded by the National Guard, which then lined up and assassinated eleven of the twelve *campesino* directors of the cooperative (the president survived by fleeing), the UCS began distancing itself from the government. By August it had split into two factions. One cooperated with the government's agrarian reform that had been promulgated the previous March. The second, with strength in the three western departments of Sonsonate, Santa Ana, and Ahuachapán as well as in Cabañas, allied itself after 1978 with FAPU.[14]

There were two important differences between the government-sponsored UCS and the popular organizations (OPs) during the 1970s. The first was ideological. The UCS was viewed by those who created it as a means of controlling the peasantry by giving its members a piece of the pie—or at least giving them reason to believe it would be possible to obtain a piece. The UCS, in short, represented a deliberate effort to maintain the economic and political status quo. The OPs, on the other hand, were dedicated from the beginning to making a different pie. The second difference was structural. The UCS was organized from the top down. Local leaders were generally handpicked not by their fellow *campesinos* but by national officers or U.S. AIFLD advisers. In sharp contrast, the OPs were completely indigenous and were developed from the grassroots. As with the Christian Base Communities, the people were encouraged to select their own leaders.

Sectarian Differences and Divisions

Among the organizations that participated in the founding of FAPU were the PDC and MNR, as observers, but they withdrew when they discovered they could not run the show. The organization grew quickly, but its unity was short-lived. FAPU, like the ERP, contained two factions. One was oriented toward the RN, the other toward the FPL. In July 1975 a split occurred, and a new OP, the Revolutionary Popular Bloc (BPR), emerged.

The Causes of Division. The differences within FAPU were political, strategic, and tactical. First, there was disagreement over whether the struggle should be defined in short-, medium-, and long-term stages (FAPU) or in terms of *la lucha prolongada,* a prolonged struggle in which all actions were directed toward the ultimate goal—the overthrow of the existing regime (BPR). Second, although both believed an alliance between workers and *campesinos* to be the fundamental and necessary force in the struggle, they divided over which to emphasize. Both originated in the countryside, but whereas the RN tendency believed that its organizing emphasis should be among the most strategic unions, such as electric, Port Authority, coffee, cotton, and sugarcane laborers, the FPL tendency considered that the emphasis should be on the *campesinos*. Third, the two tendencies parted company over the role of the progressive sectors of the middle class and the military. The FPL discarded any possibility of alliance with the military and placed less emphasis on work with the middle class; the RN considered both important and directed part of its effort to developing alliances with them.

In tactical terms, for example, FAPU's conception of working with unions was to build support from the base—the membership—through its political schools (a tactic shared with the PCS). The FPL approach was to try to seize control of a union from the top. These different approaches may be explained by the fact that all three organizations were competing with each other for hegemony in the unions; the BPR's tactics were related to its lack of resources for working at all levels because of its emphasis on the countryside. The result of these different strategies was that by 1980 the BPR had become the largest of the mass organizations, with more than 60,000 members and nine affiliated organizations. FAPU's membership was estimated at half that, and much of its leadership was older, more middle class, and in the unions.

FAPU acquired a reputation for incisive analysis of the Salvadorean reality and for its theoretical publications. Through this work it exerted a profound impact on the development of a unified political program in 1980. Ultimately, FAPU's insistence on revolution *and* democracy, as well as on forming alliances with progressive sectors of the church and political parties, the UCA, progressive labor unions, and elements of the private sector, became official policy of the FMLN.

28th of February Popular Leagues. The third of the popular organizations, the 28th of February Popular Leagues, was founded by ERP sympathizers within the University of El Salvador on February 28, 1978, the first anniversary of the massacre that occurred when the National Police cleared the Plaza Libertad of Colonel Ernesto Claramount and his supporters. LP-28's founding was the result of a belated recognition by the ERP that if it did not create its own mass organization, it was going to be left in the dust by the FPL and the RN. LP-28 was also third in size, with about ten thousand members. During the late 1970s the organization was considered by others on the left to have the least well developed political program, which was consistent, at least, with the ERP's overly militaristic view of the struggle. This meant, however, that LP-28 was given to actions designed to attract attention, such as occupation of embassies and ministries, without analysis of the context or much thought for the political fallout.

Popular Liberation Movement. The smallest, and youngest in membership, of the popular organizations was spawned by the PRTC in late 1979. The Popular Liberation Movement (MLP) was initially kept out of the CRM by FAPU, which maintained, in the face of BRP support for MLP membership, that the new organization had to demonstrate its capacity to organize and mobilize the people. By May 1980 the MLP had satisfied FAPU's criteria and joined the CRM.

National Democratic Union. While the UDN was participating in electoral politics in the 1960s and 1970s, the PCS was exerting hegemony over teacher and student organizations, and labor unions. Thus the UDN was also a popular organization, even though its political line appeared to be more "reformist" than "revolutionary" for much of the 1970s.

Unity Announced. One might conclude from the preceding discussion that the most prominent characteristic of the Salvadorean left was its sectarianism. By the end of 1979, however, a direct correlation between perceived proximity to power and a reduction in sectarianism—a phenomenon that had occurred in Nicaragua in 1978–1979—was becoming more apparent. On January 11, 1980, the popular organizations papered over their remaining differences, called a press conference, and announced the creation of the Revolutionary Coordination of the Masses (CRM).

In a document issued that day, *Nuestras organizaciones populares marcha hacia la unidad* (Our popular organizations march toward unity), the CRM described, in language remarkably free of ideological rhetoric, the "profound economic and political crisis" of the country, then argued that the "revolutionary alternative is the only solution to the crisis." "The people have created riches and live in poverty," it stated, a situation resulting from a "political and economic structure" that could not be corrected by a government that was part of that structure and did not enjoy popular support.

The press conference itself revealed something of the character of the left. One incident in particular is worth noting because it suggested the profound nationalism of people who were accused of being tools of an "international communist conspiracy." Before the conference began, a young man brought the Salvadorean flag onto the stage. At first no one noticed, but by the time he was halfway across the stage the audience began whistling, then cheering. At that point a young woman took the microphone and said she wanted to explain. "The flag is not the property of the oligarchy," she said, and "it is the only symbol of unity for us." More cheers. The conference began with the national anthem. Everyone, it seemed, knew the words.[15]

1932 Remembered

Eleven days later the popular organizations staged the biggest mass demonstration El Salvador had ever seen. According to OP leaders, the demonstration had three objectives: to "pay homage to the *compañeros* who had died in the 1932 uprising"; to "celebrate the unity" of the popular organizations; and to "demonstrate the capacity of the OPs to organize and mobilize the people."†

At least 200,000 people gathered in the capital from all over the country in a show of power that was characterized by extraordinary discipline, order, and patience. What began as a peaceful march ended in chaos as the demonstrators were fired on by National Guardsmen and National Police, ANTEL security guards, and men in civilian clothes. When the shooting was over, forty-nine were dead and hundreds injured. The government disclaimed responsibility, asserting that security forces had been confined to barracks for the day and that "armed leftists" had started the trouble. Eyewitnesses interviewed on the day of the march and later unanimously agreed that shooting had come from the roofs of at least fourteen public and private buildings in the center of the city. Subsequently, a well-placed army officer confirmed in an interview that there had been a conspiracy among Minister of Defense José Guillermo García, his subsecretary, Nicolás Carranza, and certain members of the oligarchy to disrupt the march and provoke the left into a confrontation.† It did not work.

STEPS TOWARD UNITY

By killing Roque Dalton, the ERP became the outcast among the OP-Ms, and there were questions whether the breach would ever heal. The ERP was conspicuously absent when the other three OP-Ms created a coordinated command in December 1979. Although negotiations were in progress and continued into the new year, only with the formation of the Unified Revolutionary Directorate (DRU) on May 22, 1980, did the prodigal return to the fold.

The formation of the DRU, with three commanders from each of the organizations, represented a step forward in the development of a unified command structure—in other words, a joint chiefs of staff. That unified command, however, would not become a procedural reality for more than a year. It would take much longer to be fully operational.

Lingering Discord

The creation of the DRU did not mean an end to ideological problems among its constituents. A decade-old debate over how to prosecute the struggle continued into the 1980s. On one side, the largest of the OP-Ms, the FPL, had long insisted on *la guerra popular prolongada* (prolonged popular war, or GPP), a strategy of wearing down the existing regime through hit-and-run military assault, sabotage, and similar tactics while organizing the masses. The other OP-Ms favored the strategy of popular insurrection. When the January 1981 "final" offensive failed to produce a victory, however, the OP-Ms had little choice but to fall back and regroup. At this point the FPL insisted on adhering to the GPP strategy; the other four OP-Ms opted for a strategy that combined revolutionary war with popular insurrection.

Another example of the divisions among the organizations occurred in early September 1980, when the RN walked out of the DRU in a dispute over policy and organization. One policy difference concerned efforts by the RN to exploit a crisis within the Salvadorean army officer corps. For many months the RN had been holding secret conversations with various officers. In early September a large number of young officers who were allied with Colonel Majano were transferred by Defense Minister García and junta member Gutiérrez, a tactic that isolated Majano and dispersed his supporters. The RN saw in this maneuver an opportunity to gain some more allies within the army. Other DRU members thought the RN efforts too zealous and criticized it sharply for its activities.

Meanwhile, a major organizational dispute erupted within the DRU over the adoption of the Leninist principle of democratic centralism[16] and the formation of a unified revolutionary (vanguard) party. Until this time the DRU had operated by consensus or unanimity. But the FPL, ERP, and PCS wanted to adopt democratic centralism as an operating principle. The RN argued that first it was necessary to create a revolutionary party and then apply "not only one but all the Leninist principles of organization."[17] When it was overruled, the RN withdrew, although it remained in contact with the other groups. In the end, the RN lost far more than it gained, for when it returned to the fold on November 8, it was forced to accept a series of decisions that had been made in its absence—including the formation of the FMLN on October 10 and the adoption of democratic centralism.

The persistence of these and other differences into 1981 not only indicated the extent to which political maturation was needed by all parties but also reemphasized an ancient lesson of politics—that unity is not an absolute end but a process.

Once the movement toward unity began in early 1980, a certain momentum was achieved, helped along by the unfolding political events within El Salvador. The growing and uncontrolled repression in the countryside and the inability of the junta to control the security forces led to the resignation of Christian Democrat Héctor Dada Hirezi from the junta on March 3. Three days later the first stage of an agrarian reform was promulgated; this was followed a day later by seminationalization of the country's largely decapitalized banking system. Along with these two reforms, the government instituted a state of siege, ostensibly to facilitate the occupation of the nationalized *haciendas*. In fact, it provided a cover for greatly increased repression, which began on the day the agrarian reform was announced.

One measure of the repression was that four days after that announcement, *campesinos* began streaming into the Arzobispado in San Salvador seeking refuge. Conversations with these people produced a host of horror stories: security forces or men in civilian clothes driving into the middle of a village and opening fire in all directions; women and girls being raped, then killed; houses being searched, ransacked, and burned; animals destroyed; women and children shot while sleeping; young people being taken off and "disappearing." Because most of the refugees were women and children, they were asked where the men were. There was one answer: "They've gone to the mountains"—that is, they had gone to join the guerrillas.[18]

The Christian Democratic Party Splits. The resignation of Dada and the murder of Mario Zamora (see Chapter 5) precipitated an open split in the Christian Democratic Party that had been festering for two months. José Napoleón Duarte, the titular head of the party, engineered a national convention called on March 9 to elect a new member of the junta. Duarte and his followers handpicked most of the delegates, thus ensuring his own selection to fill Dada's place. This was achieved over the unanimous opposition of all the Christian Democratic ministers in the government and the most progressive wing of the party. Duarte won the election, but the progressives walked out and almost immediately reconstituted themselves as the Popular Social Christian Movement (MPSC).[19]

The Democratic Revolutionary Front. The assassination of Archbishop Oscar Romero two weeks later was a further impetus toward unity of the center-left (social democratic political groups) and the CRM. On April 11 a coalition of political parties, professionals and technicians, small business organizations, the national university, six unions and union federations, and a student association, with the UCA and the Catholic Church as observers, announced the formation of the Democratic Front (FD). Five days later this alliance joined the CRM in creating the Democratic Revolutionary Front (FDR), thus unifying all the opposition forces from the center-left to left of the political spectrum.

A week after its formation the FDR held a general assembly to elect the Executive Committee. That committee was composed of eight members, five from the organizations making up the CRM and one each from the MNR, MPSC, and MIPTES (Independent Movement of Professionals and Technicians of El Salvador). Enrique Alvarez Córdova, who had twice been minister of agriculture, was elected president of the FDR. Throughout the spring and summer, delegations from the FDR toured Europe and Latin America in a fairly successful effort to gain international support. Four European countries declared their support for the FDR, and the Socialist International, at its June 1980 meeting in Oslo, voted to support it. In Latin America, the strongest early support came from Mexican president José López Portillo, who permitted the FDR to establish political offices in that country.

THE STRATEGY FOR AN INSURRECTION

Within El Salvador the FDR changed tactics, abandoning mass demonstrations in favor of general strikes. On June 24 and 25 a general strike shut down the country for forty-eight hours. Another strike two weeks later was called off at the last minute because of a lack of coordination between the FDR and the DRU. The strike was rescheduled for August 13–15, and the FDR announced that the DRU for the first time would be "taking appropriate actions" during the period. The June strike was a classic example of the traditional Latin American strike: Workers occupied their factories and shut them down, *campesinos* sat down on the farms, and office employees stayed home. The objective was to demonstrate broad popular support for the FDR, and with 90 percent of the country's work force out, the strike was a success. The August strike, although it included these traditional actions, was called by FDR leaders an insurrectional strike because its goal was to test an organizational structure that would be employed in a general insurrection.[20] The structure had three main elements—the guerrillas, the militia, and the popular neighborhood committees.

The Guerrillas. Each unit, organized in squads of three to eleven individuals, platoons of twenty to thirty, and large units, was capable of functioning on two levels. One was as traditional guerrilla forces operating in both city and countryside, who had as primary objectives in the preinsurrectionary period training and obtaining arms and munitions from government troops and garrisons; who during the 1970s carried out kidnappings of oligarchs and officials of transnational corporations for ransom; and who selectively killed members of right-wing paramilitary groups such as ORDEN. On the other level, the guerrillas functioned as a regular army with a military structure and strategy, a war plan, base camps, and uniforms. By mid-1981 this organization had a name: the Revolutionary Popular Army (EPR).

The Militia. Composed of peasants and workers with some military training and minimally armed, the militia until late 1980 had the primary role of harassing government troops and protecting unions and their leadership. Over time the tasks of the militia became more complex. According to Commander Jacinto Sánchez, a member of the DRU in San Vicente, "The militias are organized by brigades for different tasks: production, self-defense, securing the periphery of towns, vigilance in the areas controlled by us, and at times extending into the territory where the enemy is located." Their work included "military engineering, constructing places of refuge and underground tunnels for storage and protection from air attacks."[21]

Popular Neighborhood Committees. These committees, which were also organized at the block and zone levels, had responsibility for stockpiling food, water, medicines, and "popular arms." They provided logistical support for the military units by erecting barricades and digging ditches. Political education was also conducted through these committees by means of neighborhood study groups. As the FMLN began preparations for a popular insurrection in 1981, these committees assumed responsibility for self-defense preparations in their respective neighborhoods.

During the August 13–15 strike, all three levels of this revolutionary organization were mobilized for the first time. Proclaimed a failure by the government and private enterprise, the strike engaged 70 percent of the Armed Forces; resulted in an economic loss of $60 million over the three days, according to the business sector's own estimate; led to the militarization of all electric, water, and telephone plants as well as the Port Authority; and resulted in the proscription of the militant electrical workers' union and the jailing of four of its leaders.

The January Offensive. With the creation of the FMLN, preparations for the long-awaited general offensive began. At 6:30 P.M. on January 10, 1981, guerrilla units commandeered radio stations in San Salvador. Salvador Cayetano Carpio, by then a member of the FMLN General Command, issued the call to battle:

> The hour to initiate the decisive military and insurrectional battles for the taking of power by the people and for the constitution of the democratic revolutionary government has arrived. We call on all the people to rise up as one person, with all the means of combat, under the orders of their immediate leaders on all war fronts and throughout the national territory. The definitive triumph is in the hands of this heroic people. ... *Revolución o Muerte. Venceremos!* (Revolution or Death. We will triumph!)[22]

In the first hours of the general offensive, the FMLN had the Salvadorean army on the run. San Francisco Gotera, Morazán, fell. Two officers and eighty soldiers in the Second Brigade at Santa Ana revolted, burned a large part of the garrison, and went over to the insurgents; for a time the FMLN flag flew over that city. Towns around the country and suburbs on the northern and eastern periphery of San Salvador, where the popular organizations had spent years organizing the people, rose up in insurrection. For forty-eight hours it appeared that the FMLN was on its way to repeating the Sandinista triumph in Nicaragua a year and a half before.

Then the tide turned. Within days, the FMLN announced the end of the "first phase of the general offensive" and began a tactical retreat to its home bases in the north and east. In subsequent analyses, FMLN commanders acknowledged that there had been no unified war plan and little coordination among the commanders, a problem exacerbated by a lack of radio-communications equipment, and that there had been many tactical errors, such as the failure to cut the supply lines of the Salvadorean army.[23] There was also the continuing problem of unity: The ERP declined to share arms arriving from Cuba with the rest of the FMLN.[24]

One FMLN leader noted that they had commandeered the radio stations for a second time on January 11 to tell workers to prepare for a general strike, but they were unable to take the stations a third time to announce the beginning of the strike.† Furthermore, although the suburbs of San Salvador were well organized and many were in FMLN hands within twenty-four hours after the offensive began, the capital itself was poorly organized. Thus the Salvadorean Armed Forces were able to militarize public transportation, factories, and services. The result: The strike as a tool of insurrection was less successful than in August.

But for all the FMLN's errors, the Salvadorean army was little better. Said Miguel Sáenz several months later, "If the enemy had been well prepared, efficient, and coordinated, we would have been annihilated." General García announced that the FMLN had been routed, that the Salvadorean army had won a great victory and was in control of the entire country, and that the threat of revolution in El Salvador was past. The departing Carter administration concurred in this assessment, then rushed in $10 million in military assistance and nineteen military instructors and maintenance personnel just to make sure.[25] Sources in Washington, D.C., asserted that the new Reagan administration's scenario for El Salvador included a "military victory" over the FMLN in sixty to ninety days.† In March the administration sent another $25 million in emergency aid and raised the number of U.S. military advisers to fifty-six. By early summer, however, after a period of analysis, self-criticism, and regrouping, not only had the FMLN not been defeated, but it was once again inflicting large numbers of casualties on government forces.[26] Guerrilla leaders insisted that they controlled more territory after the offensive than before.[27] At the very least, in mid-1981 there was a military stalemate in El Salvador.

THE POLITICAL SIDE OF
THE REVOLUTION

Four days after the general offensive began, the FDR and FMLN called a press conference in Mexico City to announce formation of the Political-Diplomatic Commission (CPD). The body was composed of seven members, one from each of the OP-Ms and two from the FDR. In practice, the CPD functioned as a foreign ministry with its members traveling around the world in search of support from governments, political parties, and international organizations. The FDR-FMLN sent official representatives—the equivalent of ambassadors—to thirty-three countries. An FMLN leader commented that this was "not only more missions than the Salvadorean government has embassies," but that the representatives "exercise a stronger presence."† In other words, the FDR-FMLN was aggressively seeking out government ministers and legislators as well as talking to the media and citizens groups on a daily basis. This effort paid dividends throughout the decade; the first dividend came in on August 28, 1981, when France and Mexico issued a joint declaration recognizing the FDR-FMLN as a "representative political force" that should be directly involved in any political settlement.

In addition to the CPD, the FDR-FMLN created two other joint organs with similar membership. One was the International Relations Commission, which was responsible for developing international solidarity among the citizenry of various countries and for overseeing social and relief work connected with the hundreds of thousands of Salvadoreans who, beginning in early 1980, were fleeing their country and seeking refuge in countries from Canada to Panama. The second was the Commission on Information, which was responsible for the production of several publications, news bulletins, and posters.

Besides these overtly political structures, a series of working groups were created in health, education, agrarian reform, the economy, and other areas. They were offshoots of "professional groups" that the BPR and FAPU had put together in 1979 to analyze the country's socioeconomic problems and needs and to develop national plans that would be implemented once the Revolutionary Democratic Government (GDR) came to power. Economists, doctors, agricultural technicians, teachers, and others were involved in these projects. One of the institutions in which this research and analysis was carried out was the MNR-sponsored Centro de Investigación y Acción Social (CINAS—Research and Social Action Center), based in Mexico City, where Salvadorean and Mexican social scientists produced a large number of thoroughly researched articles and monographs on the Salvadorean and Central American reality during the 1980s.

The development of the joint commissions and the working groups emphasized several things: that in a revolutionary process the political dimension is as important as the military; that, in addition to the guerrillas, several thousand people were working full-time in the struggle; that revolution was an expensive activity, running into millions of dollars annually; that, as FDR-

FMLN members noted frequently, through working together day in and day out, they were achieving unity not in theory but in practice.

Whereas the FMLN operated on the principle of democratic centralism (which none of the constituent groups consistently honored), the FDR and joint commissions continued to operate on the basis of consensus. By late 1981 mechanisms of coordination between the FMLN and the FDR were such that all important decisions could be made together. One example of this coordination, and of the balance between the political and the military dimensions, was the decision to destroy the Puente de Oro, which spanned the Lempa River, on October 15, 1981. There was an extended discussion of both the internal and external political dimensions and potential costs as well as the economic cost ($10 million) of destroying the bridge. Once the political decision was made, the military planning became the exclusive domain of the FMLN. When the action was carried out, on the second anniversary of the October coup, units from the four organizations with bases in the area participated. One set the explosives; another, assisted by militia, evacuated the thousand people living under each end of the bridge; meanwhile, the others distracted the guard posts at each approach and at nearby garrisons.[28]

The Mountains Are the People

That the FMLN, under the noses of the National Guard, could evacuate more than a thousand people in the dead of night is one small indication of the extent of popular support for the revolutionary organizations. The question of support was disputed throughout the war. The U.S. and Salvadorean governments insisted that the FDR-FMLN had little popular support. The fact that the population did not heed the call to insurrection in January 1981 was often cited as proof of this and contrasted with Nicaragua in 1978 and 1979.

But El Salvador was different. First, the regime did not provide the population with a single figure like Somoza, whom everyone loved to hate. The problem in El Salvador was an economic and political system, a far more amorphous enemy. Second, the system of repression in El Salvador tended to be cyclical, spanning half a century, and more pervasive. A third factor was size. The Sandinistas could always retreat to the Segovia Mountains in north-central Nicaragua, or into Costa Rica, where they were virtually untouchable by Somoza's National Guard. The FMLN, in contrast, had to operate in a country where there are almost no uninhabited areas.[29] Fourth, most of the Salvadoreans learned an important lesson from Che Guevara's disastrous experience in Bolivia where he and his followers failed to build support among the population. When U.S. Special Forces went looking for Che in the jungle, there was no network to warn him and no one to hide him.

In El Salvador, from the beginning, the FPL and the ERP (the latter departing from a pure *foco* theory) lived among the people; they helped plow land and harvest crops; they provided medical care and other forms of assistance; they taught the peasants how to protect themselves. For example, a woman from Sensuntepeque, Cabañas, said that the FPL taught her fellow villagers to put a lookout on a small hill below her hamlet and to fire a flare if they saw the army or security forces coming. When the army moved in on June 1, 1980, the flare went off, and all the men ran to the mountains. No one died that day, although one old man who remained behind was tortured.[30]

Juan José Martel, who in the early 1980s was the MPSC member on the FDR Executive Committee, said in an October 1981 interview that, given the small size and high population density of El Salvador,

> It is impossible, militarily, for a guerrilla movement to survive, even for a few weeks, if it does not have the massive support of the population. We can ask, who gives food to the guerrillas? Who advises them of the army's movements? Where does the population run when it is attacked by the army—because the army attacks the population as it does the guerrilla?
>
> Evidently, it is not the Russians, nor the Cubans, nor the Nicaraguans who daily send tons of food for thousands of guerrillas to eat; tons of clothes to wear; and such exact information of the movements of the enemy. It is the people who do all this, who sow the basic grains, prepare the food, and make the clothes. El Salvador has no mountains, but the mountains of the guerrillas are their people.[31]

The "people" also lived in the cities and kept the FMLN supplied with basic necessities. Charles Clements observed in Guazapa that "The vast majority of their supplies flowed to the rebels not across the border but out from San Vicente, San Miguel, San Salvador, and other cities. They relied on an impressive underground network of supporters who risked their very lives for the cause."[32] Roberto Roca, a member of the FMLN General Command, said that "we could not establish hospitals in the war fronts if there were not an enormous popular network in the cities who buy one ampule of penicillin, sterilized water in tiny amounts—which in the course of two or three weeks allows us to stock a field hospital. Everyone participates: the doctor who provides the prescription, the person who buys the medicine, and those who carry the medicines to the fronts."[33]

A subtle indication of support was that in personal conversations with hundreds of peasants they never used words like "terrorists" and "subversives" to describe the revolutionary organizations. They talked about "the Bloc" (BPR), "the Leagues" (LP-28), the "popular organizations," and "the Front" (FMLN). They referred to the guerrillas most often as *"los compañeros"* and occasionally as *"los muchachos."* The first four terms are neutral, the last two positive.[34]

Size and Strength of the FMLN

The size of the revolutionary army was disputed. Salvadorean government sources tended to downplay its numbers and rejected the FMLN estimates. In a mid-1981 interview, Fermán Cienfuegos said that the FMLN had "4,000 guerrillas in arms" and "more than 5,000 militia."[35] Although these figures were close to estimates by various observers, the real problem, as FMLN leaders were complaining in interviews by January 1982, was not combatants but a shortage of arms. Miguel Sáenz in February 1982 described one result as being a rotation system so that in a platoon of twenty-one combatants, five would receive "three-to-five-day passes," and their places would be taken by others who did not have weapons. Raul Hercules recalled this situation vividly in a January 1992 interview. "In Guazapa in early 1981 there were 300 to 400 combatants and only 60 rifles."[36]

The observations of several U.S. journalists who spent a combined total of several weeks in guerrilla-controlled areas in the early 1980s gave lie to Reagan administration efforts to portray the FMLN as armed to the teeth by the communist bloc. As Clifford Krauss wrote after three weeks in Chalatenango: "I saw no Cuban or Nicaraguan advisers, no planeloads of guns and ammunition and no abundance of supplies." The combatants were "poorly equipped but highly disciplined. Hundreds of young militia fighters had nothing more than pistols and machetes with which to fight, against an army equipped with U.S.-leased helicopters and artillery."[37] When two colleagues and I encountered two guerrillas on the road to La Palma, Chalatenango, in January 1984, one was carrying a pistol, the other an M-1.

Arms Sources. The sources of arms that attracted the most attention in Washington (and therefore the media) were Cuba and Nicaragua. There is no question that in late 1980 and early 1981, both countries were sending arms and munitions to the FMLN in preparation for the January offensive.[38] There is also no question that when the offensive failed, Cuba and Nicaragua quickly reassessed their policy. Then, when U.S. intelligence provided irrefutable evidence of this trafficking and the United States warned both parties of the consequences of continuing, they stopped out of self-interest. Nicaragua, in particular, wanted to maintain good relations and keep the economic aid flowing. Unfortunately, the Reagan administration never allowed facts to interfere with its ideology—an ideology that dictated the overthrow of the Sandinista government in Nicaragua and the military defeat of the FMLN. As a result, various U.S. officials, including President Reagan, made a series of charges concerning arms shipments—even about the presence of Cuban military advisers in El Salvador—from spring 1981 onward for which it presented absolutely no evidence. Not until November 1989 did any evidence—in the form of a crashed airplane loaded with antiaircraft missiles and a flight plan from Nicaragua—appear.[39]

The FMLN had four primary sources of arms. The first two were the international arms market and corrupt army officers in the region who sold arms to the insurgents. The money for these purchases came primarily from an estimated $65 million in ransom money received from the kidnapping in the late 1970s of ten Salvadorean oligarchs and several other foreign businessmen, most of whom were released. By 1981 the FMLN was also receiving voluntary contributions from around the world. The people of West Germany, for example, contributed more than $1 million during 1981 in an "Arms for El Salvador" campaign.

A third source of arms was manufacture by the FMLN itself. The group became adept at making its own weapons, and there were many villages in zones under FMLN control where many of the residents were, according to visitors, voluntarily working full-time making hand grenades and land mines.[40] The fourth source, which became increasingly important by late 1981, was the more direct and increasingly successful method of attacking the Armed Forces in their barracks or ambushing them on patrol to obtain weapons. One guerrilla commander told a visiting journalist that the more arms the United States sent, the more the FMLN recovered. "We want to thank the United States government," the commander said, "for sending us so many weapons."[41]

The Rationale Behind Kidnappings. The kidnappings were internationally condemned as wanton acts of terrorism. They were certainly violations of human rights. Nevertheless, we should try to understand the rationale behind them. The Salvadorean oligarchy's large fortunes and control of the national economy were reinforced in the 1960s and 1970s by the arrival of multinationals, which brought their executives and paid workers an average salary of $4 per day. The vast majority of the people continued to live in abject poverty with no hope of improving their lot. FMLN Commander Roberto Cañas explained that the kidnappings were viewed as a means of "recouping some of this wealth for the people, to shape and develop the political struggle for their liberation." He denied that all the money was used "to buy arms; much of it has been used to build the popular organizations. The armed struggle is necessarily a part of the struggle," he concluded, "not because we would have chosen that path but because there is no other way to wrest political and economic power from the dominant forces and change the structures to a more just and humane system."[42]

OUTLINES OF A
REVOLUTIONARY SOCIETY

By 1981 it was possible to discern the shape and character of the proposed revolutionary society in El Salvador from the organizations that already existed, from the forms of governance that operated in areas of the country under FMLN control, from the ideology of the revolution as manifested in everyday practice, and from the organizations' documents.

The Political Program of the FDR-FMLN

A month after the January 22, 1980, demonstration, the CRM published its platform of the Revolutionary Democratic Government (GDR). The proposal contained a series of "immediate political measures," including adherence to the U.N. Declaration of Human Rights and due punishment for those responsible for the "disappeared," the tortured, and the murdered; the decentralization of power to municipalities; a foreign policy of nonalignment; and the development of a popular army incorporating honest, patriotic troops and officers of the present army.

Under "structural changes," it proposed nationalization of the banks, external commerce in major exports, the entire energy system, and "monopolistic enterprises in industry, commerce, and services." It promised extensive agrarian and urban reform but pledged to honor the holdings of small and medium-sized property owners. It committed the GDR to an extensive tax reform and to the establishment of effective mechanisms of credit, especially for mall and medium-sized businesses. Finally, in the area of "social measures," he GDR proposed to reduce unemployment by creating jobs and to implement massive projects in housing, health, education, and culture. Many of these proposals would find their way into the 1991 peace accords.[43]

On August 7, 1981, the FMLN General Command issued a declaration in which it listed seven points that would guide the implementation of the GDR platform. Those seven points restated the main themes of the first document, then added that the GDR would "guarantee to the Salvadorean people peace, liberty, welfare and progress by implementing social, economic and political changes that ensure a just distribution of the wealth, the enjoyment of culture and health, and the effective exercise of democratic rights of the great majorities." The declaration promised "freedom of belief and the free exercise of all religious denominations." The GDR also would "support all private businesses that are opposed to genocide, imperialist intervention, who cooperate with the implementation of its program and who contribute to the functioning and development of the national economy."

These and other documents reflected a growing political maturation of the revolutionary organizations as well as growing self-confidence. On no issue was the FMLN's policy evolution greater than with regard to the future of the Armed Forces. The February document (emphasis added in the following provisions) called for a "Popular Army, in which will be incorporated those elements of the troops, non-commissioned officers, officers and commanders of the present Army who maintain 'clean conduct,' reject foreign intervention ... and support the liberating struggle of our people." In August 1981, the FMLN's General Command spoke of "the integration of the Popular Revolutionary Army and the patriotic and democratic sector of the army ... in an army of a new type." Two months later this position was further modified in a document read before the U.N. General Assembly by Nicaraguan president Daniel Ortega: "The ... Armed Forces [will be restructured], based on the officers and troops of the present Army who are not responsible for crimes and genocide against the people, and ... the commanders and troops of the FMLN [will be integrated into it]."[44]

The FMLN's growing flexibility was a result of three factors: increasing military capability and confidence; recognition by France and Mexico of the FDR-FMLN as a "representative political force"; and a growing unwillingness to prolong the war unnecessarily (thereby increasing the bloodshed) by holding out for an absolute military victory such as the FSLN had achieved in Nicaragua in 1979.

By October 1981 the FMLN was strong enough to defeat the Salvadoran army militarily. But U.S. intervention guaranteed that the war would continue indefinitely.

New Political Structures

In urban areas the popular neighborhood committees, the basic unit of political organization, continued to function clandestinely. In the rural areas of Chalatenango, Morazán, Cuscatlán, San Vicente, and Usulután and in the Guazapa front, however, the outlines of revolutionary local government began to emerge. The character of these popular governments depended on three factors: the importance assigned to them by the principal organization in the area, the conditions in the zone, and the length of time the organization had been there.

Chalatenango. The FPL placed great emphasis on the development of local government. As a result, PPLs (*poder popular local*—local popular power were established in 1981–1982 as the guerrillas consolidated their power in eastern Chalatenango. As Jenny Pearce, who spent several weeks collecting oral histories in Chalatenango, wrote:

> The PPLs are an experiment in popular democracy and political participation. ...
> Their development ... was not simply due to an advantageous military situation
> The FPL had never seen the zones of control as mere military rearguards. Rather
> they saw them within a broader framework of political mobilization, and as a
> means by which the civilian population could guarantee their needs and orga
> nize their society independent of the military command of the FPL. The peasants
> ability to respond to the opportunity and play an active role in shaping their own
> lives rested on their prior experience first in the Christian base communities and
> subsequently in the peasant union.
>
> The primary task of the PPL is to administer and organize the population in
> the zone of control. But there are evidently broader political objectives as well
> Each PPL is democratically elected by the civilian population from among their
> own ranks. They represent the first opportunity for poor peasant farmers to orga
> nize their own communities and participate in their own government. Through
> the PPLs, the peasants have gained experience and confidence in their capacity to
> work collectively and solve their own problems.[45]

In El Jícaro, Chalatenango, for example, virtually all 2,000 inhabitants were directly involved in community decisionmaking.[46] Each PPL was elected by a "locality," about 500 people, which was divided into four *bases*, or hamlets. In each locality the "popular assembly," or town meeting of the entire population, was the highest authority. Between meetings of the popular assemblies, decisionmaking resided in a PPL junta of seven elected officials: a president, a vice-president, and secretaries for legal affairs; political education and information; health and education; production, commerce, and trade, and self-defense. Candidates were nominated from each hamlet and elected by the popular assembly for a period of six months. Assemblies convened twice a month to discuss problems with the junta; the secretaries met once a week.[47]

Morazán. In keeping with its *foco* theory of revolution, the ERP placed more emphasis on military than political organization. In late 1974 it decided to turn Morazán into a control zone and develop a mass front there. According to Comandante Balta (see Prologue), "the policy of organizing a mass front was not done on the basis of a trade union scheme but with clearly political demands. This allowed us to grow rapidly in Morazán, and from [mid]-1975, we began to develop the proposal for the formation of military committees. ... From the beginning, we conceived the mass front as a structure with a certain autonomy, with its own platform of struggle. Nevertheless, very rapidly the development of the repression in Morazán led to the accelerated creation first of the self-defense teams, then of the militia teams of [LP-28]."[48] By the early 1980s, both teams had fused with the ERP to defend the zone.

San Vicente, Cuscatlán, and Usulután. As the FPL did in Chalatenango, the PRTC encouraged the establishment of local revolutionary government in an area of San Vicente known as the Cerros de San Pedro (Hills of St. Peter) and elsewhere in central El Salvador. There Consejos Farabundistas (administrative councils) were created and divided into four sections, the first three of which were popularly elected. They included the following:

- The civil registrar had responsibility for civil procedures and vital statistics on births, deaths, marriages, and divorces.
- The religious section was composed of a catechist or delegate with responsibility for promoting the religious life of the community and for helping the people relate their faith to the revolutionary process.
- The economic section was responsible for agricultural and other production and for the distribution of the produce.
- The self-defense section, the only section appointed by the FMLN, was composed of militia whose primary responsibility was to teach the people what to do during an invasion by government forces. "Popular military engineering" became a skill born of necessity, as the militia, for example, working with the people, constructed *tatus* in nearby hills.

(*Tatus,* a device borrowed from Vietnam, are elaborate tunnel systems constructed in hills or mountains where people can hide and be protected from bombardment.)

According to Commander Jacinto Sánchez, the principal task of the Consejos Farabundistas was "the leadership of the population to normalize civic life and control and administrate resources and collective production."[49] María Caminos, a member of the FMLN who worked in information and political education, elaborated. "There are literacy campaigns and clothes-making. There are councils of elders who know all about popular or traditional medicines and who are teaching university-educated doctors how to cure certain illnesses. This," she noted, "is one example of how the revolution recovers the values of the people." There was also a "glass of milk" campaign, which was intended to give every child under seven in the zones under control one glass of milk per day, something, Caminos said, that "has never been done in El Salvador."[50]

Guazapa. The pattern of organization in this area, just twenty miles north of the capital, was less structured than in Chalatenango. Until the 10,000 civilian inhabitants were literally bombed out of the 333-square-kilometer area between 1983 and 1985, village organization resembled "pre-Columbian collectivism," in which "the people cooked and washed communally. The cultivation of the local corn or bean patch or the gathering of firewood was also communal. An individual's responsibilities in these various tasks reflected his or her interest in collective life. Not everyone chose to join the collectives or, if they did, devoted themselves full time to them."[51]

All-front congresses, where the people met with the *comandantes* to discuss problems and air grievances, were held regularly. The willingness of the *campesinos* to confront the military leaders is reflected in an anecdote related by Charles Clements. A health worker named Mario had reportedly drowned, but the peasants discovered that he had been shot and wanted to know why the FMLN leaders had covered up the execution. Raul Hercules admitted he and the others had lied because "Mario was a traitor. It was decided for morale purposes not to reveal his true identity." The people's response was emphatic: "We are not fighting and dying to be lied to. We will not win our struggle just to replace killers and liars with more killers and liars."[52] Hercules apologized.

The *campesinos* organized several cooperatives in the front. An agricultural cooperative had survived from the days of José Alas. A cattle cooperative provided milk for the children and pregnant women, and a fishing cooperative provided protein. There were also honor and justice commissions in most of the villages, elected by the people, which handled civil disputes such as "community land-use policies, the right of a *campesino* to take shelter in an abandoned house, or the ownership of a stray pig or cow." Clements wrote that "their courts weren't bothered by incidents of domestic violence and child abuse. ... In Guazapa I didn't treat a single battered wife or abused child."[53]

In Guazapa, as in all fronts, alcohol and drugs were banned. There were two reasons for this. One was to discourage among the civilian population the high incidence of alcoholism with all its attendant problems. The other was security: Guerrillas had to be alert at all times; they could not afford to fall asleep on watch, much less run the risk of a drunken guerrilla opening fire indiscriminately.

In short, the patterns of civilian political organization in zones under control varied, depending on the political perspective of the particular group operating in that zone. There was a universal effort, however, to organize collective or cooperative farms; to introduce literacy classes for civilians and guerrillas and compulsory education for children; and to institute medical care in areas where most people had never seen a doctor. By 1981 the FMLN had produced workbooks and teachers' guides for literacy campaigns that were in widespread use.[54]

When journalist Alex Drehsler asked a peasant on one of the collective farms if he missed having his own small plot of land, the answer was unequivocal. "Before the government drove me out ... I was always struggling to grow enough food for my family," the middle-aged man replied. "Often we went hungry. Now, we all work the same land and all of us have food. We don't go hungry. Do I miss having my own land? No. This way my children get enough to eat. I can't feed them a handful of earth."[55]

The Role of Women

All of the revolutionary organizations encouraged the participation of women at all levels and established an impressive record of promotion based on accomplishment and leadership qualities, not gender. This achievement occurred in the context of a powerful social tradition of protecting women. Said a male guerrilla commander in Chalatenango, "We are trying to teach the women that they do not have to accept only the traditional roles for women, that they should try to examine their potentialities. We have some peasant women who join us as cooks. Soon they realize that they have opportunities to do other things. They become combatants, medics, or leaders."[56]

The Combatants. Approximately 30 percent of the FMLN combatants and 20 percent of the military leadership were women. These figures, however, varied among zones, units, and the constituent organizations of the FMLN, with the ERP appearing to have the largest percentage of combatants and officers. In Guazapa, 5 to 30 percent of units were women.[57] In 1981 an all-women battalion was created in Guazapa. All of the organizations had senior women commanders; there were three women (of fifteen members) in the DRU. Mercedes del Carmen Letona (Comandante Luisa) managed Radio Venceremos until the mid-1980s when she moved on to diplomatic duties; two commanders, Ana Guadalupe Martínez and Nidia Díaz, were on the CPD; among the women commanders who fell in battle were Clelia in Morazán, Susana in Chalatenango, and Iliana in San Vicente.

Support Groups. In some ways it was easier for urban women to join the revolutionary movement at some level than for women in rural areas. As María Serrano, a former PPL mayor, put it:

> The [rural] women here have had to put up with most of the exploitation by the system. And the men here are mostly *macho,* so that women find themselves doubly exploited by the system and the *compañero.*
>
> So the integration into political life of women is not very easy, as we grew up with a mentality, given to us through generations, that a woman is no more than a person to look after the house, raise the children. But with the revolution this stopped; women found that they could do the same things as men.[58]

Of herself, María said, "If my husband likes my hair long, well then I won't cut it. But if he were to tell me, 'I don't want you doing political work,' I would tell him, 'Sorry,' and go on."[59]

Support roles included everything from doctors, medics, and nurses to cooks, radio operators, couriers, and farmers. In Guazapa, Isabel and Blanca, both in their sixties, got tired of hearing men's comments about women's awkwardness and slowness in the fields and organized a women's farm collective. Its first harvest was among the largest in the zone, and the collective outproduced many all-male farms.[60]

Attitudes. A revolution in attitudes occurred, as the preceding comments suggest. One guerrilla said in an interview that the "process of coming to see women as *compañeras* and not as sex objects" was one he and his fellow guer-

Three women of the FMLN in Miramundo, Chalatenango, October 16, 1984. From left: Veronica, a combatant; Comandante Susana, who died in battle in 1985; and María "Chichilco" Serrano, a peasant leader who served as mayor of her zone in the early 1980s. She became an FMLN political officer in 1988 and is now a community leader in eastern Chalatenango.

rillas had to go through in the mountains. In his particular unit, two-thirds of the combatants were women. "There is great concern," he said, "to destroy *machismo.*"†

Machismo was universally regarded by the revolutionaries as a legacy of colonialism and capitalism. (Studies of pre-Columbian Indian civilizations in Mexico, Central America, and Peru indicate that although there was a gender-based division of labor in those societies, women were widely regarded as equals.) One particularly virulent form was the attitude that having as many women as possible or having a mistress in addition to a wife demonstrated one's manhood. Such behavior was actively discouraged in the control zones for three reasons: There was a conscious effort to change attitudes, to strengthen the family, and, among the combatants, to reduce personal jealousies. When a couple became intimate, they were defined as *acompañada* or almost married.[61]

Organizations. Several women's organizations with some relation to the FDR-FMLN were formed in the late 1970s and early 1980s. AMES (Association of Women of El Salvador) was founded in 1979 and began working with women in Chalatenango as well as in San Salvador slums. By 1980 it had been driven underground by the repression in the city but continued to grow in the controlled zones where the FPL operated. AMPES (Association of Progressive Women of El Salvador), AMS (Association of Salvadorean Women), and ASMUSA (Association of Salvadorean Women) were also founded.[62]

Ideology and Practice

The presence of women, of Christians, of the "democratic"—as distinguished from "revolutionary"—sectors of Salvadorean society within the FDR-FMLN, as well as different political tendencies among the revolutionaries themselves, all contributed to a vigorous dialectical process of thought and action that gave the Salvadorean revolutionary process its own unique characteristics.

Liberation. The central concept in this process was "liberation." The term was common to the discourse not only of the revolutionaries but also of the church. In El Salvador and among the refugees in other countries of Central America, the people in Christian Base Communities spoke most frequently of "liberation" rather than of "revolution."

For these people, spread from Mexico to Costa Rica, interviews over two years showed that "liberation" had a concrete meaning: no more hunger, illiteracy, illness, or housing of cardboard, sticks, and dirt floors. For FDR-FMLN leaders, it also meant that "the people are struggling ... to expel foreign dominance and a small, dominant class that has kept the people subjugated for many decades."[63] These themes would reverberate in the 1991–1992 peace accords.

In addition, the concept of national liberation included both women's and men's liberation. Norma Guevara, who was a member of the FDR-FMLN Commission on Information, said that "the resources for which we are struggling belong to all so that the possibility of resolving the problems of women and children exists only in the context of a project that takes account of all the social, political, and economic problems of our country."[64]

Pluralism. In Norma Guevara's view, pluralism "is directly associated with the concept of liberation" because it reflects "the breadth of the social forces in the struggle." She defined pluralism as the integrated, coordinated action of different political forces. María Caminos added that pluralism means that these different sectors, "while still having some ideological differences," agree on "national independence, the right to self-determination, a more just distribution of the wealth, and the necessity for structural changes that will permit social progress."

Both Guevara and Caminos were members of organizations that made up the FMLN. Rubén Zamora was secretary general of the MPSC and a member of the CPD. In 1982 he argued that pluralism was necessary in the Salvadorean revolutionary process because it guaranteed a spirit of self-criticism and because there was a "historic demand by the people for democracy and pluralism."[65]

U.S. officials often charged that the pluralism reflected in the composition of the FDR was merely a facade for the "hard-line Marxists-Leninists" of the FMLN who, after victory, would shove all the "democrats" aside and seize total control of the state. Several dozen interviews with members of both organizations produced the same response: "rubbish." Said María Caminos: "That charge is a maneuver of imperialism to deny the authenticity of our revolutionary process and to sow divisions among the revolutionary forces. It is also an effort to present our struggle as a struggle for communism manipulated from the outside. I believe that the democratic sectors can never be isolated from the process because they represent the aspirations of the people; as long as they do that, they will be present." Juan José Martel discussed what this meant for the MPSC and other organizations of the FDR: "Actions are not taken behind our backs. Not only are we consulted, but we are actively involved in the making and execution of all [political] decisions."[66]

The FMLN and FDR emphasized political access for all sectors of society, from the local to the national level, especially the majority who traditionally had been excluded. Among the Salvadorean revolutionary organizations, the concept of political mobilization differed from that of liberal democracies in its emphasis on a process of political education designed to prepare citizens for direct participation in daily decisionmaking and cooperation toward common goals. This concept of participatory democracy, a concept reinforced by the Christian Base Communities, is one to which citizens of the United States have had little exposure.

These ideas, as we shall see, endured and were manifest in the platforms of the MPSC and MNR after 1987 as well as of the FMLN in 1992. The organizational ideas were adapted by several communities of repatriated refugees, much to the chagrin of the ARENA government and the U.S. Agency for International Development (AID).

While the FMLN was developing militarily and politically, tangential events were occurring within the Salvadorean government, military, oligarchy, and church. The United States decided to use El Salvador as a laboratory for its strategy of "low-intensity conflict," all the while defending what it insisted on calling a "moderate, reformist government." It is to these developments that we turn our attention in the next chapter.

5

Descent into Anarchy, 1980–1982

"Now there is only the law of the jungle. There is no law." Orlando de Sola pulled out a very large gun and placed it on the table. Pointing to it, he said, "Today in El Salvador, this is the Constitution." Then he pulled out two loaded clips and placed them beside the gun. "These" he added, "are the amendments."

—San Salvador, January 17, 1980

Although it was not immediately apparent, relationships and patterns of behavior that had been developed, cultivated, and maintained between 1932 and 1979 were altered forever by the coup of October. The cycle theory ceased to be an adequate analytic tool, although it appeared to be until at least 1982. A dialectic—or several parallel dialectics—developed both within and among the five principal actors. The resulting patterns of behavior can be summarized as a series of two-track strategies for the oligarchy, Armed Forces, and United States. Meanwhile, the church continued to display tensions between the traditionalists and the progressives, and the revolutionaries changed their strategy from mass struggle to armed struggle.

The two-track strategies can be summarized as follows:

- The most right-wing sector of the oligarchy developed a political-military plan that led to the development of paramilitary death squads and a political party. More moderate sectors would not be heard from until the mid-1980s.
- The Armed Forces, breaking with the oligarchy for the first time, decided they could carve out a new role for themselves by championing reforms—on their terms—that included a systematic policy of repression directed against anyone identified as or suspected of being a leftist. In this, they coincided and cooperated with the oligarchy's paramilitary apparatus.
- The United States pursued a two-track strategy under the rubric of "low-intensity conflict": a counterinsurgency strategy that coupled socioeconomic reforms and a buildup and improvement of the mili-

127

tary with a "transition to democracy" that meant cramming elections down the throat of the army.

These strategies did not develop in a linear fashion; rather, they were shaped by each other, by other outside forces, and by dynamics that they unleashed. They produced unanticipated consequences, which had their own dialectical impact on a process that continued through the decade. In this chapter the development of each strategy is examined in depth, up to the 1982 elections. What happened in these two years would shape the course of events for the next decade.

DERECHIZACIÓN

The struggle within the Armed Forces began, as we have seen, before the October coup. In the fall and winter of 1979–1980, however, it appeared merely to verify an astute observation by a U.S. Embassy official long acquainted with the Salvadorean military: "Whenever the army feels threatened as an institution, it joins together and moves to the right."† The process, or "derechización," required the elimination of the reformers and took more than a year. Meanwhile, the most right-wing sector, which included most of the senior officers, entered into a new relationship with the extreme right-wing oligarchy in which mutual dependency to achieve the medium-term goal of eliminating their opponents—the political center as well as the left—coexisted with a growing independence of purpose and action on both sides. For members of the military in 1980 this meant setting themselves up as the proponents of agrarian and other socioeconomic reforms. It also meant an escalating number of political murders that, at its peak, would exceed 1,000 per month.

The battle was joined as conservatives, led by Minister of Defense José Guillermo García, argued for strengthening the army, postponing the reforms, and taking a hard line against the OPs, whereas junta member Majano and his followers (Majanistas) argued for the reforms to which they had committed themselves in the Proclama. Their wishes, initially shared by a majority of the officer corps, became clear in a January 15, 1980, meeting when about 75 percent of those present voted to demand the resignations of Colonels García and Carranza. That same day identical letters, addressed to the junta, circulated in all army posts. The letters charged that the "objectives of the Proclama ... have been obstructed by irrational actions motivated by personal interests of our defense officials," then "DEMAND[ED] THE IMMEDIATE DISMISSAL OF THE MINISTER AND SUBSECRETARY OF DEFENSE."[1]

Signed by 186 officers, the letters precipitated the most serious crisis within the Salvadorean military since the October coup. But Majano and Gutiérrez were indecisive; the subsequent standoff ended with García and Carranza still in office. Two months later I asked the officer who showed me the original letters why his colleagues had not forced the issue. "We are still waiting for the junta to act," he replied. Héctor Dada later said that he and the other civilian members of the junta had never seen the letter or been informed of the crisis.[2]

The Christian Democrats Join the Government

Two days after the first junta resigned, the PDC met with Majano, Gutiérrez, García, and Carranza and laid down conditions under which it would participate in a new government.[3] These included a public commitment by the army to an agrarian reform and nationalization of the banks; a halt to the repression; a promise by the army to open a dialogue with the popular organizations; a ban from the junta and cabinet of any private-sector representative; and the resignation of García, Carranza, and the head of the Treasury Police, Colonel Francisco Moran.[4]

These demands were formalized in a pact reached between the army and the PDC and published on January 9. The PDC chose José Antonio Morales Erlich, a former mayor of San Salvador and vice-presidential candidate in 1977, and Héctor Dada Hirezi, the immediate past foreign minister, for the junta.[5] José Ramón Avalos, a political independent who happened to be Gutiérrez's personal physician, replaced Mario Andino. The army promptly reneged on its agreement to remove García, Carranza, and Moran. In a pattern that would be repeated, the Christian Democrats did nothing. Meanwhile, selecting a cabinet proved difficult. Few who had resigned on January 3 were willing to return. Many others were unwilling to join the new goverment. By the time the cabinet was completed in mid-January, it was common knowledge in San Salvador that most of the appointees were second and third choices.

Betrayal

The last few of the new ministers were sworn in on January 17 in the midst of the crisis in the army. Five days later the popular organizations demonstrated the magnitude of their support, but after the assault downtown, 25,000 *campesinos* took refuge on the campus of the national university. That night *majanistas* from the San Carlos garrison surrounded the campus to prevent the National Guard and National Police from storming it.† The next morning Major Roberto Staben of the National Police and Captain Arnoldo Pozo of the Treasury Police met with the junta and announced they would invade the university with or without orders. Héctor Dada demanded that García discipline these officers for insubordination. The defense minister declined saying he lacked the authority to control the security forces.[6]

One week later LP-28 occupied the PDC party headquarters and held several hostages, including Marina Morales, José Antonio's daughter. LP-28 demanded the release of political prisoners and said that "the occupation is for the repression against the people and to denounce the counterrevolutionary character of Christian Democracy."[7] A negotiated agreement between rebels and PDC to release the hostages in return for safe conduct away from the building was broken when the Treasury Police, under Colonel Moran, stormed the building, ushered Christian Democrats out, then shot five members of LP-28. Twenty-three were captured and "disappeared." Other LP-28 members escaped by lying about their identities. The Christian Democrats threatened to abandon the junta if Moran was not dismissed. "To mollify us,"

Duarte later wrote, "his commanders promised he would be ousted. ... Of course he stayed on."[8] Again the Christian Democrats backed down.

Political Intervention by the United States

These events took place as the Department of State was reviewing U.S. policy toward El Salvador. Frank Devine had retired as ambassador, and Robert White, the new appointee, had not yet arrived. The resignation of the first junta had caused "consternation," according to one embassy official; this same official later admitted that the United States should have "made it clear what our policy was" concerning support for the reforms and the junta but that "we were trying to play the game very openly and honestly—to avoid the appearance of intervention."†

Mixed Signals. As the United States was supposedly clarifying its policy, Assistant Secretary of State William Bowdler visited El Salvador January 22–24. In two meetings, one with Archbishop Romero, the other with the National Association of Private Enterprise (ANEP), Bowdler, accompanied by Devine, continued the contradictory policy line. According to an individual present at the meeting with Romero, the conversation began with Bowdler telling the prelate, "We don't want to continue talking in favor of urgent changes but for the future." Romero asserted that "The people want the changes quickly, and the more rapidly they come, the less violence there will be." Devine argued that "The popular groups want power, not changes." Bowdler tried to get the archbishop to endorse the Christian Democratic–military government, but Romero refused, saying that was not the business of the church. When the diplomats realized Romero would not budge, Devine said, "We'll support the changes."†

In a subsequent meeting with ANEP, Bowdler, according to then executive director Juan Vicente Maldonado, said it was better to have the present government than what might follow—an extreme-right military coup and the possibility of civil war. Bowdler suggested it was best to keep the Christian Democrats in power, although, he added, "We've got to move the Christian Democrats to the center and get them to act less demagogically than they are acting." The important thing, Bowdler concluded, was to reestablish law and order.[9] An embassy official later insisted that the same message had been given to both church and private sector: support for the government and the changes it was proposing. Nevertheless, certain elements among the oligarchy, bourgeoisie, and military received a different message.

"Clean, Counterinsurgency War." Another indication that the United States was more concerned with order than reform came in a meeting of the Christian Democrats in the government with James Cheek, the chargé d'affaires, in late February. The principal theme of this meeting, according to Héctor Dada and Rubén Zamora,[10] was Cheek's insistence on the need to create "adequate conditions" for a "clean, counterinsurgency war." Cheek suggested reforming the Salvadorean penal code in order to permit the Armed Forces to retain prisoners for an indefinite period of time[11] and establishing a training program for the Salvadorean army, presumably to be conducted by

U.S. military advisers. Mario Zamora, Rubén's brother and the *procurador general de los pobres* (a combination of public defender and family court lawyer), responded that "sufficiently repressive laws" already existed in El Salvador. In an interview, Cheek recalled a meeting with the High Command in which he had talked about undertaking a "clean campaign" against the left and the right. The military's response was that the laws did not permit that kind of operation. Cheek told the civilians that they should cooperate with the military by revising the penal code so that persons like BPR secretary general Juan Chacón, who had been arrested but released three days later for lack of evidence, could be held for trial. But, Cheek asserted in his interview, "Héctor Dada and Rubén Zamora did not agree with that."

The conflicting versions of this encounter illustrate the problems with U.S. policy in early 1980. The desire to build a political center by eliminating the left and right ignored two facts: Important sectors of the military were linked to the right and would not move against it, and those same elements believed the only way to deal with the left was to eliminate it. Cheek felt the Christian Democrats did not understand him. But Rubén Zamora insisted that they understood Cheek perfectly. They also understood, said Zamora, that in El Salvador a "clean war" was impossible.

Romero's Plea. In the midst of these activities, the United States announced a new military aid package for El Salvador totaling $5.7 million—eleven times the average annual aid since World War II and less than 1.5 percent of the aid El Salvador would receive in 1986.[12] The most outspoken critic of the aid was Archbishop Romero, who wrote President Carter, appealed to his Christian faith and his stated "desire to defend human rights," and then requested suspension of military aid that, Romero said, "instead of promoting greater justice and peace in El Salvador will surely increase injustice here and sharpen the repression that has been unleashed against the people's organizations. ... Neither the junta nor the Christian Democrats govern the country. Political power is in the hands of the armed forces [who] use their power unscrupulously. They know only how to repress the people and defend the interests of the Salvadorean oligarchy."[13] Carter had Secretary of State Cyrus Vance answer the letter.

THE RIGHT GETS ORGANIZED

Romero was largely correct in his assessment of the situation. It was impossible to see in February 1980 that two momentous changes had occurred: a rupture in the traditional relationship between army and oligarchy, and fissures within the oligarchy itself. Evidence was scarce, and the cracks would not become apparent for several years. In late 1979 the most reactionary sector of the oligarchy seized the initiative, but there were indications of more moderate responses. Although ANEP withdrew its members from various governmental agencies after the Christian Democrats refused to include the private sector in the new government,[14] in early February Duarte and Julio Adolfo Rey Prendes (San Salvador's mayor) secretly traveled to Guatemala where they met with members of the Salvadorean private sector living there.[15]

After Duarte joined the junta in March, conversations resumed between ANEP and the government.

The most determined response, as noted in Chapter 2, followed a May 1979 meeting in the Casa Presidencial when a small group of reactionary oligarchs concluded that if they wanted to preserve themselves and the system their fathers and grandfathers had created, they would have to take matters into their own hands. A two-track political and military strategy emerged. On the military side they sought—successfully—to reconstruct the ORDEN apparatus in the countryside, to create their own death squads, and to cooperate with like-minded army officers. As a senior officer commented in December 1983, "The men with a lot of money formed their own armies and asked the minister of defense [García] for permission to import arms for their own protection."† On the political side they founded women's and youth organizations and the Broad Nationalist Front (FAN), which "resembled a poorly organized American election committee, down to the coffee klatches and seat-of-the-pants fund raising. Its activists gave speeches at business luncheons and staged rallies to 'take back the streets' from leftists."[16] These developments symbolized the end of the cycles that had characterized Salvadorean political life since 1932.

The Guatemalan Connection

In fall 1979 Roberto D'Aubuisson and a group of young Salvadorean businessmen met in Guatemala City with Mario Sandoval Alarcón, the founder of the fascist Nationalist Liberation Movement (MLN).[17] The Salvadoreans were interested in getting arms and organizing a paramilitary underground, but Sandoval warned them against "falling into the error of [becoming only] a terrorist organization. ... If they kill you, you kill back," he said. But, he said, if they did not organize politically, they would lose within a year.

Sandoval supplied advice, raised money among right-wing Miami exiles for the political activities of D'Aubuisson's cabal, helped smuggle weapons into El Salvador, and later supplied planes and pilots to ferry hit men in and out of the country. Sandoval also put D'Aubuisson in contact with veterans of the French Secret Army Organization (OAS).[18] They developed what D'Aubuisson described as a "good plan" to seize control of the Salvadorean government through "organizational and operational guidelines for assassinations, kidnappings and military assault teams, to be coupled with a political organization engaged in international diplomacy and public relations."[19]

"Millionaires' Murder, Inc." These activities required millions of dollars, much of which came from Salvadorean exiles in Miami.[20] It was stated in a January 1981 embassy cable released under the U.S. Freedom of Information Act (FOIA) that six Salvadorean millionaires in self-imposed exile "have directed and financed right-wing death squads [in El Salvador] for nearly a year, that they are trying to destroy the moderate reformist government by terrorizing its officials as well as the businessmen who cooperate with its reform program [and] that a wave of recent kidnappings is very likely their work." The cable noted that the embassy had "heard this conspiracy described by several earlier sources and ... [that] many Salvadorans and some official Americans have been aware [since March 1980] that rightist death squads are financed and directed by a group ... in Miami, that the publisher of the *Diario de Hoy* [the second largest newspaper in El Salvador] N[apoleon] Viera Altamirano is a principal figure," and that "they organize, fund and direct death squads through their agent Roberto D'Aubuisson."[21]

Salvadorean Rambo. D'Aubuisson and company, having absconded with the ANSESAL files after the coup and having spent time in Guatemala preparing for battle, returned to El Salvador in early 1980 ready to save their country from communism. D'Aubuisson, who acquired the nickname "Mayor Soplete" (Major Blowtorch), made several television programs in which he named priests, civilian leaders, and others as part of "El Salvador's terrorist conspiracy."[22] Watching these programs reminded one of Senator Joseph McCarthy, who manufactured similar lists in the 1950s. McCarthy, however, only assassinated character; some of the people D'Aubuisson denounced were soon murdered. Others quickly chose exile.

On February 22 the major denounced Mario Zamora. At 2:00 A.M. on February 23 six heavily armed masked men broke into Zamora's home during a midnight meeting of leading Christian Democrats, forced those present to identify themselves, then took Zamora into the bathroom and shot him ten times. Héctor Dada subsequently said that within two days the junta had "concrete proof" implicating Colonel Nicolás Carranza in the assassination.[23] Colonel Roberto Santivañez, the CIA-trained director of the main Salvadorean intelligence agency, ANSESAL, in 1978 and 1979, later charged that former Nicaraguan National Guardsmen were paid $180,000 to be the hit men, arguing that Salvadoreans would have known who Zamora and his guests were.[24] No charges were ever brought.

On Sunday March 9 at 5:00 P.M., Archbishop Romero was to celebrate a memorial mass for Zamora in the Basilica of the Sacred Heart. After mass that morning the sexton noticed a briefcase under one of the pews. When opened it was found to contain seventy-two sticks of dynamite and a timer set for 5:00.

Had it gone off, the entire leadership of the Christian Democratic Party, their families and friends, and Archbishop Romero would have perished.[25]

The second attempt, two weeks later, would succeed. D'Aubuisson had warned Romero on television that "You still have time to change your ways." The only precaution the archbishop took was to begin sleeping in different places. D'Aubuisson denied involvement, but there is overwhelming evidence, confirmed in 1993 by the Truth Commission (see Chapter 8), that he orchestrated the crime and that the "honor" of killing Romero was determined by drawing lots. The Armed Forces were also implicated by secret embassy cables not released under FOIA and in material captured with D'Aubuisson when he was arrested at the San Luís farm, near Santa Tecla, in May 1980.[26]

On May 11 the five most active death squads published a list of "traitor communists" to be eliminated. On March 29, 1981, an Armed Forces communiqué listed 138 names of those held responsible for the "chaos" in the country. The two lists were identical in both names and order.[27] As Christopher Dickey noted, the right-wing death squads were "an enterprise that dealt in quality, not quantity. … The group that operated out of Guatemala went after names, people whose faces everyone knew, the sensational cases of people they thought were Communists at the top of Salvadoran society."[28]

The New Matanza

Roberto D'Aubuisson was, in his own words, a "civilian collaborator"[29] with the military—the main link between the Armed Forces of El Salvador, the group based in Guatemala, and the Miami exiles. In early 1980, for example, García and Carranza authorized video programs based on the filched files from ANSESAL that were circulated among army barracks in an effort to persuade officers that the government and army were infiltrated by communists. "Don't ever feel guilty for having fought these subversives!" D'Aubuisson exhorted the soldiers. "You are national heroes!" These appeals, which Carranza called "very objective," gave officers carte blanche to act on their own. The result of these combined efforts over the next three years far exceeded the 1932 matanza (massacre).

ANSESAL was reorganized in Department 5, the "civic affairs" section of the High Command. Every security force had its G-2 intelligence section—its own death squad. In the National Police this section was called "CAIN," the National Center for Analysis and Investigations. Political prisoners interviewed in prison in the mid-1980s spoke of the torture and interrogations they had received in CAIN. Most "visitors," however, did not survive.[30] The Treasury Police acquired the reputation for being the most brutal; the National Guard, whose director after the coup was Carlos Eugenio Vides Casanova, for being the most active and the most closely tied to D'Aubuisson's civilian apparatus. The civilians fed names of "subversives" to the intelligence forces, and written orders would go out to "pick them up, get information, and kill them later."[31]

Another kind of help came from Argentine advisers who were contacted by D'Aubuisson in Buenos Aires in October 1980, then invited to help by senior National Guard officers. The Argentines provided expert advice on safe houses, torture, extracting information, and murder. D'Aubuisson associates told Craig Pyes that interrogation techniques were so brutal that they were afraid of going near the houses. "They would kill anybody. … I never went. I wouldn't. You knew they were killing your own people," said one young Salvadorean who, disillusioned by the brutality, quit the movement.[32]

In addition to the security forces, "Every garrison of any size had Death Squads."[33] This meant that as information provided by the reconstituted ORDEN apparatus filtered into local barracks around the country, campesinos disappeared or turned up dead in growing numbers.[34] It also meant that a large number of commanding officers became directly involved in death-squad activity. These death squads were not random, uncontrolled groups: They were highly organized; they formed an integral part of the Armed Forces; and they were controlled by officers reaching all the way up to the highest echelons of the Salvadorean officer corps.

The story of the U.S. role in these developments is far from complete, but some details are known: that civilian and military officials of the U.S. government supplied electronic, photographic, and personal surveillance of individuals who were later assassinated by death squads; kept key security officials on the Central Intelligence Agency (CIA) payroll; furnished intelligence files that D'Aubuisson used for his television programs; instructed Salvadorean intelligence operatives in the use of investigative techniques, combat weapons, explosives, and interrogation methods that included "instruction in methods of physical and psychological torture"; and violated the Foreign Assistance Act of 1974, which prohibited spending U.S. funds "to provide training or advice or ... financial support for police, prisons, or other law enforcement forces ... or any program of internal intelligence or surveillance [for] any foreign government."[35]

The Aborted Coup. In late February 1980 rumors of an imminent right-wing coup began circulating in San Salvador. Duarte wrote that the Majanistas threatened to overthrow the junta if García, one of the conspirators, was not fired. To quell the rebellion, Gutiérrez and Majano promised that García would be removed. He was not.[36] There were two other reasons for this nonevent. One was the split in the army. The second was U.S. pressure on the military and the oligarchy. "The [United States] ... contributed significantly to thwarting this coup A) by quickly, forcefully, and unequivocally opposing the coup, both [in San Salvador] and in Washington ... and, B) by using our considerable influence with the Salvadorean military, particularly key leaders such as Colonel Gutiérrez."[37] The United States also turned up the heat in Miami, sending an envoy to inform the exiled oligarchs that their residence visas would be revoked in the event of a coup.

The situation the United States confronted was one it had helped create. By sending $5.7 million and pushing a law-and-order line with the Salvadorean military, U.S. officials were encouraging the most conservative officers. Meanwhile those same men were under growing pressure from the extreme right in El Salvador to impose law and order and end the threat from the left. A right-wing coup, followed by the murder of 100,000 or more people, would, the right believed, enable it to pursue its economic interests with little interference.[38] "This victory over the right," James Cheek wrote to Washington, "is ... limited and probably of short duration. We have ... temporarily outmaneuvered them and derailed their plan." A second coup attempt, April 30–May 1 was orchestrated by Roberto D'Aubuisson[39] but foiled by the *majanistas*. It suggested that the extreme right was sufficiently desperate to ignore U.S. threats because it believed that, in the long run, U.S. aid was not central to its interests.

Assassination and Resignation. A week after Mario Zamora's assassination, Héctor Dada resigned from the junta and moved to Mexico. In his letter of resignation he charged that "we have not been able to stop the repression and those committing acts of repression irrespective of the authority of the Junta go unpunished; the promised dialogue with the popular organizations fails to materialize; the chances for producing reforms with the support of the people are receding beyond reach."

Duarte threatened several times to leave the government if the repression did not stop; he wrote that "the objective" of murdering Zamora was "to force us out of the government. We were determined not to let them succeed." When the Christian Democrats met on March 9 to choose Dada's successor, Duarte engineered his own election over the opposition of the party's ministers, Colonel Majano, and Morales Erlich. Still, Duarte later wrote that his "personal desire was to stay out of the junta" because if he joined, "the violence would be my responsibility. I wanted my legacy to be democracy, not deaths."

A motion in the convention to resign from the government en masse was opposed by Duarte and Rey Prendes, who argued that "We have fought twenty years for [the agrarian reform and nationalization of banks that had been promulgated three days earlier] and now that we have them you want us to resign."† In Duarte's view, "The party would suffer either way, but with the agrarian reform enacted, and a chance to create the conditions for democracy, could we turn our back on the junta?"[40] When the convention ended, the center-left wing of the PDC had walked out. This group officially resigned from the party on March 10, charging that

> the maintenance of repression and complacency in the face of foreign interventionist plans [of the U.S. to send military aid and thirty-six advisers] constitute ... behavior absolutely contradictory with the posture our Party has maintained throughout twenty years of struggle on behalf of the Salvadorean people. To accept this course of action in return for a share of the power—more formal than real ... allows the governmental process to degenerate into something neither democratic nor Christian.[41]

During 1980 seven of the thirteen members of the party's national directorate resigned and about half the national leadership left; mass desertions, about 5 percent of the national membership, occurred in four departments.[42]

REFORM AND REPRESSION

The agrarian reform and nationalization of the banks and external commerce, which Duarte defended, and the accompanying repression, which the departing Christian Democrats condemned, were the result of pressure from the United States to promulgate the reforms as quickly as possible and a decision by the army to pursue a policy of reforms (for which it could take credit) but with repression to eradicate the left. On the day the agrarian reform was promulgated, Decree 155 imposed a state of siege. Of the decree, James Cheek wrote that "It is difficult to imagine how a responsible government facing the current near-anarchy could have done less."[43] The state of siege was not lifted until the 1982 elections, and then only briefly.

The Reform. Ambassador Robert White frequently called it "the most sweeping land reform in Latin American history," a demonstrably false claim from the beginning, but the real significance of the reform had little to do with its purported benefits to the Salvadorean peasantry. The reform was impor-

President José Napoleón Duarte
talks with the press on October 15,
1984, before meeting with the
FDR-FMLN.

tant for two other reasons. First, as Martin Diskin, who studied the course of
the agrarian reform from 1980, said, it "must be seen as a calibrated effort [by
the United States] to squelch the left but not alienate the right."[44]

Second, the army had committed itself to an agrarian reform in the
Proclama, and with its promulgation the military began to chart a new course
for itself and left the oligarchy to its own devices. As a result, the army swelled
as an institution, both in numbers and financially (see Chapter 7). This new
self-definition was spelled out in early 1980 by Colonel Gutiérrez, who told
the new vice-minister of agriculture, Jorge Villacorta, that "the land reform is
a military operation because it must be the High Command's plan."[45]

Phase I, promulgated on March 6, nationalized 376 farms of more than
500 hectares. The 244 former proprietors were compensated with thirty-year
bonds. These farms were largely pasture, cotton, or diversified crop farms.
Phase II, which would affect about 2,000 farms of between 100 and 500 hectares, was announced and then postponed indefinitely. Villacorta and Rodolfo
Viera (director of ISTA) saw Phase II as the heart of the reform because it included most of the coffee *fincas*, but its postponement signaled that El Salvador's first source of wealth would not be touched.

Phase III (Decree 207), called "land to the tiller," was promulgated on
April 27 and was the brainchild of Roy Prosterman, a University of Wisconsin

professor best known for his agrarian reform efforts in Vietnam. His role is re-vealed in several cables the embassy began sending in early March. On March 3 the embassy noted that Prosterman was meeting "almost hourly" with Viera, then summarized Prosterman's activities in El Salvador and the con-tents of a briefing he had given the embassy the night before. The cable is in-teresting for three reasons. First, it reflected extreme optimism about the breadth of the reform and rapidity of implementation; second, it reported Prosterman's belief that "major violence is unlikely"; third, it revealed that the professor, not Villacorta or Viera, briefed Archbishop Romero, junta member Gutiérrez, and others.[46]

Phase III mandated that all rented land now belonged to those who cul-tivated it. This phase was widely touted as "self-implementing," which proved to be an overstatement. The junta promulgated Phase III under pres-sure from the embassy and over the objections of Villacorta, who understood the practical and political problems of the reform. The day before Phase III was announced, Villacorta, who was appalled by the repression, took himself and his family into exile. He resigned from the PDC, joined the MPSC, and subsequently became the FDR-FMLN representative in Costa Rica.[47]

Defense and Criticism of the Reform. On March 15 Prosterman once again briefed the embassy and described implementation as a "stunning success"; he asserted that "poorly trained and highly nervous civilian technicians are not essential to ongoing operations" (meaning he felt technical assistance to *campesinos* who had never been responsible for managing anything in their lives was unimportant) and stated that "no violence has taken place so far."[48] In a memorandum, Prosterman said that "there has been … *no* evidence that the Junta or the army have used the reforms as a 'cover' or 'pretext' for inau-gurating violence against the far left, or against any peasant or other groups." He charged "far-left groups" with as many as fifty deaths in "armed efforts to take over estates already intervened."[49]

It is not clear whether Prosterman had his head in the sand or was lying. The army certainly thought the agrarian technicians were necessary: Jaime Mauricio Salazar, the head of research at the National Center for Agricultural Technology until his resignation on March 5, reported that he and 179 other employees of the Agriculture Ministry were sequestered in San Salvador's Hotel Presidente and told that they "had to participate in the agrarian reform. Up to this moment," Salazar continued, "nobody knew a thing about the plan." Salazar and six other researchers fled; the army was ordered to bring them back. Salazar left the country March 7 "fearing for my life."[50]

Furthermore, had Prosterman paid a visit to the soccer field behind the San José de la Montaña Seminary, which housed the archdiocesan offices, he would have learned that peasants began streaming in looking for protection from the army four days after the reform was promulgated. Within two weeks over 400 people had arrived; within months there were 1,200, and the archdio-cese was forced to open other refugee centers around San Salvador—and to maintain them for over five years. Three years later the Department of State acknowledged the violence: "More than 5,000 peasant farmers (campesinos) had been killed in 1981," it said in a report. "Thousands more had been evicted forcibly from land they had claimed, and there was serious doubt that any additional 'beneficiaries' would dare to apply."[51]

Such information was available in 1980 for those who sought it. One who did was Norman Chapin, an AID official who spent five weeks in May and June 1980 visiting numerous nationalized farms. Chapin found that although a small minority of the farms were working as planned, most suffered from a shortage of credit, seed, fertilizer, and technical assistance. The practical results were that production of maize, a staple of the Salvadorean diet, increased in 1980 and 1981, but the amount of crops produced for export declined. In contradiction to widespread reports from official sources that the left was disrupting the agrarian reform, Chapin found broad sympathy for the OPs among the *campesinos* and many agrarian technicians. The guerrillas did attack farms that had been given to members of ORDEN, but there is a remarkable shortage of evidence that farms populated by neutral or sympathetic peasants were attacked. An AIFLD official told Ray Bonner of the *New York Times* in mid-1983 that there never had been "a concentrated plan of attack on the land reform from the left."[52]

A July 1980 memorandum from the University of Wisconsin Land Tenure Center analyzed the problems with Decree 207, listed forty-seven criticisms, then concluded: "In general, this is a very hastily and poorly drafted law. ... Substantively, the law is very paternalistic. It sets the stage for a top-down land reform process tightly controlled by government, with no significant participation by *campesinos* at any level. Also, it creates a cumbersome two-tier bureaucratic structure for acquiring and distributing land, which is very inefficient and likely to lead to large inequities."[53]

As the memorandum anticipated, Decree 207 led to the formation of FINATA, the National Financial Institution for Agricultural Lands, which was charged with processing applications for titles from the estimated 150,000 new landholders. By mid-1981, according to a State Department official, 6,000 preapplication forms had been filed by claimants and only 7 by owners. A total of 345 provisional titles had been granted. Furthermore, violence toward these new "landowners" by the security forces was the subject of cable traffic between the U.S. Embassy and the Department of State.

Murder in the Sheraton. In January 1981 ISTA director Rodolfo Viera and two AIFLD advisers were gunned down in the coffee shop of the Hotel Sheraton in San Salvador by masked gunmen who then strolled out of the hotel and disappeared into the night. Days later Deputy Chief of Mission Mark Dion cabled the State Department that the "murders bear all [the] earmarks" of the Miami-funded death squads.[54] Six months later the UCS branches in Ahuachapán, Sonsonate, and Santa Ana threatened to pull out of the agrarian reform program because of the repression.

In December the UCS directorate completed a report requested by Napoleón Duarte, which said that "the failure of the agrarian reform process is an immediate and imminent danger." "At least ninety [UCS] officials" and "a large number of beneficiaries" of the agrarian reform "have died during 1981 at the hands of ex-landlords and their allies, who are often members of the local security forces." The report also charged that more than 25,000 former *aparceros* had been evicted from their *milpas*, "in the majority of cases with the assistance of members of the military forces," before they could obtain provisional titles. By the end of the year, sixty-seven agrarian reform cooperatives, 20 percent of the total, had been abandoned. This meant that 38,460 hectares were out of production[55] (see Table 5.1).

Destruction of the National University. Systematic repression was not confined to the rural areas. In the wake of the general strike that paralyzed the country June 23–25, 1980, the army and security forces, tired of the University of El Salvador's role as an organizational center for the OPs, invaded the campus on June 26, murdered twenty-two people, and ransacked laboratories, classrooms, and libraries. Everything from typewriters to file cabinets, furniture, and plumbing fixtures was carted away in military trucks; the library's valuable rare-book collection on Central American history was destroyed by fire and rain after the building's windows were shattered in the rampage. The estimated cost of the destruction was as much as $20 million. The military occupied the campus and would remain for the next four years.

Repression of university personnel did not stop with the occupation. The university rector, Felix Ulloa, was assassinated; another eighty students, faculty, and staff were killed; forty-two were jailed and many others were forced into exile. On February 10, 1981, the UES Executive Council (a faculty-student senate) was arrested; two years later four members of the council were still in prison without having been charged. The UES set up shop in rented buildings all over San Salvador and continued to provide classes for previously enrolled students. Meanwhile, the government slashed its budget from $26 million to $6 million, which was not enough to cover rent, subsistence salaries, and supplies. Nonetheless, the university held on until the campus was reopened in June 1984.[56]

CONCURRENT DEVELOPMENTS

The regime's policy of reform with repression on one side and the growing pressure from the revolutionary organizations on the other created a social-political-economic context of virtual anarchy by late 1980. Visitors to San Salvador reported that during the day the city seemed remarkably normal. With nightfall, however, the shooting began. In the countryside, entire villages were being destroyed by government forces in a Salvadorean version of the pacification program in Vietnam a decade earlier. In this setting various institutions of Salvadorean society were coping in different ways.

Economic Collapse

According to the Inter-American Development Bank (IDB), the economic performance of El Salvador in 1979 "was adversely affected by prolonged strikes in industry, interruptions in the harvesting of certain crops and an extraordinary flight of private capital due to the political developments during the year." One of those political developments was the deliberate policy of both the revolutionary organizations and right-wing elements to para-

TABLE 5.1   Basic Information as of 1983 on El Salvador's Agrarian Reform

	Phase One	Phase Two[a]	Phase Three	Total
Size of ownership holding subject to redistribution (hectares)	500+	100–500	All rented land	—
Estimated number of holdings to be affected by the agrarian reform	328[b]	1,700	30,000	—
Estimated amount of land to be redistributed (hectares)	224,326[b]	125,500	Up to 200,000	549,826
As a percent of the country's 1,455,000 hectares of land in farms	15.4[b]	8.6	13.7	37.7
Amount of land actually redistributed through December 1982 (hectares)	224,326	0	76,936	301,262
As a percent of the country's 1,455,000 hectares of land in farms	15.4	0	5.3	20.7
Estimated number of small farmers to benefit from the reform[c]	60,000	N.A.[d]	125,000	185,000
Actual number of farmers who have claimed land under the reform	29,755	0	48,357	78,112
As a percent of the estimated target	49.6	0	38.6	42.2
Number of provisional titles issued	0	0	35,823	—
Number of final titles issued	22	0	1,410	—

[a]Not implemented.
[b]Actual figures.
[c]Original estimates, probably too high.
[d]Not available.

Source: "El Salvador: Brighter Prospects for Land Reform," Bureau of Intelligence and Research, U.S. Department of State, March 17, 1983.

lyze or destroy the economy. This led to a decrease in the real gross domestic product of 1.5 percent, as compared with an increase of 4.8 percent in 1978 and an average annual growth of 5.2 percent during the period 1975–1977. Gross domestic investment declined 20.18 percent in 1979 and 62 percent in 1980. Meanwhile, the consumer price index (CPI) rose 17.2 percent in 1980 (compared with 15.9 percent in 1979, 13.2 percent in 1978, and an annual average of 12.7 percent during the mid-1970s).[57]

Capital flight began to resemble a stampede as members of the oligarchy sent their money to Miami and other safe havens. The IDB reported that the net outflow of private capital was estimated at $176 million for 1979, compared with a net inflow of $159 million in 1978. But in January 1980 the assistant manager of the Central Bank reported that in the preceding two years $1 billion had left El Salvador through the black market. As the fear of impending bank nationalization grew, by late January 1980, $800,000 per day was being withdrawn from savings accounts.[58] By May 1981 only four banks remained solvent. The Central Bank was not among them.

Employment in the industrial sector dropped sharply. By early 1980 all the industries located in an area known as the Zona Franca (free zone) had closed.[59] A January 12 story in San Salvador's *Prensa Gráfica* reported that twenty businesses employing 8,200 workers had ceased operations in the preceding months. Two weeks later the paper reported that another 7,000 workers had been laid off. This was in a country where the total number of full-time industrial employees in 1980 was just over 300,000 (see Table 2.6). Between 1979 and 1981, 148 businesses closed, leaving 18,213 people unemployed.[60]

By late 1980 the Salvadorean government was heavily dependent on the United States to remain solvent, a situation that would worsen through the decade. A State Department source admitted that without continuing U.S. and multilateral assistance from such institutions as the International Monetary Fund, the government would be bankrupt within days.† By 1982 the foreign exchange shortfall was estimated at between $298 million and $344 million; the limited dollars available were spent on financing the war and imported food at a total cost of $200 million.[61] Table 5.2 reveals how critical the situation had become. It would get worse.

The Private Sector Organizes

The Alianza Productiva. In mid-1980 conservative businessmen created through ANEP the Alianza Productiva (Productive Alliance), the first of several organizations founded by members of the private sector during the decade. A self-described "broadly based association of businessmen's groups and professionals" committed to continuing "its own productive processes," the alliance argued that "the country's economy can only be saved through the collaboration of both the productive sector and the government." It was not trying to overthrow or destabilize the Junta," the alliance maintained, "but [was] trying to restore, in a short period of time, [El Salvador's] economic situation." In June the organization sent a delegation to Washington, D.C., to call "the attention of the U.S. government to the importance of private sector

TABLE 5.2   Economic Indicators, 1979–1982 (in millions of dollars)

	1979	1981	1982
Gross domestic product	138.4	123.2	111.6
Private purchases of machinery and equipment	212.4	61.6	52.8
Exports	339.2	234.4	176.4
Imports	426.0	256.0	204.8
Budget deficit	43.6	204.8	228.8
Gross consumer spending	1,084.8	876.0	770.4

Source: "Balance Económico: 1982," Proceso, no. 94, December 1982, pp. 8–10.

cooperation in achieving a climate of tranquility in El Salvador and reducing unemployment."[62]

El Salvador Freedom Foundation. In Miami, where dozens of families from the oligarchy had taken up residence by mid-1980, the El Salvador Freedom Foundation was established on the advice of a Washington, D.C., public relations consultant, Ian MacKenzie. The 250 members of the group hired Mac-Kenzie-McCheyne, Inc., for $7,500 per month to introduce them to friendly legislators like North Carolina's senator Jesse Helms and to help them counter critical press stories. "We are not oligarchs in the sense of exploiters," asserted Alfonso Salaverría, a scion of one of the largest landowning families prior to the 1980 agrarian reform. "We developed our country, we penetrated its jungles, and planted coffee. We are like the pioneers of the United States. We don't want unjust privileges. We just want our country to return to a democratic regime."[63]

The Church After Romero

The nomination of Arturo Rivera Damas as apostolic administrator following the assassination of Archbishop Oscar Romero was greeted with joy and relief throughout the archdiocese and the progressive sector of the Catholic Church. Rivera, after all, had been the first choice of this sector to succeed the aged Luis Chávez back in 1977. Rivera began with a pledge to continue in the pastoral line of Romero, and it appeared for a time that he would indeed do so. But Rivera was a different personality with a different background. Romero, although his homilies were models of clarity, was first and foremost a pastor. Rivera, a canon lawyer by training, did not convey the personal warmth that Romero had projected. More important, Rivera immediately came under strong pressure from Rome to heal the rift in the hierarchy—which inevitably meant being more cautious about what he said.

Romero and Rivera had been close friends; indeed, Rivera was the only supporter the archbishop had among the five Salvadorean bishops. After Rivera became bishop of Santiago de María, they wrote a pastoral letter in which they took the post-Medellín position that the people had a right to form their own political organizations and that the church had a responsibility to "accompany" the people as they engaged in that activity. The two bishops also addressed the question of violence and condemned what they termed "institutionalized violence," which they specifically distinguished from "revolutionary" violence. They praised the doctrine of nonviolence as the highest form of morality but then argued that under certain specified conditions violence as "legitimate defence" was justified.[64]

In early 1980 it was clear from listening to Monseñor Romero's weekly homilies that he was moving toward a position of ultimately supporting the right of the Salvadorean people to insurrection. This was a position the archbishop of Managua, Miguel Obando y Bravo, had taken prior to the final insurrection in Nicaragua in 1979. The reasoning in both cases was that the evil confronting the people was greater than the evil of insurrection and war. Rivera, however, backed away from that position. The Vatican made it clear that it wanted Rivera to heal the political and theological divisions in the Episcopal Conference. The Vatican also kept Rivera on a short leash by refusing to name him archbishop. (In other countries, new archbishops had been named in as little as three weeks.) Further, Rivera was a personal friend of Napoleón Duarte. Finally, Rivera knew what had happened to Romero.

Rivera's public statements between April 1980 and September 1981 regarding a political solution to the civil war mirrored the fortunes of the left. After the January 1981 offensive, Rivera was reluctant to argue for its inclusion in a political solution. But six months later, after the FMLN initiated an extremely successful offensive and then received French and Mexican recognition as a "representative political force," Rivera parted company with his fellow bishops, saying that "we have spoken of the necessity ... for seeking a political solution to our situation"; therefore if the Franco-Mexican declaration "signifies the call to dialogue in order to find a peaceful solution, we would not find it inconvenient to accept." The other bishops issued a statement in CEDES's name that condemned Mexican and French "intervention" and added that the FDR-FMLN "has lost its popular support and is dedicated to sowing terror among the population."[65]

By November 1981 Rivera was saying that elections for a constituent assembly, scheduled for March 1982, could not be carried out without "previous understanding among the parties most involved in the conflict." Soon after he declared that the elections "are not the solution" to the conflict.[66] Nor did Rivera ignore the excesses of the government. On the contrary, after the general strike in August 1980, he sharply criticized the regime for militarizing all public services and demanded that the junta lift the five-month-old state of siege.

After the murder of four U.S. missionaries in December, Rivera joined the priests and nuns of the archdiocese in the most strongly worded condemnation of official repression to be expressed by the church since the assassination of Romero. "We hold the Security Forces and ultra-rightist groups responsible for the persecution against the Church and specifically for the assassination of priests and lay pastoral workers. We therefore also hold responsible the Government Junta which, given its ultimate authority over the Armed Forces, is responsible for actions by members of the military."[67]

Meanwhile, the formation of the National Conference of the Popular Church (CONIP), an organization of priests, nuns, and Christian communities, caused further tensions because CONIP took the position that the FDR-FMLN constituted, for political purposes, the "authentic representatives" of the Salvadorean people.[68] A very few priests—the numbers are in dispute—joined the FMLN as combatants. At least one became a commander. Other priests and nuns, however, while eschewing arms, moved to controlled zones to continue their pastoral work or began working for the FDR-FMLN outside the country. Sister Silvia, a nurse, was killed at Cutumay Camones in January 1981. Father Rafael Moreno, who had edited *Orientación*, became the FDR-FMLN representative at the United Nations.

DERECHIZACIÓN CONTINUES

The second coup attempt on April 30, 1980, pushed Colonel Majano to act. He dispatched a loyal contingent from San Carlos to arrest Roberto D'Aubuisson and his fellow conspirators, who were captured at a farm near Santa Tecla with a suitcase full of incriminating documents, including a draft manifesto apparently to be published at the time of the coup. The men were promptly arraigned. Three days later a judge, under pressure from Defense Minister García, found there was insufficient evidence to hold D'Aubuisson for trial and released him. The PDC voiced support for Majano but did nothing when he was soon stripped of his position as commander in chief of the Armed Forces and replaced by Colonel Gutiérrez. Majano threatened to resign from the junta but was talked out of it by U.S. Ambassador Robert White.[69]

In September all the *majanistas* were transferred to insignificant posts in El Salvador or out of the country. The new commanding officers of the garrisons in San Salvador were García's men. In November Majano narrowly escaped death from a car bomb. A month later he was named ambassador to Spain but refused to go and went into hiding. García issued a warrant for Majano's arrest, but he was not found until February 20, 1981. The army threatened to court-martial him but came under extreme pressure from Panama's General Omar Torrijos; instead Majano was put on a plane and sent to Mexico.[70]

In the wake of Majano's removal in December, a shuffling of positions occurred in the Salvadorean government. (The U.S. government has declined to release documents dealing with its role in the restructuring.) Duarte became president of the junta, and Gutiérrez was named vice-president. José Antonio Morales Erlich became head of the agrarian reform program. Nothing more was heard from Dr. Avalos. Carranza was named director of ANTEL, hardly a demotion. This shake-up was heralded in Washington as a sign that the influence of Duarte was increasing—the implication being that civilian control over the military was emerging. But Duarte told Ray Bonner a few days later, "The only reason I am in this position is because I have the support of the army."[71]

Duarte got it right. As a Mexican diplomat put it at the time, "If García is minister of defense and Gutiérrez is commander-in-chief, then Mr. Duarte is an adornment. ... The military has been left in control of the military, and that is the country's problem."[72] Beyond this, Duarte's presence in the government assured the continuing support of the Christian Democrat–led Venezuelan and Costa Rican governments, not to mention the U.S. Congress. The United States needed Duarte to justify its policy of support for a "moderate, reformist, civilian/military government."

The **Derechización** *of U.S. Policy*

The arrival of Robert White in early March 1980 as the new U.S. ambassador meant that one thing could be said about U.S. policy: It was being forcefully enunciated for a change. After infuriating both left and right within three weeks of assuming the post, White insisted that El Salvador had a "revolutionary government" that had implemented the "most sweeping land reform since the Mexican Revolution." He defended Duarte as a champion of democracy and insisted that the junta headed a "moderate, reformist" government caught between two warring extremes of left and right. Privately White was more candid. In a November 1980 cable, he wrote that "the military have the power; no government can exist without their approval. The failure to take strong action against the violence which comes from within its ranks is the Achilles' heel of the JRG," White continued. "The military will not act against those who are killing its enemies lest a Pandora's box of accusations be opened. ... There is very little possibility of compromise."[73]

After Ronald Reagan was elected president in November 1980, however, a "hit list" of ambassadors to be replaced, prepared by a Reagan transition team, surfaced. White's name was on it. He stormed into Washington charging that his authority had been undermined. He was correct, but his outburst did not endear him to the emerging powers in the Reagan foreign policy camp. When the news hit San Salvador, fliers were distributed in three of the wealthiest residential areas calling on those who favored White's dismissal to fire guns or fireworks at 8:00 P.M. Mark Dion reported a noisy ten-minute "message" beginning on the hour.[74]

After the assassination of the four churchwomen on December 2, the Carter administration suspended the balance of the $5.7 million in "nonlethal" military aid that had been reprogrammed by Congress shortly after Archbishop Romero's death. The administration also suspended economic assistance but reinstated it two weeks later because the Salvadorean economy was on the verge of collapse. The suspension of military aid remained in effect until three days before Carter left office—and a week after the beginning of the FMLN's general offensive. "We must support the Salvadorean government in its struggle against left-wing terrorism supported covertly with arms, ammunition, training, and political and military advice by Cuba and other Communist nations," the State Department announced.[75]

White at first supported and then opposed the resumption of military assistance in general and the authorization of an additional $5 million in lethal weapons in particular. He went public with his opposition, as a result of which he was recalled to Washington at the end of January and told he would not be returning to El Salvador. When he declined a make-work job in the State Department, he was automatically retired ninety days later.

Continuity and Change

In the first weeks after Ronald Reagan's inauguration, U.S. Embassy officials in San Salvador maintained that there were no major policy changes from Carter to Reagan. In a narrow sense that was true; by the end of its term the Carter administration was propping up the Salvadorean economy and had begun supplying lethal as well as nonlethal military assistance. The ideological basis of the policy, however, was different. In December the Carter administration outlined its "basic objectives": "to support a political process most likely to lead to a democratic outcome … ; to support socio-economic reforms which involve the majority of people in the country's politics and economy; and to promote an end to violence from all quarters."[76]

The Reagan administration's ideology demanded casting the Salvadorean conflict in global terms. As Alexander Haig, Reagan's first secretary of state, wrote in his memoirs, "Salvador was not merely a local problem. It was also a regional problem that threatened the stability of all of Central America, including the Panama Canal and Mexico. … And it was a global issue because it represented the interjection of the war of national liberation into the Western Hemisphere." By early spring the Reaganites had privately defined a threefold policy for Central America: overthrow the revolutionary government in Nicaragua, establish a permanent military base in Honduras, and militarily defeat the FMLN. Publicly, however, the emphasis was on building democracy; as Haig put it, "the Duarte government … was the only hope for the transfer of power by democratic means. If it survived, elections could follow." Administration officials apparently shared Haig's view that the government "included military officers as well as civilians who represented every political tendency in the country except those of the far right and the violent left."[77]

Arturo Rivera Damas tried to disabuse Vice-President George Bush of this notion in a conversation and later a letter in April 1981. Rivera expressed in writing his conviction "that the Administration does not understand the composition and nature of the Junta. Specifically, I think you underestimate the power and resistance of the right-wing military to true political change, including the kind of political dialogue which I am sure is the only road to peace in our country. … The United States must clearly indicate it is in favor of a political solution through negotiations or [they] will not occur."[78]

Rivera's words were prophetic, but the Reagan administration was not interested in a political solution. A 1981 document, "Annual Integrated Assessment of Security Assistance for El Salvador," provided the rationale and detailed the needs for doubling the size of the army, increasing the navy and air force, and providing necessary materiel. According to the document, which was written by embassy staff and signed by the new ambassador, Deane Hinton, embassy officials "concur[red] with the Salvadorean assessment that substantial increases in the armed forces are a precondition for a *military solution* to the civil war." But the report also cautioned that "We are not yet in a position to face the likely central policy issue: Are we prepared to provide El Salvador the means to achieve a military solution or are we content gradually to support their buildup during what now looks to us like a long drawn out struggle?" The "overriding short term goal of the security assistance program," Hinton wrote, "is to prevent the takeover of a friendly neighbor by an externally supported communist guerrilla army."[79]

"KISSSS": THE ROLE OF THE U.S. MILITARY

How to achieve that goal was the object of a U.S. counterinsurgency doctrine revised in the wake of the defeat in Vietnam and renamed "low-intensity conflict" (LIC), or "small wars." Colonel John Waghelstein, who served as head of the U.S. Military Group (MilGroup)—advisers—in El Salvador in 1982 and 1983, defined LIC "as revolutionary and counterrevolutionary warfare ... that uses *all* of the weapons of total war, including political, economic and psychological warfare with the military aspect being a distant fourth in many cases."[80]

From the early 1980s, the guiding philosophy behind the U.S. role came to be known as "KISSSS"—"Keep it simple, sustainable, small, and Salvadorean." In the waning months of the Carter presidency, the first military trainers were sent to El Salvador. Then, in early 1981, General Fred Woerner "went to El Salvador with the task of doing three things: develop a national military strategy for El Salvador, a situation report for the United States, and put in effect a security assistance program." The latter, Woerner said, "was to be conceptualize[d] for an unspecified period of time, but which could be reasonably interpreted to be an approximate five-year program." At the end of the program, Woerner concluded, the "Salvadoran armed forces will be absolutely capable of finally suppressing the guerrilla movement and minimally maintaining it at the nuisance level."[81]

The "Woerner Report" became the handbook for the MilGroup advisers, who sought to achieve three goals, all subsumed under the rubric of "professionalization": persuade the Salvadorean officer corps to subordinate itself to civilian authority; convince the Armed Forces to respect human rights; and rationalize the military's "internal methods of governance so that talent was nurtured, success was rewarded, incompetents were weeded out, and the officer corps in general became operationally effective."[82]

From the U.S. perspective, these were desperate needs. Not only was the army on the defensive after July 1981, but also its love affair with conventional military operations coupled with continuing human rights violations did not contribute to the process of "winning hearts and minds," the fundamental need in any counterinsurgency war. U.S. influence, however, was impeded by three problems: constraints on leverage; intragovernmental limits on reform in El Salvador; and the character of relations between government and populace on one hand and between guerrillas and populace on the other.[83]

Soldiers on patrol in Soyapango, on the east side of San Salvador, in 1988. Photo by Corinne Dufka, reprinted with permission.

The process of subordination to civilian authority began with persuading the army not only to support elections in 1982—and later—but also to see itself as defender of the newly emerging order. The human rights problem for the Reagan administration was much more a public relations problem than a moral issue. Too many dead bodies in the streets or too many massacres in the countryside meant serious problems with Congress over new—and increased—appropriations for El Salvador.

The third task, transforming the Armed Forces, in some ways proved to be the most daunting. Ambassador Hinton commented in 1987 on the early years: "There were all kinds of efforts by MilGroup commanders, both to try to reform the way the war was conducted and to get people off of their butts and out of the *cuarteles* [barracks]. By the time I left [in mid-1983], it seemed to me it was still in doubt as to whether the Salvadorean Army would ever be an effective field force."[84]

One problem, the size of the army, was resolved by expanding the Armed Forces from 10,000 in 1979 to 24,000 in 1982 to a high of 56,000 in 1987. A shortage of arms and munitions was overcome by significantly increasing U.S. assistance.[85] A third problem, leadership, proved to be the most intractable. As Colonel Waghelstein, to whom the responsibility of transforming the army first fell in 1982 and 1983, pithily recalled, "Out of the 14 departments there were only two departmental commanders that were worth a damn, the others being notably ineffective. ... There were lots of young lieutenant colonels who knew what to do, but they were viewed with some suspicion by

García who ... was more intent on maintaining his power base within the military."[86] By May 1982, when the Armed Forces were taking a drubbing from
the FMLN, the embassy reported that the Salvadorean government was "fully
committed to the 'victory strategy' plan ... developed ... by B[rigadier]
G[eneral] Fred Woerner."[87]

The "White Paper"

In late February 1981 the Department of State issued a document that
claimed to offer "definitive evidence of the clandestine military support given
by the Soviet Union, Cuba, and their Communist allies to Marxist-Leninist
guerrillas now fighting to overthrow the established government of El Salvador."[88] Unhappily for the Reagan administration, there were three problems
with this White Paper. First, the "supporting documents" did not substantiate
the extravagant claims of arms shipments to the FMLN or of Soviet or Cuban
control of the revolutionary forces.[89] Second, most U.S. allies did not believe
the "evidence" or did not view El Salvador in such cataclysmic terms. Third,
Congress, under growing public pressure, refused to be railroaded.

Six weeks after the White Paper was issued, 29 percent of the U.S. public
told a Gallup poll that they thought the United States should "stay completely
out of the situation." A year later that figure had grown to 54 percent.[90] Congressional mail was running ten to one against U.S. policy; at one point in
spring 1981 a White House press spokesperson admitted that its mail was
twenty-five to one against. Additional pressure came from human rights
groups and Catholic and major Protestant churches that were outraged by the
escalating human rights violations; also spurring action were the army's publication of a "hit list"[91] and the repeated calls of Rivera Damas for a political
solution. Thus, legislation was introduced that would bar all military assistance and advisers unless President Reagan certified every six months that the
Salvadorean government had met six conditions designed to prevent human
rights violations, to bring the Armed Forces under civilian control, and to promote democratic reforms.[92] Unfortunately, certification became little more
than a game both in Washington and El Salvador. Human rights abuses that
were increasing every month declined in the weeks immediately preceding
certification. Documented massacres by the army became events to cover up
to avoid outright lying in the certification document.

Days after release of the White Paper, new increases in military assistance totaling $25 million were announced. By late March fifty-six military ad-
visers and instructors were in El Salvador "to train Salvadorean personnel in
communications, intelligence, logistics, and in other professional skills designed to improve their capabilities to interdict infiltration and to respond to
terrorist attacks."[93] Rapid- response batallions (BIRIs) were trained along with
small, mobile units, and a Vietnam-style pacification program aimed at "winning hearts and minds" was attempted.

Sources within the administration privately revealed that the game plan
was to "win a military victory in sixty to ninety days." Ambassador Hinton
and Colonel Waghelstein were not so naive. Waghelstein said later that he and

Iinton reached an understanding: "We were trying to reorient the Salvadoran military to the reforms across the board in order to steal the guerrilla's hunder and if we didn't do that then we might as well pack it all up and go ome because it was a no-win situation."[94] In June 1981 Hinton reported that Both sides have fought to a draw. ... The guerrillas have the initiative on heir side ... and the government has the capacity to contain the insurgent asaults on a case-by-case basis, but not to destroy the insurgents' force." "Conequently," Hinton concluded, "as we perceive the situation, there is no miliary end in sight to the war of attrition in El Salvador."[95]

Because LIC doctrine called for a political component, and because the Reagan administration understood the domestic political need to keep Congress on board and public opinion at bay, the overall strategy included an lectoral process that would produce a new constitution and then elections for president, Assembly delegates, and mayors—and legitimate the Christian Democrats in the process. Publicly, the first step would be to elect on March 8, 1982, a constituent assembly that would write yet another constitution.

The Resurgence of the FMLN

In late July 1981, after six months of analysis, self-criticism, and reorgaization, the FMLN launched its second offensive, for the first time took prisners of war, and then announced that the Geneva Conventions regarding risoners of war (POWs) would be observed and asked the International Red Cross to assume responsibility for them. Twelve of forty prisoners chose to renain with the insurgents.[96] During the fall the FMLN maintained pressure on he army throughout the eastern third of El Salvador. Economic sabotage beame an increasingly important instrument of war. Between May and December, the army averaged three offensives per month against the rebels, using ,500 to 4,500 troops in each drive. The army attempted eight times during his period to dislodge the guerrillas from Guazapa, an effort Commander Raul Hercules termed "a total fiasco."[97] The army also carried out multiple ofensives in Chalatenango, Morazán, San Vicente, and Cuscatlán. In early 1982 he FMLN and the U.S. Embassy agreed on one thing: The army had not chieved one objective.[98]

The Army Strikes Back

This does not mean the army was not trying, in its own way. Its biggest ffensive against the insurgents during this period came in early December in Morazán, where 4,500 troops in coordination with the Honduran army atempted to trap the FMLN in a "hammer and anvil" strategy. A major government objective was to destroy the FMLN's Radio Venceremos, which had been roadcasting by shortwave without interruption for almost a year. The government announced on December 14 that Radio Venceremos had been detroyed; in fact, the radio equipment was carted in backpacks and on mules rom Morazán to Usulután; then was returned in the same manner. Regular roadcasts resumed on December 26.

There was a darker side to the Morazán offensive, however. The FMLN had advance notice of the offensive and began advising the people to seek safety in other areas and evacuating several thousand people. None of these people died during the offensive. But many others thought they were safe because the army had left them alone during an October offensive. This time the army moved through three small towns in central Morazán and left behind 482 bodies in El Mozote alone; 280 were under fourteen years of age.[99] This pattern of attacking the civilian population persisted through the 1980s, although the frequency of such attacks and the number of civilians killed declined sharply after 1985. More often than not, such attacks were carried out by U.S.-trained units.

The Morazán massacre raised such an outcry in the United States that the army behaved itself for several months. Then in late May 1982, the Ramón Belloso battalion, which had just returned from four months and $8 million worth of training at Fort Bragg, North Carolina, was sent into eastern Chalatenango in an offensive clearly aimed at civilians, most of whom supported the FMLN. Hundreds were killed, and the 5,000 who fled were unarmed.

Colonel Jorge Adalberto Cruz Reyes, commander of the garrison in San Francisco Gotera, Morazán, justified attacks on civilians by citing the FMLN's presence in an area: "Civilians who don't want to cooperate leave the area and those who remain are collaborating." A few months later Colonel Sigfrido Ochoa, who at the time was commander of the base at El Paraiso, Chalatenango, told a Mexican reporter, "I can massively bomb the red zones because only subversives live in them."[100]

On January 27, 1982, the FMLN opened up another offensive with an attack on the Ilopango air base, destroying 70 percent of the air force.[101] Immediately thereafter, insurgents attacked San Miguel, laid siege to Usulután and San Francisco Gotera, briefly brought the war to San Salvador, and began staging attacks in the western third of the country for the first time since early 1981.

Meanwhile, the electoral campaign for the Constituent Assembly got under way; the United States sent increasing amounts of military aid; U.S. military trainers began having some success "professionalizing" the army; and it soon became apparent that the FMLN was much better at fighting a guerrilla war than at mounting a political offensive.

A New Political Offensive

While preparations were under way for the March elections, the Reagan administration attempted to recover the public relations initiative. After failing to convince many people with the White Paper in February 1981, the administration brought Duarte to the United States for thirteen days in October. There were two objectives: to influence U.S. public opinion and the Congress and to send a message to the Salvadoran right that Duarte had firm U.S. support. The visit, however, was a disaster. While Duarte was in Washington and

Camp residents wait at water well in Mesa Grande refugee camp, Honduras, July 1982.

despite public opposition by both presidents, the Senate approved imposition of conditions on aid.

The administration ignored repeated declarations by the FDR-FMLN that the revolutionary forces were prepared to negotiate. A "Proposal for Peace," prepared by the DRU and the FDR Executive Committee and read by Nicaraguan leader Daniel Ortega before the United Nations on October 10, 1981, called for negotiations with an open agenda and without prior conditions. Said Miguel Sáenz of the U.N. speech, "That was the moment to be absolutely serious about negotiations."[102] A later appeal was directed to President Reagan in a January 18, 1982, letter signed by the five top FMLN commanders.

The administration responded to these initiatives by sponsoring two new regional alliances that were designed to encircle El Salvador and to isolate Nicaragua. One was the "Triangle of the North," a military alliance among Guatemala, Honduras, and El Salvador. The other, created in January 1982, was the Central American Democratic Community, composed of Costa Rica, Honduras, Guatemala, and El Salvador.[103] Neither effort succeeded, partly because Guatemala refused to be dictated to by the United States and partly because four Latin American countries that came to be known as the Contadora group decided in January 1983 to seize the initiative in seeking a political solution to the Central American crisis (see Chapter 6). Meanwhile, a senior U.S. diplomat in Costa Rica asserted in late 1981 that although the Reagan administration understood the inevitability of and necessity for change, "insurrectionists' methods are not the way to go. We don't want another communist government in the region."

The way to go, the Carter and Reagan administrations decided, was elections that would legitimate the Christian Democratic Party and install junta president Duarte as an elected president. The elections that followed must be seen as part of the overall counterinsurgency strategy for El Salvador that was designed to encourage "the transition from an illegitimate de facto regime to constitutional rule"[104] while reducing the guerrillas to a "nuisance."

The electoral process, discussed in the next chapter, ushered in a new era: the return to civilian government for the first time since 1931. The process had mixed results, however. On one hand, it initiated a series of events that were both unanticipated and undesired by the dominant powers in El Salvador. On the other hand, it did nothing to change the real locus of power: the military, the oligarchy, and the United States.

6

High-Intensity Politics and Low-Intensity Conflict, 1982–1984

Ambassador Hinton had never been given instructions to win the war. He had been given instructions to maintain the status quo and not let the thing slide. But when Ambassador Pickering came in, the game plan had very evidently changed. His first words to me ... were, "I want you to get Fred Woerner up here and I want a strategy for bringing 90 percent of the terrain and population under control of the government in two years. ..."
—Colonel Joseph S. Stringham III,
Commander, U.S. Military Group in El Salvador, 1983–1984[1]

Between 1982 and 1985 two realities dominated Salvadorean life. One was the war. The other was elections. Within this framework other significant events occurred, each of which had an impact on overall developments. These included the expanding role of the United States in both El Salvador and Honduras; the legitimation of the extreme right in Salvadorean politics; major crises in the FMLN and the army in 1983; a visit by the pope in March 1983; the first formal meeting between the government and the FDR-FMLN; and regional efforts to resolve the Central American crisis.

ELECTIONS

Focusing on the elections that took place during the 1980s would permit one to argue that El Salvador has moved from a country dominated by the military for half a century to one that successfully made the transition to civilian rule. This focus, however, ignores the central question in politics: Who holds power? In countries as diverse as the United States, Zimbabwe, Sweden, and Mexico, it is reasonable to assume that the person who holds the top office in the land also wields considerable political power. In El Salvador this assumption ignores the real social forces and the role they have played—at least until the early 1990s—in predicting the outcome of any important political crisis. In other words, in spite of elections, the locus of power—the army and oligarchy—did not change. There were two differences, however. One

155

was a new actor wielding significant power—the United States—not the political parties or the civilian leaders who took office in 1982 and later. The other was a determined revolutionary movement that fought the army to a stalemate.

Demonstration Elections

In 1981 and 1982 the question of who actually wielded power was inconvenient. Over opposition from many quarters—from Salvadorean businessmen who feared the PDC would "fix" the election; from the army who feared a new Christian Democratic dynasty would undermine the military institution; from the National Federation of Lawyers who declined to help draft a new election law on the grounds that meaningful elections were impossible under a state of siege; and from Monseñor Rivera Damas who said in a homily that meaningful elections were impossible in a context of violence—the United States pushed ahead with its "transition to democracy" formula.[2] The plan, announced by the junta in March 1981, was to elect a constituent assembly in 1982 and a president and Legislative Assembly in 1983. The context in which the 1982 (and later) elections occurred was fundamentally different from the past in two respects. First, they took place in a country at war with itself. Second, they were held not on the initiative of Salvadoreans but at the behest of a U.S administration anxious to keep the money flowing from the Congress to El Salvador.

In short, the proceedings were what Edward S. Herman and Frank Brodhead called "demonstration elections," the primary purpose of which "is to convince the citizens of the United States that their client government is freely chosen" and only secondarily "to select political leaders or even to ratify the political leaders chosen by the ... administration."[3] By late 1981 the Reagan administration was the object of growing public criticism and congressional skepticism of its Salvador policy. The growing human rights violations, the poor military performance of the Armed Forces against the FMLN, and the obvious *derechización* of the government put the White House on the defensive. Elections gave the administration some space to regroup and redesign its political offensive in Washington.

Herman and Brodhead suggested "six criteria of election integrity": freedom of speech, freedom of the media, freedom of organization for intermediate groups, an absence of state-sponsored terror, freedom of party organization and ability to field candidates, and an absence of fear and coercion among the population.[4] In El Salvador in 1982 none of these conditions obtained. A state of siege had been in effect since March 1980; the media were under government control; the popular organizations had been decimated and disbanded by late 1980; state-sponsored terror was the norm, with over 30,000 civilians killed and 600,000 refugees since the October coup; leaders of legal parties on the left of the political spectrum were threatened with death if they returned; as in many other Latin American countries voting was required by law, but in El Salvador Defense Minister García advised citizens that failing to vote was treasonable. Furthermore, voters were told their *cedulas* (identity cards) would be stamped, and the voting system was such that it was possible to determine who had voted for whom.[5] In this context, preparations for the election began.

The Political Parties

The Right Organizes Politically. The antecedents of a right-wing political party were sown in fall 1979 with the creation of the FAN and related organizations of women and youth. In creating these organizations, Roberto D'Aubuisson received encouragement from three sources outside El Salvador: Mario Sandoval Alarcón in Guatemala; the French OAS, whose members helped draft a military-political plan that included a political organization; and the New Right in the United States.

Sandoval hosted a meeting in Guatemala City on May 22, 1981, at which the Alianza Republicana Nacionalista (Nationalist Republican Alliance), ARENA, was secretly founded.[6] Thirty-five members later signed the roll in San Salvador. Sandoval gave ARENA the MLN siogan, "God, Homeland, and Liberty" (which the MLN inherited from the Dominican dictator Rafael Trujillo), and its symbol, a sword, which ARENA transformed into a cross. "Republican" was chosen in honor of the Republican Party in the United States. ARENA and D'Aubuisson had good reason to be grateful to the GOP: The "pivotal suggestion" to found ARENA came from the U.S. New Right. It included staff members of Senator Jesse Helms's office; the staff director of the U.S. Senate's Republican Conference, which serves as the GOP's coordinating machine; the public relations firm of MacKenzie-McCheyne; and other right-wing public policy groups. Together they supplied political support in the United States, lobbying on Capitol Hill, and instruction on U.S. methods of political campaigning. ARENA's creed was a mixture of the 1980 Republican platform and neo-Nazi principles. On the advice of its U.S. friends, the military underground that had been functioning since early 1980 surfaced to campaign for the 1982 election. The "coming out" occurred at a "Dinner of National Salvation" in late October 1981 at the Sheraton Hotel in San Salvador.[7]

Other Parties. By fall 1981 seven parties had registered for the elections. All were located on the right of the political spectrum. Three of them, with virtually no political base, could easily be dismissed.[8] The others began slugging it out in the fall within the Central Elections Council (CCE) that had been created to conduct the proceedings. In addition to ARENA, the three contenders were

1. The Christian Democrats: After the exit of the party's left wing in March 1980, ideological and organizational dominance shifted to the most conservative members of the party, led by Duarte.
2. The Party of National Conciliation: The PCN has the distinction of being the only official party to survive a coup d'etat. It was reduced to playing a pivotal power role between the PDC and ARENA.

3. The Democratic Action Party: The AD also was created in Novem
    ber 1981 and quickly became known in San Salvador as the "Ro
    tary Club" of the oligarchy's lawyers. It was ideologically closer to
    the Christian Democrats in that it supported the first phase of the
    agrarian reform.

The MNR (social democrats) and the MPSC were invited to leave the
FDR and participate in the elections. They were told that they could campaign
by long distance (for example, by television from Guatemala) if they were
afraid to campaign openly inside El Salvador. Apart from the transparent at
tempt to split the FDR, MNR and MPSC members had good reason to be
afraid; sixty Christian Democratic mayors and other officials had been assassi
nated by death squads in the previous year. If the government could not guar
antee the safety of members of the party in government, it could hardly offe
guarantees to parties in open opposition. In September 1981 CCE presiden
Jorge Bustamante publicly recognized the FDR as a representative politica
force but refused to do the same for the FMLN, arguing that it was a group
that sowed terror, hatred, and violence.[9]

The FMLN took the position that (1) it was not opposed to elections; (2
elections must be in the context of a total political solution to the crisis in E
Salvador; (3) the setting in El Salvador made it impossible for elections to be
held; and (4) with the election as projected, the war would continue to worsen
The General Command's January 1982 letter to President Reagan said, in part
"To pretend that the solution to the Salvadorean conflict is the March elec
tions, is ... outside reality. How can a democratic process be guaranteed in the
context of indiscriminate repression?"[10]

In late fall, Duarte narrowly survived the first of several maneuvers by
Robert D'Aubuisson to force him off the junta. That came in a meeting of al
the political parties with the CCE to discuss the election law. Duarte was
saved by the vote of General José Alberto Medrano, who was known for his
idiosyncrasies. By February 1982 ARENA was gaining strength on the ex
treme right and campaigning effectively, and speculation grew that the ex
treme-right parties would win a majority in the Assembly.

The U.S. Role

In February 1981 CIA director William Casey drafted a presidentia
finding[11] that called for political support and propaganda to legitimize and fi
nancially support the Christian Democrats and moderate military officers
President Reagan signed the finding on March 4, 1981, which initiated a flow
of money to Duarte. In June the assistant secretary for inter-American affairs
Thomas Enders, met with Reagan and recommended working for free elec
tions.[12] In the following months at least $250,000 were funneled through AID
$50,000 through AIFLD, and unknown amounts through the CIA and the De
fense Department's supersecret Intelligence Support Activity team.[13] The
money was spent for posters, radio jingles, television commercials, and comic
books for illiterate peasants. The main theme was "Your vote will help end the

violence because it will strengthen the democratic Government while the loyal army eliminates the Communist threat."[14]

The Campaign

The flavor of the campaign was reflected in two scenes. One was D'Aubuisson on the hustings leading the party faithful in ARENA's campaign song, "Tremble, Tremble, Communists." The other was the major picking up a watermelon with one hand and a machete with the other, lopping off half the melon, which splattered on the ground, then telling his listeners that the Christian Democrats were just like the melon: green (the PDC's color) on the outside and red on the inside.

Analysts in the UCA's University Center for Documentation and Information (CUDI) wrote that the campaign was characterized by "intimidation and confusion."[15] The intimidation came from several sources: a barrage of propaganda from the CCE and the junta whose message was that not voting equaled "support for subversion"; an electoral law that mandated stamping *cedulas* with an "invisible and indelible" ink; and a statement by the Episcopal Conference that "human and divine law ... requires that we also comply with our obligations to our country."[16]

The confusion also had several roots. Neither the government nor the CCE nor the parties bothered to explain the nature and purpose of the Constituent Assembly for which people were being asked to vote. In some departments the names of the candidates were not publicized, a move that thus forced voters to choose among parties. The PDC deliberately sowed confusion when it promoted Duarte as a "candidate for provisional president" during the sixty-day campaign. No party presented a platform, and all parties opposing the PDC attacked the reforms with negative campaigns that were distinguishable only by the varying demagoguery of their charges.

Election Day. In this context thousands of people walked for miles, then often stood in the intense sun for hours to vote. The media reported long lines all over the country, a clear indication, most said, of the people's desire for democracy and their rejection of the guerrillas. In fact, the long lines were generally a result of disorganization bordering on chaos and a limited number of voting places. For example, in the capital where, according to the final tally, 374,850 voted, there were 500 voting tables divided among 13 sites. According to official observers, many voting places did not open at the appointed hour of 7:00 A.M.; some did not open until midday; others closed before the 7:00 P.M. deadline.

The FMLN's response was contradictory. Its public statements indicated it was not disposed to disrupt the elections, but the guerrillas laid siege to the city of Usulután for over a week and prevented voting in many areas of the four eastern departments. They also carried out three other attacks; one of these, on the San Salvador *barrio* of San Antonio Abad, was conducted by a turncoat guerrilla commander, Paco, without the knowledge of his superiors.[17] No voting occurred in twenty-eight municipalities, most of which lay in rebel-controlled territory.

Roberto D'Aubuisson addresses ARENA rally, Santa Tecla, March 1985.

The Results. Before the election, predictions of voter turnout ranged from a low of 640,000 to a high of 1 million. The CCE's final vote tally was 1,551,687. The U.S. Embassy was euphoric. The UCA undertook an extensive analysis and concluded that the maximum number of voters could not have exceeded 1.2 million and that probably between 600,000 and 800,000 actually voted. Ambassador Deane Hinton reacted with characteristic diplomacy: "Bullshit!" he said. "It would take a professor in an ivory tower who didn't go out to vote because the guerrillas told him not to to come up with a theory like that."[18] Before he left El Salvador in 1983, Hinton privately admitted to UCA personnel that their analysis was correct.

The Christian Democrats gained a plurality (see Table 6.1), but with only 40 percent of the vote Duarte's party was unable to form a controlling majority in the Assembly with AD, its closest ideological soulmate. Furthermore, ARENA, with 30 percent of the votes, immediately sought to throw out the Christian Democrats. In an effort to restore some civility after a bitter campaign, Hinton invited the various party leaders to lunch the day after the election where he suggested avoiding charges of fraud. The following day all the extreme-right parties, including AD, announced that they had signed an agreement to form a majority coalition in the Assembly.

The Military Names a President, Again

The U.S. Embassy began pressuring the parties to keep the Christian Democrats in the government. D'Aubuisson, who had promised during the campaign to try Duarte and company for treason, and his allies refused on the grounds that they had won the right to form a government and name the pro-

TABLE 6.1   Electoral Results for Major Parties, 1982–1989

Party	1982	1984[a]	1985	1988	1989
PDC	546,218	549,727	505,338	326,716	338,369
	40.1%[b]	43.41%	52.35%	35.1%	36.03%
ARENA	402,304	376,917	286,665	447,696	505,370
	29.53%	29.76%	29.7%	48.1%	53.82%
PCN	261,153	244,556	80,730	78,756	38,218
	19.17%	19.31%	8.36%	8.5%	4.07%
CD	—	—	—	—	35,642
					3.8%
AD	43,929	100,586	35,565	16,211	4,363
	3.46%	7.38%	3.68%	1.7%	0.46%
MERECEN	—	6,645	689	—	—
			.52%		
MAC	—	—	—	—	9,300
					0.99%
POP	12,547	4,677	836	1,752	—
	0.92%	0.36%	0.087%	0.19%	
PAISA	—	15,430	33,101	19,609	—
		1.21%	3.43%	2.1%	
PPS	39,504	24,395	16,344	—	—
	2.9%	1.9%	1.7%		
LIBERACION	—	—	—	34,960	—
				3.8%	
UP	—	—	—	—	4,609
					0.49%
PAR	—	—	2,963	5,059	3,207
			0.31%	0.54%	0.34%

[a]Results of first round.
[b]Percent of valid votes cast for each party.
Source: Central Elections Council (CCE), San Salvador.

visional president. D'Aubuisson was their candidate, and if the United States decided to cut off aid, El Salvador had other sources of support. ARENA, however, did not count on either U.S. tenacity or the extent to which the army, in spite of its paramilitary links to the right, was already beholden to the United States. The Reagan administration sent a congressional delegation headed by House majority leader Jim Wright with the message that a D'Aubuisson government would be unacceptable. Wright, however, undermined the message by rejecting the most serious charges against the major and praising his dedication to democracy.[19]

According to Duarte, inspiration came from Honduran chief of staff General Gustavo Alvarez, who paid a visit to San Salvador, ostensibly to offer congratulations on the elections. When Abdul Gutiérrez asked him how the Honduran military had found an acceptable president the year before, Alvarez said a military committee had imposed its decision on the political parties. Gutiérrez, reported Duarte, then suggested that the army back Alvaro Magaña for president.[20] Magaña, head of the Banco Hipotecario for seventeen years, was, in William LeoGrande's words, the "mortgage banker for the officer corps."[21]

D'Aubuisson Elected President of Assembly. Having had a provisional president crammed down its throat, the Constituent Assembly began to exact its revenge. First it named Roberto D'Aubuisson Assembly president. Next it set out to sabotage the agrarian reform by naming ARENA people to run it, by suspending several provisions of Decree 207, and by naming an agriculture minister, Miguel Muyshondt, who opposed the reform. The suspension of parts of the law led to widespread evictions of tenant farmers. By mid-1983 AID reported 25,572 evictions and 21,091 reinstallations. On the cooperatives, credit dried up, seeds did not arrive, forms were not processed, and problems began to multiply.[22] Martin Diskin wrote that between 1982 and 1984, "the management of ISTA ... supported increases in the agrarian debt of co-ops, reduction of social services, late delivery of credit, and considerable corruption in administration of Phase I. Nevertheless, using the criteria of business success and managerial efficiency, it constantly criticized Phase I as an economic failure."[23]

Meanwhile, D'Aubuisson named Héctor Antonio Regalado, a dentist from San Miguel notorious for organizing his own death squads, head of Assembly security. The two of them turned the second floor of the Assembly building into a storeroom for "bombs, dynamite, face masks, and a munitions factory," according to an Assembly member, who said they also had vehicles with double license plates, airplanes at their disposal, and a staff of forty to forty-five men.[24]

Damage Control, U.S. Style. The U.S. government knew all about what it described as "ARENA death squads," but that did not stop it from revising D'Aubuisson's biography. Before the election one U.S. intelligence agency's profile "mentioned the charges that D'Aubuisson had been involved in the assassination of the archbishop. Two months later the same profile made no mention of the charges or the assassination."[25] Ambassador Hinton assisted in the rehabilitation. He acknowledged that "D'Aubuisson made the death squad leader [Regalado] head of assembly security. ... But now [D'Aubuisson] is a respectable democratic politician—or trying to be. He is not beyond hope—although he has relapses."[26]

As the political right flexed its muscles, the White House became increasingly concerned about its ability to justify certification the following July. A confidential memorandum from Secretary of State Haig to the U.S. Embassy emphasized how pressure should be exerted on the Salvadoreans in the three areas that the president had to certify: development of democratic institutions, human rights, and agrarian reform.[27] The document is revealing in its preoccupation with appearances—Haig's concern was not whether El Salvador was making progress in these areas, but that it *appeared* to be making progress. This attitude would continue through the 1980s.

Learning to Govern

The Pact of Apaneca. It was critical to the overall U.S. strategy that El Salvador have a functioning civilian government—or one that appeared to be functioning. To this end Ambassador Hinton exerted great pressure on the army to play its role in keeping D'Aubuisson in line and in arranging a government of "national unity." These efforts culminated on August 3 in the pact of Apaneca, which was signed at President Magaña's hacienda near the village of Apaneca, Ahuachapán. ARENA, the PDC, the PCN, and the PPS (one deputy) signed the pact. Democratic Action (two deputies) refused to sign, charging that the national situation after the elections had "rapidly worsened," that foreign [U.S.] intervention was increasingly clear, and that "instead of a crisis[-management] government, we have a government in crisis."[28]

The pact contained five points: economic recovery; reforms; confidence and security; improvement in international relations; and creation of peace, human rights, and political commissions. In December an economic reactivation commission was formed. The U.S. Embassy reacted with characteristic effusiveness: "The signing of this pact represents a big step forward for the government of national unity. The creation of commissions and the fixing of dates for elections will enable the government to show, and achieve, real progress. *The objectives stipulated in the pact coincide almost perfectly with the requirements for U.S. presidential certification.*[29]

A more sober assessment appeared three weeks later. After reporting that a heated discussion in the Assembly "led to personal insults and threats of armed assault" among the deputies, *Proceso* observed that the pact "has not succeeded in solving the divisions within the parties in power and even less in promoting measures directed toward pacification or democratization called for in the document. To the contrary. Multiple contradictions have flowered from its roots within the parties, especially the PCN, and the fights are still not resolved between ARENA and the PDC."[30]

Problems Multiply. Several serious political and governing problems emerged in the following weeks. First, supporters and opponents of the pact within the PCN split. The dissidents took ten of the fourteen PCN Assembly deputies with them and formed the Partido Auténtico Institutional Salvadoreño, PAISA (Salvadorean Institutional Authentic Party).

Second, the PDC was excluded from the newly formed Political Commission, which had responsibility for coordinating and overseeing compliance with the pact and developing policy for the other two commissions. Third, there was a fight over apportionment of the 263 mayoralties. The PDC argued for apportionment based on the percentage of votes received in the election. The PCN, with ARENA's support, proposed, and in September won, an equal three-way division among the top three parties in the Assembly. The mayors were important because of the spoils they represented for the party or respective officeholder.[31]

A far more serious problem was the economic plan. With the Christian Democrats committed to the agrarian reform and other minimal economic improvements for the masses, and with ARENA committed to dismantling the agrarian reform and returning to the economic status quo ante, the stage was set for continued conflict. This, along with the war, meant an increasing deterioration of the economy.

By the end of 1982 these difficulties had not abated. "The Pact," *Proceso* wrote in its year-end review, "has not succeeded in eliminating the disagreements. Because of this the USA continues pressuring for a slow realignment of forces to assure a 'democratic center' composed of the PDC, PCN, and AD."[32] These efforts, as we will see, had only marginal success. All these problems meant that the Constituent Assembly, whose first order of business was to write a constitution, barely addressed that issue in 1982—which meant that the U.S. plan for presidential elections in 1983 faced indefinite postponement. While the government floundered, the war continued—and U.S. direction was as pervasive in the military as in the political realm.

LOW-INTENSITY CONFLICT
EQUALS HIGH-INTENSITY WAR

When the FMLN roared back from its poor showing in the January 1981 offensive, it placed the Salvadorean army on the defensive and kept it there for the next three years. Not until the cumulative effect of the FMLN's success and a significant U.S.-provided increase in air power forced a dramatic change in the guerrillas' strategy could the army be said to have gained any initiative at all. This is not to say that the army was not active; as noted in the last chapter, it began carrying out sweeps of areas under FMLN control that did little damage to the guerrillas but caused increasing civilian casualties.

Conducting the War, Salvadorean Style

The hammer-and-anvil strategy was developed in cooperation with the Honduran army even before the United States became directly involved in training. In May 1980, following a secret meeting in El Poy, Honduras, among top officials of the Salvadorean, Honduran, and Guatemalan militaries, about 250 Honduran soldiers took positions along the Sumpul River. Then Salvadorean forces moved into northern Chalatenango and massacred almost 600 civilians. People who attempted to cross the river were turned back by the Hondurans, although some ultimately made it across with the help of Honduran civilians.[33] In March 1981 a Salvadorean army sweep through Cabañas sent between 4,500 and 8,000 *campesinos* running for Honduras. This time eyewitnesses helped the (mostly) women and children cross the Lempa River between air assaults by U.S.-provided helicopter gunships.[34] In late May 1982 the second Sumpul massacre occurred when the Belloso battalion was sent into eastern Chalatenango.

The Officer Problem. The task for the U.S. military in El Salvador was to turn "a militia of 11,000 [in 1979] that had no mission" and was "sitting in the garrison abusing civilians" into a fighting force that could hold its own against the FMLN.[35] As described earlier, this was translated by General Woerner and others into three concrete problems: get the Salvadorean military to subordinate itself to civilian authority; teach the forces to respect human rights; and transform the officer corps. Clearly, the success of the first two depended on the third, and in that respect there was little to show by the late

1980s. In a study during a year at Harvard, four colonels suggested that by 1988, things had not changed significantly:

> The "tanda" system, a sort of West Point Protective Association gone berserk, remains the chief barrier to a competent officer corps. Once each class or tanda is commissioned from the Salvadoran Military Academy, it moves upward through the ranks together, the group advancing at intervals regardless of any evidence of individual competence or lack thereof. Whatever an officer's failings ... his career is secure through the rank of colonel. ... Proponents of American methods must choose between being ostracized and giving in to those demanding adherence to Salvadoran military traditions. ... To American chagrin, the officer corps persists in viewing autonomy over its internal affairs as essential to its institutional integrity.[36]

This arrangement meant that incompetent officers were left in the field and even promoted; officers who were implicated in serious human rights violations were never reprimanded, much less punished; and the "war-lord" system that historically gave every departmental commander virtually absolute control over his region of authority was almost impossible to destroy.

The Honduran Connection. Honduran involvement in the war began in 1980, and by 1982 the Honduran army and air force had become regular collaborators in the large operations near the border, a fact confirmed by the vice-minister of defense, Colonel Adolfo Castillo, who acknowledged that he "participated in coordinating plans with the Honduran Army [which was acting] with the support and consent of the United States."[37] There was another aspect to the Honduran connection: the presence of U.S. military personnel along the border. Ray Bonner visited the La Virtud area in late July 1981 and met Green Beret captain Michael Sheehan, who told him the "National Security Council had approved a Green Beret presence in Honduras to support the military effort against the Salvadorean guerrillas."[38]

It is not surprising that the U.S. government, because it faced myriad problems, stretched and violated the rules concerning involvement by trainers in the war and the fifty-five-man limit that was established by the Pentagon to assuage congressional concern about the expanding U.S. role. Nor is it surprising that the United States found other ways to expand its involvement—and the war. The CIA established a center in Honduras from which patrols into El Salvador operated "to destroy Salvadorean guerrilla bases," according to a top-secret memorandum prepared for a meeting of the National Security Council on July 8, 1983. The fifty-five-man limit was first abridged by sending twenty-six Special Forces medics who were assigned to train field medics. Although this may have been part of their assignment, they had received elite combat training that they likely put to to use in El Salvador.[39]

Then in September 1983, Secretary of State George Shultz cabled the embassy in San Salvador with a lesson in creative accounting: "We have concluded that we should continue with the 55-man ceiling on trainers in El Salvador," he wrote, but "we will apply this ceiling only to those military personnel actually carrying out training responsibilities. It is the intention of

State and DOD," Shultz continued, "not repeat not [sic] to publicize the above decision."[40] The embassy was instructed to provide information only "on an if asked basis" and was given answers to potential questions from the press. This meant, in practice, that the number of U.S. trainers in El Salvador exceeded 100, and the new math provided the bureaucratic cover.

Who's in Charge Here? On May 29, 1983, the *Philadelphia Inquirer* carried this front-page headline: "How U.S. Advisers Run the War in El Salvador." Journalist Rod Nordland described how, over the previous six months, "American officers have moved quietly into the top levels of the Salvadoran military and are ... actually making critical decisions about the conduct of the war. ... [They serve] as strategists, tacticians and planners." Nordland learned that there were "at least six U.S. Army lieutenant colonels working full time in the Salvadoran High Command," and that other officers were stationed with the air force and navy.[41] By the late 1980s, U.S. military advisers were with every brigade and battalion in the country.

Mercenaries. Less than a month after arriving in El Salvador, Ambassador Hinton proposed in a secret cable "contracting non-Salvadorans" to fly and maintain military helicopters. One U.S. pilot acknowledged he was paid $12,000 for two weeks' work flying Salvadorean troops into combat on Air America planes, the company used by the CIA in Southeast Asia. A second aviator ferried men and supplies from Homestead Air Force Base, Florida, to Ilopango in unmarked planes and was paid cash for his work. Other U.S. citizens worked directly with Salvadorean troops in the field.[42]

Advisers in Combat. U.S. law prohibits military trainers from entering zones of potential combat, engaging in combat, or carrying offensive weapons. There is abundant evidence, however, that this law was given the same adherence as the 55-man limit and was flouted from the beginning. On February 11, 1982, CNN (Cable News Network) filmed three U.S. advisers carrying M-16s in a combat zone. The embassy said they had been "repairing a bridge," but Ambassador Hinton shipped the senior officer back to the United States and reprimanded the other two.[43]

In January 1983 Charles Clements was summoned to the secret FMLN command post in Guazapa and asked to listen to transmissions of government soldiers who had just begun yet another assault on the zone. Clements wrote that as the radioman picked up the frequencies being used by the army, "I heard distinctly American voices issuing coded directives to the troops as well as asking questions of the Salvadorean commanders." Clements added that "these men obviously were, at the very minimum, acting in a command and control function. They could not have been more than a mile or two from us."[44]

The reports of U.S. trainers in combat or potential combat situations continued through the 1980s. According to a January 1985 document from the U.S. Army War College, the CIA and Special Forces trained and led "Long Range Reconnaissance Patrols [PRALs]" that engaged in combat. Former advisers from this unit with experience in El Salvador told journalist Frank Smyth that "U.S. military advisors, in addition to CIA paramilitary operatives, engaged in combat operations in El Salvador."[45] Nor did publicity stop the practice. During the November 1989 offensive, journalists in San Salvador intercepted by radio a conversation between a U.S. military adviser in an observation helicopter and the U.S. military command center. The adviser told his group contact that the Salvadorean air force needed to "hit" an area several blocks "north of the church."[46]

Advisers were intentional targets. The announced purpose of FMLN assaults on the army's national training school in La Unión in 1985 and the Third Brigade in San Miguel in July 1986[47] was to kill U.S. advisers. Both attacks left many dead Salvadorean soldiers and considerable destruction. But Staff Sergeant Gregory Fronius was the first U.S. soldier among seventy casualties when the FMLN overran the Fourth Brigade at El Paraiso for a second time on March 31, 1987. Another 100 enlisted men were wounded; most officers sought refuge in an underground bunker.[48]

Intelligence Gathering. Before 1981, "Israeli technicians began installing a computer system ... with capabilities ... [that] would enable the military and police to seek out government opponents more systematically."[49] Nonetheless, the Salvadoreans had little knowledge of and less equipment for sophisticated intelligence gathering. The United States sought to address this problem by setting up an operation in El Salvador run by the CIA and military intelligence. The system included unarmed flights over El Salvador, first from Panama, then by early 1984 from Palmerola Air Base in Honduras.[50] Nevertheless, one U.S. Army analyst concluded in late 1987 that "The [Salvadorean army's] significant weaknesses are ... in their intelligence capability which would ... not only enable an enemy force to cause damage almost at will in El Salvador ... but also fails to provide [them] the capability to take the initiative in a manner that would ... defeat the guerrilla forces in a military sense."[51]

The Game Plan

Defeating the FMLN militarily was the objective of the Woerner Report, which focused on turning the Salvadorean army into a capable counterinsurgency force. The United States first developed BIRIs and expanded the officer corps by training 500 cadets at Fort Benning, Georgia. Then MilGroup, its commander, John Waghelstein, and the U.S. Embassy drafted the National Campaign Plan (NCP). The difference between the Woerner Report and the NCP, as the colonels at Harvard wrote, was that the former "had aimed to create an army that could kill guerrillas; the aim of the NCP was to win."[52]

The extent of U.S. involvement is suggested by a heavily excised memo that describes a meeting in the embassy "to discuss implementation of the combined integrated POL/ECON/SECURITY plan."[53] In theory, it was to be a comprehensive, integrated plan that involved the Armed Forces, several government ministries (including Agriculture, Economy, Health, and Education), and the civilian population in the countryside. The plan "placed emphasis on civic action and developmental projects behind a security screen."[54] A critical component of the NCP was the training by U.S. advisers of mobile Cazador (hunter) companies with thirty men each. By early 1984 thirty-six companies were trained. Their mission was to stay in the field for extended periods, hunt down the guerrillas, and call in one of the BIRIs in the event of contact with a large number of insurgents.

The province chosen as the NCP "pilot project" is in the geographic center of the country. Its dominating physical characteristic, Chinchontepec (the San Vicente volcano), and the Cerros de San Pedro region of low mountains to the immediate west were areas of major guerrilla activity by late 1982. Operation "Maquilishuat," as the NCP was called in San Vicente, began with high hopes and widespread publicity in June 1983. "For its first hundred days," the four colonels noted, "this ambitious project lived up to its promise. The Salvadoreans made real headway; they seemed to have broken the code."[55] An intragovernmental agency, the National Committee for Restoration of Areas (CONARA), was formed to coordinate the civilian and military efforts. Two years later AID assessed the results: "The initial successes were followed by disappointment. The guerrillas began an Eastern Zone offensive in September 1983 that lasted until January 1984. Military units needed elsewhere were withdrawn from San Vicente. The civil defense program, delayed by lack of planning and resources, was insufficient to protect the area. A string of guerrilla attacks on lightly defended towns and garrisons followed, and the National Plan effort in San Vicente and Usulután was effectively stalled."[56]

The largest problem, however, was that the army lacked sufficient troops and resources either to maintain San Vicente or (much less) to extend the NCP to other departments. The NCP was doomed to failure from the beginning, but the United States continued to pretend that it was alive and well and tried to resuscitate it in 1986.

Crises

As if the Salvadorean Armed Forces did not have enough problems fighting guerrillas, they also had to contend with dissension in the ranks. Meanwhile, although the FMLN was riding high militarily, it also was suffering from internal discord. The problems in both organizations exploded in the first half of 1983, but the FMLN performed as it had on the battlefield and proved able to handle its crisis more quickly and efficiently than the army.

Barracks Revolt. On January 3, 1983, Lieutenant Colonel Sigfrido Ochoa, commander of the garrison in Cabañas, refused to accept an order sending him off to diplomatic exile in Uruguay. Ochoa was widely regarded as the army's most effective field commander; he had driven the FMLN out of the province the year before. Ochoa holed up in his garrison and demanded the resignation of Defense Minister García, who increasingly, if belatedly, was seen by his colleagues and the U.S. military as corrupt and inept. The crisis split and distracted the officer corps. According to Colonel John Cash, the defense attaché at the time, "Waghelstein told Flores Lima, who was the Chief of Staff, 'You got a war to fight, and you can't just let these political battles among your officer corps stop you at the war effort.' ... Flores Lima t[old] him that this was more important than the war right now. This threatens the very fabric of our officer corps. What was surprising was that Blandón ... an old García crony, went up [to Cabañas] with a commission of officers, and came back and told García that Ochoa was right."[57] After sixteen days, Ochoa accepted a one-year appointment to the Inter-American Defense College in Washington, D.C., and García agreed to resign within ninety days. As the ninety days ran out, amid growing indications that García intended to renege, air force commander Bustillo threatened a mutiny. President Magaña then intervened and demanded García's resignation, which García tendered on April 18. Magaña immediately named Colonel Carlos Eugenio Vides Casanova, who had been director of the National Guard since fall 1979, to succeed García. Vides promised to take the army out of politics.[58]

Murder in Managua. On April 6 the FMLN's most senior woman commander, Mélida Anaya Montes (Comandante Ana María), who was also second in command of the FPL, was murdered in her house in Managua. Montes, a teacher, had been a founder of ANDES-21, the national teachers' union. Days later Nicaraguan police captured Rogelio Bassaglia, who not only confessed to the crime but accused FPL commander in chief Salvador Cayetano Carpio of ordering the murder. Carpio, who was in Libya when the deed occurred, had flown back to Managua for the funeral. When he was confronted with evidence of his own complicity, Carpio committed suicide.

The root of the crime lay in a profound political division in the FPL. Carpio had become rigid and dogmatic concerning his view of the "correct" political and military policy for the FMLN. Anyone who did not agree with him was counterrevolutionary. But the FMLN was becoming more unified, and Carpio was increasingly the odd man out. He withheld troops during military actions, resisted advances toward greater unity, and opposed negotiations. Montes supported the opposite positions, and by early 1983, in an FPL congress in Chalatenango, her positions won a majority of the delegates' votes. Carpio could not accept it. Murder and suicide followed. Ironically, this event achieved what Montes had stood for: The FMLN immediately closed ranks; the new commander in chief of the FPL, Leonel Gonzalez (Salvador Sánchez Ceren), came from the Montes faction; and, according to Miguel Sáenz, greater unity was achieved in the month after the murder than had been achieved in the previous year.

In September, after another FPL congress in Chalatenango, a faction loyal to Carpio's politics broke away and formed the Salvador Cayetano Carpio Revolutionary Workers' Movement (MOR). The FMLN disavowed the splinter group, and when the MOR went public in December, the FPL and FMLN issued statements condemning Carpio for his role in Montes's death and for having developed a "cult of personality" that "admitted no other political position than his own."[59]

The FMLN Strikes Back

While the United States was in the process of expanding the Salvadorean Armed Forces, training new officers, and developing new combat units, the FMLN was expanding from a few hundred combatants in January 1981 to an estimated 9,000 to 12,000 by 1984. The insurgents were so effective that by January 1983 General Wallace Nutting, commander of the U.S. Southern Com-

Former minister of defense Carlos Eugenio Vides Casanova (*center*) and regional commanders, San Vicente, July 1983.

mand (SOUTHCOM), communicated his concern to the Joint Chiefs of Staff, who sent him to the State Department, then on to the White House. "On the 26th of January of 1983 I told Judge [William] Clark that if we did not step up our effort and make a commitment that was visible, the thing was going to go down the tubes."[60] U.N. Ambassador Jeane Kirkpatrick's visit in early February reinforced Nutting's message. Publicly she asserted that the insurgents "were not winning anything." Privately she told President Reagan that the situation was bad. By the end of the month the president called for $60 million more in military aid.[61]

In the previous six months the FMLN had mounted two devastating offensives. In early June the rebels took Perquín and San Fernando, Morazán, then set up an ambush for the expected reinforcements. The army fell into the FMLN's trap, and the guerrillas captured a large number of arms, munitions, and POWs, including Vice-Minister of Defense Castillo. The army's counteroffensive included the Belloso battalion, but the FMLN forced the Belloso to flee "like a covey of quail"; it also instigated the first of many transportation stoppages aimed at undermining the national economy.[62] August brought another major action, then after a six-week hiatus in September and October, the FMLN began another offensive that continued into 1983.

For the visit of Pope John Paul II in early March, the FMLN declared a unilateral cease-fire. There was a lull in military activities until late April, when rebels overran the customs station at El Amatillo on the Salvadorean-

Honduran border, causing an estimated $2 million in damage. In May the FMLN spent six days slipping combatants past army guardposts on the slopes of Cacahuatique in Morazán; the attack on the main military communications center atop the mountain destroyed it.

The Fall Offensive. On September 3 the FMLN launched another offensive with an attack on the Third Brigade in San Miguel. Colonel Joseph Stringham, who had replaced Waghelstein as MilGroup commander, later recalled the event: "During the month of October the military situation continued to reverse rapidly. We lost a Cazador battalion ... and we lost a Salvadorean battalion at Cacahuatique [in a second assault]. This took place over a period of three weeks, and I am talking about 'wipe out'! The Sunday before Thanksgiving the FMLN drove up in busses to a small outpost south of Corinto and the lieutenant surrendered the garrison. The troops were a company of Cazadores."[63]

The air force responded with bombing runs on towns that the FMLN had taken and, in one case (Tenancingo, Cuscatlán), had already abandoned. On New Year's Eve the rebels attacked (for the first time) the El Paraiso garrison, which had been designed by U.S. counterinsurgency experts and was said to be impenetrable. After destroying most of the installation and killing or wounding 300, they left with three truckloads of supplies and 200 prisoners of war. The next night FMLN commandos blew up the Cuscatlán suspension bridge across the Lempa River on the Pan American Highway.

The War in 1984. By early January the FMLN controlled extensive areas of eastern, central, and northern El Salvador. Late that month, however, the army began a series of sweeps through these areas to retake control of as many towns as possible in preparation for the March 1984 presidential elections. This offensive continued for several weeks and was partially successful; for example, the guerrillas were forced to abandon Jucuarán and other towns where they had been ensconced for months.

After the election the U.S.-guided strategy acquired greater coherence and more energetic implementation. For at least two years there had been a clear division among army officers between those who favored big military operations involving 1,500 to 6,000 troops during daylight hours only (from whence came the term "9-to-5 army") and those favoring the U.S. strategy of constantly maintaining troops in the field to keep the guerrillas on the run. That division was effectively eliminated when officers supportive of the U.S. model were given key assignments and the Ministry of Defense and High Command were reorganized to improve efficiency. Still, nothing, except air power, helped the government's war effort. As CONARA floundered, the army once again began using large operations, now accompanied by massive airstrikes, to drive the guerrillas out of their strongholds.[64]

The War and Human Rights

Nowhere were constraints on U.S. leverage more apparent than in the continuing human rights violations. In 1982, 4,419 people were killed and 1,045 disappeared. Between January and July 1983, 1,787 were killed and 840

Drawing by refugee child at Mesa Grande, Honduras, July 1982, depicts the flight of Salvadoreans from Chalatenango across the Sumpul River into Honduras. Salvadorean troops are at top, Honduran soldiers at bottom right.

Drawing by refugee child, Sacred Heart Basilica refugee center, 1985. In contrast to accompanying drawing, this shows guerrillas fighting back. The broken trees are caused by fragmentation bombs that explode about one meter above the ground and send out razor-sharp shrapnel in a 360-degree radius.

were captured or disappeared. Between August and December, however, the numbers dropped; 588 died and 476 were captured.[65] Strong pressure from Congress and peace groups concerning the continuing high levels of political violence finally caused the administration in early November to initiate a conerted campaign to lower the "grim-gram" totals—embassy cables that reported the dead and disappeared.

On the human side, the impact of the escalation in 1984 was massive. According to the Red Cross, displaced persons from the conflict zones inreased from 80,000 to 105,000 between January and July; displaced persons in government-controlled regions climbed to 342,000 from 262,000 between November 1983 and May 1984. The FMLN contributed to the exodus in Morazán and San Miguel by initiating a policy of forced recruitment. In April and May alone, 1,570 refugees fled these areas.[66] The ERP, which was doing most of the forced recruiting, came under harsh and widespread criticism—including from within the ranks of the FMLN—for this practice, and it was abandoned after a few months. By early 1985 most of the civilian casualties were a result of the air war and other deliberate attacks on civilians. The worst example of the latter occurred when an FMLN plan listing villages to be used as staging areas for an attack on Cerron Grande fell into army hands. On July 19, 1984, days after the attack, the Atlacatl battalion and departmental units carried out a three-day operation in the area. Sixty-eight members of Christian Base Communities were murdered, including twenty-seven children. The army denied the massacre, but after foreign journalists provided evidence, newly inaugurated President Napoleón Duarte ordered an investigation.

The Air War. In March 1983, shortly after he left El Salvador, Charles Clements testified before Congress that since the previous July he could not "remember a day that a village has not been bombed by A-37 jets, strafed by Huey helicopters, or rocketed by Cessna spotter planes. ... I live in a zone," he continued, "where any assembly of people, whether children in a school or patients outside a clinic, where any sign such as diapers or bandages hanging out to dry, where many times even the smoke of a cooking fire, invite aerial attack."[67] Guazapa received the most intense bombing, but the air war was extended throughout the country. According to Department of Defense figures, "average flying hours for UH-1H (Huey) helicopters and A-37 strike aircraft—the core of El Salvador's attack capability—increased by over 220 hours per month between July 1983 and February 1984." The Reagan administration, meanwhile, denied that "indiscriminate" bombing occurred and maintained that the A-37 pilots had developed "near surgical precision" in their bombing runs.[68]

Prisoners of War. In 1983 the FMLN turned over 1,300 POWs to the International Committee of the Red Cross (ICRC), some of whom chose to remain with the guerrillas.[69] Government forces, in contrast, had a policy of killing captured guerrillas. Under pressure from their U.S. advisers, however, this policy slowly changed after 1983. One reason for the change was the "human rights political situation; as long as the Salvadorans were violating human rights," an unidentified spokesperson for army intelligence explained, "this presented a problem in terms of getting aid, not only from the United States, but also from European countries. ... The second reason for the change was common sense. ... The advisers convinced the Salvadorans that ... when treated properly the value of a prisoner who decides to give information is much greater than the prisoner who is dead."[70]

INTERNATIONAL DEVELOPMENTS

While the United States pursued its dual strategy, it could not control all events on the world stage. One of these was the formation of the Contadora group by four Latin American countries seeking to find a political solution to the Central American crisis; another was the visit by Pope John Paul II to Central America.

Contadora

As the U.S.-sponsored militarization of Central America increased after 1981, the foreign ministers of Mexico, Panama, Venezuela, and Colombia met in January 1983 on the Panamanian island of Contadora to search for political means to end the Central American crisis, not only within El Salvador but regionally. They concluded their first meeting with a call for negotiations among all parties, then followed up with visits to the five Central American countries in April. In March, Costa Rican president Luís Alberto Monge offered himself as a mediator in the Salvadorean conflict, an offer the Magaña government promptly rejected.

After the four participants (the countries they represented became known as Contadora) visited El Salvador on April 12, the foreign ministers of Costa Rica, Honduras, Guatemala, and El Salvador met in San Salvador on May 20 to discuss the Contadora proposals. In September all five Central American presidents ratified the document of objectives that had been hammered out by Contadora. The objectives included respecting human, political, civil, economic, social, religious, and cultural rights; promoting the relaxation of tension in the area; reducing the arms buildup and beginning negotiations on the control and reduction of current arms stockpiles and troops; banning foreign military bases and all other foreign interference; reducing the number of foreign military advisers; establishing internal mechanisms to control the arms traffic in the region; disallowing the use of one's country by groups seeking to overthrow another government in the area, and denying support to such groups; and refusing to promote or support acts of terrorism, subversion, or sabotage in other countries of the region.[71]

The Reagan administration repeatedly affirmed its support for Contadora's efforts, but the continuing U.S. military buildup in Honduras and El Salvador, plus the organization, training, and arming of the Nicaraguan counterrevolutionary forces, led many in Latin America, particularly Mexico, to conclude that U.S. support was little more than lip service for domestic and congressional consumption.[72] While Contadora labored, the U.S. administration, concerned over its failure to sell its El Salvador policy to Congress or the nation, appointed in April former Florida senator Richard Stone special envoy to Central America. In July the president named a bipartisan commission on Central America, headed by former secretary of state Henry Kissinger. In January 1984, after hearing from selected regional and foreign policy specialists and after a whirlwind trip through the region, the commission issued its report, which called for significant increases in military and economic aid. The president responded positively to these recommendations, but the continuing emphasis on military over political means dismayed many, including Costa Rican president Monge, who was otherwise a strong Reagan policy supporter.[73]

Finally, on September 7, 1984, Contadora endorsed a compromise draft treaty and submitted it to the five Central American governments, all of which accepted it. U.S. support for the Contadora process and the treaty evaporated, however, when the Nicaraguans accepted it on September 21. The administration dispatched representatives to Honduras, Costa Rica, and El Salvador who successfully pressured these governments to reject the treaty on grounds that had never been an issue—namely that verification procedures were inadequate. President Duarte reasserted his willingness to sign the treaty but only if there were guarantees that Nicaragua would not supply the Salvadorean insurgents.[74] Efforts to revise the treaty in a way that would make it acceptable to all parties, including the United States, failed, and Contadora limped along for the next two years, its members unwilling to let it die and unable to achieve the peace they all sought. Not until Costa Rica's new president Oscar Arias offered a bold new initiative in 1987 would hopes for peace again surge to the fore.

The Pope Pays a Visit

In Chapter 3 I suggested that from the 1960s, the church passed through several stages or periods that were defined by specific events. The period from the assassination of Archbishop Romero to the visit of Pope John Paul II on March 6, 1983, was a time of caution for the church. Romero's successor, Arturo Rivera Damas, had been named apostolic administrator rather than archbishop; the position limited his authority and influence. But the pope's visit brought significant, even dramatic changes.

On his way from the airport to the site where an outdoor mass would be celebrated, John Paul stopped at the cathedral to pray at Romero's tomb.[75] Later, he began his homily by telling the crowd of approximately 30,000 of his visit. The impact of his words can be measured by trying to visualize the scene: Immediately in front of the newly constructed platform that held the altar were seated the power elite of El Salvador: government officials, military, diplomatic corps, and the oligarchy, all dressed in their Sunday best. Immediately behind this group were a raised platform for the press, then a chain-link fence, and the rest of the people—standing. The pope extolled Romero as a pastor, his defense of human rights, his "pastoral line" in general. As he finished the people seated in front of the press sat with folded arms. The people standing behind the press cheered for several minutes. In short, the pontiff "resurrected" Romero. For three years it had been considered a subversive act to mention Romero's name publicly. At the masses in the cathedral in 1981 and 1982 on the anniversary of his death, only a few hundred people attended. But two weeks after the pope's visit, the memorial mass drew thousands.

In the main part of his homily, John Paul made "dialogue" his central theme. With this focus he not only placed the church behind efforts to seek a peaceful solution to the civil war, but he also strengthened Rivera Damas's position as a potential mediator between the government and the FMLN. Rivera had long made known his willingness to act as a mediator, and in May 1984, at the request of the FDR-FMLN, he delivered a formal proposal for a meeting to the government.

The resurrection of Romero had another unanticipated effect: It contributed to a renewed militancy by many in the church concerned with the continued human rights violations. On March 24, 1984, one day before the presidential election, the Basilica of the Sacred Heart in San Salvador overflowed with worshipers for the memorial mass. Afterward, there was a march from the basilica to the cathedral twelve blocks away; about 300 people, accompanied by the international press corps, participated. Along the route someone began shouting, "Who killed Monseñor Romero?" The marchers' response: "D'Aubuisson!" The streets of San Salvador had not heard chants like that since early 1980. It was only the beginning. Each year thereafter the number of marchers doubled.

ELECTIONS, AGAIN

Before elections for president could be held, the Constituent Assembly had to write and ratify a new constitution. In July the U.S. Embassy reported, with apparently mixed frustration and hope, "that elections called for 1983 may be postponed," although "the president [Magaña] has publicly reaffirmed his intention to proceed as planned and the elections ... are still expected to be held this year."[76] It was not to be.

The fundamental problem was the profound divisions among the parties in the Assembly; they bickered and fought through most of 1983 over political and economic provisions in the document. In addition, there were a number of logistical problems, as the same cable noted: no voting list; no electoral law; no direction from either Magaña or the Assembly concerning either the date or scope of the election. By fall the embassy's concern turned to anxiety as the Assembly found itself stymied, primarily by deep divisions over the agrarian reform.

There were other difficulties. On September 27 the Popular Democratic Union (UPD) put 20,000 demonstrators in the streets of San Salvador, easily the largest demonstration since 1980. Allied with the PDC, the UPD was a coalition of centrist unions that had been organized in September 1980 under strong influence from AIFLD as an alternative to the FDR and its union members.[77] Its primary demand was that the Assembly approve articles for the new constitution that would protect the agrarian reform. In October and November persistent rumors of an impending coup by officers disgusted with

The first public demonstration on the anniversary of Archbishop Romero's death; about 600 people marched. In 1985 the number doubled, and in 1986 it doubled again. By the late 1980s the number grew to over 5,000.

Assembly shenanigans were consistently denied but would not go away.[78] On the military front, the FMLN was routing the army in eastern and central El Salvador.

Moving (Somewhat) Against the Death Squads. The biggest problem for the Reagan administration, however, was the continuing human rights violations. By mid-1983 domestic political reaction to the "grim-gram" totals forced the administration to begin pressuring the Salvadoreans. The efforts included the farewell speech by Ambassador Hinton in July; a visit by Defense Department officials Fred Iklé and Nestor Sánchez and the assistant secretary of state for human rights, Eliot Abrams, during which the extremely conservative Iklé criticized the death squads; a publicized investigation into links between Salvadorean oligarchs in Miami and the death squads; a speech by Ambassador Pickering attacking the death squads; the decision to deny D'Aubuisson a visa to enter the United States; a promise from Defense Minister Vides that the Armed Forces would combat the death squads; and, finally, a visit from Vice-President George Bush on December 11.

Bush brought with him a letter from President Reagan to President Magaña that included a list of military and civilian officials identified by the United States as being involved with the death squads. One of the persons named was Héctor Antonio Regalado, the head of Assembly security. Bush also delivered an ultimatum: Fire or cashier them by January 10, 1984, or risk suspension of military aid. Magaña did nothing, but on December 15 thirty-one senior army officers, two of whom were publicly linked to the deatl squads, signed a statement supporting Vides Casanova in his efforts to curl death-squad activity. Six weeks after Bush's visit, a CIA cable complained tha only two of the officers had been transferred and that they had been replacec with two extreme-right officers. The cable also noted that Mauricio Staber and Dennis Moran, previously mentioned, as well as René Emilio Ponce anc Juan Orlando Zepeda, who would become minister and vice-minister of de fense, respectively, in the late 1980s, were "all close associates of rightist stan dard bearer Roberto D'Aubuisson."[79]

This minicampaign by the United States was not unequivocal. Presiden Reagan had twice certified in 1983 that human rights violations were improv ing. After Abrams visited El Salvador, he asserted that the ability of the United States to exert influence was constrained by the fear of an FMLN vic tory. Then in early December, Reagan pocket vetoed a bill extending the certi fication process. Most significant, the United States continued and increasec military aid after no officer was cashiered, suspended, or charged. Nonethe less, U.S. pressure had an impact: In the first half of 1984 murders and disap pearances dropped between one-third and one-half.

A New Constitution. After a tumultuous fall, during which the Assembly spent many weeks arguing over two articles concerned with the agrarian re form, the representatives finally agreed to postpone further discussion of Ar ticles 104 and 105. Then, in a burst of activity in mid- and late November forty-three articles were approved one week and nineteen the next.[80] On No vember 22 the Assembly decreed that election for president take place the fol lowing March 25. On December 15, in a formal ceremony in the Assembly building, the new constitution of El Salvador was signed. By then the electora campaign was already under way as parties rushed to name their candidates To no one's surprise, José Napoleón Duarte was the PDC candidate, Robertc D'Aubuisson the ARENA candidate, and José Francisco Guerrero the PCN standard-bearer.

The Campaign

The 1984 elections, like those in 1982, fit the definition of "demonstra tion elections," with one difference and one caveat.[81] The difference lay in me dia freedom, which was somewhat greater than it had been two years earlier. The caveat is that the concept of a demonstration election was insufficient tc adequately explain the dynamics unleashed by the electoral process itself.

Ambassador Thomas Pickering suggested toward the end of the cam paign that "Americans would be at home with the rhetoric, the enthusiasm, the fanfare, and even the invective characteristic of a tough political battle."[82] But Mexico's prestigious newspaper *Excelsior* said the campaign was "charac terized by vulgarity, insulting epithets and low language."[83] *Excelsior*'s per ception no doubt grew out of watching the two main candidates sling ad ho minem attacks at each other rather than debate issues like the war and the economy. Duarte's references to "nazi-fascists" and "Roberto D'escuadron' as in *"escuadron de muerte,"* death squad) were matched by D'Aubuisson's references to *"el loco* Duarte" or *"el comunista* Duarte."

Eight parties nominated candidates for the first round on March 25 (see Table 6.1). Five had sufficient funds to conduct a real campaign. Once again, three were significant contenders: ARENA, the PDC, and the PCN. The electoral law went into effect on February 13, and the first week the CCE announced there had been violations such as government workers using official cars to campaign.

The last week in February the PDC signed a "social pact" with the UPD in which the latter pledged its support in exchange for PDC promises to name rural and urban labor representatives to the ministries responsible for the agrarian reform and labor relations, to respect human rights, and to begin a process of dialogue with the FMLN.[84] UPD support was critical because of its ability to mobilize thousands of voters, especially in the countryside. In the end, Duarte's failure to uphold his end of the bargain would cause him many problems and would produce great disenchantment in the UPD.

Four weeks before the election, ARENA challenged the PDC's vice-presidential candidate, Pablo Mauricio Alvergue, based on some ambiguities in the election law. Rather than fight it, Alvergue withdrew to avoid endangering a PDC triumph, and Rodolfo Castillo Claramount was chosen to replace him.

Electoral Procedures

AID provided more than $3 million for computer and microfilm hardware, with which the CCE prepared a voter registration list by examining every birth certificate since 1900 and subtracting all death certificates, adding *cedula* names and numbers to the memory, then eliminating duplicates. The final list contained almost 2.5 million names. Because there could not be a full list at every voting booth, municipal, departmental, regional, and national booths were devised. If one voted in a municipality where one's *cedula* was issued, one voted at a municipal booth. If one was in a different municipality of the same province, then one looked for a departmental urn. Tens of thousands of displaced people were in the country, and those who could not vote at municipal urns often had to travel great distances on election day.

The FMLN and the Elections

In early 1984 it appeared that the FMLN had learned from its 1982 mistakes. On February 9 in Mexico City the FDR-FMLN announced that the elections would "not be the object of direct military attacks" and that the guerrillas would continue their fight before and after the elections.[85] A month earlier Juan Ramón Medrano (Comandante Balta) had said that "The solution is to increase the incorporation of the people, to strike harder blows, to deepen the war, and to search for a solution to it through the only vote of ours that [the government] listens to, the vote of rifles. Only when we are … at the point of defeating the army will they listen to us."[86]

In late February, at the behest of the United States, the army opened up a new offensive with the primary objective of securing as many towns as possible by election day. The FMLN was forced to withdraw from towns where it had operated with impunity for many months. The rebels suffered relatively few casualties, but their political work among the masses, which had become their primary focus at the end of 1983, was seriously affected. To counter this the ERP devised a systematic program of confiscating *cedulas*, a policy that was strongly but ineffectively opposed by the other organizations. The FPL, however, followed another tack: On the night of March 24, after voting materials had been delivered to Santa Rita, Chalatenango, rebels moved in and confiscated or destroyed all the voting materials. The FMLN's rationale was that the army offensive required them to respond in ways that demonstrated their power. But these actions deprived people of a stamp in their *cedula*, which demonstrated that they had voted and were therefore "patriotic," not "subversive."

Election Day

The FMLN turned off the lights in San Salvador the night of March 24, but that cannot account for the pandemonium at many polling places the next day. The CCE failed to anticipate the confusion of its complicated system, and its North American election advisers, enamored of their hard- and software, did no better. The logistics of delivering ballot boxes, ballots, rubber stamps, stamp pads, indelible ink, and official forms to record each table's vote at the end of the day were poorly planned; the result was that many polling places opened late.

The Voting Process. Vigilantes (poll watchers) from each party circulated freely, and the three parties with the most votes in 1982 (PDC, PCN, and ARENA) were able to name one member each of the three-person junta that processed the voters by checking *cedulas* and giving out ballots. The setting provided many opportunities for confusion and shenanigans. In general, the irregularities depended on local ingenuity rather than any partisan master plan. Still, the "organized disorganization," as Ricardo Stein, a political analyst and former director of the UCA's Center for Documentation and Information (CUDI), put it, was clearly the result of using the latest computer technology to try to prevent even the appearance of fraud in a country with an estimated 60 percent illiteracy rate.

Except for San Miguel during the runoff on May 6, there were no reports of FMLN attacks near voting places on either day. People interviewed in four provinces on both election days suggested that the two primary motivations for voting were fear and a desire for peace. There is little reason to doubt the reported vote of 1.4 million on March 25. Lines were long throughout the country. There is strong reason, however, to doubt the vote total on May 6. Lines were much shorter, and the hundreds of people waiting for transportation or walking along the highways in March were absent in May.

In the capital there was a riot in the late afternoon because the CCE had grossly underestimated the number of urns needed. The local junta simply

Election day in Apopa (twenty kilometers north of San Salvador), March 25, 1984.

created new urns and allowed everyone to vote. In San Miguel the voters were orderly but could not figure out where they were supposed to vote. At 3:30 P.M. people began to vote at any booth. ARENA and the PDC did whatever they could get away with to gain votes. On both days there were charges and countercharges from the PDC and ARENA over their comportment in polling areas. On May 6 in Chalatenango PDC workers accosted a Canadian television crew and accused both ARENA and the National Police of trying to tell campesinos how to vote as they stepped up to the urn. ARENA denied the accusation. The police vanished. Vote buying was witnessed, especially in outlying areas. In Jiquilisco, Usulután, ARENA was giving four ballots to every (reliable) voter until PDC deputy Antonio Guevara Lacayo appeared. An altercation between Guevara and an ARENA *vigilante* led to Guevara's arrest and incarceration for almost two hours.

The Role of the Army. During the previous two years the Armed Forces had increasingly come to identify itself as the protector and defender of the new constitutional order—including free and democratic elections with *civilian* candidates. Thus in March and May the army defined its role as guaranteeing a free election, and soldiers were in evidence throughout the country. In some places they were models of circumspection; in others violence and intimidation were in evidence. In Santa Rita, where there was no voting in March, on May 6 army presence was strong; a mortar was parked in the front school yard and soldiers hovered over the urns. In San Miguel de Mercedes, Chalatenango, the army was present but unobtrusive, despite being less than two kilometers from FMLN territory. In Mejicanos people began lining up at 5:30 A.M. When the polls opened at 8:00 there was a rush, and people jammed together at the entrance. The National Guard used rifle butts to push people back, knocking down some and injuring several.

Near Chalatenango soldiers and officers stopped trucks carrying people to vote. Women were lined up along one side of the highway, men on the other. Officers went down the lines checking *cedulas.* Each truck had a *vigilante* wearing his party's tunic. An ARENA truck stopped and everyone got off except the *vigilante.* On the next PDC truck, however, even its *vigilante* was checked.

The Results and the Cost

Despite the army's efforts before the elections, no voting occurred on March 25 in 58 of 261 municipalities, up from 28 in 1982. On May 6 the FMLN prevented voting in 46 municipalities, many of which lay deep in rebel-controlled territory. This is a measure of the extent to which the FMLN had expanded in two years.[87]

In March and in May it took about a week for the official results to be announced. In the first round the results were not very different from 1982: Duarte and the PDC won 43.41 percent of the vote; Roberto D'Aubuisson and ARENA garnered 29.76 percent; the PCN's Francisco Guerrero, 19.31 percent. All other parties trailed far behind with less than 8 percent each.

In the runoff Duarte won 53.59 percent and D'Aubuisson 46.4 percent, the result of a split in the PCN vote. The next day D'Aubuisson claimed victory and charged that Duarte had won through fraud. In both rounds there were threats to impugn the results and call for another election. Then the threats were turned toward CCE members. One Christian Democrat left the country, and an AID employee, John Kelley, who was responsible for data management for the voting list, went into seclusion under heavy guard.

Militarily, the army was exhausted. It also paid a high price in casualties—150 lives lost between March 12 and 25 alone. Politically, the campaign created paralysis in the government for several months. The FMLN, as in 1982, demonstrated its incapacity to respond coherently and creatively to an eminently political event.

The United States paid for the elections with $4 million in overt aid and $2 million in covert aid to the PDC and PCN. The Reagan administration was officially neutral but in fact preferred the PCN candidate, Guerrero, who promptly declared his neutrality after the first round. Faced with a well-funded (from the oligarchy), slick, and high-powered ARENA campaign machine, the CIA delivered money directly to the Christian Democrats, a fact that Senator Jesse Helms (R.–N.C.), who supported D'Aubuisson, revealed on the Senate floor soon after the runoff.[88]

President, at Last

Twelve years after he was denied his electoral victory by the army, José Napoleón Duarte was elected president with the acquiescence and, in a sense, support of that same army.[89] His election helped convince wavering members of the U.S. Congress to support him with more aid. On May 10 the House of Representatives voted 211 to 208 to approve $229.4 million in military aid in fiscal year 1984 and $132.5 million for 1985.[90] In late May, before his inauguration, Duarte went to Washington and persuaded Congress to increase aid even more.

The Inauguration. Duarte was inaugurated as El Salvador's first civilian president in fifty-three years on June 1, 1984. His inaugural address was long on rhetoric and short on specifics. The objectives of his government, Duarte said, were fourfold: pacification, democratization, economic reactivation, and respect for human rights. He promised a foreign policy of "absolute independence" and diplomatic and commercial relations "with all countries of the world." On the possibility of negotiation with the FDR-FMLN he said, "I will not negotiate the mandate of my people in order to receive international assistance."[91]

The absence of concrete proposals may be excused on the ground that few inaugural speeches by any president anywhere deal in specifics. But in the following months Duarte did not follow up his generalizations with any programs to deal with El Salvador's myriad economic, social, and political problems. Three months after his inauguration, *Proceso* wrote "that the PDC has no defined political program for the country."[92]

Portents of Things to Come. Duarte's first months in office revealed patterns of behavior that would come to characterize his presidency and would doom it, in the end, not just to failure but ignominy. His success in the United States and the halls of Congress contrasted with his utter failure in his own legislature during his first year in office. His inability to assert his authority as commander in chief meant that the Armed Forces continued to be the most powerful institution in the country. His perhaps arrogant intransigence toward his political adversaries, especially the PCN, suggested that he had not learned that politics is the art of the possible. And his failure to follow through on a dramatic gesture—the invitation to the FDR-FMLN to meet him in La Palma, which seized the imagination of the world for a week—revealed his ultimate inability to deal with El Salvador's most fundamental problem: its civil war. In short, Duarte failed to deliver on any one of the four goals he set for his administration.

In the next chapter we will examine the Duarte years and the reasons why, between 1984 and 1988, he and his party went from triumph to defeat.

7

Electoral Authoritarianism and the Revolutionary Challenge, 1984–1989

A government under siege by insurgents must persuade the mass of people to freely choose the existing order in preference to those who would destroy it. Such willing support presumes an honest and responsible government, capable of meeting basic human needs.

The government of El Salvador did not manifest those qualities when U.S. involvement in the war began. Unfortunately, neither does it manifest those qualities today.

—Four U.S. Army Colonels at Harvard, 1988[1]

The 1984–1989 period was bracketed by presidential elections, with two elections for the Legislative Assembly and mayors in between. If one accepts the formula that elections equal democracy, then El Salvador returned to a democratic, civilian-led regime for the first time since 1931. The history of this period, however, offers abundant evidence that although elections are a necessary condition for democracy, they are far from sufficient. Democracy also requires that fundamental civil rights and civil liberties be honored and that the military be subordinated to civilian rule. As noted in the last chapter, these conditions did not exist in 1982; the extent to which they developed over the next seven years was due largely to pressure from mass organizations, the FMLN, and democratic-left political parties whose leaders decided to return after middecade and to operate with increasing openness. Nevertheless, the political context continued to be one of a highly militarized society in which civilian rule was subordinated to military will and to the desires of the U.S. Embassy. William Stanley and Frank Smyth have termed this period one of "electoral authoritarianism."[2]

The Duarte years began with hope and ended with frustration for the president and his supporters. In between, the war expanded, the economy continued its precipitous decline, and corruption became endemic. Still, there were positive developments. The sharp decline in human rights abuses after Vice-President Bush's visit in December 1983, coupled with the electoral process itself, opened political space into which innumerable new popular orga-

185

nizations rushed. The churches, both Catholic and Protestant, became increasingly outspoken about the negative effects of the war and seized the initiative in 1988 to push for a negotiated end to the war. Tragically, however, at the end of his tenure the only success a dying Duarte could claim was that he had passed the presidential sash from one civilian to another for the first time in fifty-nine years.

REIGNING OR RULING? THE FIRST YEAR

José Napoleón Duarte took office on a wave of euphoria. He had won a decisive victory over Roberto D'Aubuisson; many who voted for the Christian Democrat did so not out of party or personal loyalty but because they believed his promise to end the war through negotiations. In Washington, D.C., Duarte's election was viewed as proof positive that a democratic "political center" had been institutionalized in El Salvador.

Duarte's Travels. Despite the pledges of his inauguration speech, Duarte's actions during his first months in office suggested his real priorities were to curry international favor and to gain the support of the army. He had journeyed to the United States and other Central American countries, with the exception of Nicaragua, before his inauguration, and he returned to the United States in July. Duarte also traveled to England, France, Belgium, and West Germany—but Italy and Spain refused to receive him, and he was forced to leave Portugal early because of embarrassing errors in protocol.[3] In September he visited three of the Contadora countries, excluding Mexico. The results of these trips were mixed. Politically Duarte received significant support. France announced that it would reopen its embassy, which it had closed in 1980. Duarte's reception in the United States was enthusiastic. Materially, however, with the exception of increased U.S. aid, the trips were not fruitful.

Cultivating the Armed Forces. Duarte appeared to make some modest inroads on the army's traditional prerogatives. Before the election his campaign manager, Julio Adolfo Rey Prendes, had promised that Duarte would not be "an Alfonsín," a reference to Argentina's new president who vowed—and then delivered on his promise—to hold the military accountable for the "dirty war" of the 1970s in which 7,000 to 9,000 civilians were murdered or disappeared.[4] During his first weeks in office, Duarte visited the principal garrisons in the country in a deliberate effort to woo support from suspicious officers. Three weeks after his inauguration, he disbanded the Treasury Police's S-2 intelligence unit, which was widely regarded as the most brutal of the security forces. But he did not touch similar units in the National Guard or National Police or in major garrisons around the country. Next, Duarte dismissed the heads of the three security forces and ordered their successors to report to the person named to the newly created post of vice-minister of defense for public security: the former head of the National Police, Colonel Carlos Reynaldo López Nuila, who had been directly implicated in the death squads by the *Christian Science Monitor* two months earlier.[5]

In September the president named a five-member commission to review procedures for identifying and prosecuting death-squad members, then sent he Legislative Assembly a bill to create an institute for criminal investigation hat would include both an investigative unit and a forensic laboratory. In the ame period, however, he presided over the dedication of a bridge at which he military honor guard was commanded by one Lieutenant Roberto López ibrian, a man directly implicated by court testimony in the murders of Rodolfo Viera and two AIFLD advisers in January 1981. Duarte had recently efused to sign promotion papers for López transmitted by the minister of defense, and López had predicted that Duarte would promote him the next time. But to everyone's surprise, the president cashiered López in November.[6] This ction, however, was exceptional. In general, the time-honored practice of golden exile" continued. Most notable in this regard was the case of Nicolás Carranza, the former vice-minister of defense and Treasury Police director vho had been directly linked to the death squads and the CIA. He was reasigned as military attaché to West Germany, which refused to receive him. He vas then posted to Spain.[7]

The Legislative Assembly. Duarte's efforts in the international arena and vith the army were not matched in the Legislative Assembly, where his party ontrolled only twenty-four of sixty seats. He ignored advice of some Salvaorean supporters to cultivate defeated PCN candidate Guerrero, and except or naming Guerrero as chief justice of the Supreme Court, Duarte virtually ignored him.[8] The result in the Assembly, where the PCN held fourteen votes nd therefore the balance of power, was predictable: The Assembly remained is intractable as before and in late 1984 and early 1985 handed Duarte two major defeats.

The first centered around the 1985 budget, which Duarte presented to he Assembly on September 27. It called for a 40 percent increase for defense US$269.9 million), a 10 percent decrease for education ($24 million), and a 50 percent increase in the deficit. These figures did not include U.S. aid, which according to Ambassador Pickering was $1 million per day by late September.[9] Not until the middle of January did the Assembly approve the budget— nd only then after cutting programs strongly supported by the PDC and increasing budgets of agencies controlled by ARENA, PAISA, and the PCN, uch as the Supreme Court (ARENA) and the Court of Accounts (ARENA-PCN). The Assembly reduced the vice-president's salary, cut the budget for he Casa Presidencial by $2.4 million, and virtually eliminated the $9.16 million agrarian reform budget, leaving a symbolic $4 for the program. Duarte charged that "the thirty-four deputies who approved the budget have no idea of the magnitude of the problem, since the President of the Republic is left vithout salaries, food for the troops ... or the means of paying for water, lights nd telephone."[10] The Assembly also approved the sale of $140 million in onds to finance the budget.

Government and Guerrillas Meet

Duarte's inability to deal with his own legislature was matched only by his success in dealing with the U.S. Congress—but he was best at stunning the world with the unexpected gesture. On October 8 the president made yet an-

other trip, this one to the United Nations. His speech before the General As
sembly was widely expected to be little more than a rerun of his inaugural
But Duarte made the top of the evening news when after having ignored th
FDR-FMLN's May proposal for five months, he called on the FDR and FMLN
to meet him one week later in the north-central Chalatenango town of L
Palma. The next shock came the following day when the insurgents and thei
political allies accepted.

   La Palma. The logistics of the meeting were daunting: how to get tw
warring sides into one place with all the necessary security guarantees an
without anyone getting shot or kidnapped in the process. Through extraordi
nary cooperation from several Latin American governments, the ICRC, th
Catholic Church, and the immediate parties, it all came off with only on
hitch: The failure to provide adequate security arrangements to transpor
FMLN commander Joaquin Villalobos from Morazán to Chalatenango lef
him waiting in Torola, Morazán.[11]

   October 15, 1984, was the only day during many visits between 1979 and
1992 that I did not see a gun in El Salvador. A cease-fire was declared, and
people lined the 100-kilometer route from San Salvador to La Palma, dressed
in their Sunday best, cheering, chanting, "We want peace!" and waving white
flags and white paper doves. La Palma itself was packed. Guerrillas withou
rifles mingled with the people and soldiers in civilian clothes. The FMLN
staged a small demonstration, complete with political speeches, on a corner o
the square by the church. Duarte, accompanied by Vides Casanova, José Fran
cisco "Chachi" Guerrero, and other aides, arrived early and gave an im
promptu press conference. The FDR-FMLN delegates spent the night ir
Miramundo, about eighteen kilometers north of La Palma, and arrived with
an ICRC escort. Boy Scouts kept order around the church.

   The people waited for five hours while the talks went on behind closed
doors. The two sides sat at a table, the government on one side, the rebels or
the other, with Archbishop Rivera Damas at the head. Duarte asked the rebels
to give up the armed struggle, accept an amnesty, and participate in elections
At the end each delegation addressed the crowd, the FDR-FMLN appearing
first. FDR president Guillermo Manuel Ungo and FMLN commander Fermár
Cienfuegos (Eduardo Sancho) spoke; after they left, Duarte addressed the
crowd. All expressed hope that this was a new day for El Salvador, the begin
ning of a process that would lead to peace. In 1993 and 1994 some Salvador
eans and at least one Latin American ambassador would credit Duarte with
planting the seed that produced peace accords in 1991.[12]

   Late in the afternoon the FMLN invited a small group of journalists to
return to Miramundo for a press conference with the commanders. Ungo and
Rubén Zamora left immediately for the airport. The next day Ricardo Stein
commented that it remained to be seen if La Palma was indeed the beginning
of a process or merely an "event." His words were prophetic. An agreement a
La Palma to meet again within a month was delayed briefly over logistical is
sues. Duarte then announced he would not attend because "it is to discuss the
mechanisms, and the President will not go out to discuss who is going to tall

After a five-hour discussion on October 16, 1984, with President Duarte, Minister of Defense Vides Casanova, other government officials, and Archbishop Arturo Rivera Damas, the FDR-FMLN delegation addressed the 5,000 people who had come to La Palma from as far away as San Salvador. From left: Facundo Guardado, Fermán Cienfuegos, Guillermo Manuel Ungo (speaking), Rubén Zamora, Lucio Rivera, and Nidia Díaz. Salvadorean Boy Scout holds one microphone.

first, who is going to talk second." The FDR-FMLN, however, wanted substantive discussions on ways to "humanize" the war, to "incorporate other social sectors" into the talks, to "accelerate the process toward peace," and to arrange a Christmas truce and a more extended cease-fire.[13]

    A Second Meeting. On November 30 the two sides met for twelve hours in Ayagualo, a small town south of the capital. Once again Rivera Damas presided. FDR-FMLN representatives presented a "Comprehensive Proposal for a Negotiated Political Solution and Peace," which addressed the issues listed previously, then suggested a gradual process and indicated their willingness to reformulate their positions in the course of the discussions. The proposal was widely interpreted as "hard-line," and Duarte went on national television the same night the talks ended to reject the proposal and charge that the insurgents were threatening the prospects for peace. It is possible that Duarte felt compelled to respond in this way because opponents of the talks among the oligarchy and army were increasingly critical. But it is also clear that Duarte believed absolutely in the constitutionality of his government and that it was nonnegotiable.[14] It was the last meeting of the two sides for almost three years.

A War Economy

During Duarte's first year in office, the Salvadorean economy passed di
saster and headed for catastrophe. In late 1984 Planning Minister Fide·
Chávez Mena described the situation in these terms:

> The domestic situation is characterized by a slumping economy with falling pro·
> duction, accompanied by high unemployment and a dangerous increase in the
> public deficit. All these phenomena are correlated with the deterioration of the
> purchasing power of the *colon* and minimal domestic capital formation. To a
> large extent this low level of domestic capital formation results from the lack o·
> confidence and insecurity of the private sector given the high degree of destruc
> tion and deterioration of the national productive capacity. ... These economi·
> problems have been aggravated by massive human movements both inside the
> country and abroad; all of this has accentuated the need for foreign aid.[15]

What Chávez Mena did not say was that people in the private sector·
most of whom were members or sympathizers of ARENA, had no more confi·
dence in Duarte as constitutional president than they had accorded him as a
member of the junta four years earlier. As oligarch and Assembly membeı
Armando Calderon Sol remarked on the first anniversary of Duarte's tenure·
"The Duarte government is not capable of finding solutions to the nationa
problematic."[16] Time would prove Calderon Sol correct, although not for the
ideological reasons implicit in his remark.

Deterioration. Meanwhile, the president of the Central Reserve Bank an
nounced that the war was claiming 50 percent of the national budget in 1985, a
figure that would remain constant for the rest of the decade. This enormou·
expenditure meant increased hardship for the average Salvadorean, reduc·
tion in already minimal social services, and a growing national debt. The GDI
did grow 1.5 percent—after a cumulative 23 percent decline between 1979 and
1984. This rise was due primarily to a 16 percent increase in worldwide coffe·
prices (even as coffee production declined 2.4 percent, thanks to *roya* [coffe·
rust]).[17]

Furthermore, consumer prices rose at an annual average rate of 12 per·
cent, and food prices increased 14.1 percent. Wage increases for urban work·
ers in real terms barely restored the loss of purchasing power that resulted
from price hikes during 1984. Agricultural workers' real income fell by oveı
10 percent—bringing the total decline for this group since 1980 to over 30 per·
cent. The *recognized* unemployment reached 30 percent in urban areas and
more in the countryside. The foreign debt increased to $1.986 billion, double
the total 1984 revenues from the export of goods and services. Debt service
reached $262.3 million.[18] The extent of the crisis could be clearly measured ir
education. According to ANDES-21, the teachers' union, between 1980 and
1984 over 4,500 teachers were forced to leave the country; over 1,200 primary
schools were closed, and illiteracy grew to over 65 percent. The Ministry oı
Education indicated that in some provinces illiteracy topped 90 percent.[19]

All of these conditions continued to worsen under President Duarte, a
situation noted in a 1987 report by the U.N. Economic Commission for Latir
America (CEPAL):

After the virtual standstill of the previous year, in 1987 the Salvadorean economy renewed the slow recovery that has characterized its trajectory in the last five years. The real gross internal product expanded almost 3 percent, but its level was 7 percent below that of 1980, which means that, per inhabitant, it was equivalent to the level a quarter of a century ago. The need for additional resources to repair the damages caused by the 1986 earthquake, the prolongation of the armed conflict, and the deterioration of the terms of trade increased the dependency of the country with respect to foreign assistance.[20]

El Paquetazo. The only significant economic program of the Duarte years was announced in January 1986. Called the "Program for Stabilization and Economic Reactivation," the proposal set forth four objectives to be achieved in three years: reduce the balance-of-trade deficit; achieve relative price stabilization; increase production and employment; and improve the distribution of income. The heart of the *paquetazo* (program) was a 100 percent devaluation of the colon, a move the U.S. Embassy had promoted in the expectation of improving the negative balance of payments, stimulating exports, and reducing imports. The program included an increase in the price of gasoline, prohibition of some luxury imports, minor wage increases, and basic-goods price controls that soon failed. Most of the oligarchy denounced the *paquetazo*; only the Salvadorean Foundation for Economic and Social Development (FUSADES)[21] gave it conditional support.

The greatest outrage came from those who had voted for Duarte. Even before the proposals became law, workers took to the streets. An initial demonstration of 8,000 was followed on February 21 by the largest demonstration since 1980. An estimated 60,000 public and private workers, teachers, and cooperatives organized by the newly founded National Unity of Salvadorean Workers (UNTS) defied a ban on demonstrations to demand that Duarte retract the *paquetazo* and resume negotiations with the FDR-FMLN.[22] Duarte did not back down, but neither did his program have the desired effect. The economy continued to deteriorate.

REAPPEARANCE OF THE MASSES

When the United States sponsored elections in 1982, it implicitly assumed that parties would organize and nominate candidates who would campaign and that voters would turn out, then go home and passively wait for the next election. All this happened in 1982 and 1984 (and after) except that the people did not stay home. The electoral process had the unanticipated and, for the government, military, oligarchy, and U.S. Embassy, undesired effect of opening political space that had been closed by the repression between 1980 and 1982. Even in this period progressive union militants had met clandestinely one-on-one with their members—a method of union organizing known as "ant work."[23] By 1983 a variety of labor unions and other grassroots organizations began to make their presence known through strikes, street demonstrations, and leafleting. By 1988 it seemed that every sector of Salvadorean society was organized: market vendors, those displaced by the war and the 1986 earthquake, shantytown residents, families of the disappeared and political prisoners, students, teachers, women, public service employees, cooperatives, and, for the first time in the history of El Salvador, its indigenous peoples.

Most frustrating for the government and embassy was that the majority of these groups were beyond their control. Hence considerable effort was expended trying to link many of them to the FMLN. There is little question that direct links existed between some organizations and the rebels. There is also little question that many organizations developed out of a felt need to demand redress of grievances. Whatever their relationship with the FMLN, there was a convergence of interests; often the demands were for the same things: decent wages, better working conditions, housing, health care, education, an end to inflation, and peace.

The mass movement that began to reemerge in 1983 was headed by a new generation of leaders and was different in character from the mass movement of the 1970s. The latter, as we have seen, was divided among five umbrella organizations, each of which included its own associations of students, teachers, peasants, and workers. Between their ideological sectarianism and revolutionary rhetoric, their concrete socioeconomic and political demands were often lost. After 1984, however, the demands were stated clearly, in nonideological terms that everyone could understand. The new leaders did not have twenty or ten years to learn; they "grew up" in compressed time, entering the labor force and rising to the top in less than five years. Yet the quality of the leadership was as high as it had been at the end of the 1970s. The story of this period is convoluted and often confusing, primarily because AIFLD and the embassy attempted, with limited success, to divide and conquer the new mass movement. It is, however, the paramount political story of the Duarte years.

In a worsening economy—industrial wages frozen at less than $3 per day, agricultural wages half that, inflation almost 100 percent, many companies falling in arrears on salaries or benefits or both, the government refusing to enforce the law on benefits, and unions powerless to respond—discontent began to grow, even in the progovernment UPD. A new center-left coalition of unions, the Unitary Trade Union and Guild Movement of El Salvador (MUSYGES) appeared, and disenchanted UPD union leaders responded to its overtures. Then, in September 1983, MUSYGES leader Santiago Hernández was captured. Thirteen days later his mutilated body appeared, an obvious warning to UPD leaders who had been flirting with the coalition. MUSYGES disbanded in November 1984, the victim of repression and sectarian division caused by the suicide of Cayetano Carpio, but it contributed greatly to the opening of political space for the organizations that would follow.[24]

As the 1984 presidential campaign approached, the UPD grew more independent. Its price for supporting José Napoleón Duarte was a "social" pact in which the PDC pledged itself in writing to guarantee labor union rights, expand and accelerate the agrarian reform process, and negotiate an end to the war. It is generally agreed that the thousands of votes the UPD delivered in the countryside provided Duarte his margin of victory. But once in office, Duarte became preoccupied with appeasing the private sector and keeping the United States happy, which meant postponing reforms and making the war his first priority. In August UCS leaders publicly criticized Duarte for failing to pursue peace talks and called for an end to U.S. military aid. AIFLD demanded that the UCS leave the UPD and join another federation. AIFLD also told the UCS and other unions not to push "Duarte to the left"—that is, to fulfill the commitments of the pact. AIFLD's brass-knuckle tactics ultimately split the UPD and caused great bitterness toward the AFL-CIO.

Public Employees Find Their Voice. As economic conditions deteriorated for workers, public employees, who historically had been progovernment or nonpolitical, began organizing anew. A postal employees' strike bracketed Duarte's inauguration, and other public-sector unions, old and new, joined to coordinate solidarity actions. This thrust led to the creation in early 1985 of the State and Municipal Workers Coordinating Council (CCTEM). This was a significant step—first, because CCTEM set forth a political position critical of the government and in favor of negotiations with the FMLN and, second, because it signaled a new organizing strategy for labor. Rather than traditional federations and political groupings (as in the 1970s), the new labor alignments, all center-left, were by public, agrarian, and industrial sectors. Thus farm workers and cooperatives regrouped in the Salvadorean Agricultural Workers Union (SITAS) and the Cooperative Associations of El Salvador (COACES), respectively. In November 1984 twenty-one of the strongest industrial unions came together in the Workers Solidarity Coordinating Committee (CST).

On May Day 1985, the CST joined with several centrist unions for a march in the capital. As the unions became more militant, the government's response changed from accommodation to repression. Between March and November 1985 there were sixty-three strikes, fifty-three among public-sector unions involving at least forty-six organizations and 60,000 workers.[25] Nothing caused more outrage than the government's response to social security health workers (STISSS) who occupied twenty clinics and five hospitals in early May; on June 2 Duarte authorized several hundred military police and National Guardsmen, many of whom were from a U.S.-trained SWAT team, to attack the occupied buildings. Medical and administrative personnel were beaten and detained; patients were thrown from their beds; and two top union officials were arrested. Other unions immediately mobilized in support of STISSS, and rather than breaking the union, the military action strengthened it. The UPD "repudiated and condemn[ed] the repressive actions," said there was "no legal excuse that could erase the offense," and told the Christian Democrats to decide whether they wanted "a classist party" or to "open a process of change for popular participation necessary to democracy and peace." During the fall 25,000 workers from several government ministries and agencies (telecommunications, treasury, post office, tourism, public works, agriculture) struck to protest the arrests of union leaders on subversion charges and to demand increased wages and nullification of Decree 162, which gave the government authority to move public employees from one ministry to another in an effort to control union activity.[26]

Progressive Unions Unite. On February 8, 1986, leaders of STISSS, the UPD, and COACES and several hundred more union officials gathered in front of the Legislative Assembly building to announce the founding of the

A large demonstration in San Salvador, July 1988, organized by the UNTS. The banner in front condemns both the PDC and ARENA as equally responsible for the continuing war and the renewed increase in death-squad murders.

National Unity of Salvadorean Workers (UNTS). Composed of about 100 unions that claimed to represent 350,000 workers, the UNTS issued a broad critique of the government's austerity program and the role of the United States and the International Monetary Fund (IMF), in it; set forth a comprehensive program of social and economic development; and demanded that the government resume peace negotiations with the FMLN.[27] Days later the UNTS held the largest demonstration since 1980. Within six months the UNTS was the most powerful center of political opposition to the government.

Reaction. AIFLD's reaction was predictable. It charged "Marxist-Leninist" subversion of the UPD and accused its leaders of being either "ideologically friendly to the guerrillas" or "interested primarily in taking money from both sides."[28] UPD leaders responded that AIFLD was, essentially, issuing their death warrants. The UNTS called for AIFLD's expulsion from the country. Instead, AIFLD, with government and PDC collusion, organized the National Union of Workers and Peasants (UNOC) one month later. UNOC incorporated unions affiliated with the Christian Democrats and the Democratic Workers Central (CTD), which had been created by AIFLD at the end of 1984. AIFLD used its funding leverage to force the isolation or removal of union leaders who became critical of the government. UNOC mustered 40,000 people in support of the government in mid-March, but it was widely reported that *campesinos* were bused or trucked to the capital without being told why and that municipal employees were told to appear or be fired. On May Day the UNTS brought out another 80,000, but UNOC was conspicuous by its absence. Still, *Proceso* had already noted that

> in spite of their apparent antagonisms ... both organizations are in favor of dialogue as the only way to bring peace; both propose a deepening of the reforms, and they agree that Phase II of the agrarian reform should be implemented immediately. ... The differences between UNTS and UNOC lie more in their sponsors' intentions: while the UNTS is the response of the organized people to the demonstrated incapacity of the PDC to fulfill its promises, UNOC is the response of the PDC to the people's demands, demands that at this moment it does not appear capable of satisfying.[29]

These words anticipated the end result: By mid-1988 the UNTS and UNOC were talking; in August 1989, after ARENA won the presidency, UNOC threw its lot with the UNTS.

In the meantime, with help from AIFLD, UNOC formed several new unions to replace or compete with antigovernment unions. In general, their gains were minimal, but in some key areas the parallel unions took over; these included peasant cooperative organizations, most municipal workers in the capital, a good part of the construction industry, and several individual firms in textile and candy making. Efforts to derail labor opposition went well beyond organizing and funding alternatives; when asked in a 1988 interview about reports that the U.S. Embassy had been involved in efforts to split the UNTS, an embassy official laughed and said, "Of course!"

Despite efforts to buy off labor leaders (some of which succeeded), to split the increasingly militant labor movement, and finally by 1988 to proclaim the decline if not demise of the UNTS, labor and other mass organizations continued to grow and to press their demands before the government. The embassy acknowledged the existence of 150 active unions with 40,000 members, or 20 percent of the work force.[30] The UNTS alone claimed 467 affiliated organizations, not all of which were unions.

ELECTORAL SIDESHOW, 1985

Duarte's difficulties with the Legislative Assembly over the budget paled in comparison with the fiasco of the electoral law. The bill drafted by the CCE in preparation for the 1985 Legislative Assembly and mayoral elections was modified in two significant ways by the Assembly in early December. First, the deputies prohibited close relatives of the president from running for mayor anywhere in the country. This immediately barred Duarte's son, Alejandro, from running for reelection as mayor of San Salvador. Second, parties were allowed to form a coalition and run the same candidate for an office but to maintain their respective symbols on the ballot. Because voters mark the party's symbol (a means of coping with a largely illiterate populace), one candidate could, in effect, be listed two or more times. The threat to the Christian Democrats was that the right-wing parties would join together and maintain control of the Assembly and most of the city halls. Duarte vetoed these parts of the law, whereupon his Assembly opponents appealed to the Supreme Court and threatened to impeach him, charging that he had violated the constitution. On February 7, 1985, the court overruled Duarte but found that he had not intentionally violated the law.

The Campaign. If excitement had characterized the 1984 elections, malaise characterized those of 1985. During a visit to El Salvador a week before the vote, there was more talk about large COACES demonstrations in previous weeks and the growth of the popular organizations than about the campaign. There were several reasons for this change of mood. First, it was the third election in as many years. Second, after the euphoria of La Palma, Duarte did not demonstrate any commitment to follow through on his grand gesture, thus producing frustration among many citizens. Third, Duarte's less than adroit handling of his legislative battles contributed to a decline in his popularity. Six weeks before the election, virtually no one, friend or foe, gave the Christian Democrats any chance of winning a majority in the Assembly. Under the new electoral law, ARENA and the PCN formed a coalition that almost everyone assumed was unbeatable.

In addition, the United States did a political about-face. Whereas it had funneled an estimated $2 million via the CIA to the PDC in 1984, Ambassador Thomas Pickering took the public position that his government, including the CIA, was "not supporting or opposing any party in any way" in 1985.[31] Other reports circulated that the embassy preferred an ARENA-PCN victory because it feared what the right might do without power. The embassy denied the charge.[32]

Electoral Surprise. Everyone, including the Christian Democrats, was stunned when they swept the elections, winning 52 percent of the vote, a clear majority of 33 seats in the Legislative Assembly, and 153 of 262 mayoralties. The reasons for the upset were multiple. First, some people felt that the PDC had not done anything for them economically, but one shopkeeper noted that "now they leave us in peace and for me that's a change. Before they used to take people away in the middle of the night." Second, the reduction in fear also meant that many people, especially in the countryside, did not feel compelled to vote, whereas before they had voted for ARENA or the PCN under some sense of duress or because D'Aubuisson's simplistic solutions appealed to them. Many of these people, especially in conflictive zones, voted for the PDC in 1985. Third, the PDC held on to its urban base. Fourth, ARENA and the PCN no longer had control of government ministries and the resources attached to them. Fifth, the rightist coalition tried to turn the election into a referendum on Duarte, to whom D'Aubuisson regularly referred as the "green stain." In February, however, ARENA was embarrassed when one of D'Aubuisson's cronies was arrested in Texas with eight suitcases filled with $6 million in cash, an event that the Christian Democrats gleefully publicized with full-page *campos pagados* in local newspapers.[33]

The Army Steps In. The Armed Forces maintained a relatively low profile during the campaign and on election day. The FMLN had carried out widespread attacks and sabotage in the weeks prior to the election but staged few attacks on election day and none on polling places. As ballot boxes began arriving in San Salvador, however, the ARENA-PCN coalition accused the PDC and army of collusion to perpetrate an electoral fraud. Under the electoral code, the vote count was stopped pending a ruling from the CCE. Three days after the election and one day after ARENA and the PCN formally petitioned to annul the elections, Minister of Defense Vides Casanova and fifteen high-ranking officers went on television and threw their support behind the PDC. "This is not the time to toy with the will of the people as expressed at the polls," Vides said. "We cannot permit elections to be repeated on the whim of each party, as though it was a game of cards." Within hours a PCN official issued a communiqué withdrawing the petition to annul the elections. That night the CCE unanimously voted to declare the petition "out of order."[34]

Fallout. On the surface the significance of the High Command's action was twofold. It put the army squarely behind a civilian government headed by a man the same army had prevented from taking office thirteen years earlier. It also represented a clear and open break with the extreme right. On another level, however, it confirmed that the army remained the center of power in the country. The electoral law provided a forty-eight-hour period following poll closings in which to receive petitions challenging the election; called for a three-day period to receive evidence; and mandated a decision no more than twenty-four hours later. The High Command preempted these procedures by calling its press conference a day after the petition was submitted. The CCE circumvented the electoral law because there was no provision authorizing it to declare a petition "out of order."[35]

There was other fallout from the election: internal shakeups in ARENA and the PCN. A small faction with a few deputies split off from ARENA and formed the Liberation Party. More significant, more moderate Areneros decided it was time for "Major Blowtorch" to take a backseat. In September an ARENA general assembly changed itself to the National Executive Council, named D'Aubuisson its "president for life," and elected as president a relative newcomer to the party, a young, wealthy, U.S.-educated coffee grower named Alfredo Cristiani. The PCN dismissed three members of its executive committee, one of whom had issued the (unauthorized) communiqué withdrawing the party from the electoral challenge.

THE WAR GOES ON

The Rebels Adapt. By 1985 the war settled into a new pattern. The FMLN developed a new tactic and a new strategy. The tactic, which analyst Ricardo Stein named the "mercury ball effect," was the ability to concentrate a large number of platoons (of ten to twenty combatants) in a short period, carry out a major assault, then disperse before army reinforcements could arrive. Using this tactic, the FMLN carried out a number of effective lightning strikes against such targets as the Cerron Grande hydroelectric project, the supposedly impenetrable El Paraiso garrison (three times), the army's national training center in La Unión, and the Third Brigade in San Miguel.

The new strategy was to turn every guerrilla into a political officer who could talk with the people about the FMLN and its policies (a task that previously had been the responsibility of designated senior FMLN officers) and to send the guerrillas out in small self-sufficient units across the countryside. In this way the rebels expanded into all fourteen provinces, mounting regular operations in thirteen of them (Ahuachapán in the west being the exception). The FMLN was able to do this even as its numbers were reduced—from about 12,000 to 6,000 combatants—between 1983 and 1987. These units were almost untouchable by the army because their intelligence networks in the countryside, which were always far better than the army's, together with their vastly improved radio communications, warned them when troops were moving into the area.

Thus, between 1985 and 1988 the FMLN adopted what Stein called "yoga warfare"; many U.S. analysts and others announced the demise of the FMLN because it was no longer making its presence known in a dramatic way. But the activities described here continued, and the rebels began to move back in force into the cities, especially after the 1986 earthquake. In a CBS "West 57th Street" program in spring 1989, reporters not only accompanied guerrillas on the slopes of the San Salvador volcano, which towers over the capital, but also met with clandestine urban commandos in San Salvador just blocks from the old U.S. Embassy. More solid evidence of this presence was a series of attacks, some in broad daylight, on the National Guard headquarters, the High Command, and other significant military targets. The FMLN also received deservedly bad press for carrying out some attacks against civilian locales or in areas and at a time when innocent civilians were endangered—and in some cases injured or killed.

The Army Tries Again. The Armed Forces responded to these developments with some new strategies and tactics of their own. First, there was an effort to resurrect the National Reconstruction Plan that had failed so abysmally in 1983. The new United to Reconstruct Plan (UPR) had the advantage of being more Salvadorean and less U.S. in design than the original. But it had the same objectives—and the same problems. The army, for all its expansion (to 56,000) by 1987, was still not big enough to fight the guerrillas and implement a program of social, economic, and psychological operations at the same time. This was complicated by the earthquake on October 10, 1986, which forced the Armed Forces to divert personnel to help with the disaster.

The army began "Operation Phoenix" in the Guazapa area in January 1986. A combination of elite forces, continual operations, and massive air bombardment sought to clear the zone of guerrillas and *masas* (FMLN supporters). Thousands of civilians fled, and the FMLN was forced to scale back operations. *Proceso* described the offensive as "perhaps the [army's] greatest success in the war," but that success was limited. One operation did not accomplish the objective; by 1990 there had been at least thirteen such operations; *masas* still lived in settlements on the skirts of the volcano; and, most significant, the FMLN was still there, though in reduced numbers. The guerrillas transformed the mountain into a strategic, logistical, and communications center for the rest of the country and used it as a base from which to establish permanent operations twenty-five kilometers to the south. The perspective of the army was that it instituted "a new policy of rescuing the *masas*, who were controlled by the guerrillas in order to obtain supplies, information, agricultural tasks and to fortify the land. ... The guerrilla screams that it is a failure," said the commander of the First Brigade in San Salvador, Colonel Leopoldo Antonio Hernández, "but it isn't ... because we have conveyed great confidence to the people. ... We have also developed civic action programs providing medical attention, deliveries of food and clothing, and recreational games for children (such as clown shows and piñata parties). And at night ... we show films which are rented in San Salvador."[36]

Dynamic Equilibrium. In sum, by the mid-1980s, the Armed Forces and the FMLN found themselves in a constantly changing situation with reactions and responses to new strategies and tactics on both sides—a dynamic equilibrium, rather than a stalemate as most analysts asserted. Neither side could defeat the other, and neither side could win. Regardless of label, the United States was in a bind, a status that drew this comment from Colonel Lyman C. Duryea, the defense attaché between 1983 and 1985: "So we've nearly arrived at a point [in 1986] where additional infusions of training, material, and various other elements of security assistance won't move us toward the ultimate goal of defeating the insurgency but will merely reinforce the stalemate. ... The guerrillas have had to change the way they operate. ... But they can continue in that mode literally forever, and we have not yet developed a strategy nor a policy with a proper objective."[37]

Two years later the departing head of Salvadorean army intelligence, Colonel Juan Orlando Zepeda, concurred: "To what degree does the Salvadorean subversion have sufficient quantitative and qualitative forces to launch a general offensive? We cannot determine this with precision. ... The current indicators lead us to believe that this conflict under the present political, economic, and social conditions is far from being resolved."[38]

THE NEW OCTOPUS

In Guatemala in the 1940s, the United Fruit Company came to be known as "El Pulpo," the "octopus," because its tentacles reached into every corner of society. During the 1980s the Salvadorean armed forces began to resemble an octopus, enriching itself in a variety of ways and using its mushrooming wealth to expand its "civilian" wing, which had originally been created in 1974 with the founding of the Armed Forces Mutual Savings Bank (CAMFA) under the guidance of Alvaro Magña.[39] CAMFA functioned as a pension and life insurance fund and, after the 1979 coup, changed its name to IPSFA, the Armed Forces Institute of Social Foresight. The real change, however, came when the United States began pouring millions of dollars in military assistance into El Salvador and began quintupling the size of the army between 1980 and 1987.

IPSFA is only one of several military institutions whose acronyms all end in "FA" and whose reach into civilian society expanded with the war. The others include COPREFA, the press and propaganda office; CEFAFA, a chain of drugstores; COOPFA, the supermarket and department store; CITFA, the electronics center; FUDEFA, the mortuary; and CERPROFA, the rehabilitation and job placement center for disabled veterans.

IPSFA made plans to open a bank in the late 1980s, as many other Latin American militaries have done, and was so sure that the Assembly would pass the necessary legislation after the 1989 presidential election that it built a glass-plated tower, complete with helicopter pad on top, to house the enterprise. IPSFA, however, failed to anticipate the opposition of the oligarchy, which had lost its banks in the 1980 nationalization and was looking to denationalize the banks as soon as possible. The last thing the former bankers wanted was competition from one of the wealthiest institutions in El Salvador. Hence, IPSFA's bank never opened, in the end a casualty of the peace accords.

IPSFA's Wealth. Where did all the money come from? As the army began to expand in 1980, IPSFA broadened its pool of contributors to include all new recruits and created a two-tier system of obligatory contributions with career personnel, military and civilian, contributing 3 percent more than conscripts. But the real money came from conscripts, who contributed 7.5 percent of their $70 per month salary, or $5.40, to the IPSFA fund, and from the government, which matched all contributions. By 1988 the monthly total from these three sources was over $2 million per month.

The IPSFA system has elitist features. A soldier doing a two-year hitch contributes $130 to IPSFA, but unless he dies or is disabled and needs rehabilitation, neither his family nor he, respectively, will ever receive any benefit from that money. Benefits are reaped by a small minority, most of whom are officers, for only they and reenlistees can apply for personal and housing loans and only they will receive a pension.

From its income, IPSFA pays pensions and veterans' rehabilitation and makes loans. The net balance ($40,000 per month in the late 1980s) is placed in banks to earn interest or used as working capital to service IPSFA's investments, including former oligarchy *fincas,* real estate in the capital, new residential subdivisions for military families, and a Pacific coast resort.

Between 1979 and 1989, IPSFA's reserves grew from $2.5 million (before the devaluation) to $100 million. As a Salvadorean businessman observed in 1989, "They're the biggest source of liquid capital in the country. They've got so much money they don't know where to put it." The windfall that came from 20,000 new recruits each year reduced the incentive to encourage reenlistments. As a result, the vast majority of soldiers in the field had minimal training and little field experience—a fact that the FMLN, most of whose ranks were veterans, exploited with some success.

The Corrupt Octopus. William Walker served twice in El Salvador, first in the late 1970s as political officer and then from 1988 to 1992 as ambassador. In a 1989 interview, he said that when he first left in 1977, "corruption was so prevalent, it was just about inconceivable that an officer would rise to a senior level without being corrupt."[40] In the early 1980s U.S. advisers hoped to dilute the possibilities for corruption and break up cliques by expanding the army and officer corps. Instead, opportunities for corruption expanded with the army, and for the first time lower-ranking officers had opportunities to enrich themselves. In addition to the kinds of corruption described in Chapter 2, patronage and graft provided endless sources of enrichment. The system began at the brigade level, where annual recruit quotas were divided among the various commanders. By maintaining a list of *plazas ficticias* (ghost soldiers) on the roster, a brigade commander could draw their salaries into his slush fund. According to one major, "Just about every brigade lists at least one fifty-man company that isn't there," each of which brings $100 per month—or $60,000 per year. Real recruits, many of whom had been forcibly inducted, were often subjected to mandatory deductions from their pay for food, boot polish, toothpaste, uniform accessories, even soccer uniforms and barracks television. Senior officers rented out soldiers for guard duty on coffee *fincas* and factories for $200–$300 per month. The soldiers, of course, never saw a cent of this. "It's the same mistake we made in Vietnam. Military aid is easy; all you have to do is give the bucks, and all they have to do is take them. But we got ourselves into a position where we have no leverage, so we have been acquiescing for years in corruption and methods of operations we don't believe in, all because of the *Realpolitik* of winning the war."[41]

PANDEMIC CORRUPTION

The absence of leverage extended to the civilian sector as well as the military. The Christian Democrats, who had criticized a succession of military governments for twenty-five years for larceny, graft, and kickbacks, wasted no time demonstrating that civilians, given the opportunities, could steal just as much. President Duarte himself was never implicated in any of the corruption that pervaded his administration, but he denied that it was happening and did nothing to control or stop it. Other Christian Democrats acknowledged it: "Yes, it's true there is corruption," one party member said. "The bureaucracy and members of the party are taking advantage of their position."[42] The U.S. government was well aware by 1987 that corruption was rampant but did little about it. There were some reports that the ambassador, Edwin Corr, was collecting evidence to present to Duarte; meanwhile a State Department official told the *Wall Street Journal* that "We've never read them the riot act … the same way we did on human rights with the military. … Many of them see [corruption] as the price the gringos will have to pay for their larger strategic objectives being met."[43]

How large a price "the gringos" paid will never be known, but it easily ran into the millions of dollars. Corruption was as wide as it was deep; the documented cases touched the Casa Presidencial, government ministries, and agencies across the country. There were reports that government jobs were given only to those with letters of recommendation from PDC officials; that scarce teaching positions went only to party members; and that displaced persons were threatened with a cutoff of benefits, including U.S.-funded food aid, if they did not participate in progovernment demonstrations. The more egregious cases, however, included the following:[44]

- Guillermo Antonio Guevara Lacayo, president of the Legislative Assembly, who abused his privilege of importing cars without paying high import taxes. Other Christian Democrats confirmed that Guevara did this.
- The minister of education, who was accused by the teachers' union (ANDES-21) of using ministry materials and employees on "company time" in the construction of an addition to his home. Some of the workers admitted to both on a local television newscast.
- Ricardo J. López, the treasury minister, who bypassed the bidding process and gave contracts for ministry equipment to his own firm, which went from struggling company to millionaire status between 1984 and 1987. The ministry's union gathered evidence and published it in a *campo pagado*.
- Fedeccredito, a credit agency that was put in charge of a jobs program in 1985 for the half million people displaced by the war. Funded by the United States, it soon became a deep well of patronage for PDC members or displaced persons who were forced to join the party before being hired. In several provinces, Fedeccredito projects stalled or were abandoned after administrators overran their budgets by padding payrolls, authorizing payment for nonexistent materials, and/ or paying local PDC militants for work they did not do.
- The Regulatory Institute for Basic Goods (IRA), a government-run, AID-supported distribution network for subsidized basic foods that was exposed by its union, ASTIRA. ASTIRA acquired official documents revealing large illegal purchases of powdered milk by IRA officials who sold them to middlemen, who in turn sold them on the black market at illegally inflated prices.[45] The diversion was so great that in the summer of 1987, there was a shortage of dry milk in the markets. Journalist Sandra Smith found the milk and other products in the central market in San Salvador at markups of 20 to 60 percent.
- Diversion of aid sent in response to the massive earthquake (7.5 on the Richter scale) that hit San Salvador on October 10, 1986, causing 1,500 deaths, 10,000 injured, 200,000 destitute, and an estimated $2 billion in damage. Aid poured in from thirty-one countries. According to U.S. officials, however, large quantities of canvas and corrugated zinc roofing flown to El Salvador on C-5A transports were unaccounted for; heavy equipment vanished from warehouses; and a significant portion of $20 million given to the nationalized banks for housing-reconstruction loans to earthquake victims ended up in the hands of PDC members, bank employees, and favored customers. When the United States complained, the banks promised to return the funds to AID. These cases received little attention in the international press and only marginally more in the local media. ARENA, however, used the issue to pummel the Christian Democrats during the 1988 campaign, with great success.

JUSTICE FOR NONE

Given the history of military rule and the absence of anything resembling a Uniform Code of Military Justice, the weakness of civilian institutions, and no tradition of due process, the failure of the Salvadorean judiciary to prosecute the perpetrators and beneficiaries of the rampant corruption just described—not to mention the gross violations of human rights during the 970s and 1980s—should come as no surprise. At a luncheon for Secretary of State George Shultz hosted by provisional president Alvaro Magña in January 984, Shultz was blunt: "Death squads and terror," he said, "have no place in a democracy. ... The armed forces must act with discipline in defense of the Constitution. And the judicial system must prove its capacity to cope with the errorist acts of extremists of the right or left."[46]

Reforming the Unreformable

Toward this end, AID funded a Salvadorean government project to reform the judicial system after the 1984 election. Four areas of reform were targeted, all of them under the direction of the Commission on Investigations:

- The Legal Revisory Commission, which was intended to evaluate the system and the existing code of laws, then draft appropriate reform legislation. Most of the commission's work, however, focused on theoretical studies of the judiciary, an exercise with few immediate applications that could improve the human rights situation. Only one draft law passed the Assembly.
- Training of judges and court personnel and improvement of other technical support. At best, this reform could have improved the court's efficiency, but as late as 1990, testimony being taken in connection with the murder of six Jesuits in November 1989 was recorded by hand; there were no stenographs.
- The Special Investigative Unit (SIU), which was staffed by military detectives theoretically working under civilians in the Commission on Investigations. The SIU had a mandate to tackle the most sensitive human rights cases, including the assassination of Archbishop Romero and the 1983 massacre of indigenous peasants at Las Hojas, Sonsonate. In reality, it focused on common crimes and a few corruption cases. Despite $3.5 million in U.S. aid, by 1991 there was no significant change in the ability of the Salvadorean judiciary to investigate and prosecute serious violations by the Armed Forces.
- The Judicial Protection Unit, which was intended to protect participants, from judges to jurors to witnesses, in sensitive cases. After being used in a few cases, it was disbanded.

In 1987 the New York–based Lawyers Committee for Human Rights concluded that "without the political will to ensure the fundamental integrity of the justice system of El Salvador, no amount of technical aid, training, revision of the laws, or special units will inspire confidence in that system."[47] A Salvadorean human rights worker observed: "What they have done i strengthen *injustice*. The military, which should be conducting investigations is actually interfering with judicial power. For the first time, an institution ha been created that unifies civilians and the military to violate human rights. ... The Minister of Justice has become a mouthpiece for military men."[48]

Some jurists were equally candid; with cases involving ordinary people one judge said, the law can be applied as needed. "In cases involving lower ranking soldiers acting on their own," he continued, "you are subjected to cer tain pressures, but not serious problems. But in cases involving high-ranking officers or low-ranking officers acting on orders of a higher authority, practi cally speaking you can't do anything."[49] Three of the most notorious early cases serve to illustrate the problems. They are the Romero case, the churchwomen, and the Las Hojas massacre.

The Romero Case. Despite the fact that Roberto D'Aubuisson and several close associates were soon implicated in Archbishop Romero's death, the courts made no progress in resolving the case. After the Christian Democrat-controlled Assembly appointed Roberto Giron Flores attorney general in June 1987, things began to move. Then ARENA recaptured control of the Assembly in March 1988. Giron Flores issued an extradition request for Miami exile and D'Aubuisson cohort Captain Alvaro Saravia; government investigations had implicated him in the assassination. Days later, on December 23, 1988, the Assembly fired Giron for "incompetence," and "misconduct"; the latter charge included improper filing of the extradition request. In Miami, Saravia, who had been picked up by U.S. authorities after the extradition request was issued, was released on $10,000 bail. Giron, who appealed his dismissal to the Supreme Court, told the *Washington Post* that he had been "fired for a simple and fundamental reason—because the Romero case was about to be resolved. The Romero case is now closed, and I was fired so the case could be closed." The Assembly promptly filled the post with Roberto García Alvarado, a lawyer who had no demonstrable commitment to human rights.[50]

The Nuns and the Guard. The bodies of four U.S. churchwomen were dug up near Zacatecoluca, La Paz, in early December 1980. Within days "the identities of the killers were known to officials of the Salvadorean National Guard. Nonetheless, the official response to this information ranged from indifference to active cover-up." An internal investigation went nowhere. The head of a public investigation, Colonel Roberto Monterrosa, told an official U.S. investigator, Judge Harold Tyler, that he steered clear of implicating any officers because to do so "would cause serious consequences for the armed forces from a political point of view."[51] It would be more than a year before five guardsmen were arrested and charged and another three years before they were tried. In the interim, U.S. officials investigated the case, interviewed witnesses, prepared evidence, and at trial helped present the cases that resulted in conviction and maximum sentences of thirty years.[52]

Soon after First Penal Judge of Zacatecoluca Consuelo Salazar de Revelo denied amnesty to the five guardsmen in January 1988, she began receiving death threats. The U.S. Embassy supplied her with bodyguards for two months. Six months later the guardsmen again applied for amnesty, arguing that "the assassinated nuns belonged to a leftist religious order which participated in terrorist plans."[53] They were denied.

Las Hojas. An agricultural cooperative administered by the National Association of Indigenous Salvadoreans (ANIS), Las Hojas was engaged in a dispute with a large *hacendado* whose land adjoined it and who had tried and failed to gain right of way across the cooperative. On February 22, 1983, 200 soldiers from the Sonsonate garrison, guided by masked members of the local civil defense unit, entered the cooperative and murdered seventy-four men, women, and children. When Duarte became president, he put Las Hojas on a list of five critical human rights cases.

Eyewitnesses and other evidence implicated Captain Carlos Alfonso Figueroa Morales, Colonel Elmer González Araujo, and Major Oscar Alberto León Linares, all from the garrison. Figueroa was charged with responsibility by the governmental human rights commission but was cleared of wrongdoing by military superiors and later placed in charge of intelligence in Sonsonate. Araujo was subsequently promoted to director of the army's procurement office; in 1986 he was identified as one of several high-ranking officers to share almost $400,000 in bribes from a U.S. defense contractor. The U.S. Embassy concluded from its own investigation that these officers were indeed involved in the massacre and withdrew its military advisers from Sonsonate.

In July 1988 a lower court granted amnesty to the three officers and eleven other soldiers implicated in the crime; the decision was upheld by the Supreme Court. "They gave those bastards amnesty!" fumed one U.S. official, who went on to describe the court's decision as "a political balancing act": Some FMLN political prisoners had been released, so the Las Hojas culprits were granted amnesty.[54]

All in the Family. The case that, until its time, revealed just how untouchable military officers were involved a kidnapping ring headed by the National Police chief of detectives and head of the intelligence department, Lieutenant Colonel Aristides Márquez. One of his right-hand men was detective Edgar Pérez Linares, who the CIA identified as the link between CAIN and Hector Antonio Regalado.[55] Between 1983 and 1986 at least five wealthy Salvadoreans were kidnapped and held for ransom. Widespread assumptions that the FMLN was behind them were wrong. Running the kidnapping ring were Pérez Linares and three former guerrillas who had been captured in 1980 and tortured so badly that they became right-wing fanatics and his private death squad, known as the Secret Anticommunist Army (ESA); they were assisted by other "free-lancers."

By March 1986 Salvadorean investigators, with the help of Venezuelan intelligence agents and the FBI, broke the ring, which by then had raised approximately $4 million for "profit-hungry senior military officers." Tom Gibb and Douglas Farah, two longtime journalists in El Salvador who spent four months working on a story about the resurgence of the death squads, of which the kidnapping ring turned out to be an unexpected part, wrote that "The investigation was requested by the kidnap victims because they realized almost from the beginning that their abductors were getting collaboration from high-

level military officers. The victims, many of whom had in the past given fund
ing and support to D'Aubuisson and ARENA, recognized the voices of thei
kidnappers." They became "the victims of a monster they themselves hac
helped create."[56]

Even with all the evidence, the case fell apart. Just before arrests were to
be made, three major suspects, one a colonel, another D'Aubisson's forme
private secretary, were warned and fled the country. The most powerful colo
nel implicated, Roberto Mauricio Staben, who had long been connected to the
death squads, was arrested but refused to testify or take lie-detector tests. A
group of senior officers demanded that President Duarte release him; despite
three sworn statements implicating Staben, within weeks all charges were
dropped and he was returned to his prestigious command.

The other three were captured. Pérez Linares was arrested in Guate
mala, returned to El Salvador, and died in handcuffs "while attempting to es
cape" from a speeding van on the Pan American Highway. Said one senio
military investigator, "He had to die. There is no way that group could have
let someone as knowledgeable as [him] live." The second suspect was killed ir
a shoot-out; the third "committed suicide" by hanging himself with his socks
in his cell at the National Police headquarters.[57]

The FMLN and Human Rights

Over the years the FMLN committed many human rights violations
still, international human rights agencies consistently found that in both mag
nitude and type, the rebels' violations represented a fraction of the total.[58] Ir
my research during 1991 among Salvadorean refugees in Belize, an analysis o
1,500 registered refugee files revealed that 90 percent left El Salvador because
of a "well-founded fear by persecution" of the army or security forces, not by
the guerrillas.[59]

In the 1970s the revolutionary organizations were most notorious for
kidnapping wealthy Salvadoreans and foreign businessmen. As mass strug
gle moved to armed stuggle and the rebels began to expand in the country
side, the violations increased in kind though remained limited in numbers
During the 1980s these violations included the following:

1. Summary executions, called *ajustacimientos*, of persons identified
    as being *orejas,* or army collaborators
2. Maltreatment or murder of captured soldiers
3. Killings of civilian passengers in vehicles that failed to stop a
    guerrilla roadblocks
4. Political assassinations
5. Assassinations of U.S. military personnel
6. Forced recruitment, which impelled people to move
7. Kidnappings of mayors and Inés Duarte
8. Forcing civilian officials in FMLN-controlled areas to leave their
    homes or be killed
9. Mines

According to Americas Watch, most FMLN abuses during the first half of the 1980s fell into the first four categories.[60] Although human rights violations by the guerrillas accounted for a fraction of those inflicted by government forces in the early years of the war, the disparity narrowed as the decade progressed for two main reasons. One has already been discussed: U.S. pressure on the army and security forces to curb violations. The second resulted from increased use of land mines by the FMLN, which were designed to impede the army but which caused many injuries and deaths among unsuspecting civilians in the countryside.

The sorry record of massacres belongs largely to government forces.[61] The FMLN, however, was not exempt from such actions, although they were few and far between. In 1984 the guerrillas executed seven civilians in northern Morazán, then waited over a year to acknowledge the crime. In June 1985 urban commandos attacked four U.S. Marines dining alfresco in San Salvador, killing them and several civilians who had the misfortune to be sitting nearby. During the 1989 offensive, the FMLN attacked the government press agency and killed six, five of whom were journalists.

The kidnapping of President Duarte's daughter, Inés, and a friend on September 10, 1985, was the most notorious act of its kind since 1979. Under great pressure from the right and military not to negotiate, Duarte nevertheless did so and secured the release of both women and twenty-three municipal officials in exchange for twenty-one government-held prisoners and the departure of ninety-six wounded guerrillas for medical treatment abroad.

Political assassinations tended to bring the most sustained criticism. Toward the end of the 1980s, the FMLN set up the Office for the Promotion and Protection of Human Rights, headed by Comandante Nidia Diáz (María Marta Valladares), who had been the most famous of the prisoners exchanged for Inés Duarte. The rebels also met several times with representatives of Americas Watch, their most consistent internationally respected critic, to debate their procedures for condemning alleged informers. After reviewing the FMLN's cases and arguments, Americas Watch concluded that "the organization of and procedural guarantees offered by the rebels' *ad hoc* courts flagrantly violate the non-derogable provisions of Common Article 13 [of the 1949 Geneva Conventions] and Article 6 of Protocol II [of 1977, which spells out restrictions on both parties in civil conflicts such as this]."[62]

THE ELECTORAL LANDSCAPE CHANGES

The political space that opened after 1983 not only affected the popular organizations but also had a significant impact on party politics. After 1985 the FDR and FMLN had a tacit agreement that in certain areas, each enjoyed autonomy of action. This understanding was formalized in a pact signed on November 30, 1986, and announced in December. The pact consisted of two parts. The first defined the "nature and character of the democratic-revolutionary alliance." Part two defined "the mechanisms for making decisions, joint institutions and shared tasks." The FDR and FMLN described their alliance as "Historic, Strategic, Political, and Voluntary." They defined the difference between the FMLN, which "maintains and develops an aspiration and policy to ... form a unified party," and the FDR, "which is formed by political and social organizations that maintain and develop ... a policy that seeks to preserve and strengthen their respective identities." The pact committed both groups to strengthening themselves as well as their alliance; to making decisions by consensus (a reaffirmation of the policy since 1980); and, in the event of disagreement, to dissenting publicly when disagreements arose and to offering "constructive criticism."[63]

The Democratic Left Returns. The pact formally sanctioned a process already under way: the return to El Salvador of parties representing the democratic left. In 1985 the MPSC, whose political program was closer to the social democrats than to the Marxist FMLN, began quietly sending some of its leaders back to El Salvador, from which they had been exiled for five years, to test the waters. Finally, in November 1987, Rubén Zamora returned permanently to El Salvador, along with Jorge Villacorta and Juan José Martel, who had been prominent in 1980. MPSC members actively and aggressively began building the party at the grassroots in major cities, working with limited resources and in a climate of fear. The MNR's Guillermo Manuel Ungo and Héctor Oquelí Colindres returned at the same time. Meanwhile, the new Social Democrat Party (PSD) was formed in March 1987 and headed by Secretary General Mario Reni Roldán.

By fall 1987 these three parties were discussing the possibility of engaging in electoral politics. On November 7, the MPSC, MNR, and PSD met in Guatemala and founded the Democratic Convergence (CD). They subsequently declined to participate in the 1988 election, judging that the necessary democratic conditions did not exist. But the CD put forward a platform in September 1988 in which it defined "four great problems" facing El Salvador: civil war; loss of national sovereignty; absence of real democracy; and extreme poverty of the Salvadorean people.[64]

Electoral Debacle, 1988. The Christian Democrats frittered away their electoral mandates of 1984 and 1985, and ARENA mounted yet another effective campaign, using the floor of the Assembly to begin questioning the growing revelations of corruption. It may have been the only time in the 1980s that the extreme right and the unions were on the same side of an issue. In this they were abetted by the media, particularly as the campaign heated up. In March 1988 a disillusioned electorate gave the PDC only twenty-two seats in the Assembly and seventy-nine mayoralties. ARENA won thirty seats and, in coalition with the PCN, control of the legislature.

On the heels of the election, an internal struggle erupted in the PDC over who would be the standard-bearer in the 1989 presidential election. The fight between Fidel Chávez Mena, who represented a younger, technocratic, and honest wing of the party, and Julio Adolfo (Fito) Rey Prendes, a party hack, former mayor of San Salvador, and Duarte confidant, split the party. Rey Prendes left and formed the Authentic Christian Movement (MAC); the exodus included twelve of the twenty-two PDC Legislative Assembly delegates and a majority of the seventy-nine PDC mayors who had been elected in March.

Duarte's Illness. In the midst of this intraparty fight, President Duarte journeyed to Walter Reed Army Hospital in Washington, D.C., where he was diagnosed with stomach and liver cancer. Surgery confirmed that the cancer had spread, and he was given only months to live.[65] With the same determination that had guided him through other battles, however, Duarte succeeded in serving out his term and passing the presidential sash to his successor. He died on February 23, 1990.

TRANSITION—TO WHAT?

There was an almost palpable feeling in San Salvador in midsummer 988 that an era was over. There was also a sense of hope, even expectation, in some quarters of civil society that the seven-year-old war was not necessarily interminable.

Regional Pressures. Two developments in 1987 and 1988 contributed to these feelings. The first was regional: Picking up where Contadora had failed, Costa Rican president Oscar Arias, who would win the Nobel Peace Prize for his effort, prodded the Central American presidents to agree during an August 1987 meeting in Esquipulas, Guatemala, to seek a regional solution to the Central American conflicts. The presidents were helped by "Irangate," which distracted the Reagan administration from Central America for a few months. The Esquipulas agreement, among other things, put pressure on the Duarte government to resume negotiations with the left. Indeed, Esquipulas paved the way for a regional peace settlement and brought the United Nations into the process with election observation in Nicaragua (ONUVEN, 1990) and the deployment of U.N. military observers throughout the region in 1990–1991 (ONUCA).

The FMLN responded positively to the accords. It promptly proposed a five-day truce during talks in mid-September. President Duarte, however, merely reiterated his demand that the insurgents lay down their arms and return to the "democratic process." After a two-week postponement, the FMLN-FDR and government met for nine hours at the apostolic nuncio's residence on October 4 and agreed to establish two commissions, one to deal with the issue of a cease-fire, the other to focus on the requirements of the Esquipulas accords. Commander Shafik Handal said afterward that the two sides differed markedly on their views of a cease-fire; for the FMLN, "it's to find a solution that attacks the principal causes of the conflict," including economic reforms, human rights, and U.S. intervention.[66] The two sides met again in Caracas, Venezuela, the last of October and agreed to meet in Mexico on November 4. In the interim, however, Hebert Anaya, president of the nongovernmental Salvadorean Human Rights Commission, was murdered near his home.[67] In protest, the FMLN refused to attend the talks; the FDR condemned Anaya's assassination but disagreed publicly with the FMLN on the boycott. The FMLN viewed its action as a suspension, but President Duarte broke off the talks completely. They would not resume during his tenure.

National Pressures. The second development was instigated by the churches. The Permanent Commission on the National Debate, an ecumeni-

Archbishop Arturo Rivera Damas and Lutheran Bishop Medardo Gómez are interviewed before the February 1, 1992, ceremony to install the Peace Commission (COPAZ). The woman behind Rivera Damas is María Julia Hernández, director of the archdiocese's human rights office, Tutela Legal.

cally based organization, in both religious and secular terms, was founded to seek a national consensus on the question of peace. Led by the Catholic and Lutheran churches, 102 organizations (excluding only government and politi cal parties) were invited to come together. In September 1988 sixty "living forces," representing a large percentage of the population (the private secto was conspicuous by its absence), gathered, debated, and achieved a remark able consensus on propositions related to sources of the war, views toward the principal actors, and appropriate steps toward peace.[68] The significance of the "National Debate," as it came to be known, was that it convincingly demon strated an overwhelming popular sentiment for peace. In the following months, this would build, with the help of UCA public opinion polls, into a grassroots consensus in favor of negotiations that neither the government no FMLN could ignore.

The End of an Era. Meanwhile, Duarte continued to reign but did not rule and across the political spectrum people talked as if he was already gone. spent two weeks in El Salvador in July, and during that time his name wa never mentioned unless I introduced the subject. The president's illnes stripped away a facade: There had been a vacuum of leadership at the top fo three years, but as long as Duarte was on the scene the appearance of leader ship was maintained. Once the president was confined to a hospital bed and a long period of convalescence, however, the vacuum was obvious to all.

Caught in a web of complex events—the economy continuing its downward trend, the FMLN heating up the battlefield once again, pressure for peace growing regionally and internally, the popular organizations pressing their demands, the Christian Democrats in disarray, ARENA united behind its new, moderate-sounding leader, the United States distracted by a presidential campaign—El Salvador muddled through a long, unplanned interregnum. As we shall see in the last chapter, it would be the FMLN that would force the other actors to do things they did not really want to do. In political science, that is one definition of power.

8

The Road to Peace, 1989–1994

The war has been, in good measure, clandestine. The negotiations to end it are, in good measure, confidential. But don't worry: Peace, if it is to merit the name, must be a great collective exercise in full public view.

—David Escobar Galindo, December 1, 1990[1]

FULL CIRCLE

With the victory in the 1988 legislative and mayoral elections, ARENA began to look toward the 1989 presidential elections and decided it needed a more moderate image. In June 1988, therefore, the party chose a young oligarch, U.S.-educated Alfredo Cristiani, to be its standard-bearer. A political neophyte, Cristiani was selected because of his image and his lack of association with the death squads. Still, Roberto D'Aubuisson was often at Cristiani's side on the campaign trail and had no compunction about inserting himself in events, sometimes in excessively vulgar ways that had the effect, if not the intent, of embarrassing the candidate.[2] There was little doubt that D'Aubuisson ran the party; he dictated his choice of candidate for vice-president (Francisco Merino) and installed his people in key security positions after the election.[3] The question was who would really run the government.

Another Critical Election: 1989

As the presidential campaign began, ARENA, through the Assembly, began investigating charges of governmental corruption. The Christian Democrats, who for twenty years in opposition had stood for honesty in government, proved to be at least as corrupt in office as their military predecessors. Their fate was sealed when the party split over who should be its candidate. The decision of the CD to participate in the 1989 presidential campaign drew considerable attention; it was, after all, the first time since 1977 that parties on the left had participated in electoral politics.

The FMLN Derails a Campaign. The FMLN stole everyone's thunder and effectively derailed the campaign for a month with an audacious proposal, published on January 23, 1989, to postpone the elections for six months, keep the military in their barracks on election day, put the CD on the Central Elections Council, and provide for absentee voting for Salvadoreans living abroad, in return for which the rebels agreed to participate in the elections and to honor the outcome. According to Miguel Sáenz, the FMLN had spent the previous fall analyzing itself and the national reality and had concluded that it had broad support that would convert into votes were it to participate in elections.[4] The president of the CCE and Christian Democrat leader Fidel Chávez Mena responded positively to the proposal; two days later the Duarte government rejected it; two days after that the new Bush administration's State Department spokesman said the proposal required "serious and substantial consideration."[5]

The government stalled for three weeks, then talks between the FMLN and representatives of thirteen political parties took place in Mexico February 20–21. At this meeting the FMLN presented a second proposal, the points of which would echo through the off-again, on-again peace talks of the next three years. The rebels agreed to renounce armed struggle, incorporate into the political process, and recognize the existence of a single army. In exchange, they sought to reach agreement with the government on a series of military reform measures. For a few days there were signals that the talks might succeed, but in the end negotiations collapsed, largely because ARENA sensed victory and was unwilling to postpone for six months what it believed to be inevitable. Meanwhile, the FMLN for the first time dominated internal political debate and eclipsed the campaign. A longtime Latin American diplomat, reflecting on the events, commented: "It is ironic that the one main force in Salvadoran politics not participating in elections—the FMLN—has managed to set the agenda. They showed greater creativity and agility than the government or the political parties."[6] With this proposal, the FMLN revived itself as a force with which other actors had to contend and put peace back at the top of the national agenda.

Political maneuvers were not the only thing on the FMLN's agenda. Several commanders have acknowledged that planning for the 1989 offensive began in 1987. Still, had the political offensive succeeded, said Comandante Roberto Roca (Ernesto Jovel), who was one of the two FMLN negotiators in Mexico, "they could have prevented the '89 offensive ... which was much more politically justified after [the election proposal failed]."[7] The immediate result was that the guerrillas turned up the heat.

The Oligarchy Triumphs. Election day was bloody. The rebels did not attack polling places, but there were firefights across the country between guerrillas and army. The FMLN blacked out San Salvador and 80 percent of the country and ordered a highly effective, four-day national transportation stoppage. Three journalists were killed and one was seriously wounded by the Armed Forces. Voter turnout continued to decline.[8]

ARENA ran another effective U.S.-style campaign, but it was the PDC's woes that virtually guaranteed Cristiani victory in the first round with 54 percent of the vote. Chávez Mena, the PDC candidate, garnered 36 percent, while the PDC splinter party, MAC, won only 1 percent. Guillermo Ungo and Mario Roldán, the CD candidates for president and vice-president, respectively, ran on the platform spelled out in fall 1988: civil war; loss of sovereignty; absence of real democracy; and poverty. The CD won 3.8 percent of the vote and was dismissed by ARENA and the U.S. Embassy as a blip on the political screen. Nonetheless, the CD continued its organizing efforts around the country, especially in urban areas, and this thrust would pay off in 1991.

A New Beginning

On June 1, 1989, Alfredo Cristiani received the presidential sash from José Napoleón Duarte. Handing formal power to the political right could not have been what Duarte dreamed for thirty years, but he carried out his duty with dignity. Cristiani's assumption of office brought full circle a history that had begun in December 1931—when the last oligarch to be elected president was removed in a coup d'etat. Ironically, but not surprisingly, some on the extreme right were prepared to carry out a coup if victory was denied; others threatened to leave ARENA and create a new extreme-right-wing party.[9] Still, the new president may have surprised and even irritated the fanatics among his coreligionists. Two days after the election, Cristiani called for immediate peace talks with the FMLN, which responded on April 6 in Washington, D.C., with a new proposal.

Cristiani adopted a more moderate line than D'Aubuisson; the new president's inaugural speech on June 1 pledged a government "based on the principles of liberty, honesty, legality and security."[10] He promised to get the economy moving, then unveiled a five-point plan for talks with the FMLN, something the rebels themselves had proposed the day before, and did not call for their surrender. This was an enormously popular position; one day before the inauguration, the UCA's public opinion research institute published a national poll showing that 76 percent of those surveyed believed the new government "should open a dialogue and negotiate with the FMLN."[11]

Initial Steps Toward Peace. Following a meeting of the five Central American presidents in Tela, Honduras, in August, the results of which both the government and the FMLN found positive, the rebels issued a proposal "to initiate as soon as possible a definitive process of negotiation to put an end to the war and place all our forces at the service of constructing a true democracy."[12] These moves came as a result of pressures on the FMLN to negotiate despite their strong military position. The social and economic costs of an interminable war were escalating; Salvadorean public opinion increasingly favored negotiations; Latin American leaders were calling for a negotiated solution; and the Soviet Union was no longer willing to bankroll revolutionary governments. (Before the talks concluded, there would be no more Soviet Union.) Meanwhile, Cristiani and his more moderate business colleagues recognized the impossibility of economic recovery without a resolution of the war. The president also knew that in spring 1991 there would be Legislative Assembly and mayoral elections. The majority ARENA enjoyed in both could evaporate overnight if economic conditions (which had regressed almost twenty years) did not improve and there was no sign of an end to the war.

Metamorphosis. None of these factors explain fully the profound ideological transformation that the FMLN underwent between 1988 and 1991. In essence, this revolutionary movement, which had embraced several varieties of a peculiarly Salvadorean brand of Marxism-Leninism since the early 1970s, shucked it all in favor of democratic socialism. It is important to recall that the FMLN had never embraced certain Marxist-Leninist beliefs such as a one-party state or a completely socialized economy. They had never been antielections; they had argued that conditions did not exist in El Salvador for truly democratic elections. Furthermore, they knew the world was changing; they knew military victory would bring isolation; they watched the Sandinistas lose an election in Nicaragua in 1990; they heard many promises from Europe and Latin America of help for reconstruction after an accord was reached; they realized that in 1989 the United States had a less ideology-driven foreign policy; finally, they saw the changes in Eastern Europe in 1988 and 1989 as a clear sign that Soviet-style socialism was not the wave of the future. Thus, the reasons for the transformation lie in the pragmatism that the Salvadorean revolutionaries often showed from the beginning. In the end that was more important than ideology.

Talks Begin

Representatives of the Cristiani government and the FMLN met in Mexico in mid-September and agreed on procedures for negotiations that included, as witnesses, representatives from the Salvadorean Episcopal Conference, the United Nations, and the Organization of American States. The FMLN presented a proposal calling for a cease-fire by November 15 and an end to the war by January 31, 1990. The government indicated that the plan marked a positive change of tone.[13] When the two sides met again a month later in San José, Costa Rica, with the proposed cessation of hostilities on the agenda, the government demanded an immediate cease-fire. Cristiani, however, was unable to offer any guarantees concerning safety for the insurgents and their supporters. The parties agreed to create a special operative commission, which would be responsible for implementing accords guaranteeing life, liberty, and freedom of organization and assembly; reform of the electoral system; and improvement of the justice system. Under the peace accords this would be known as the National Commission for the Consolidation of Peace (COPAZ). There was also a minimal agreement to resolve the economic crisis and to reduce the Armed Forces. The FMLN, which had been carrying out widespread assaults even as the talks were getting under way, offered and then implemented what Ana Guadalupe Martínez called "the suspension of half of the war."[14]

A third meeting was scheduled for November 20 and 21 in Caracas, Venezuela, but on October 31, 1989, just days after the San José meeting, a noontime bomb at the headquarters of El Salvador's largest and most militant trade union federation, FENASTRAS, killed its secretary general, Febe Elizabeth Velásquez, and nine others and wounded thirty.[15] That assault had been preceded by several bombings, including of Rubén Zamora's home and the offices of the Lutheran Church, and a grenade attack on the UES. The bombing of FENASTRAS persuaded the FMLN that the government was not serious about negotiations. "We are faced with a new situation that forces us to de-end the people's struggle," an FMLN communiqué said. "We had become more flexible in our positions in an effort to open real negotiations, but. ... We reaffirm before the nation that we will never lay down our guns in the face of state terrorism."[16] President Cristiani went on national radio, asked for calm, and promised a full investigation of the bombing. Nothing happened.

THE NOVEMBER OFFENSIVE

In a June 1988 classified analysis of the FMLN, General Juan Orlando Zepeda had asked to what extent the "Salvadorean subversion [had] sufficient qualitative and quantitative forces to launch a general offensive?"[17] The FMLN answered Zepeda's question on November 11, 1989, when it opened a nationwide offensive and brought the war to San Salvador for the first time (see Map 8.1).

Preparations. According to Ernesto Jovel, the FMLN began preparing for the offensive during "the entire second half of 1987," when "the *comandancia* had the job of inculcating among all the combatants the idea of the need for a strategic counteroffensive. We weren't preparing militarily, we were creating the subjective conditions to begin [to do this]."[18] Their inspiration, according to Comandante Damian Alegría, "was a little like Vietnam with the final offensive in 1975. ... We tried to copy their design, first opening routes from north to south; second storing arms in all locations, even next to garrisons; third sending combatants to learn the entire zone so they could be placed within the capital before the offensive." San Salvador was not Saigon, Alegría continued, so the offensive was launched from Guazapa and the San Salvador volcano.[19]

There was, said a U.S. official, "a torrent of arms and ammunition" into San Salvador. "That couldn't have happened," he admitted, "had not a lot of people helped, or at the minimum, kept quiet."[20] The presidential election, in Jovel's view, "created a propitious environment for us. After the elections the number of collaborators tripled; there were people offering their houses near the city where we could establish a clinic or store three [thousand] or four thousand cartridges or corn and beans." In addition, the FMLN bamboozled Salvadorean and U.S. intelligence specialists by using newly released political prisoners to set up nongovernmental organizations (NGOs), on which intelligence operatives focused, while urban commando units were organized and deployed throughout the capital. The target date for the offensive was August or September because, said Jovel, "there was still rain but it was no longer heavy, which would have created problems moving people across two or three departments; the mountains were very green, which provided natural cover from the helicopters." But the FMLN was not ready: "We hadn't completed the logistical part that was so determinant."

The breakdown in peace talks, the escalating repression against center-left political party activists, grassroots organizations, and labor unions that culminated in the bombing of FENASTRAS, and the increasingly publicized view of the Salvadorean military, government, and U.S. Embassy that the FMLN was militarily and politically finished[21] all provided public justifica-

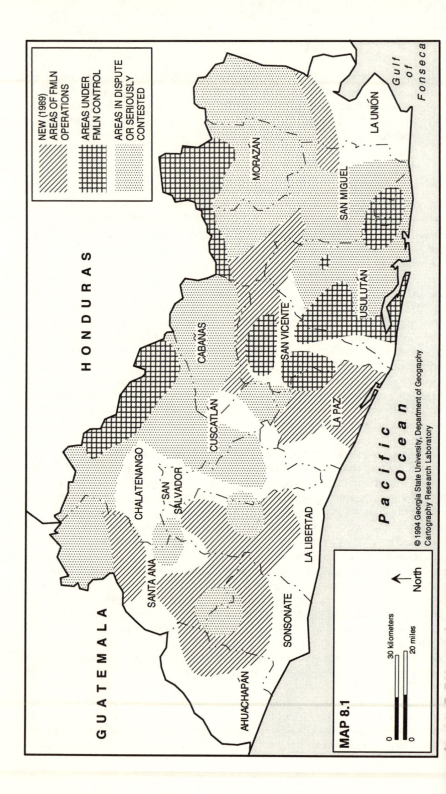

MAP 8.1

North

| 0 | 30 kilometers |
| 0 | 20 miles |

NEW (1989) AREAS OF FMLN OPERATIONS

AREAS UNDER FMLN CONTROL

AREAS IN DISPUTE OR SERIOUSLY CONTESTED

GUATEMALA

HONDURAS

Gulf of Fonseca

Pacific Ocean

SANTA ANA

AHUACHAPÁN

SONSONATE

CHALATENANGO

SAN SALVADOR

LA LIBERTAD

CUSCATLÁN

CABAÑAS

SAN VICENTE

LA PAZ

MORAZAN

SAN MIGUEL

USULUTÁN

LA UNIÓN

© 1994 Georgia State University, Department of Geography
Cartography Research Laboratory

tions for the offensive. Believing its own propaganda led to the government's position at the October meeting that the only thing to negotiate was the terms of the FMLN's surrender and contributed to extreme rightists' view that they could clean house with impunity.

War Comes to the Capital. The Armed Forces responded as usual: Incapable of mounting an effective counterattack on the ground, it called in the air force to bomb and strafe working-class neighborhoods and shanty towns around the northern and eastern periphery of the capital from which the guerrillas launched their assaults. The results were predictable and devastating: Hundreds of civilians were killed or wounded by the bombardments in these neighborhoods. Not surprisingly, the army demonstrated a double standard when the FMLN twice occupied wealthy neighborhoods for extended periods. "I do not understand how this happened," said one resident of the upscale Escalón district. "This area was heavily militarized yesterday when the terrorists came, and the soldiers did nothing." The area was never bombed.[22]

Assessment. The offensive was instructive on several levels. First, there was the utter failure of U.S. and Salvadoran intelligence. Just hours before the offensive began, a U.S. Embassy official told journalist Frank Smyth that he did not think the guerrillas had "the capability" to mount an offensive and that the Armed Forces had "taken measures to prevent it."[23] Second, the FMLN quickly demonstrated its ability to define the terms of combat on the ground and expose the incompetence of the Salvadoran army. The FMLN held government forces at bay in many neighborhoods for a week, until aerial bombardment forced the insurgents to withdraw. Their retreat, through known routes on the north side of the capital, could have been cut off by the army but was not. And when the FMLN regrouped and entered Escalón, less than two kilometers from army headquarters, the guerrillas virtually had the run of the area.

Third, and most significant, the offensive exposed the utter failure of nine years of U.S. policy. Apart from the Armed Forces' incompetence, it soon became clear that "professionalization"—teaching the army to respect human rights and subordinating itself to civilian authority—was an illusion. On the fourth night of the offensive, an army unit of the Atlacatl battalion, trained by U.S. Green Berets, entered the grounds of the Jesuit-run Central American University and killed six priest-scholars, including the rector and vice-rector, their housekeeper, and her daughter. This single act would have an impact both within and beyond El Salvador that was at least as great as the offensive itself.

Fallout. The FMLN shook the Salvadoran army, government, and oligarchy to their roots. The only military weakness the FMLN displayed during the offensive (a not insignificant one) was its inability to penetrate or destroy the perimeters near army installations in the capital and advance beyond them. Cristiani's decision, made under great internal and external pressure, to press for the arrest of several army officers (including a colonel) and soldiers in connection with the Jesuits' murders produced deep divisions within the army and Cristiani's own party.

The offensive and the Jesuits' murders reopened, for the first time in years, the debate over El Salvador in the U.S. Congress. President Bush could no longer assume continued funding for El Salvador at previous or increased levels, as he asked for in 1990. But, as always, it required a tremendous amount of pressure on Congress to reduce or condition aid. In its conclusion to a study titled "Violations of the Laws of War by Both Sides" during the offensive, a report that criticizes the FMLN as well as the government forces, Americas Watch wrote:

> After nine years of a stubborn defense of the Salvadoran regime, and after more than $4 billion have been spent in propping it up, the urban offensive of November 1989 has put the Bush Administration once again in the awkward position of defending the indefensible. It is clearly not enough to say that A. Cristiani is an elected official. If he has effective control over his country's armed and security forces, then he is ultimately responsible for the unspeakable abuses that those forces commit, as well as for those committed by shadowy death squads with close links to his own political party. If he is in fact powerless to exert any meaningful control over them, then the Bush Administration fiction that the U.S. supports a legitimate government is really no more than a thin veil to cover up its support of a murderous military.[24]

RETURN TO THE PEACE TABLE

In 1992 interviews, several senior FMLN commanders freely acknowledged that the military objective of the offensive was to overthrow the government; the official position was "unconditionally committed to a political-negotiated settlement of the war and the offensive seeks to reopen serious negotiations."[25] The offensive achieved this goal.

In early 1990 the U.N. secretary general's office, at the behest of both sides, initiated several months of shuttle diplomacy that led to an April 4 agreement in Geneva, Switzerland, between the government and the FMLN to achieve a cease-fire by September 15, then continue negotiations during the cease-fire period to end the war. Both sides cast the U.N. in a passive role that excluded its negotiator from putting forth his own proposals. In May the two sides met in Caracas and issued a joint agreement on the schedule and agenda of future talks. They also agreed to address political issues prior to a cease-fire and aimed to achieve agreement on this by September. In June talks were held in Querétaro, Mexico, and proposals regarding the future of the Armed Forces were exchanged.[26]

At San José, Costa Rica, in July the government submitted a thirty-three-point proposal regarding the Armed Forces: They would regulate themselves and set the limits of their functions; abusive units would be transferred, intact, within the existing system. The fundamental problem was that the government viewed the problem within the military as a matter of criminal and corrupt individuals; the FMLN defined the problem as systemic. Nonetheless, the first substantive agreement was reached: A U.N. human rights observation team would begin immediately after a cease-fire.

The following month the sides met again in San José, where the FMLN withdrew its June proposal on the military and submitted what the government viewed as a more hard-line position. The FMLN had long insisted that any peace settlement include a reduction and "purification" of the officer corps, a purge of those associated with human rights abuses. When the government refused to entertain this, the FMLN put forth an even more radical proposal: the complete dissolution of all armed forces in the country, both government and revolutionary, as was done in Costa Rica; the creation of a new civilian police; and the formation of a special tribunal to prosecute ten major human rights cases. The deadlock continued into September, and the target date for a cease-fire came and went. As a result, U.N. negotiator Alvaro de Soto convened a series of secret meetings with each side as well as with other social forces in the country; these sessions continued until the end of the year.[27]

On October 29 in Mexico, a special meeting between the government and FMLN was held to unblock the negotiating process. Two days later, at the request of both sides, de Soto sent each a working paper that called for abolition of two of the three security forces and of the military intelligence apparatus and the naming of a three-person commission empowered to investigate individual human rights records of senior military officers and to recommend prosecution where necessary. The working paper did not break the logjam, but it was significant for the change it represented in the U.N. role; from that point on, to the end of the U.N. mission in El Salvador, that body was no longer a passive mediator but an active player in the process.

U.S. Policy Shifts. In September 1989 *Proceso* editorialized in favor of "A clear signal by the United States, in support of the negotiations [which] could bring about a key turning point in the process of resolving the Salvadorean conflict by political means."[28] U.S. policy had changed with the Bush administration; this was clear from its support for discussion of the FMLN's election proposal earlier in the year. Still, support for the peace talks, although fairly constant, was not consistent, especially during Bush's first year.

Military aid to El Salvador was coming up for a vote in Congress, and President Cristiani traveled to Washington in an effort to repeat his predecessor's lobbying successes. Cristiani failed. On October 19 the U.S. Congress finally did what it had occasionally threatened to do for nine years: It cut 50 percent of the military aid to El Salvador and conditioned the remainder on progress in the Jesuit murder investigation and the peace talks. Analysis of the vote's impact varied from those who argued that it could strengthen hardliners on the right and the left, to those who believed that it would cause deeper divisions in the Armed Forces and thereby make it easier for the government to negotiate. The latter proved closer to reality.[29]

A New "Military Campaign." FMLN frustration with what it viewed as governmental intransigence, especially on the issue of the Armed Forces, led on November 20 to a series of coordinated guerrilla attacks near a dozen towns around the country that inflicted significant casualties and damaged considerable military equipment. On November 23, for the first time in the war, the insurgents brought down an air force plane with a surface-to-air mis-

sile. On December 4 they hit a second plane. Days later the guerrillas humili-
ated the U.S.-trained Bracamonte battalion when two of its companies re-
treated from Chalatenango into Honduras after forty hours of combat. Air
force pilots had begun refusing to provide air support.[30]

Ironically, whereas the Armed Forces had sought to minimize the size
and impact of the offensive a year earlier, in 1990 Defense Minister René
Emilio Ponce attempted to exaggerate the size and effectiveness of the
FMLN's attacks: "This is an operation of great strength that can only be characterized as an offensive."[31] The hyperbole was presumably to encourage the
restoration of full military aid. Labels aside, the FMLN did not disagree with
Ponce's assessment. Rafael Benavidez gave this analysis: "From the military
point of view, the effects of this campaign were greater [than in 1989] ... because we had the missiles ... and we neutralized almost completely the air
force. ... [This] had a severe psychological impact on the army; they felt like
orphans; they had to evacuate their wounded and dead like we had done
throughout the war—by carrying them [instead of evacuating them on heli-
copters]."[32]

Even as the campaign continued, in early December the FMLN proposed accelerated negotiations about the future of the Armed Forces that
would conclude on December 31 with a cease-fire. There was too little time to
achieve this, but the combined military and political offensive moved the process along. On January 1, 1991, de Soto presented a proposal to both sides on
the future of the Armed Forces. In January and February there were two meetings in Mexico and one in Costa Rica. Meanwhile, a U.N. preparatory mission
opened in San Salvador. These advances, however, were overshadowed for a
time by the cold-blooded murder of two U.S. servicemen who had been shot
down and wounded by a guerrilla platoon in mid-January. An outraged Bush
administration restored the $42.5 million in military assistance that had been
withheld by Congress, although it did not meet any of the criteria Congress
had stipulated for restoration of aid. Then the administration leaked its dis-
pleasure with de Soto to the press, accusing him of going too easy on the
FMLN. Despite these setbacks, the net effect of the events between November
and February was a narrowing of differences between the two sides on critical
issues like military reform.

THE 1991 ELECTIONS

Meanwhile, the campaign for the March 1991 Assembly and mayoral
elections got under way. For the first time since 1982 the FMLN did not attempt in any way to impede the electoral process, although voting did not
take place in twenty-one municipalities (roughly equivalent to a U.S. county)
that lay deep in conflict zones. Five parties plus the Democratic Convergence
participated. The campaign was marred by violence; a week before the election the CD issued a nine-page list of documented cases that ranged from assassination to destruction of property to intimidation. The offices of El Salvador's only opposition newspaper, *El Diario Latino*, were destroyed by arson in
early February. On election day there was evidence that the computerized vot-

ing lists had been tampered with; in areas where the CD was expected to do well, hundreds of voters found that although they had registered and held voting cards, they were not on the list and were not allowed to vote. On election eve in a number of these same areas, the polling station was arbitrarily moved without public notice.[33]

As election day approached, it became clear that the big question was how well the CD would do. The MNR had suffered two major blows in the previous fifteen months: In January 1990 its undersecretary general, Héctor Oquelí Colindres, was kidnapped and murdered on his way to the airport in Guatemala City. In February 1991 Guillermo Manuel Ungo, who had been Duarte's vice-presidential candidate in 1987, a member of the first junta in 1979, and president of the FDR for much of the 1980s, and who was a candidate for the Assembly on the the CD ticket, died after surgery in Mexico City. By election day, however, the question was whether the CD or the PCN would come in third, after ARENA and the PDC.

In the end, despite various other irregularities in the vote count, the CD gained 12 percent and eight seats in the Assembly. Rubén Zamora, who had left the PDC and the country in 1980 after his brother was murdered, won a "national" seat and was subsequently elected a vice-president of the Assembly. Roberto D'Aubuisson, who had denounced Mario Zamora on television just before his assassination, voted for Rubén. D'Aubuisson traveled to the United States days after the election where he was diagnosed with and underwent surgery for throat cancer. Despite a 3.6 percent growth in GNP in 1990 that the vast majority of Salvadoreans did not benefit from, ARENA experienced the same fate as the PDC in 1988: Its percent of the vote dropped ten points, and it won only thirty-nine seats in an Assembly that had been expanded to eighty-four deputies. The PDC took 26 percent of the vote and twenty-six deputies. The PCN won only 9 percent of the vote but nine seats, thanks to a byzantine system of proportional representation. ARENA's alliance with the PCN ensured continued control of the Assembly, but it would have to deal with an articulate and politically astute democratic left whose leaders had made it clear that they would both inform and consult with the people on a regular basis. In a symbolic gesture of this commitment, the one UDN and eight CD deputies took their oaths of office before a May 1 gathering of 10,000 in San Salvador; thousands more were prevented from entering the city by army roadblocks on all major highways.[34] At the municipal level, ARENA won 181 mayoralties, the PDC 70, and the PCN 11. Mayoral elections for the municipalities in conflict zones took place in departmental capitals, which often meant that a few dozen votes were cast by citizens also living in exile. These mayors, along with forty-seven others who were elected in their municipality, were forced to govern from exile because the FMLN wielded enough power in the area to prevent them from returning.

Following the election President Cristiani's deputy chief of staff, Ernesto Altschul, commented that ARENA was not looking at "one or two more terms but a longer period of domination for a center-right party."[35] In a subsequent interview Altschul denied that his statement implied any intent to manipulate elections;[36] nevertheless, it reflected, at the very least, an attitude that assumed ARENA's domination of the electoral process for the foreseeable future, just as the oligarchy has dominated the economy for more than a century.

COUNTDOWN TO PEACE

Days before the election President Violeta Chamorro of Nicaragua introduced a new FMLN proposal to foreign ministers of the European Community participating in a Central American summit meeting in Managua. Secretary of State James Baker and Soviet Foreign Minister Alexander Bessmertnykh expressed both countries' support for the negotiations and the U.N. role in them. All the ministers approved a resolution expressing strong support for the United Nations in its effort to achieve a peace agreement. April brought a marathon twenty-four-day negotiating session in Mexico that produced significant military, political, electoral, and judicial agreements that achieved in large measure what the left had been fighting for: constitutional reforms to establish civilian control over the military; changes in the electoral and judicial systems; and creation of a truth commission to investigate major human rights cases.

Talks continued through the summer in Mexico with some advances and a few setbacks. The United Nations Observer Mission in El Salvador (ONUSAL) formally opened on July 26. As awareness grew that a final cease-fire agreement was in sight, however, the extreme-right in El Salvador began to react in typical fashion: In July the Salvadorean Anticommunist Front (FAS) issued a threat against all who supported ONUSAL; the decade-old Crusade for Peace and Work published a thinly veiled threat against ONUSAL in local papers; and death squad threats and murders of Salvadoreans increased.

In late August U.N. Secretary General Javier Pérez de Cuéllar invited President Cristiani and top officials from both sides to New York for "consultations" on how to "unblock and breathe new life" into the negotiations. When talks resumed in New York on September 16, things began to move, in large part because the Salvadorean government came under enormous pressure from Spain, Mexico, Venezuela, and Colombia, collectively known as the "Group of Friends," and the United States. On September 25 the two sides signed an accord that went beyond Mexico. The FMLN dropped its long insistence that it be incorporated into the army in exchange for incorporation of FMLN forces into a new National Civilian Police (PNC) and participation in the Peace Commission (COPAZ). The agreement on the police was a significant victory for the left because the PNC would become the sole agency responsible for public security. The FMLN presence in COPAZ ensured it a voice in implementation of the political accords.

Meanwhile, in El Salvador, under "Operation Palomino," ONUSAL/ONUCA helicopters began ferrying FMLN field commanders out of the country via Tegucigalpa, Honduras, to assist in the peace talks. A terminally ill Roberto D'Aubuisson gave what would be his last public speech to the party faithful and urged them to support Cristiani and the peace process. U.S. Ambassador William Walker decided that "maybe it had reached the point in the peace process to reach out" to the FMLN. This idea led to the first meeting inside El Salvador with FMLN commanders, headed by Raul Hercules (Fidel Recinos), in Santa Marta, Cabañas, on August 31. According to Walker, they spent three hours talking about peace, reconciliation, changes in the world, differences in the FMLN, the conditions for laying down their arms, and the difficulties of the peace process. Walker returned for a second visit in September.[37] Another informal meeting with Bernard Aronson and Colonel Mark Hamilton would take place after the final accords were signed in the New York hotel where the FMLN delegation was lodged.

After two more rounds of talks in Mexico in October and November, the negotiators returned to the United Nations on December 16. The remaining issues, according to Roberto Cañas, were critical: Details concerning the civil police, reduction of the army, socioeconomic issues, and the cease-fire itself were all on the agenda. Still, Cañas maintained that the negotiations could end in three days "if there is the political will to sign the accords; there is no necessary relation between the time remaining and the volume of things that must be negotiated and agreed to."[38] For two weeks, however, the talks proceeded at a snail's pace. The government's delegation had no authority to make decisions and had to consult on every detail by fax or phone. Finally, under pressure from the U.N., the Group of Friends, and the United States, President Cristiani flew to New York on December 28. On December 29 the Bush administration sent six senior State Department officials and diplomats to the U.N. to talk with Cristiani and Minister of Defense Ponce. The talks went into round-the-clock sessions. With the clock stopped moments before midnight, final agreement was reached twenty minutes after the new year began and Secretary General Pérez de Cuéllar's term expired. The final accords reduced the size of the Armed Forces; limited their role to territorial security; revised the education of officers and provided for purification of the officer corps; eliminated the three security forces and replaced them with the PNC; provided for judicial and electoral reforms; and addressed economic and social issues. Because the accords did not cover all outstanding issues, talks continued in New York until January 12, during which a timetable for the cease-fire period was agreed upon. On January 16, 1992, the Salvadorean peace accords were signed during an elegant ceremony in Mexico City.

The cease-fire, which began unofficially on December 31, became formal on February 1 and was heralded with a national celebration. FMLN supporters were everywhere, sporting red bandanas. About 1,000 showed up at the airport on January 31 to welcome FMLN leaders who flew in on a Mexican air force plane and from Managua on a U.N. aircraft. A ceremony was held on February 1 to install the National Commission for the Consolidation of Peace (COPAZ); FMLN members who had not been seen in public in twelve years were in the audience; clandestine supporters were seen openly fraternizing with FMLN members to the surprise, even shock, of many. In the afternoon and evening the FMLN celebrated in the plaza Civica, in front of the cathedral where the 1979 massacre and the violence at Archbishop Romero's funeral had occurred. The cathedral was draped with an enormous banner that bore the image of Monseñor Romero and the words "You are resurrected in your people." Radio Venceremos broadcast live from the plaza. The only blight on

Installation of the Peace Commission, February 1, 1992. From left: Joaquin Villalobos, Francisco Jovel (Comandante Roberto Roca), General Juan Orlando Zepeda, Colonel Juan Martíne Varela, Rubén Zamora, Carlos Díaz Barrera, Gerardo LeChevallier, and Fidel Chávez Mena.

the day was the sycophantic praise that San Salvador's mayor, and ARENA ally, Armando Calderon Sol, lavished on a dying Roberto D'Aubuisson during the COPAZ installation.[39]

A "NEGOTIATED REVOLUTION"

The Chapultepec accords, so named for the castle where they were signed, sought to deal with the fundamental causes of the war by ending the armed conflict as quickly as possible; by promoting democratization; by guaranteeing absolute respect for human rights; and by reunifying Salvadorean society.[40] These objectives are unprecedented; no previous civil war has ended with an agreement not simply to stop shooting but to restructure society.[41] The accords established a precise calendar for implementation during the ceasefire period that was to end October 15. They mandated demilitarization, including halving the size of the Armed Forces, eliminating the state security forces and the FMLN's guerrilla army; legalizing the FMLN as a political party; amending the constitution; reforming the electoral and judicial systems; settling the land distribution issue, one of the root causes of the war; and establishing independent commissions to identify those responsible for major human rights abuses and to purge the army of its most serious human rights violators.

MLN commanders at celebration in the Plaza Cívica, San Salvador, February 1, 1992. From left: Salvador Samayoa, Joaquin Villalobos, Facundo Guardado, Ana Guadalupe Martínez, Francisco Mena Sandoval, Nidia Díaz, Mario López, Javier Castillo, Merdedes del Carmen Letona, Miguel Sáenz (behind Letona), Eugenio Chicas, Sonia Aguinada Carranza, and Salvador Guerra. Martínez, Mena Sandoval, Díaz, Sáenz, Chicas, and Aguinada were elected to the Legislative Assembly in 1994.

The cease-fire itself was never broken, to the credit of both sides, but portions of the accords were subject to further negotiations into 1994. The cease-fire period was extended for two months, and both sides were responsible for the delay. The FMLN did not concentrate its forces on time; it postponed on several occasions the demobilization of its troops, which was to occur on five specified dates during the cease-fire period; the weapons it surrendered in the early months defied credibility in both number and quality; some peasants identified with the FMLN occupied lands in violation of the accords. For its part, the government appeared to follow a policy of doing as little as possible as slowly as possible.

Demilitarization. In an August 1992 press conference called to explain why the FMLN was delaying demobilization of the second 20 percent of its combatants, Joaquin Villalobos observed that the peace "accords are about the transformation of Salvadorean society," not simply the dismantling of the FMLN's military apparatus.[42] Nonetheless, the transformation began with demilitarization. Beween June 30 and December 17, 12,362 former guerrillas were demobilized. By August 17, 1993, the FMLN had turned in and destroyed 10,230 arms, over 4 million bullets, almost 10,000 grenades, 5,107 kilograms of explosives, and 74 missiles.[43] The army's intelligence apparatus rapid-reaction battalions, National Guard, and Treasury Police were dismar tled. The Armed Forces were reduced by half—from 60,000 to 30,000—a num ber regarded by many as excessive in a country at peace with no outside ene mies. Even more significant in political terms, constitutional changes in Apr 1992 made the army responsible only for protecting the national territory an barred it from any internal security function; it no longer was to be the guar antor of the constitutional order.

Disappearing Act. The United States, which had acted as a proconsul fc most of the previous eleven years, including when it applied appropriat pressure at critical moments in late 1991, behaved as though its job was fin ished with the participation of Vice-President Dan Quayle in the February ceremony. For the next six months there was no ambassador or deputy chief c mission (DCM) in El Salvador.[44] In December 1992 a senior U.S. official admit ted that "There was a general feeling after January 16 that things would fa into place. People didn't realize how ambiguous the accords, especially land were." The Bush administration finally sent a DCM, Peter Romero, in July, bu there would be no ambassador until October 1993, when Alan Flanigan ar rived.

The vacuum created by this inattention encouraged the government' recalcitrance and brought top U.N. negotiators back to El Salvador four time between March and November 1992 to get the peace process back on track The government's foot-dragging was reinforced by military and civilians t the right of President Cristiani who viewed the accords as nothing more than a vehicle for militarily dismantling the FMLN—a view publicly stated b ARENA supporters in the Legislative Assembly.

Reconstruction

Under the accords "reconstruction" had three meanings: (1) undertak ing physical restoration of the social infrastructure, including schools, clinics housing, and roads; (2) using physical restoration to advance the reconstruc tion of civil society through the interaction and cooperation of all sectors in th effort; (3) addressing the social and economic conditions that caused the wa The accords implicitly recognized distinct and unrelated forms of governanc in government- and FMLN-controlled areas. The two were distinguished pri marily by the high level of grassroots and nongovernmental organization (NGOs) that were and continue to be involved in the delivery of social ser vices in former FMLN areas. The accords further assumed government an FMLN collaboration to reach consensus on a reconstruction plan. In Marc 1992, without consultation, the government initiated a five-year National Re construction Plan (NRP) that purported to address the three aspects of recon struction. It created the Secretariat for National Reconstruction (SRN) through which funding was to be channeled and all programs were to be ad ministered. This unilateral, top-down behavior came to characterize much o the SRN's efforts in the first year and led to severe criticisms of the governn ment plan, both in and outside El Salvador.

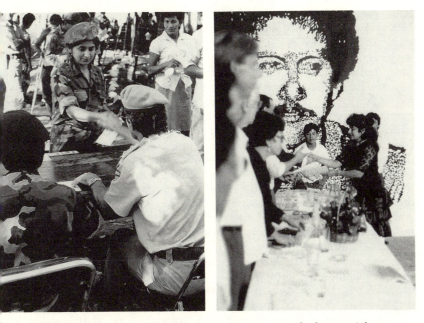

Left: FMLN combatant Yesimía Arias, who at age twenty-two had spent eight years as a guerrilla, shakes hands with ONUSAL officer after receiving her demobilization paper and temporary identity card, December 14, 1992, Aguacayo, Guazapa. Right: Arias receives high school diploma in the University of El Salvador Law School Auditorium, five days after being demobilized. She was one of over 100 former combatants who had studied during the cease-fire to complete high school.

In a comprehensive study of the first year, Peter Sollis of the Washington Office on Latin America (WOLA) found that the SRN had "failed to promote a consensus-building reconstruction process."[45] This was due primarily to the use of CONARA, which had originally appeared in San Vicente in 1983 as the civilian component in the counterinsurgency strategy and was therefore viewed with great suspicion by people living in former conflict zones. Further, the SRN contradicted in practice its own goal of promoting broad, grass-roots participation. It declined to work with NGOs that had the greatest experience with the targeted population: repatriated refugees, the displaced, and other affected civilians. It undercut several local and potentially successful collaborative efforts between local government (sometimes headed by an ARENA mayor) and NGOs related to the FMLN. Further, the NRP did not include provisions for new housing, a desperate need. And for months the SRN declined to disburse thousands of AID dollars, which sat in bank accounts accruing interest.

It was abetted in these policies by AID officials who viewed the NGOs as anathema because they were considered to be FMLN front organizations, and most of the people with whom they worked as FMLN sympathizers.

AID's position that "we only work with governments"[46] dovetailed with the SRN's ideological proclivities. Ironically, one of the casualties of this myopic policy was an AID-supported municipal development project, Municipalitie in Action, which envisioned local government–grassroots cooperation to de fine priorities but which in fact remained under the control of mayors.

Soldiers in Reconstruction. Even more serious, given the constitutional re forms that excluded the army from participation in socioeconomic develop ment and the emphasis on demilitarization, the Armed Forces were permitted to carry out "civic action" projects under the reconstruction framework. Solli concluded that "civic action" did "not contribute to sustainable reconstruc tion and democratization" because these activities were not coordinated with the SRN and the military was often competing with civil organizations. Fur thermore, the army was being encouraged in this new role by the United States; General George Joulwan, SOUTHCOM commander, told Congress in April 1993 that SOUTHCOM intended to support an "appropriate role of the military in a democratic society" by sponsoring joint projects on engineer and other training activities, deploying U.S. military engineering personnel by late 1993, and using El Salvador for a new national assistance operation called "Fuerte Caminos–94" (Strong Roads). The latter, Joulwan said, would contrib ute to reconstruction through "involvement by the [army] and public works personnel in a joint and combined exercise to rebuild after ... a decade of war."[47] If Joulwan's comments were indicative of Pentagon thinking in 1993 then the U.S. military had learned nothing from its experience in El Salvador about the nature of Salvadorean society and the character of its military. More serious, as Sollis concluded, "A US policy which enhances the capacity of the [army] to carry out civic action programs ... clearly contradicts the spirit and purpose of the agreements which ended the war."[48]

Reestablishment of Public Administration. At the end of the war, sixty-eight mayors of municipalities in conflict zones were living in exile. Under the ac cords the FMLN accepted the existing governmental structure from the na tional to the local level and agreed to the return of both mayors and judges who had been excluded or expelled by the insurgents on the grounds that they were cooperating with the government's counterinsurgency strategy. With the cease-fire on February 1, twenty-four of the mayors returned within days. The remainder, however, were prevented from returning by local NGOs al lied with the FMLN that continued to view the mayors as instruments of gov ernment oppression, and by the mayors themselves who refused to negotiate with the NGOs. This impasse led in mid-July to a request from the govern ment and the FMLN that ONUSAL prepare a program for the reestablishment of public administration in these municipalities.

The program called for a carefully orchestrated series of events: ONUSAL-supervised negotiations between NGOs and mayors to establish a date for the latter to return; a town meeting within fifteen days of the mayor's return to elect a reconstruction and development comission that then met to determine priorities for local projects such as roads, schools, or water; and in forming the SRN of the community's decisions. According to Henry Morris, who as ONUSAL coordinator for the San Miguel region was intimately involved with these developments in eastern El Salvador, the promise of funds from the European Community and AID helped the process in many municipalities.[49]

ONUSAL's "pro-active role" was also critical, especially in the few locales where ARENA extremists sought to derail the process. For example, in Concepción de Oriente, La Unión, the ARENA governor, who had previously been Vice-President Merino's bodyguard, flew in on an army helicopter to tell the mayor that he did not have to hold a town meeting. In this same period a mob invaded the FMLN's small office and threw all of its things into the street. Three days later forty FMLN members in three trucks drove into town, grabbed the mayor, and threw everything from his office into the street. The situation was defused when a businessman in San Salvador, who was a cousin of the mayor, called ONUSAL one day and offered his help. Henry Morris flew the man into Concepción on a U.N. helicopter where he told the mayor that democracy could work. ONUSAL also asked the office of the president to ask Merino to call his former bodyguard and tell him to stay out of Concepción. Merino did and the governor obeyed. In the town meeting, not one FMLN member was elected to the reconstruction commission.[50]

In Perquín, Morazán, the newly created right-wing Perquín Foundation and the FMLN's NGO, PADECOMS, almost came to blows in two successive town meetings; the conflict caused the ONUSAL delegation, which was there observing the proceedings, to leave. At the third meeting, ONUSAL suggested holding meetings in four villages of the municipality simultaneously. The FMLN had enough people to cover all the meetings and therefore did not object. The foundation, however, realized that it could not be in four places at once to disrupt the meetings and therefore had to compromise. The FMLN won a strong presence on the reconstruction committee.

The reestablishment of public administration in the former conflict zones, the passage by the Legislative Assembly of a new municipal code that gave mayors more autonomy and therefore contributed to decentralization of government, and, later, the role of the mayors in the voter registration process revealed a fact about Salvadorean politics that had been obscured by the war: Salvadorean mayors are, in many respects, the most powerful officials in the country. Because local elections are winner-take-all, the mayor and town council members are from the same party.[51] The municipal code requires that town meetings be held at least once every three months, but a mayor who does not comply, particularly if she or he is a member of the party that controls the executive branch, will encounter little outside pressure to fulfill this provision or other legal requirements. A mayor may behave in a profoundly undemocratic fashion, but there is little accountability until the next election, unless there are strong local NGOs prepared to confront this tendency. The FMLN learned quickly the importance of local government and, as a result, mounted campaigns for mayor in 240 of the 262 municipalities in the 1994 elections.

Reintegration of Former Combatants. The peace accords implicitly and the National Reconstruction Plan explicitly anticipated the need for short- and long-term programs directed to the special needs of former guerrillas and soldiers and wounded civilians. Short-term programs included the distribution of agricultural implements and basic furniture and equipment for the home and vocational training in agriculture, industry, and services. These programs, with the exception of industrial training, were completed by May 1993; the latter was slated to continue until April 1994. Long-term programs included credit at below market rate for small businesses and farms and scholarships for university study. Despite a total of 42,000 former combatants from both sides, by May 1993 the government had initiated programs that would affect less than 11,000. Programs for the wounded and disabled were even further behind.

In November 1993, ONUSAL identified three fundamental problems with the process: The absence of a "global strategy" affected the design and planning of the programs; the short-term training programs did not begin at the same time and were not synchronized with demobilization dates; and the lack of general planning led to repetition of the same mistakes in each of the reintegration programs. Programs for extending credit to small businesses and farms and for technical assistance and scholarships suffered serious delays because of administrative problems, delays in financing, and a shortage of political will. A further complication was inordinate delays in land transfers.[52]

Many former FMLN combatants were relatively better off than their army counterparts, simply because the NGOs in former conflict zones were able to forge ahead with a variety of development projects for which they secured outside funding. In northern Morazán, over 2,000 people were living in houses that they had occupied during the years of war and from which they could be instantly evicted were the owners to return. In response to this crisis, PADECOMS developed a housing project that by February 1994 had 64 houses under construction. The project was producing its own roof tiles and building blocks. With the help of an ONUSAL political officer, PADECOMS was writing a proposal for 400 houses and was in touch with a potential international funder.[53]

The absence of this kind of grassroots organization left former soldiers dependent on the government and by mid-1993 produced growing frustration and resentment. Their anger boiled over in February 1994 when they demanded that the government resolve the issue of indemnification (one year's salary, under the accords), threatened to "sabotage the elections," and asserted that they were "willing to take up arms" and that "Guazapa awaits us with open arms."[54] The government promised to address their complaints immediately and, indeed, began handing out checks averaging $1,500 on March 2.

Lands. Throughout the period following the cease-fire, as since the last century, the most intractable problem was land. Historically, any hint of land redistribution was anathema to the oligarchy. The accords required redistribution to former combatants and soldiers and to *tenedores,* people who had occupied and farmed abandoned land for ten or twelve years. The purpose was partly to address historical inequities and partly to acknowledge de facto occupation and cultivation in former conflict zones. In some parts of the country, notably Chalatenango, the problem was less the oligarchy than small land holders whose plots ranged in size from one-half to five *manzanas* and who were often as poor as the *tenedores*. By late 1992 many medium-size farmers, most of them ARENA supporters, were stirring the cauldron by exhorting the owners not to sell to FMLN members even if they had no intention of returning to their plots. The situation in Chalatenango was further exacerbated by the sheer number of plots; 60 percent of the total lands inventoried by the FMLN lay in this department, and as of January 1994, only two formal land transfers had occurred.

In October 1992 ONUSAL hammered out a "supplement to the peace accords" that was accepted by the government and FMLN. It defined three phases for land transfers, the size of plots, depending on soil conditions, and the legal and financial arrangements for the purchasers.[55] Continuing resistance prevented resolution of these issues by deadlines set under the accords, and the problems continued through 1993 and into 1994. The November 1993 ONUSAL report noted that one year after the October agreement, land titles had been given to less than 10 percent of the possible beneficiaries. The principal problems were (1) deciding who had the right to receive lands; (2) the FMLN's failure to remove from the lists it had presented to the government all those who had not been "verified" as recipients; (3) a shortage of funding; and (4) a bureaucratic nightmare in the Land Bank, which provided financing for the transfers.[56]

Political Changes

One of the government's negotiators during the peace talks, David Escobar Galindo, observed in early 1994 that "To end the war without sharing the benefits would result in failure."[57] He was talking about the commitments to political, social, and economic reform that both sides had made in the accords. The accords succeeded in legitimating dozens of organizations that until the 1980s were called "popular organizations" and were considered illegal and subversive. For the first time the poor became involved in a legal political process—the peace process; their successful insistence on inclusion in the process of reconstruction at the local level was matched in early 1993 by massive demands that the "purification" of the Armed Forces proceed on schedule; both levels of activity signaled that they would be an active presence in the political life of the country.

COPAZ. The voices of those who had had no voice were heard in two institutions created under the accords. The most important was the National Commission for the Consolidation of Peace. COPAZ, composed of representatives from every political party in the Legislative Assembly, the government, and the FMLN, was the primary mechanism for implementing the political aspects of the peace plan. This required a large number of legislative actions, from a constitutional amendment that redefined the role of the Armed Forces to new laws for the electoral process. Because the voting in COPAZ was evenly split between government-ARENA-allies and opposition (FMLN-CD-PDC), deadlocks were frequent. Hammering out compromises became a political necessity—and a newly acquired skill for many politicians who had been accustomed to getting their own way and steamrollering the minority opposition in the process. The accords mandated observer status for ONUSAL and the Catholic Church; Blanca Antonini, a senior ONUSAL political officer who had been an assistant to Alvaro de Soto throughout the negotiating process, was assigned this responsibility.

The Economic Forum. The second manifestation of popular involvement was representation of unions in the Economic and Social Forum, which was created under the accords to seek agreement on basic economic and labor issues among three traditionally antagonistic forces: government, private sector, and labor unions. The private sector boycotted the forum until early September 1992 and the larger economic issues were never addressed, but once the forum began to work, the three parties were able to reach a historic agreement in February 1993 that for the first time recognized the legal right of workers to organize. Labor then proposed that twenty-nine conventions of the International Labor Organization (ILO) be adopted by El Salvador; the forum agreed on twenty-five but stalemated over the remaining four. The stalemate continued through the summer, during which ONUSAL's chief of mission, Augusto Ramírez Ocampo, proposed that ILO specialists be brought in as mediators. The forum accepted and on August 25 agreed to propose to the Assembly a series of amendments to the labor code, the founding law of the Ministry of Labor, and the social security law, all of which improved workers' rights. The three parties also agreed to establish a labor council within the Labor Ministry to institutionalize the work of the forum.

The forum, however, like other institutions created under the accords, never was given the resources to carry out its work. Internecine squabbles within the labor movement limited its ability to speak with one strong voice and thereby reduced its potential power. Ministry of Health employees staged a strike in mid-1993 that strengthened the government's and private sector's antiunion biases and contributed to a lack of political will to push the reforms through the Assembly. The FMLN, distracted by larger issues of lands, reintegration, and elections, did not give labor the support it had a right to expect. These difficulties led *Proceso* to ask in its year-end analysis "if some important result can come out of [the forum's] current way of operating."[58] Indeed, there was some question whether the forum would continue; ANEP announced in early November that it would retire for the duration of the electoral campaign. This decision reflected the private sector's inability, or unwillingness, to separate issues related to an election from broader national issues that transcend the electoral period.

At the end of the year the United States threatened to exclude El Salvador from the General System of Preferences (which gives a country trade benefits and is therefore advantageous to its exporters) if the labor code and ILO conventions were not approved. President Cristiani met with the private sector, not the forum, then presented an "intermediate proposal" for labor reforms to the Assembly that included some points on which the forum had reached consensus, other points on which the forum had achieved consensus but that Cristiani modified, and a third set of recommendations not approved by the forum. By late February 1994 two Assembly committees had held hearings on the proposal in which the government and labor presented their views. The private sector had not yet testified. In an interview, Assembly deputy Juan José Martel said there was a consensus in the Assembly to study the proposal but not vote on it until after the electoral campaign. The idea, he said, was to try to approve it in time to take effect May 1, International Workers' Day. Martel noted labor leaders' willingness to settle for less than their original objective, a position that he characterized as "quite mature."[59] Indeed, although the government and private sector displayed a decided lack of political will throughout 1992 and 1993, the fact remains that the forum brought together two forces, labor and business, in an institutionalized effort to develop consensus after twelve years of confrontation. Although much remained to be done, the work of the forum represented another example of old enemies learning to talk to each other and seek common ground.

The Judicial System. The peace accords mandated dramatic changes in the judicial system—something the United States, a master plan, and $6 million in aid had not been able to do. As with other parts of the accords, especially those mandating institutional changes, agreement was easier than implementation. The Salvadoran judicial system was corrupt to its core, inefficient, rife with incompetence, and highly politicized. Impunity for those with power or connections was the order of the day. Justices of the peace were rarely lawyers; higher-level judges often received their appointments because of who they knew, not what they knew about the law; and the president of the Supreme Court, Mauricio Gutiérrez Castro, repeatedly demonstrated through his actions and public statements not only his incompetence as a jurist but also that he understood neither the meaning of an independent, nonpolitical judiciary nor the word "discretion."

For example, in June 1993 the Supreme Court "legally" notified Segundo Montes, the founder of the UCA's human rights institute, and Margarita Aguilar, the former coordinator of Socorro Jurídico Cristiano, a human rights organization, that a case they had jointly brought in November 1987—to have a part of an amnesty law approved by the Assembly the previous October declared unconstitutional—had been resolved and their petition denied. The legal notice was delivered three and a half years after Segundo Montes was murdered along with five other Jesuits in November 1989. The law requires that judicial review of a case charging unconstitutionality take no more than 100 days.[60]

In early 1994 another institution set up under the accords, the National Judiciary Council (CNJ), clashed with Gutiérrez Castro. The CNJ, as required by law, had begun an evaluation of justices of the peace and judges of *primera instancia* (first level, roughly equivalent to a city court judge) that included interviews and questionnaires. Gutiérrez Castro sent a letter to these judges advising them that the Supreme Court had "not authorized this type of investigation" and that the judges were under no obligation to cooperate. The CNJ published a *campo pagado* in which it asserted that in carrying out its responsibilities, it was under no obligation to subject itself to the "orders, instructions or directives of the Supreme Court."[61] Gutiérrez called a press conference in which he lamented the confrontational attitude of the CNJ. By early March it was unclear how this standoff would end.

An egregious weakness of the judicial system was the country's prison system. Not only were the country's prisons characterized by almost 100 percent overpopulation in early 1994, but 80 percent of the prison population had not come to trial. In Santa Ana, of 594 prisoners only 26 had been tried and sentenced. On November 18, 1993, one gang of prisoners massacred twenty-seven members of another gang in the San Francisco Gotera, Morazán, prison, while the guards locked the doors and ignored the slaughter. The response of the director of prisons as well as the local warden was to absolve themselves of any responsibility and accuse the guards of being on drugs, a charge that was subsequently proved through lab tests. Sixteen guards were dismissed. The surviving gang members were moved to other prisons; in one, Santa Ana, another massacre of nine prisoners, involving some of the gang members from Gotera, occurred on February 24, 1994.[62]

These events obscured a slow but recognizable effort at judicial reform as mandated by the accords. In late February 1994, the Ministry of Justice requested approval by the Assembly of a new penal law that included internationally recognized penal principles, a modern system of administration, including judicial oversight, and $2.8 million to implement these reforms, with emphasis on relieving prison overpopulation.[63] Beginning in late 1993 all justices of the peace who were not lawyers were replaced with individuals holding law degrees. Judges were removed for malfeasance or outright criminal activity. The minister of justice also announced that the cost of judicial reform would total $22 million by 1997, the projected date for completion.

Unfortunately, these small but significant steps were overshadowed in early 1994 by a highly politicized campaign for new Supreme Court judges. Ironically, the procedures for electing a new court by the Legislative Assembly were designed to depoliticize the process; half of the eighty-four candidates were selected by the CNJ, the other half by the Federation of Associations of Lawyers, which was composed of eight different bar associations. In a move that raised questions about the seriousness and competence of the lawyers involved, Gutiérrez Castro was nominated by six of the eight associations.

The Procuraduría de Derechos Humanos. The accords mandated the creation of a legal office (*procuraduría*) for human rights that was an independent agency of the national government. In a country where tens of thousands had had their human rights violated with impunity by agents of the state over many years, the FMLN saw this office as a guarantee that such violations could not continue and that any complaints would be investigated and publicized and the evidence turned over to appropriate judicial authorities. Like other institutions created under the accords, the agency was not given the budget or resources it needed in 1992; nor were the head of the office and other officials named with dispatch. Nonetheless, by late 1993 offices had opened in all fourteen departments, and ONUSAL human rights officers were working closely with local directors and staff to provide training and other support.

A New Police Force

The creation of a new police force, the National Civilian Police (PNC), with a new doctrine went to the heart of a necessary, fundamental change in El Salvador: attitudes toward and the exercise of authority. In a country that was historically authoritarian, where the police were part of the Armed Forces, where in 1994 impunity was still the order of the day, and where few in authority took responsibility for their actions, much less those of their subordinates, how authority was exercised by the new police force would determine to a large extent how far the country moved toward becoming a modern, democratic state. As one Salvadorean commented in late 1993, "The entire peace process hinges on the PNC. If that doesn't work, everything collapses."

The importance of the PNC was reflected in its place in the Chapultepec accords: It was the subject of Chapter II; Chapter I dealt with the Armed Forces. The new doctrine, as set forth in the accords, emphasized "public security as a service provided by the state to its citizens," professionalism, respect for human rights, the use of force appropriate to the situation, an absolute ban on torture and "cruel, inhuman or degrading treatment," the responsibility of agents not to follow illegal orders of their superiors, and protection of the right of assembly.[64]

Selection, Training, and Deployment. Under the accords, 20 percent of the new force members were qualified former FMLN combatants, 20 percent former National Police and the remainder civilians. At least 15 percent were women. Educational standards were higher for the PNC than the security forces: A ninth-grade education was required for agents; sergeants needed a high school diploma; executive-level officers needed at least three years of college or its equivalent; and superior officers were required to have a university degree. In November 1992, however, ONUSAL complained that ten candidates for senior-level positions in the PNC had come from the National Guard or Treasury Police through the PN, thus contravening the accords. ONUSAL held "several discussions" with the goverment to ensure that these officers were seen as "exceptions," not a "precedent."[65] The FMLN accepted this in exchange for the placement of two former guerrilla officers in high-level administrative posts.

Unfortunately, this effort by the government to circumvent the letter and spirit of the accords was not unique. In December 1992 ONUSAL hammered out a "complementary accord" between the government and FMLN concerning the incorporation into the PNC of an antinarcotics unit (UEA) and a special investigations unit, both of which had been created by and received special training from the United States and had been a part of the National Police and the office of the president, respectively. The FMLN agreed to their incorporation under strict conditions that included individual evaluations prior to incorporation; a special course that emphasized the new doctrine and human rights; keeping the units intact; confining the units to their prescribed functions; and barring their officers from being assigned to command of regular PNC units. The government violated all of these conditions during 1993,

National Civilian Police (PNC) chief of Chalatenango province, Carlos López (second from right), talks with Norwegian development minister in San José las Flores, August 1993. López was in the FMLN. The officer on his left, Miguel Angel Guerrero Vallecillos, was in the old National Police. Woman in center is translator.

but ONUSAL had some success in forcing the government and PNC to make appropriate changes.

In December 1991, after it was clear that there would be a new police force, the government gave the PN's new and spacious training facilities to the army for a new military academy. ONUSAL's suggestion that the academy be signed back to the PNC fell on deaf ears. Then the Cristiani government did nothing to facilitate the selection and construction of new facilities and it delayed naming a new civilian police director for three months. Finally, a former army base next to the international airport was selected and the first class began its six-month training course on September 1, 1992. Although the U.N. Development Program (UNDP) had primary responsibility for developing the new academy, faculty, and curriculum, various problems brought ONUSAL in to monitor admission exams and recommend improvements when necessary; to strengthen academy courses on human rights; and to participate as an observer in the Academic Council.

In March 1993 the first PNC detachments were deployed to Chalatenango in north-central El Salvador, one of the most conflictive provinces during the war. By February 1994 the PNC was in ten departments covering the eastern two-thirds of the country and was deployed by early March in all the municipalities that ring the northern and eastern sides of San Salvador. Full deployment, with the last site the city of San Salvador, was scheduled for July 1994. The first reports during the summer and early fall 1993 indicated that the new police were operating effectively. More significant, former enemies—former National Police and former guerrillas—were becoming personal friends, able to talk about the past without rancor.[66] Some anecdotes convey the character and success of the new force in its first months:

- At a roadblock in Chalatenango soon after deployment, PNC agents were checking registrations and licenses. When an agent approached one driver, the man handed him a letter signed by General Mauricio Ernesto Vargas, the former vice-minister of defense. In pre-PNC days it was common practice for senior military officers to provide a letter or write a note on the back of their personal cards asking that the bearer be given all "consideration" or "respect." This time the agent looked at the letter, then at the driver. "Señor," he said, "when you crossed the Colima Bridge [between San Salvador and Chalatenango departments] you entered Chalatenango. Here this letter is worth nothing." The agent returned the letter and the driver was obliged to recross the bridge.

- In Citalá, Chalatenango, north of La Palma, the PNC relieved a UEA agent of his semiautomatic weapon, which he was carrying off duty without a permit. In the following three days the local judge and mayor came and asked the police chief to give them the weapon. On his second visit the judge asked for the weapon's identification number, and the chief gave him the number with several digits intentionally altered. Two days later the judge returned with written permission from the Ministry of Defense for the UEA agent, whereupon the chief told him that the number was incorrect and that the judge had violated the law on two counts: The UEA agent had lost his right to obtain permission by failing to carry a permit, and the judge had secured permission with a false number.

- In Cabañas there were two notorious gangs operating. One, headed by a Juan García, had operated for many years with impunity. Within two months of deployment the PNC, with ONUSAL police logistical support, went after García. He fled, shot one officer in the leg, and was killed by another officer. The second gang was composed of five brothers, the Velascos. Armed with another arrest order, the PNC captured the brothers and raided several houses where they found arms and a sack of marijuana.

Undermining the Force. Unfortunately, by early 1994 there were troubling signs. ONUSAL documented several cases of excessive use of force and at least one case of torture. In almost every one of these cases, however, the offending agents were former National Police. Some cases could be attributed to a lack of experience and a shortage of necessary resources. There were even more troubling signs that the PNC leadership and the government were not committed to the new doctrine or the fullest possible training for the force. A police officer found guilty in an administrative hearing of mistreating a prisoner was transferred to another province, rather than suspended or fired.

In October 1993 the PNC's vice-director, Oscar Peña Durán, a former army officer handpicked by the United States because of his administrative experience and demonstrated willingness to charge officers and soldiers with human rights violations, informed ONUSAL that the six-month period stipulated in the accords for supervising and verifying the work of the PNC was over. This meant that ONUSAL police officers were barred from offering the kind of help they had provided in the Cabañas cases. ONUSAL, the FMLN, and others viewed this as a distorted reading of the peace accords, which they understood to mandate supervision and verification for six months after final deployment of the PNC, not six months after initial deployment. Further, not one police officer or agent interviewed after this directive was issued agreed with it. Agents in the field understood that six months' training was the minimum, that they had much to learn, and that they had free advice and a form of on-the-job training available through international police officers with years of experience. In practice, however, most agents and officers in the field maintained a close relationship with the ONUSAL police and were not above asking for advice or debating issues like appropriate times for the use of long arms.

The most serious problems for the PNC in the field were threefold: a lack of resources, poor working conditions, and politicization. A shortage of resources accompanied every deployment. Complaints about insufficient vehicles, radios, arms, and uniforms were heard in every police post from Chalatenango to La Unión. In the latter, 230 police were deployed among twelve posts on July 20, 1993. They were given seven vehicles and two motorcycles to cover an area roughly the size of metropolitan Atlanta, Georgia. Five posts did not have even one radio. In Santa Clara, San Vicente, one week after ten PNC were deployed in October 1993, they had one pickup truck, two radios, and no telephone. On a return visit in February 1994, they had one radio, a telephone, and no vehicles; their one pickup was transferred to the departmental capital. These cases were typical and they had a direct impact on the PNC's effectiveness. In San Vicente, said one officer, "When we arrived there was great publicity and the gangs disappeared. But when they discovered there were no vehicles or arms, they reappeared."

PNC stations were usually located in buildings acquired for them; in cases where they occupied old National Police posts, the PNC arrived to find that the buildings had been stripped down to lightbulbs. In Citalá the police arrived to find their building locked and no one waiting with a key. A citizen drove to La Palma to get the key. In Ilobasco, Cabañas, the PNC found the former PN headquarters stripped and dirty as a pigsty.

PNC officers and agents were promised salaries significantly higher than those of the old security forces as a means of reducing the temptation to corruption. Three days before the first deployment, the PNC director announced that they would be getting several hundred colones less than promised. In October 1993 the PNC received a 12 percent raise, but agents were simultaneously docked the equivalent of 50 cents per day for food. This left them with a net increase of about $6 instead of the expected $21. Some officers in late 1993 acknowledged that morale was dropping and that some agents had resigned in disgust. The salary problem was exacerbated by long work days, sometimes sixteen hours in duration.

The last problem was one of politicization. In Chalatenango the police chief was asked to hire as secretaries young women who had not gone through the established screening procedures but who arrived with letters of introduction from PNC headquarters and whose primary qualification was that they were ARENA party members—a violation of the accords and PNC procedures. When the chief refused to hire them he was called "insubordinate" by a visitor from headquarters in Santa Tecla. The women were not hired.

The most blatant form of politicization appeared on the streets of San Salvador in early November 1993 when new white pickups carrying PNC agents were painted not with the PNC colors of navy blue and yellow but red, white, and blue, ARENA's colors. In a country where ARENA mayors paint the inside of city halls and even city trucks in their party's colors—that is, where party activists have difficulty separating government from party—to put the PNC in such vehicles sent a message that most PNC officers wanted to avoid. As one officer said in early 1994, "Our future is in the hands of the government. They will reap what they sow."

The Ad Hoc Commission

One of the primary objectives of the FMLN in the peace accords was the purification of the Armed Forces. Under the accords this was accomplished by the Ad Hoc Commission, composed of three Salvadoreans appointed by the U.N. who reviewed the personnel files and performances of the senior 10 percent of the officer corps. Its report, which included over 100 unpublished names, was delivered in late October 1992 to U.N. Secretary General Boutros-Ghali and President Cristiani. The named officers were to be removed within sixty days. In December, however, rightist pressure on Cristiani plus growing disarray within the FMLN produced conflicting reports about whether the *depuración* would take place on schedule. A series of conversations between the government and FMLN produced reports of "negotiations" in which the former rebels allegedly gave up on having many officers removed in exchange for a package of benefits for former combatants—to which they already were entitled under the accords. These reports led to a fire-storm of protest from NGOs, the churches, and opposition parties. Meanwhile, the FMLN was dealing with an argument between Joaquin Villalobos, who was willing to negotiate retirements for benefits, and Salvador Sánchez Ceren (Leonel Gonzalez of the FPL), who was not. Villalobos lost, and on January 13 the FMLN issued a strong statement demanding that the removals proceed on schedule.

According to a January 7, 1993, letter from Boutros-Ghali to the Security Council president, 23 officers had been cashiered; 25 transferred to other military posts in the country; 38 placed on leave without pay until they retired in no more than six months; one, Vice Minister of Defense Juan Orlando Zepeda was allowed to stay until his retirement on March 1; seven were sent into "golden exile" as military attachés abroad; and eight, including Defense Minister Ponce, were scheduled to remain on active duty until May 1994. Boutros Ghali said he was willing "to accept as satisfactory the measures adopted and implemented" by the government regarding all but the last fifteen officers. The arrangements for attachés and continuation until 1994, he said, did not conform to the recommendations, and he had "asked President Cristiani to take early action" to comply.[67] These officers were not retired, however, until June 30, 1993.

The Truth Commission

This arrangement was complicated by another provision of the accords that created a commission (the Truth Commission for El Salvador) to investigate major human rights violations, including massacres, murders, and kidnappings. The United Nations rejected government pressure to keep secret those implicated in the various crimes and released the commission's 200 page report in March 1993.[68] Days earlier President Cristiani had asked the U.N. to keep the names of those implicated confidential for an indefinite period. In an interview with Mexico's *Excelsior*, he argued that this was necessary "for reasons of internal reconciliation, to try to avoid confrontations."[69] He also appealed to the FMLN, saying it could benefit from sealing a report that might name some of its leaders; the FMLN rebuffed Cristiani and called for full disclosure.

The commission found that 95 percent of the human rights abuses since 1980 were attributable to the Armed Forces of El Salvador or paramilitary death squads; the FMLN was found to be responsible for the remainder. Among the major findings were the following:

- Mario Zamora was murdered by members of a state security force.
- Roberto D'Aubuisson ordered the assassination of Archbishop Romero, and members of his personal security force carried it out.
- The detention and murder of the four churchwomen was planned before their arrival at the airport on December 2, 1980; senior National Guard officials, including its director, Vides Casanova, knew that members of the guard had done this under orders from superiors and engaged in a systematic coverup.
- Units of the Atlacatl battalion, under its commander Domingo Monterrosa, killed more than 200 people in El Mozote in December 1981; the Atlacatl and other units killed many more in neighboring hamlets; Minister of Defense García knew of the massacres but did not investigate.
- "Agents of the state" carried out the bombing of FENASTRAS in October 1989, and "competent authorities did not carry out a complete and impartial investigation."

- Defense Minister René Emilio Ponce, in the presence of other members of the High Command, ordered Colonel Guillermo Alfredo Benavides to carry out the murder of Ignacio Ellacuria, the Jesuit rector of the UCA, and "leave no witnesses"; these same officers and others took steps to cover up their involvement.
- The FMLN's General Command "approved and adopted a policy of assassinating mayors whom they considered to be working against them"; the "nucleus" of the ERP, which included Joaquin Villalobos, ordered local commanders to implement the policy, under which eleven mayors were murdered.

In its recommendations the commission castigated the Salvadorean executive, legislative, and judicial branches of government for allowing military domination of society. It noted that the judicial reforms called for in the accords had not been implemented, and "given the enormous responsibility of the Judicial Organ in the impunity under which grave acts of violence occurred," the commission called on members of the Supreme Court, who had been chosen under preaccord rules, to resign. The president of the court, Gutiérrez Castro, announced that "The only one who can fire us is God." Cristiani said that "all state institutions have every right to express their point of view."

Gutiérrez Castro's outburst was characteristic of commentaries that issued from the government, ARENA, the PCN, and the Armed Forces after the report was released. The Armed Forces formally rejected it in a press conference on March 23. General Ponce said that the conclusions "misrepresent the historical reality and present accusations without substance and objectivity, affecting negatively the process of pacification. ... The report is unjust, incomplete, illegal, unethical, partial and insolent."[70]

Five days after the report was released, the ARENA-dominated Legislative Assembly approved a sweeping amnesty law over the vociferous but futile opposition of the PDC, CD, and UDN. It was the first law related to the peace process that was not approved by consensus.

THE UNITED NATIONS
OBSERVER MISSION (ONUSAL)

ONUSAL represents the first time the United Nations has been asked to help resolve an internal conflict; it was the first mission to include human rights and police divisions; it was therefore the first mission to integrate these divisions with traditional, military U.N. peacekeeping functions. ONUSAL was created with a mandate from the U.N. Security Council to observe and verify the peace accords. It was originally scheduled to begin monitoring human rights after a cease-fire, but the prolongation of the peace talks led both sides to request that the U.N. open the mission before the cease-fire. ONUSAL began operations with a human rights division exactly one year after the Security Council approved the mission on July 26, 1991. From four regional and two subregional offices, human rights and military observers worked to-

ONUSAL chief of mission Augusto Ramírez Ocampo discusses conditions at the El Espino cooperative with members of its directorate, October 1993. To Ramírez Ocampo's immediate left is Anders Kompas, head of the U.N. Development Progran in El Salvador.

gether (another first) to monitor forced recruitment, people detained withou families being notified, murders, and prison conditions. They established an maintained contact with the army and the guerrillas. According to on ONUSAL official, "We're not here to denounce. We're here to develop an provide positive alternatives [to previous practices]." This comment went t the heart of ONUSAL's roles in institution building and the transformation c political culture—roles that were not defined in the accords but were clearl carried out in the day-to-day monitoring, consulting, and discussions with c vilians, military, and police.

Human Rights Observation

From four to eight human rights officers were assigned to each offic and charged with receiving complaints of abuses from the governmen FMLN, and civilians; initially 150 observers from twenty-nine countrie spread out across El Salvador to deal with human rights violations as the were reported. When a complaint was received, observers went to the site an investigated, taking testimony where appropriate, then talking with the a leged violators to try to ensure that such violation, assuming it was confirme would not reoccur. ONUSAL had no judicial powers. Its mode of action wa to present facts in a case to the responsible party, try to impress on the part the fact that its behavior was in violation of international human rights norms and the peace accords, and to secure agreement that such behavior would not be repeated. In the case of affected civilians, they were free to take the case to the Salvadorean judicial system. ONUSAL's human rights office prepared periodic reports to the U.N. secretary general in which it discussed the types of complaints it received and summarized human rights violations by type and over time. The first reports in late 1991 and early 1992 angered the right because the overwhelming majority of cases were violations by government forces.

How ONUSAL dealt with forced recruitment of underage boys (less than sixteen) illustrates the methodology employed by the human rights division and, with variations, by the entire mission. In fall 1991, the San Miguel office received complaints from parents of forcibly recruited boys. Every ten days the regional coordinator, Nguyen Dong, traveled to the army's national training center (CEMFA) in La Unión to present its commander with a list of names. In the first meeting the commander virtually denied that forced recruitment of underage youth was taking place and put the list in his drawer. On the second visit the commander took the list and released five boys a few days later. By the third visit, the commander was willing to search immediately for the boys in question and release them within twenty-four hours. By November, according to Nguyen, the problem was significantly reduced. In a later interview he acknowledged that "forced recruitment ended on January 16."[71]

After the cease-fire ONUSAL human rights officers continued to receive complaints and to investigate them within the limits of their resources. In late 1993 the murders of three top FMLN officials as well as threats against and assaults on individuals in the FMLN and several other parties brought the human rights issue once again to the forefront of ONUSAL's concerns.

The Police and Military Divisions

The second and third divisions, military and police, began operations with the cease-fire on February 1, 1992. The army and the FMLN combatants were required by the accords to concentrate in sixty-two and fifteen locations, respectively, all of which were supervised by ONUSAL military observers from thirteen countries. ONUSAL was quickly forced to go beyond its mandate when it realized that there was no water, food, or sanitary system in the FMLN zones of concentration. An ONUSAL-UNDP working group was formed that addressed the problem and minimized the delay in the guerrillas' movement to these zones.

ONUSAL officers acted as mediators with the army and the FMLN in regard to any alleged human rights violations. The army could not leave its barracks without notifying ONUSAL and, in most cases, without ONUSAL officers accompanying the units. Similarly, until the final demobilization of FMLN forces on December 14, 1992, guerrillas could only leave their zones individually, unarmed and in civilian clothes. As the FMLN demobilized, ONUSAL officers received and stored arms and munitions, which the FMLN

subsequently destroyed under ONUSAL supervision. ONUSAL officers co
ducted demobilization ceremonies during which they presented each gue
rilla with a certificate and temporary identification paper. ONUSAL polic
meanwhile, were assigned to National Police stations throughout the countr
except in former FMLN-controlled zones, and monitored police behavior on
twenty-four-hour basis. ONUSAL became involved in training the PNC wi
particular emphasis on human rights education and correct police proc
dures—another step beyond its mandate. The daily interaction of military an
police with their Salvadorean cohorts provided opportunities for assisting th
processes of demilitarization and teaching new ways to treat and relate to c
vilians under a concept new to El Salvador: public security.

The National Guard and Treasury Police were eliminated by Septemb
1992 after some effort by the government at sleight of hand to keep the tw
forces intact under new names (Frontier Police and Military Police, respe
tively). The National Police was to be reduced and phased out as PNC uni
were deployed. In mid-1993, however, it had grown as former members
BIRIs, the National Guard, and the Treasury Police were incorporated, and i
training center was still graduating 60 to 100 officers monthly. This produce
a blunt critique from ONUSAL that, with pressure from the Group of Frienc
and the United States, forced the government in early October 1993 to preser
a plan for the elimination of the National Police. The plan provided for closin
the academy by the end of 1993 and for the staged demobilization of almo
10,500 police before September 1, 1994, a tacit acknowledgment of ONUSAL
earlier criticism.[72]

One case illustrates the limitations of ONUSAL's supervisory role—an
how desperately a new police force was needed. In early May 1993 a group
former soldiers and former guerrillas held a joint demonstration in front of th
Casa Presidencial to protest the government's failure to deliver the package
benefits agreed to under the accords. The demonstration was peaceful, but th
National Police antiriot squad was called out and, without provocation, fire
into the crowd. One guerrilla was killed, six soldiers and guerrillas wei
wounded, and twelve were captured. There were reliable reports that a fe
people accompanying the demonstrators appeared to have arms, but not on
policeman was injured. The ONUSAL police did not know the antiriot squa
had been sent until after the assault. Once called, they went immediately t
the scene and were joined by human rights officials. When asked wh
ONUSAL police had not accompanied the National Police, a political office
said that they were not informed or invited (as they should have been und
the accords).[73]

ONUSAL and the 1994 Elections

In January 1993 Salvadorean president Alfredo Cristiani formally aske
the United Nations to observe and verify the 1994 elections for president, Leg
islative Assembly members, mayors, and delegates to the Central America
Parliament. The Security Council passed a resolution enlarging ONUSAL
mandate "to include the observation of the electoral process due to conclud

with the General Elections in ... March 1994."[74] In September 1993 the fourth and last ONUSAL division was created with a mandate to observe and verify the process before, during, and after the March 20 elections and a possible April runoff for president should no candidate receive a majority in the first round. Theoretically, the mandate required ONUSAL election officials to be present during voter registration, and to observe the campaign, voting, and every stage of vote counting. In reality, ONUSAL had to step in with massive logistical support to ensure success in registering an estimated 786,000 adults; it had to flatter, cajole, and bully the Supreme Electoral Tribunal (TSE) to do the job it was created to do. In addition, ONUSAL officials were reduced to "ant work"—going to municipalities to look up individual birth certificates, without which one could not register to vote—because the TSE was incapable of doing it, many mayors were unwilling to help, and the legitimacy of the election after twelve years of civil war depended in large part on a high level of voter registration and participation.

On election day ONUSAL deployed 900 observers throughout the country, approximately two observers per voting site. Their job was to accompany the voting materials from the moment they were dispensed in San Salvador, through election day, to the counting of the votes and the delivery of the official totals to the capital. ONUSAL observers also maintained a parallel count that they reported to their headquarters.

Assessment

ONUSAL's presence in a country that endured an eleven-year civil war and another eleven-year period before that of growing civil unrest and government repression meant supervising the transition from a war-torn, highly militarized society to a peaceful and demilitarized one. Although the successes of the peace accords were due first to the commitment of many Salvadoreans, it is inconceivable that the peace process could have advanced as far as it did by early 1994 without ONUSAL. The opposition of extremists and the lukewarm support of many ARENA followers sapped the political will of the government, while the FMLN had to deal with competing internal interests and some serious political mistakes, the most egregious of which was the discovery of an enormous arms cache in Managua in May 1993.

Reaction to ONUSAL's role was generally positive across the political spectrum. The extreme right, however, took exception to ONUSAL's very presence in the country. David Escobar Galindo identified two sectors involved in these groups: discontented military officers who resented the change in their role, and a "sector of the traditional right, an obsessive right that has nothing to do with"[75] the progressive capital sector that Rodolfo Cardenal identified in the Introduction. These small groups resorted to vituperative paid ads in newspapers and occasional anonymous threats to senior ONUSAL officials. ONUSAL vehicles were deliberately hit by private vehicles; ONUSAL officials were subjected to rude behavior by private citizens. The political culture of people who engaged in these activities was rabidly nationalistic and politically reactionary. They viewed ONUSAL's presence as intervention in the internal affairs of the country. They did not or chose not to understand that ONUSAL was in El Salvador at the invitation of its govern ment and the FMLN. Support from many conservatives, however, was consis tent and clearly stated. Notably, two new conservative and largely Evangeli cal political parties were outspoken in their support of ONUSAL and its work This support was one source of optimism for the future because it spoke to the larger issue of political tolerance and commitment to democratic values and process.

THE "ELECTIONS OF THE CENTURY"

By mid-1993 the national and local elections scheduled for March 20 1994, were being characterized by virtually all national and international sec tors in El Salvador as the "elections of the century." This hyperbole was per haps imprudent because of the expectations that such a label could generate Nevertheless, under the Salvadorean system, the country elects a president Assembly deputies, and mayors at the same time only once every fifteen years. The president, who cannot be reelected, serves five years; deputies and mayors serve three years each. For the first time since the war began and the only time until 2009, Salvadoreans would elect all officials at the same time.

The peace accords acknowledged problems with the electoral system, in particular domination of the CCE by the party in power, and mandated a more broadly based TSE and other changes designed to democratize the sys tem. Unfortunately, the new five-man TSE was no less partisan than the old CCE. Its president, Luís Arturo Zaldivar, professed his independence but was a former ARENA deputy. ARENA, the PCN, the PDC, and the CD each had a magistrate; these individuals were elected by the Assembly on the recommen dation of their respective parties. Observation of the TSE over several month suggested two dynamics at work. The first was partisanship: ARENA and the PCN stuck together, which meant that any vote was at least three to two. The second was the "old boys' club" atmosphere: Regardless of political differ ences, the five magistrates had a common institutional interest—to make the TSE look as good as possible and present a united front, especially in the fac of increasing criticism of their work in late summer 1993. One might have ex pected the CD's magistrate, Pedro Solórzano, to be a strong advocate for the left's interests—in getting as many people registered as possible and in mak ing the registration process as simple as possible—but such was not the case Solórzano's selection, in the view of several CD members and officials, was a disaster. Said one in fall 1993, "If we lose the [presidential] election, Solórzano may be the single most responsible factor."[76]

A new electoral code took effect in January 1993, eight months later than the accords required. In July the TSE had still not approved the regulation necessary to put the code in force. This foot-dragging stood in contrast to the FMLN's desire to conclude the peace talks successfully in 1991, which was shaped in part by its recognition that it would have barely two years to trans form itself from a clandestine organization into a legal political party with all that implies. Everyone, from former commanders to rank-and-file, had to

FMLN representative collects signatures on petition to legalize the FMLN as a
political party. Plaza Cívica, San Salvador, February 1, 1992.

learn new political skills, find and train candidates to run for office, get their
supporters registered, and negotiate some sort of alliance with other parties,
especially the Democratic Convergence and, possibly, the Christian Democrats. Two years, the FMLN soon discovered, was precious little time to accomplish all of this. Another delay affected the FMLN itself. Under the accords, the Assembly was required to introduce legislation legalizing the
FMLN by May 1. ARENA deputies, however, stalled on the grounds that the
FMLN had not completely demobilized—even though the calendar for demobilization of the guerrillas was agreed to before the cease-fire began with the
final 20 percent demobilizing on October 31. The FMLN finally became a legal
political party on December 14, 1992.

The Voter Registration Imbroglio

A November 1992 national census revealed that there were 673,649 Salvadoreans over 18 who did not have *cedulas* and another 100,000 without
cedulas who would turn 18 by November 1993. A U.N. poll of 20,000 persons,
released in July 1993, estimated 786,000 unregistered voters, a major concern
for political parties from the center to the left, for ONUSAL, and for international actors, including the United States. These data meant that one-third of
those in the voting-age population were unregistered and unable to register
because they did not possess identity cards. In July and August, 59,748 citizens completed applications (SIREs) for voter registration cards (*carnés*). It

was estimated that if the TSE operated at maximum capacity between July and November, it could process 250,000 applications.[77] This situation led ONUSAL's election team to observe that "If ... it is not possible to inscribe a significant number of legitimate applicants, this will produce an irremediable delegitimization of the electoral process."[78]

By August 1993 voter registration was the major political problem.[79] The TSE's failure to come up with an effective voter registration plan was widely attributed on the left to its domination by ARENA. Others attributed it to general incompetence. Rubén Zamora argued that the major problem was that the TSE defined itself and its work legalistically and had no appreciation for the political character of its task. These reasons are not mutually exclusive. There was a general feeling on the left that ARENA understood that it was not in its interest to register hundreds of thousands of new voters, many of whom were likely to vote for the Democratic Convergence or the FMLN, although Armando Calderon Sol flatly denied this in an interview. The U.S. Embassy embraced the incompetence theory but turned on the pressure; chargé d'affaires Peter Romero sent two letters to President Cristiani expressing U.S. concern, the second of which reminded the president that Congress had frozen $35 million in aid and was prepared to freeze another $35 million if registration did not improve. One U.S. official said, "It's a mess that's just not right. ... Part of this whole thing [the peace process] is to plug people into participatory democracy." Another said that he was "about as frustrated as I've ever been on an issue." In response to the pressure, the TSE prepared a new plan to begin the last weekend in August that would take registration to the people, instead of requiring that people come to their municipalities. In July the TSE registered 1,400 in factories and markets, an insignificant figure compared to the magnitude of the problem.

The Registration Gauntlet. Voter registration should be as simple as possible. In El Salvador the TSE made the process complex and byzantine. In order to receive a *carné*, a citizen had to pursue this course:

1. Secure a birth certificate (*partida*) from the municipality in which one was born, even if it meant traveling across the country at one's own expense.
2. Secure a *cedula*, which required having a *partida* or being inscribed in the municipal register, and have some other form of identification or be personally known to the mayor.
3. Complete a SIRE at any registration site that was then sent to the TSE where a search was made of the national *partida* registry. If the *partida* was found, the SIRE was approved and a *ficha*, a computer-generated card, was produced and returned to the municipality; absent the *partida* the SIRE was returned unapproved with the reason why.
4. Return to the municipal seat to claim one's *ficha* and have the laminated *carné* with photograph made.

Multiple problems attended this process. The *partida* and *cedula* nor-
ally cost $1.25 to $5.00 per document depending on the whim of the mayor;
ne mayor charged $10.00. Some, including ARENA mayors, suspended fees
uring *jornadas* (voter registration days). In many municipalities the mayors
at on dozens of *partidas* for up to a year, despite a law requiring their submis-
on once a week. The TSE did not comply with its own thirty-day period after
eceipt of SIREs for returning *fichas*. During the spring and summer 1993,
here were numerous reports of mayors and local TSE officials arriving late,
aving early, or failing to appear for *jornadas*, a problem that diminished dur-
ng the fall. TSE workers untruthfully told citizens their *fichas* had not arrived.

Blatantly partisan meddling undermined registration efforts in several
ocales. In La Unión the infamous governor effectively prevented registration
uring the summer by intimidating the mayors. After he insulted a U.S. Em-
assy political officer, ONUSAL and the embassy called President Cristiani's
ffice and asked that the governor be reined in. Fifty percent of the unregis-
ered voters were registered by November 20, which ONUSAL considered a
ictory. Before the end of the year, President Cristiani replaced the governor.

Logistical Difficulties. Most important, the TSE was unprepared to handle
he logistics of a massive registration process. It printed insufficient docu-
nents; did not purchase enough cameras, generators, office furniture, and ve-
icles; had inadequately trained personnel, most of whom were hired under a
atronage, not merit, system; and treated its employees badly, which led to an
leven-day strike in July 1993 and subsequent threats of more strikes.

Had it not been for assistance from many quarters—the willingness of
any TSE employees to work with no per diem allowance, which for many
eant no lunch; logistical support of ONUSAL, which transported people,
achines, and documents; financial support of UNDP and AID; and human
upport of Salvadoran NGOs, which aggressively promoted voter registra-
on with door-to-door visits, printed materials, and handheld bullhorns or
ound systems mounted on pickup trucks—the TSE would not have been able
o improve on the poor results of July and August.

The second report of ONUSAL's electoral division, which cited TSE fig-
res, said that 787,834 SIREs had been received between July and November;
69,098 were from previously unregistered voters and 315,360 requested
hanges (the discrepancy between the categories and the total originated with
he TSE). The TSE also claimed that as of January 19, 1994, more than 2.6 mil-
on citizens had been registered, 2.1 million of whom had received a *carné*.
he remaining half million still had to collect a *ficha* and convert it into a *carné*.
ONUSAL concluded that the number of individuals holding *carnés* on January
9 represented about 80 percent of the voting-age population.[80]

With this number registered to vote, an important question was where
he unregistered voters were located. ONUSAL's report as well as field obser-
ation by various ONUSAL electoral officials suggested that many lived in
ormer conflict zones such as eastern Chalatenango and northern San Miguel.
n these and other areas, there was a disproportionately high number of peo-

ple who had not received a *ficha* months after completing a SIRE. Although the total number of people in this situation was probably not enough to affect the presidential election, there were certainly enough of them to affect municipal elections and, possibly, elections for the Assembly, which are calculated at the departmental level. This situation, therefore, could call into question the legit imacy of elections at the local level in areas where the FMLN had good reason to expect that it would do well.

Parties and Candidates

Beyond the participation of the FMLN, the novelty of the 1994 election was the appearance of two new parties dominated by Evangelical Christians The Evangelicals' mostly Pentecostal churches had multiplied in the 1980 and had spread to the Salvadorean middle class, a phenomenon with anteced ents in Guatemala and Brazil. By 1994 approximately 20 percent of the Salva dorean population was Evangelical. With the precedent of an Evangelical having been elected president of Guatemala in 1990, it was not surprising tha Evangelicals should begin to organize politically in El Salvador. A series o national polls gave both parties little chance of winning at any level; nonethe less, both were active and visible in the campaign.

The Movement of National Solidarity (MSN). "Solidarity," as the party re ferred to itself, appeared in November 1991 when its leaders presented the re quired petitions with 3,000 signatures to the CCE and asked for official recog nition. The party, however, was not legally inscribed by the TSE unti February 1993. The party made a point of the fact that about 60 percent of it members were Catholic and even included "some atheists." Indeed, durin; the presidential campaign, a spokesman in one television spot addresse("Brother Evangelicals ... Brother Catholics." In November 1993 the party hac established a presence in over 100 municipalities and was convinced, accord ing to its spokesman, that it would "win in '94 through God's miracle. We wi] govern for the rich as well as the poor because the Bible says that God is fo both." Its presidential candidate was Edgardo Rodríguez Englehard.

Unity Movement (MU). This party constituted itself in January 1993 and was approved by the TSE in late August. It grew out of a study group in which emerged the idea that "those who were involved in the conflict [i.e., ARENA and the FMLN] are not capable of constructing peace." The party's organizing efforts reached into most corners of the country. Its modus operandi was unique; it would go into a community and poll 50 to 100 residents on the mos serious problems they confronted, then ask who they considered the most re spected citizen in the community. MU representatives would then approach that individual and try to persuade him to become the local organizer. Execu tive Board member and candidate for mayor of San Salvador José Vicente Coto said that most of the time the individuals had never been involved ir politics and most of the time they accepted. In November 1993 the MU had the distinction of being the first party to cause a split in ARENA. The first ARENA deputy for Morazán, Jim Umaña, became disenchanted with hard-liners in the departmental party, resigned from ARENA taking several others with him, and joined the MU.

MU's founder, Jorge Martínez Menéndez, was captured and tortured in 1980 by the security forces. This experience led to a religious conversion, and after being released, Martínez, a lawyer, began to work in the most economically marginal areas of the country. In 1992, after President Cristiani removed Vice-President Merino as vice-minister of the interior, Martínez was named to succeed him and became the first Evangelical ever named to a cabinet post in El Salvador. Martínez resigned at the beginning of 1993 to run for president.

The FMLN. The largest political party making its first run at electoral politics was the FMLN, which decided not to nominate anyone for president and to focus instead on Assembly and mayoral elections. The FMLN had to deal with continuing internal problems, which produced speculation in August 1993 that its unity would not survive the election. Norma Guevara, a permanent member of COPAZ, argued, however, that the FMLN had confronted serious internal problems in the past and had always been able to unify around a larger objective. Guevara proved to be right, at least through the electoral period.

The first serious division was over whom to support for president. The FPL, PC, and PRTC all supported Rubén Zamora, the CD candidate. The RN, with Joaquin Villalobos leading a majority faction in the ERP, supported Abraham Rodríguez in his fight for the nomination of the Christian Democrats. After Rodríguez lost the primary, Villalobos and company returned to the fold and embraced Zamora. Villalobos also had problems within the ERP. He had become increasingly outspoken about the need to form an alliance with the political center, the primary reason for his support of Rodríguez. Some of Villalobos's regional former commanders did not share his enthusiasm, dissented vociferously, and were expelled by Villalobos from the ERP. A more amicable split occurred when the PCS and UDN decided to go their separate ways. The UDN had always included noncommunists, and many felt they had more in common with the Democratic Convergence than the FMLN. After the split, the UDN joined the CD.

These differences could be traced to the 1970s and 1980s; indeed, the strengths and weaknesses apparent in those periods reemerged in different forms in the 1990s. One of the strengths was the ability to hang together despite the difficulties, including the murders in November and December 1993 of three senior FMLN officials, at least one of which was clearly a political assassination. The FMLN succeeded remarkably in transforming itself from a clandestine organization to an open, well-organized party. It created an NGO, ASPAD, that put 300 voter registration promoters in the field for three months. It generated extensive analyses of the voter registration situation, which were accepted by all parties on the Junta de Vigilancia (oversight board), another institution set up under the accords composed of all legal political parties as a means of giving new and small parties a role in supervising the electoral process. These data played a role in building pressure on the TSE to become more aggressive in its voter registration plans.

The most significant weakness, in electoral terms, lay in the differen sizes and strengths of the FMLN's five constituent organizations and wher their respective popular bases were located. As in the heyday of the popula organizations, the FPL emerged in 1992 as the largest and best organized po litically. Of the five, the FPL and the Communist Party (PCS) made th quickest and most effective transition to electoral politics, the FPL because i could draw on years of political organizing and because it began transformin itself before the peace accords were signed. The PCS had experience in elec toral politics dating back to the 1960s when it participated through the UDN In contrast, the ERP, just as it had created the penultimate popular organiza tion in 1978, was slow to organize politically and only in fall 1993 opened cam paign offices in the east. Internal difficulties in Morazán and Usulután furthe undermined the ERP's efforts and raised questions about whether the FMLN would win even one Assembly seat in Morazán, where it had initially been ex pected to do well. The RN and PRTC, as the smallest of the five groups, con centrated their efforts in two departments: Cuscatlán, where Fidel Recino (Raul Hercules–RN) was running for deputy, and San Vicente, where María Marta Valladares (Nidia Díaz–PRTC) was the number one candidate for th Legislative Assembly.

The Democratic Convergence. On October 3, 1993, the MPSC, PSD, an UDN, the three parties in the CD coalition, fused to become a new politica party with the same name. During the ceremony, Carlos Díaz Barrera, the PSL secretary general, noted that this was a historic moment, the first time in E Salvador that such a union had occurred. The CD subsequently elected Arone Díaz, a lawyer, former UDN secretary general, and widow of Mario Zamora as secretary general, the only woman holding this post in any Salvadorean party.

It was clear by the summer of 1992 that Rubén Zamora would be the CL candidate for president. The question was its relationship with the FMLN There was a widespread assumption within the CD that there would be a co alition at the presidential level; some also argued for a coalition in certain de partments for Assembly races and in municipalities where only a coalition o the left could win. Those within the CD who believed that the party had to go it alone in most races in order to maintain its identity carried the day; as a re sult, each party mounted its separate slate for deputies and formed a coalition for mayor in fewer than ten municipalities. A notable exception to this policy at the local level occurred in Santa Ana where CD deputy Juan José Martel ag gressively sought to build coalitions wherever possible. As a result, by early March the CD-FMLN expected to win the mayoralties of Santa Ana and Metapan, two of the three largest cities in the department. Martel had also ac tively recruited disaffected Christian Democrats, many of whom joined the CD and some of whom became its local candidates.

The CD-FMLN pact stipulated that the FMLN would choose the vice-presidential candidate, subject to final approval of the CD. After several names were floated and were rejected for various reasons—the most notable case being Facundo Guardado because he was indicted by Nicaragua in the wake of the arms cache discovery in May 1993—the FMLN surprised everyone by selecting Francisco Lima, a seventy-six-year-old sharp-tongued lawyer and businessman who had been vice-president from 1962 to 1967.

The MNR. The MNR, which left the CD in 1992 because of differences between its new leader, Victor Valle, and Rubén Zamora, nominated Valle as its candidate for president. Discussions in fall 1993 with the PDC about a possible alliance came to naught; Valle then decided to go it alone and run as many candidates for important positions as possible. Roberto Cañas expressed interest in only one position: mayor of San Salvador. Valle asked Alberto Arene, a U.S.-trained economist, to join him on the ticket. Subsequent discussions within the MNR and with individuals in the CD led to the conclusion that the MNR was so small that it might receive less than 1 percent of the national vote, which would end its existence as a party. After more discussions with the CD and FMLN, the MNR withdrew all its candidates, joined the CD-FMLN coalition on the national ticket, and supported the FMLN candidate for mayor of San Salvador. These coalitions guaranteed the MNR at least enough votes to survive.

The Christian Democrats. The only interesting contest for a party nominee occurred in the PDC. Fidel Chávez Mena, the 1989 candidate, wanted renomination but was challenged by one of the party's founders, a man of great rectitude, Abraham Rodríguez, who also was supported by the ERP and RN. The PDC organized a national primary instead of a convention, and to no one's surprise, Chávez Mena won. He, after all, controlled the party apparatus. In the fall, Chávez expelled several party members who had supported Rodríguez for violating party discipline. The members appealed to the courts, which ruled in their favor. The issue was not resolved in early 1994 and had the effect of further dividing the party and distracting it from the campaign.

During summer 1993 there were discussions between the PDC and ARENA about a possible alliance; some ARENA deputies, when asked how the talks were going, reportedly replied, "Well, we're still talking but we don't see how we can ever reach agrement with them."[81] By December 1993 the PDC was in third place in every national poll, behind ARENA and the CD-FMLN coalition.

ARENA. As in previous elections, ARENA had a well-oiled, well-funded campaign machine. The selection of San Salvador mayor Armando Calderon Sol as its standard-bearer, however, produced dissension within the ranks. Calderon Sol did not have the intelligence, polish, or political instincts of Alfredo Cristiani. He was viewed by sectors within his own party as too conservative; the San Salvador departmental leadership opposed his nomination. He had been close to Roberto D'Aubuisson and never lost an opportunity to eulogize the party's founder; it was widely reported in San Salvador in mid-1993 that in a small ARENA gathering, Calderon said, "Fredy Cristiani signed the accords, I didn't." The clear implication was that Calderon did not feel bound to support full implementation of the accords. He also reportedly said that he would fold the remaining National Police into the PNC after his inauguration, a move that would violate the accords, destroy the integrity of the PNC, and outrage at least 70 percent of the Salvadorean population, not to mention the United Nations, the United States, the Group of Friends, and other international donors. In an interview, however, Calderon professed total support: "I am the most obliged to fulfill the accords. I was in New York with President Cristiani the day that happy agreement was reached." He denied ever saying he did not support the accords.[82]

Calderon was joined on the ticket by Enrique Burgo Bustamante, the president of TACA airlines. Burgo was widely seen as coming from the Cristiani wing of the party; the behavior of both on the campaign trail, however, raised questions about Burgo's relative moderation. ARENA, like other parties, did most campaigning on weekends. Caravans were organized to visit a series of towns in one or two departments over a two-day period, with advance work to attract the crowds. On caravans in San Miguel and Morazán, both candidates consistently reviled the individuals on the CD-FMLN ticket, calling them "terrorists" and "cow killers" (*matavacas*)[83] and charging that "only riff-raff (*chusma*) will vote for those idiots." This message was not universally well received by the party faithful; a hairdresser in San Miguel acknowledged that she was an ARENA supporter but that she planned to vote for the MU because "Calderon only talks about war."

National Conciliation. The PNC, which had appeared to be slowly fading with each successive election, suddenly enjoyed a new surge in membership from former military officers who had been cashiered in the *depuración* and were unhappy with ARENA for its role in reaching the peace accords. The PCN nominated former air force commander Rafael Bustillo, who was implicated in nefarious activities from drug-running to graft to death squads during the 1980s. Bustillo, however, withdrew as a candidate on September 1, charging that the party had refused to allow him to control its apparatus. After weeks of internecine struggles that displaced some of the PCN's top leaders, the party nominated a lawyer and retired general, Roberto Escobar García, who had been a presidential candidate for PAISA, which he founded after leaving the PCN in 1984. In early 1994 Escobar García was elected the PCN's secretary general.

MAC. This splinter from the 1989 wars in the PDC nominated Rhina Escalante de Rey Prendes as its candidate for president. She had the distinction of being the first woman ever nominated for president of El Salvador. The holder of two doctorates in jurisprudence and economics, she was also the wife of MAC's 1989 nominee, Julio Adolfo Rey Prendes. Her first television ad was a direct appeal to women: "You work for me, and when I'm president I'll work for you." She never said what she would do.

The Campaign

Unlike 1989, when ARENA was the clear front-runner, 1994 was more complex. First, the full political spectrum was participating. Second, ARENA's candidate, Armando Calderon Sol, was as charismatic as a bowl of gruel and had no Bobby D'Aubuisson to rev up the crowds for him. Instead he resorted to chorus-line ARENA cheerleaders, vituperative stump speeches, and an enormous campaign budget. Second, Fidel Chávez Mena was a weak, uncharismatic candidate who was presiding over a party that appeared to be

ajor candidates for president of El Salvador, 1994: Left, Armando Calderon Sol
RENA); right, Rubén Zamora (CD).

sintegrating. Third, these factors increased Zamora's chances of coming in
cond (behind ARENA) in the first round of voting. Indeed, all national polls
om November 1993 onward placed Zamora second. Fourth, there was a
rong feeling on the left (CD, FMLN, and MNR) that in the event of a runoff for
esident, the strategy would be "all against ARENA." In 1992 this appeared
e obvious strategy; from mid-1993 on it was problematic not only because of
e PDC's internal difficulties and its flirtation with ARENA but because a pri-
ite poll taken for the PDC in early 1994 revealed that three-fourths of the re-
ondents would vote for ARENA in a second round. Fifth, there were three
ild cards in the race, the MSN, MU, and PCN, which could only drain votes
om ARENA, although national polls suggested that combined, the best they
uld hope to do was prevent Calderon from winning on March 20.

   Gentlemen's Agreements. ONUSAL tried to preempt the kind of character
sassination in which Calderon and Burgo were engaging by encouraging all
arties from the national to the local level to sign "gentlemen's agreements."
t the national level ONUSAL's chief of mission, Augusto Ramírez Ocampo,
cceeded in hammering out such an agreement among all presidential candi-
ates save Chávez Mena, who declined to sign on the grounds that it did not
> far enough. ONUSAL election officials encouraged similar signed agree-
ents at the departmental level and in larger municipalities, with consider-
le success. The CD, FMLN, and MU made conscious decisions to avoid
udslinging; their national tickets and most local candidates adhered closely
this principle. In San Miguel the FMLN and MU made a pact to avoid all vi-
ent or negative language. The result, according to two ONUSAL election ob-

servers in the east, was a colorless, unexciting campaign by the FMLN, the la thing anyone expected.

This did not stop dirty campaigning and other violations of the agree ment, the electoral code, and human rights. Complaints came in to ONUSAL regional offices on a daily basis, the most common of which were that or party had painted over another party's signs or murals. There were also mor serious charges of intimidation, threats, and murder, most often from the le about the right. In the months prior to January 31, "at least fifteen person with some political connection, about whom the suspicion or complaint [was that the crimes were politically motivated," were murdered. Ten had be longed to the FMLN, four to ARENA, and one to the MSN. In addition ONUSAL received an additional thirty-one complaints of murders that th complainants charged were politically motivated.[84]

A major violation of the electoral code that President Cristiani ha promised to avoid was alleged in late February when a group of workers from the Ministry of Public Works met with the Junta de Vigilancia and complaine that ARENA supporters were using the ministry's printing press and pape during weekends to produce campaign propaganda, and that ARENA was s phoning off four barrels of gasoline every weekend to keep the caravans run ning. The workers brought one of the printing plates and page proofs of th materials, which they left with the junta. The junta filed a formal complair with ONUSAL. Said one bemused junta member, "ARENA has so muc money. Why do they bother?"

Selling the Message. By late January television, especially in prime tim was awash with political advertising.[85] Not surprisingly, ARENA's ads wer the slickest, the most sophisticated, and the most expensive. The party's cam paign slogan was "We're going to live better" (*Vamos a vivir mejor*), and it ap propriated the universal Latin American symbol for "OK," a thumbs-up. also had several new campaign songs in different musical styles; the son most frequently heard was extremely catchy and stuck in the memor whether one wanted it to or not. The CD-FMLN coalition also had its ow catchy campaign song; the difference was that one heard the ARENA dit about five times as often as the coalition's.

Most of ARENA's images featured well-dressed, middle-class, ofte young and enthusiastic Salvadoreans. In a few ads there were images of clean neat, and well-dressed *campesinos*, always smiling and almost always givin the thumbs-up. Some ads were all image: a beautiful country with beautifu people, all of which was because of ARENA. One ad showed what Calderc had done as mayor of San Salvador; there were images of parks, a traffic circ with an enormous Salvadorean flag, new monuments, new roads, clean ma kets. There were no images of *tugurios*, street vendors (a major issue in th city), the poor, or the mounds of garbage that was a growing urban problen With a smaller war chest and with the obvious need to tell the people who h was, what issues he considered important, and what he intended to do abou them, Zamora ran a series of ads that identified certain problems, such as th high cost of living and families separated by the economic situation tha caused one or more members to live in other countries and send back remi tances. Then the campaign produced five-minute ads that addressed health, education, housing, and the economy and ran in prime time.

The tough talk for the coalition was left to Francisco Lima. The most clever and satiric coalition ad featured a dramatization of two businessmen meeting in an office and exchanging a contract for a briefcase full of money. Only the hands and middle of the bodies were shown, and at the end, the two men shook hands, said "¡Vamos a vivir mejor!" and gave a thumbs-up. Lima then appeared and said that corruption had to stop and the coalition was prepared to stop it.

This ad, however, was mild compared with the ostensibly nonpartisan ads run by an extreme-right-wing think tank, the Institute for Freedom and Democracy (ILYD). In late 1993 ILYD began a series entitled "Ayer en la Historia" (Yesterday in history). Each ad featured newspaper photographs of and headlines about bombings, kidnappings, and assassinations from the 1970s and 1980s that were attributed to "terrorists." The ads concluded with a beautiful shot of a Salvadorean volcano and the same punch line, "We want to live in peace and construct democracy." The TSE went to court to ban these ads charging that they violated the electoral code; ILYD appealed, the Supreme Court struck down the ban, and the ads reappeared.

Another group of allegedly nonpartisan, extremely sophisticated ads was presented by a number of government ministries and agencies, including the Ministry of Agriculture, FINATA, ISTA, the Secretariat for National Reconstruction, and the executive branch. Their images and voice-overs detailed all the government had accomplished in the previous five years. These ads provoked severe criticism from members of the opposition, who argued that they were nothing more than propaganda for ARENA and that the government had no business spending millions of colones on self-aggrandizement in the face of great social needs. In late February the ads disappeared. There is little question that they were in violation of at least the spirit, if not the letter of the electoral code, which barred the government from any involvement in political campaigns.

Assessment. The discussion thus far may leave one with the impression that the 1994 campaign was lively and dynamic. It was, in fact, rather boring. There were, to be sure, moments of excitement, especially for the parties' faithful. There were interesting moments, sometimes positive, other times negative. But there was no sense anywhere in the country outside the parties' headquarters that these were indeed the "elections of the century," the "culmination of the peace process." Indeed, the 1994 elections were not the culmination of the peace process because much remained to be done, especially around the issues of lands, reintegration, the PNC, and the judicial system. The elections were an important part of the process for the obvious reason that they marked the first time the FMLN was participating in elections—and for the less obvious but no less important reason that who occupied the Casa Presidencial on June 1, 1994, who controlled the Legislative Assembly, and who occupied the town halls around the country would determine the direction El Salvador would take and the shape of public policy for the next five years.

PEACE AT LAST

Johnnetta Cole, the president of Spelman College in Atlanta, tells the story of an old woman who was given a guitar. After a while her benefactors returned to find her strumming the same note, over and over. When told that there were many other notes on the guitar, she said, "Yes, I know. But I've found *my* note."

In 1982 I wrote that there could be no lasting, viable solution to the conflict in El Salvador without the participation of the revolutionary organizations and that the only question was how much more blood would be shed before the U.S. government accepted that reality.

That has been "my note."

It took eleven years and almost 80,000 dead before the United States accepted the inevitability of a permanent and legal leftist political force in El Salvador.

Things changed in El Salvador before the peace accords. Politically, the country moved from a civilian-military junta to an elected civilian president. Militarily, the Armed Forces expanded from 11,000 to 56,000 men while the FMLN expanded throughout the country. Economically, El Salvador regressed to levels of the early 1970s. The United States, which began by offering military assistance to the new junta in October 1979, began the 1980s supporting the Salvadorean government and military at the rate of $1 million to $1.5 million per day.

The Democratic Revolutionary Front evaporated in the late 1980s, its place taken by dozens of nongovernmental organizations, many of which did not dream of existing—or have reason to exist—in 1979. The left, whether ARENA and the Armed Forces like it or not—and clearly they do not like it—is and will remain a significant player in the Salvadorean drama. The fact is the FMLN played a major role in the positive changes that have occurred since 1982: the opening of political space; the reemergence of popular organizations; the political return of the democratic left; the mobilization and participation of women; the new prophetic voices in the Salvadorean churches, both Catholic and Protestant; the renewed activity in Christian Base Communities; and, most important, the debate over what kind of society El Salvador should be, what kind of political and economic system it should have—none of this would have happened without the FMLN.

The FMLN has forced an important segment of the oligarchy—what Rodolfo Cardenal in the Introduction calls "progressive capital"—to change its way of thinking. In January 1980 a private-sector spokesman said that it might be necessary to kill 100,000 in order to rid El Salvador of its problems and restore the status quo ante. By the late 1980s that man worked at FUSADES, which Cardenal described as part of "progressive capital." Like the oligarchy, the FMLN had to accept new realities. The dream of military victory, socialist revolution, and the destruction of the oligarchy vanished long before the guerrillas. The FMLN accepted the governmental structure created by the United States and the Christian Democrats in 1982. The oligarchy still controls the national economy and continues to insist, contrary to the accords, that its neoliberal, trickle-down model of development is not negotiable. The task for the left is to figure out how to challenge this model without becoming an obstacle to reconstruction and economic recovery.

There are those, of course, who argue that El Salvador would be better off had none of this ever happened—if things had remained as they were before, say, 1974. There was stability; everyone knew his or her place; there were agitators, but they were taken care of without any social disruption. El Salvador's GNP was growing. People were earning money. The peasants were happy. El Salvador could become another Chile.

There are also those who will argue that without the FMLN there would not be 75,000 dead. They are probably correct. Without the FMLN there would have been many thousands more dead. There would have been no internal counterforce to the absolute power of the Armed Forces and the death squads as they confronted the awakening in the 1970s of thousands of Salvadoreans, Gulliver tied down by strings of oppression and repression, who finally cried "¡Basta!"—enough—an awakening so profound that even the terror of 1980–1983 could not stop them. It is a sad reality that the FMLN's achievements at the negotiating table would have been inconceivable without the armed struggle. The oligarchy and the army were not disposed to transform themselves or the system to which they had given birth, nurtured, and defended at enormous social cost.

It is regrettable that some members of those same groups continue to try to stop the march of history. Meanwhile, the Chapultepec accords are transforming Salvadorean society in ways never anticipated or desired by the powerful. It comes down to this: What kind of society will El Salvador be? Who will wield power? In whose interest will decisions be made? Will it be, as Nicaraguan Jesuit and economist Xabier Gorostiaga termed it, "the logic of the minority"? Will the same power elite that has been making the decisions to suit itself for almost 500 years continue to do so? Or will decisions be made according to the "logic of the majority," in the interests of that 70 percent of Salvadorean people who have been excluded and objectified? Changes will not occur overnight or, as continuing threats, human rights abuses, and foot dragging on major reforms reveal, without cost and struggle. Progressive forces in El Salvador, with the help of the United Nations and other interested parties, succeeded in substantially demilitarizing El Salvador in the space of a year and began to change the terms of political debate, the political process, and, in some measure, the political system. The culmination of this process, that is, full implementation of the peace accords, would represent—as Secretary General Boutros-Ghali said at the signing of the accords in Mexico City—a "negotiated revolution." The question, as El Salvador came to elections in March 1994, was whether this end would be realized or whether it would be a revolution derailed.

Epilogue:
The Electronic Tamale

On March 20, 1994, an ARENA member found that, despite holding a valid carné, she was not on the voting list. When poll workers refused her a ballot, Hector Dada Hirezi, who was next in line and supported the Coalition, insisted that she be allowed to vote. She was. Her party's founder, the late Roberto D'Aubuisson, was on the voting list. Former FMLN commander and soon-to-be elected Legislative Assembly deputy Francisco Jovel was not. In Villa Victoria, Cabañas, a man who held a *carné* issued on October 24, 1987, and who said he had voted in all elections since then, could not find his name on the list. He was not alone; in Santa Tecla, in a ninety-minute period an ONUSAL election observer recorded almost 150 names of voters with *carnés* who were not on the list. At least 75 percent of the *carnés*, she said, had been issued on October 24, 1987.[1]

Before the 1980s, stuffed ballot boxes were known as "tamales," a reference to the Mexican dish made of crushed corn, ground meat, and chile peppers, then wrapped in corn husks and steamed. In the analogy, corn husks are ballot boxes, and the maize (legal ballots) is mixed with other things. By 1994, with between 2,000 and 3,000 international election observers, stuffing ballot boxes the old-fashioned way was next to impossible. There was, however, a more efficient way of altering electoral results—before the election took place—through the computer. There is abundant evidence that citizens were prevented from voting through a variety of electronic machinations, some of which were discussed in Chapter 8. Election day confirmed these and other irregularities. Apart from the 340,000 *fichas* that were never delivered to municipalities and another 81,000 SIREs that were never converted into *fichas*, there were thousands of people with valid *carnés* who were unable to vote because they were not on the voting list.

In El Salvador's largest cities, people are assigned to polling places alphabetically regardless of where they live. For example, in San Salvador a person with the last name of Cana Zamorano should have voted at the International Fairgrounds. However, if a data-entry technician had reversed the last names (Zamorano Cana), the individual would have appeared on a list at the national gymnasium, four kilometers away. The only way to find out would have been to go to the gymnasium. In addition, ONUSAL and other observers documented entire families and other groups of fifteen to thirty sequential names that had vanished from the list. There were other problems. In March the master voting list, posted near the entrance to the polling place, should have been identical to the lists at each individual voting table. In many cases they were not; names appeared on the first list but not on the second. In some towns, like Sensuntepeque, Cabañas, and in the city of San Miguel, voting tables were set up in and around the central plaza, but information directing voters to their respective tables was extremely limited. As a result many citizens gave up and left without voting. On March 20 the departmental Supreme Electoral Tribunal (TSE) in Sensuntepeque remedied this situation by midmorning: it set up microfiche machines with the master voting list in a gazebo in the center of the plaza. A TSE official later in the day said there had been a constant line of ten to twenty people looking for their name or their table.

Abstentions were estimated at 43 percent on March 20 and 50 percent on April 24.[2] These figures may seem normal to U.S. voters, but the hype surrounding the Salvadorean elections as the "elections of the century" and the "culmination of the peace process" might have led one to expect a turnout of at least 80 percent. Difficulties with voter registration, a largely boring political campaign, and serious problems with public transportation on March 20, however, produced alienation and apathy that translated into a level of abstentions not significantly different from the levels in 1989 and 1991.

THE ELECTION RESULTS

The TSE continued its incompetent and unprofessional behavior. On the night of March 20, the TSE was prepared to allow President Cristiani, who was waiting with Armando Calderon Sol in a room adjacent to the main ballroom of the four-star Presidente Hotel, to claim a first-round victory. Only phone calls from ONUSAL to the major candidates advising them of the results of its "quick count," which like the final result gave ARENA just under 50 percent, prevented a political fiasco. Cristiani slipped quietly out of the hotel.

The TSE rented a number of rooms in the Presidente, including all of the cabanas facing the swimming pool, where the final vote count was conducted by the respective departmental electoral boards (Junta Electoral Departmental, JED). The TSE had promised that final presidential results would be ready within forty-eight hours; it took ten days to complete the count and TSE president Luís Zaldivar sought to move the process along in his own way. On Friday afternoon, March 25, according to an official observer, Zaldivar appeared at the La Libertad JED and said, "We need the presidential results right now. What's one little [ballot] box if it's not going to make a difference? Just make it work and let's get a result." To their credit, the La Libertad and the other JEDs, all of which received a similar visit, took their task seriously and ignored the TSE president.

These problems, however, likely did not affect the outcome of the presidential election. They may have had an impact in some close Assembly races, and they certainly had an impact at the municipal level, to the detriment of the left. On March 20, ARENA won 49.3 percent of the presidential vote, the coalition of the FMLN, CD, and MNR (hereafter Coalition) won 24.5 percent.[3] The Christian Democrats (PDC) came in an ignominious third with 16.4 percent. In the runoff, ARENA's Calderon Sol won in a landslide with 68 percent against Rubén Zamora's 32 percent.

The elections for 84 Legislative Assembly deputies were significantly more mixed. ARENA won 39 seats, the FMLN 21, and the PDC 18. The remaining seats were divided among the PCN (4), CD (1), and MU (1). Many in the FMLN were ecstatic; its most optimistic calculation had been 18 deputies. The left won one deputy in eleven of the fourteen departments, five deputies in San Salvador, and five on the national slate. If the FMLN, CD, and MNR could have agreed to run in coalition as they did for the presidential election, they would have picked up at least three more deputies, in La Libertad, La Unión, and Cabañas.

The failure to run in coalition cost them mayoral elections. The most conservative projections had given the FMLN between 50 and 60 mayoralties; it won only 15. ARENA swept 206, the PDC won 20, and the PCN won 10. In a number of municipalities, including the port of Acajutla, Sonsonate, and Ayutuxtepeque, San Salvador, the combined vote for FMLN and CD candidates exceeded that of the candidate, usually from ARENA, who won. Earlier problems with registration had a major impact. In one Morazán town, Torola, the FMLN lost by twenty votes; 500 former combatants had been denied their carnés because the local mayor did not send in their partidas. In another, San Fernando, the FMLN lost by two votes; 190 militants did not receive their carnés.

These results suggest at least three lessons: The left must run in coalition if it hopes to win at the national level; ARENA's domination of many municipalities, including several in metropolitan San Salvador, is vulnerable; and the FMLN's new representative on the TSE has a clearly defined task between 1994 and 1997—to ensure that the unregistered are registered and that the dead are removed from the rolls.

The obvious question is why the left did not win a larger portion of the vote. Apart from the myriad problems with registration and divided candidacies, there are at least five additional factors: fear, political culture, confusion over vote splitting, a punishment vote for the FMLN, and the left's failure to celebrate its role in the peace process and take responsibility for its major successes. Fear took two forms. There was the traditional fear of communism that ARENA candidates and militants shamelessly exploited. In some areas people were told that, if the FMLN won their children would be taken away. Two weeks before the runoff, ARENA vendors appeared on the streets of upscale neighborhoods hawking plastic cups, balls, and other paraphernalia with ARENA's logo, and bumper stickers with "Patria si, comunismo no" (Fatherland yes, communism no) printed on them. That slogan, a common sight in the 1980s, had not been seen since before the peace accords.

The second type of fear was the result of threats and lies ranging from the general (Do you want El Salvador to become like Nicaragua?) to the specific: In a western El Salvador town after the first round of voting, a man told Coalition vice-presidential candidate Francisco Lima that he wanted to vote for the Coalition but that his community had recently pooled its resources to build a school and had been told by local ARENA leaders that if the community voted for the Coalition, the government would not send a teacher. ARENA also warned people that a Coalition victory would mean renewed capital flight and the subsequent loss of jobs.

Traditional political culture also played a role. In most cultures everyone loves a winner; among poor and marginalized Latin Americans this has been a critical factor in their continuing electoral support for elitist governments that, by most measures, have not ruled in their interests. ARENA looks and acts like a winner. Its campaign propaganda constantly emphasized this theme; its seemingly bottomless pit of campaign funds reinforced it.

This factor clearly had a greater impact at the presidential level than at the departmental and municipal levels; the three parties making up the Coalition won almost 32,000 votes more in Assembly elections than the Coalition did in the presidential race. ARENA, for its part, ran 35,000 votes ahead of itself at the presidential level as compared with its total vote for Assembly races. This is explained in part by the fact that the pattern for the PCN was the reverse; the old official party received 13,000 votes more in Assembly races than for the presidency.

At the same time, necessary differences in the ballots for the three elections produced confusion and thousands of null votes. The presidential ballot grouped the flags of the three Coalition parties inside one square. On the Assembly and municipal ballots, the FMLN, CD, and MNR flags were printed separately. As a result, many who voted for the Coalition at the presidential level then marked both the FMLN and CD or FMLN and MNR flags at the municipal level where two parties joined to run a candidate. This apparently cost the left Mejicanos, one of the largest municipalities in metropolitan San Salvador, where the FMLN and CD ran in coalition and lost by less than 200 votes but over 1,000 votes were nullified. According to observers, many null ballots had an "X" through both the FMLN and CD flags.

The fourth factor was a punishment vote for the left. In its most simple form, this meant that people refused to vote for the FMLN because of its role in the war and the destruction it wrought. ARENA had the good fortune not to be associated with the war in the public mind, and the left chose not to exploit ARENA's historical ties to the death squads. The question of a punishment vote was more complicated still. In former conflict zones, according to a study by journalist Tom Gibb, the municipal seat often became and remained an ARENA stronghold, whereas the outlying villages of the municipality were and remained FMLN strongholds.[4] There is evidence that citizens from such villages had significantly more difficulty receiving their *carnés* than did their compatriots in the municipal seat. On election day ARENA won many of these municipalities that had been expected to go to the FMLN. Furthermore, many FMLN sympathizers did not want former commanders running for of fice; they wanted civilians. In Morazán, this attitude prevented one of the FMLN's top commanders, Jorge Meléndez (Comandante Jonas), from being a candidate for deputy; instead the FMLN's departmental convention chose a young lawyer, Elí Aviléo Díaz.

The fifth factor was, perhaps, the least comprehensible. The left in general and Rubén Zamora in particular decided not to wrap themselves in the major successes of the peace accords for which they could legitimately claim credit. Instead, they chose to focus entirely on a series of real concerns, as identified in opinion polls, and programs to address those issues, which included housing, jobs, and public safety. For example, in addressing the safety issue, Zamora and the FMLN could have emphasized that the National Civilian Police (PNC) would not exist had it not been for the FMLN's insistence during the negotiations that the security forces be abolished and replaced with a new police force. The left could have attacked the Cristiani government for allowing the PNC to become increasingly dominated by former National Police officers, in violation of the peace accords, but it was silent on this critical issue. After the election several FMLN leaders acknowledged their error.[5]

AFTERMATH

The final results of El Salvador's 1994 elections produced fallout ranging from the farcical to the profound. The night of April 24 president-elect Armando Calderon Sol gave an unexpectedly statesmanlike acceptance speech, while President Cristiani, normally a model of decorum, appeared partially inebriated and sang "El Rey" (The King), an old Mexican song.

The MAC received less than 1 percent of the vote and ceased to exist as a party, even as it won one mayoralty in eastern El Salvador. One of the two new Evangelical-dominated parties, the MSN, disappeared for the same reason.

Few were surprised when Victor Valle and Fidel Chávez Mena resigned as secretaries general of their parties, the MNR and PDC respectively, having led them into electoral disaster. The MNR's hopes of surviving were dashed when the TSE applied the 1 percent rule to it as well. Because the MNR was a member of the Socialist International, the question of whether a new social democratic party would emerge in the coming years was of great interest, especially for two factions of the FMLN (the ERP and RN) that had already publicly embraced social democracy. The demise of the PDC was described by several Salvadorean analysts as a tragedy that might have been averted had Chávez Mena chosen, after his 1989 loss to Cristiani, to relinquish control of the party to a new and younger leadership unsaddled with the political baggage of the 1980s. A similar view was expressed by those who understood that democracy requires a broad and stable center, something that did not exist in the highly polarized politics of El Salvador in spring 1994.

The most stunning development, however, came on the first day of the new Legislative Assembly. Through a simple but clever change in internal governance, ARENA succeeded in doing what the U.S. government had been unable to do for fourteen years: It precipitated an open split in the FMLN. In

the closing hours of the old Assembly, ARENA rammed through a bill tha
gave the party absolute control over the direction of the legislature by givin;
the Assembly president two votes in the event of a tie in the ten-person leader
ship. In a party caucus a majority of the FMLN's leadership voted to abstai
from participation in the Assembly directorate (one president, four vice-presi
dents, and five secretaries) until the rules changed. When the vote came fo
president of the Assembly, however, five FMLN deputies from the ERP an
two of three from the RN voted for ARENA deputy Gloria Salguero Gross
fourteen (from the FPL, PC, and PRTC) abstained. Eduardo Sancho (RN) the
nominated Ana Guadalupe Martínez (ERP) for vice-president, and she wa
elected with a unanimous vote and fifteen abstentions (the fourteen no
joined by the one CD deputy, Jorge Villacorta). Later Sancho was nominate
for secretary by an ERP deputy and elected in the same fashion.

With passionate oratory Santa Ana deputy Dagoberto Gutiérrez de
nounced ARENA: "They have shown their true colors," he began. "They tal
of democracy, reconciliation and compromise, but their actions ar
antidemocratic. We will not participate ... until the rules change." Severa
FMLN deputies characterized the day's events as a "tragedy." Ana Guadalup
Martínez later said in a press interview that the goal was to show ARENA tha
the double-vote rule was not necessary and she hoped that in a few month
ARENA would reverse its position.[6] ERP leader Joaquin Villalobos told th
press that if the fourteen could not practice democracy they should "go bac
to the mountains."

The FMLN responded by suspending all seven deputies from the part
and removing Villalobos from the party's directorate. FMLN coordinato
Shafik Handal accused Villalobos of "reaching an understanding" wit
ARENA.[7] The five organizations then moved to negotiate a new pact tha
would open up the party, allow greater flexibility for each, and thereby pre
serve the FMLN as a party. The party's action, however, had no impact on th
standing of the seven as deputies. They would continue to serve unless, as in
dividuals, they resigned, a highly unlikely event. The Christian Democrat
immediately claimed that they were now the "second force" in the Assembl
since they had eighteen deputies to the FMLN's fourteen.

CONCLUSION

The 1994 elections reinforced one truism known to every serious studen
of politics: Elections do not equal democracy. They are a necessary but insuffi
cient condition for the successful practice of a difficult and complex process
Salvadoreans are continuing to learn how to practice democracy, a proces
that began, against all odds, in 1982. They have learned a great deal in the en
suing years, but much remains to be assimilated.

First, they need to learn that politics should not be viewed as a zero-sun
game—I win only to the extent that you lose. Politics at its best is a positive
sum game: Everyone wins something, and the democratic process wins mos

of all. There is a danger, however, that ARENA has not learned this lesson, as its behavior in the Assembly suggests.

Second, Salvadoreans must address directly and quickly the disillusion and frustration produced by the elections. It was deeply disturbing to read that a new, apparently extreme-left death squad, the Salvadorean Revolutionary Front (FRS), threatened the seven dissident FMLN deputies with death for betraying revolutionary ideals.[8] Although the possibility that the FRS was an invention of the extreme right could not be dismissed, it was no secret that there were many on the left who felt that the FMLN had given up too much for peace and that twelve years of war and 75,000 lives was a very high price for twenty-one deputies and fifteen mayors. This unhappiness can turn into civil disobedience and violence if it is not addressed. The situation is a challenge for the new government as well as the opposition.

Third, the FMLN needs to listen to its people. The ERP made the mistake of not doing this in 1992 and 1993 with resulting internal divisions. But the FMLN must also reach out to and educate the sympathetic but afraid and the undecided. This means a great deal of grassroots work, but it is the only way to preserve the core support it attracted in the elections and build on it. The alternative is the fate of the former guerrilla M-19 party in Colombia, which showed extremely well in its first electoral outing, then faded away in subsequent elections. The FMLN also needs to devote considerable energy to reform of the electoral process and to ensuring that all Salvadoreans over eighteen are registered to vote.

These developments portend political realignments that were undefined but inevitable in mid-1994. The most fundamental lesson for the left is this: If it wants to win, it must broaden its base and form coalitions. Otherwise it is doomed to remain a minority party for the foreseeable future.

There is no question that ARENA favors this scenario. After the elections a number of *Areneros* compared their party with Mexico's Institutional Revolutionary Party (PRI), which has dominated politics and government in that country since the 1930s. The fact that ARENA won the presidency with an extremely weak candidate suggests that the analogy is not far-fetched. In any event, the oligarchy was once again in control of the political and economic sectors of the country, as it had not been since December 1931.

All of this recalls Stephen Webre's penetrating commentary about the 1972 election; the flaw of the political reform of the 1960s, he wrote, was that it created an opposition but by definition forbade that opposition from coming to power. There were signs in 1994 that ARENA's design for Salvadorean politics in the foreseeable future was no different. The challenge before the opposition was to make sure that did not happen.

Notes

PROLOGUE

1. Cienfuegos had just finished a tennis game at an exclusive sports club in San Salvador when he was assassinated by three gunmen on March 7, 1985. The gunmen, dressed in tennis clothes, got away. Subsequently, a renegade FMLN faction, the Clara Elizabeth Ramírez Brigade, claimed responsibility for the act, but the FMLN itself, through its official voice, Radio Venceremos, denied complicity. "Salvadoran Army Officer Slain in Sports Club" (Reuters), *New York Times*, March 8, 1985; "FMLN niega complicidad en muerte de Cienfuegos" [FMLN denies complicity in death of Cienfuegos], *El Diario de Hoy*, March 11, 1985; "Terroristas atribuyen crimen en Cienfuegos" [Terrorists acknowledge Cienfuegos crime], *La Prensa Gráfica*, March 9, 1985. The Clara Elizabeth Ramírez Brigade emerged following an internal power struggle in the Popular Forces of Liberation (FPL) in early 1983 (see Chapters 4 and 6).

2. Interview with municipal official in Jucuarán, January 10, 1984.

3. Father Rogelio Ponseele was both a product of evangelizing efforts of the Catholic Church in the 1970s and a recipient of its consequences. In the early 1970s he became pastor of the parish of Zacamil, near San Salvador. By 1979 he was being openly attacked as a subversive, and in early 1980 the National Guard began to harass him and his parishioners—to the point of driving a tank up to the front of the church one day. As threats against his life increased, Ponseele began sleeping in a different place each night. By mid-1980 he realized that he had three choices: He could stay in Zacamil and wait to be killed; he could leave the country; or he could go to the mountains and continue his pastoral work there. He chose the third course and spent the ensuing years serving as a priest to both civilians and guerrillas in zones under FMLN control. All this he related during our long conversation in Jucuarán.

On February 1, 1992, Ponseele appeared publicly in San Salvador for the first time since 1980. He was present for the swearing in of the Peace Commission (COPAZ), the body responsible for implementation of the political aspects of the peace accords (see Chapter 8).

4. Zambel and Pedro (David Pereira Rivera) both survived the war and in 1993 were working in the Communist Party headquarters in San Salvador.

5. Interview with five FMLN recruits, January 11, 1984.

6. Janeth Samour Hasbun had been a philosophy student at the Universidad Centroamericana José Simeon Cañas (UCA), a Jesuit institution, in San Salvador. In our interview she remembered fondly several of her former professors, including former rector and junta member Román Mayorga. In late December 1984 she and a younger ERP colleague, Máxima Reyes Torres, were picked up by the National Guard in the city of San Miguel. Radio Venceremos identified her by her real name, said she was a mem-

ber of the ERP's Central Committee, and demanded her release. On January 23, 1985, *La Prensa Gráfica*, one of San Salvador's morning newspapers, cited military sources who said that Samour Hasbun was still undergoing interrogation. The next day it ran another story quoting Lieutenant Colonel Ricardo Cienfuegos as saying that the capture never occurred, that Venceremos's allegations were false; the story implied that the FMLN was trying to cover up its own internal purge. Her disappearance was also the subject of cable traffic between the U.S. Embassy and Washington. "Capture of Guerrilla Leader Janeth Samour Hasbun," confidential cable from Ambassador Thomas Pickering to Department of State. Released under Freedom of Information Act (FOIA), January 24, 1985.

7. Pedro was thirty-six years old and married and had three children he had not seen in one and a half years. He was from Santa Ana and was a carpenter by trade. In the early 1970s he became general secretary of his labor union. He joined the Salvadorean Communist Party (PCS) in 1971 and participated in the electoral campaigns of 1972 and 1977 through the PCS legal front, the National Democratic Union (UDN). He was elected to the Central Committee of the party in 1979 and became a guerrilla in June 1981.

8. The Latin American Studies Association is an international organization of academics and other specialists on Latin America and the Caribbean.

9. Colonel Herrarte was one of the officers named in the Truth Commission's report, issued in March 1993. The army tried to keep him and seven other senior officers on active duty until May 1994, but public and international pressure forced all of them to resign in June 1993.

10. The Democratic Revolutionary Front faded away by 1987 (see Chapter 8).

CHAPTER 1

1. Melvin Burke, "El sistema de plantación y la proletarización del trabajo agrícola en El Salvador" [The plantation system and the proletarianization of agricultural labor in El Salvador], *Estudios Centroamericanos (ECA)* 31, no. 335-336 (September-October 1979):476–479. PNUD/Misión Interagencial ONU, "La pobreza rural en El Salvador: Elementos básicos para una política campesina" [Rural poverty in El Salvador: Basic elements for a *campesino* policy], January 1986; cited in Raúl Rubén, "El problema agrario en El Salvador: Notas sobre una economía agraria polarizada" [The agrarian problem in El Salvador: Notes on a polarized agrarian policy], *Cuadernos de Investigación*, no. 7 (San Salvador: Centro de Investigaciones Tecnológicas y Científicas [CENITEC], April 1991), pp. 15, 56. Aquiles Montoya, "El agro salvadoreño antes y después de la reforma agraria" [Salvadorean agriculture before and after the agrarian reform], *Cuadernos de Investigación*, no. 9 (San Salvador: CENITEC, June 1991), p. 67.

The drop in percent against a significant increase in numbers of large landowners is due to the 1980 agrarian reform, which created thousands of small landowners with two hectares or less. The increase in numbers is due, in part, to efforts by members of the oligarchy to avoid the impact of the agrarian reform by dividing and "selling" their land to family members and friends. The lack of change in landless between 1980 and 1986 is remarkable, given the highly touted 1980 agrarian reform (see Chapter 5).

2. Manuel Sevilla, "Visión global sobre la concentración económica en El Salvador" [Overview of the economic concentration in El Salvador], *Boletín de Ciencias Económicas y Sociales* [Bulletin of Economic and Social Sciences] (Universidad Centroamericana José Simeon Cañas), no. 3 (Spring 1984), pp. 158–159; Burke, "El Sistema de plantación," pp. 479–481; see also *Development Assistance Program Central*

America, book 2 (Washington, D.C.: Agency for International Development, 1973), chap. 7, "El Salvador."

3. "Las dimensiones de la pobreza extrema en El Salvador" [The dimensions of the extreme poverty in El Salvador], *Cuadernos de Investigación,* no. 1. (San Salvador: CENITEC, February 1989), pp. 6–12.

4. These data are from the United Nations, *Indicators of Economic and Social Development in Latin America* (New York: U.N. Social and Economic Council [CEPAL], 1976); Segundo Montes, Florentín Meléndez, and Edgar Palacios, *Los derechos económicos, sociales y culturales en El Salvador* [Economic, social, and cultural rights in El Salvador] (San Salvador: Instituto de Derechos Humanos, UCA, May 1988), pp. 93, 149, 159; and Inter-American Development Bank (IDB), *Economic and Social Progress in Latin America, 1988 Report* (Washington, D.C.: IDB, 1988), p. 408.

5. Santiago Barbarena, *Historia de El Salvador* [History of El Salvador] (San Salvador: n.p., 1914–1917), quoted in Roque Dalton, *El Salvador (Monografía)* [El Salvador (monograph)] (San Salvador: Editorial Universitaria, 1979). Information on the colonial period is also drawn from Eduardo Colindres, *Fundamentos económicos de la burguesía salvadoreña* [Economic fundamentals of the Salvadorean bourgeoisie] San Salvador: UCA Editores, 1977); John Baily et al., *El Salvador de 1840 a 1935* [El Salvador from 1840 to 1935] (San Salvador: UCA Editores, 1978); Alastair White, *El Salvador* (London: Ernest Benn; Boulder, Colo.: Westview Press, 1973); and David Browning, *El Salvador: Landscape and Society* (Oxford: Clarendon Press, 1971).

6. Murdo J. MacLeod, *Spanish Central America: A Socioeconomic History 1520–1720* (Berkeley: University of California Press, 1973), p. 49. The concept of a repeating economic cycle is drawn from MacLeod, as is much of the information in this section.

7. Ibid., pp. 170–173.

8. Ibid., pp. 221–223, 381; Browning, *El Salvador,* pp. 260–261.

9. Blacks were officially barred from living in El Salvador for many years, although this broke down in the 1980s as African Americans were sent to the U.S. Embassy as diplomats or to be military trainers; the latter included one head of the U.S. Military Group in El Salvador, Col. John Steele. Other African Americans came as journalists, human rights workers, and staff members of nongovernmental organizations.

The African heritage of many Salvadoreans is apparent in a stroll down any street, especially in the capital. There seems to be no discrimination because of this. What discrimination existed in 1980 stemmed more from class than ethnic background. For example, in conversations with members of the oligarchy, they regularly disparaged the peasants as having "no culture," and in 1980 a government official associated with the land reform program referred to them in a conversation with Mac Chapin (then an AID official) as *"los monos"* (monkeys).

10. Colindres, *Fundamentos económicos,* p. 24.

11. Liberals and conservatives in Latin America bear little resemblance to liberals and conservatives in the Anglo-American political tradition. Conservatives were aristocrats and monarchists who wished to keep church and state tied closely together and who were dedicated to preserving the church's wealth and privileges. Liberals were anticlerical and often antireligion. They were inclined to support free trade, whereas conservatives preferred to erect tariff barriers to protect local textile production. Within El Salvador the differences were not so great as in other countries because the church did not have much wealth that could be confiscated. The liberals therefore succeeded in abolishing monastic orders, establishing civil marriage, and taking some initial steps toward removing education from control by the clergy and creating a state education system.

12. White, *El Salvador,* pp. 71–73.

13. Montes's theory is reinforced by an excellent study, Héctor Lindo-Fuent(
Weak Foundations: The Economy of El Salvador in the Nineteenth Century 1821–1898 (Berk(
ley: University of California Press, 1990), pp. 180–184.

14. Robert Varney Elam, "Appeal to Arms: The Army and Politics in El Salvad
1931–1964" (Ph.D. dissertation, University of New Mexico, 1968), p. 9; White, *El Salv*
dor, p. 120; interview with Miguel Mármol, Managua, Nicaragua, October 9, 1981.

15. In Spanish the concept of "illegitimacy" does not exist; one speaks of *niñ*
naturales, never of *niños ilegítimos*.

16. Interview, Miguel Mármol, October 9, 1981.

17. Max P. Brannon, *El Salvador: Esquema estadística de la vida nacional* [Statistic
outline of national life] (San Salvador: n.p., 1936), pp. 22–24. The amount of lar
planted in coffee kept growing. In 1950, there were 115,429 hectares, or 75 percent of t
total land, under cultivation; in 1961, 139,000 hectares, or 87 percent of the tot(
Colindres, *Fundamentos económicos*, p. 72.

18. "La crisis del maíz" [The maize crisis], *Patria*, January 18, 1929.

19. *Patria*, January 4, 1929.

20. "Sobre la carrestía periódica del maíz en El Salvador" [On the periodic sc(
city of maize in El Salvador], *Patria*, April 4, 1929, p. 5.

21. *"Como anda la justicia en esta San Salvador"* [How justice operates in this S(
Salvador], *Patria*, November 30, 1928.

22. Arthur Ruhl, *The Central Americans* (New York: n.p., 1927), p. 206.

23. For the fullest treatment of the revolt, see Thomas Anderson, *Matanza* (Li(
coln: University of Nebraska Press, 1971). Much of the material in this section is drav
from this book as well as Arias Gómez, "Augustín Farabundo Martí (Esbo
biográfico)" [Augustín Farabundo Martí (biographic sketch)], *La Universidad* 96, no.
(July-August 1971): 181–240; and Everett Alan Wilson, "The Crisis of National Integr
tion in El Salvador 1919–1935," (Ph.D. dissertation, Stanford University, 1968), pp. 21(
232. Anderson's book is an excellent historical study of an extremely complex perio
but I believe he erred in his basic premise, as reflected in the subtitle *El Salvador's Co*
munist Revolt of 1932. Obviously Martí and other leaders of the insurrection were me(
bers of the PCS, and the movement had received limited funds and a great deal
printed material from New York. But Anderson himself made a strong case that beyo(
the leadership few communists were involved in the uprising. The vast majority of t
Indians and *campesinos* who participated in the revolt were acting not out of ideologic
commitment but out of genuine social, political, and (especially) economic grievanc(
As the revolt a hundred years earlier had demonstrated, the *campesinos* did not need
sophisticated political ideology to help them understand exploitation or poverty. S
also Roque Dalton, *Miguel Mármol* (San José, Costa Rica: EDUCA, 1982), pp. 229–306.

24. Wilson, "Crisis of National Integration," pp. 51–52.

25. Ibid., p. 53.

26. Ibid., p. 54; Arias Gómez, "Farabundo Martí," p. 211; interview, Migu
Mármol, October 27, 1981.

27. Interview, Miguel Mármol, October 27, 1981.

28. It is doubtful that any sort of conspiracy existed between the oligarchy a(
the military in carrying out the coup. Rather, it is more likely that the young office
were aware of the oligarchy's sentiments and shared that group's fear of anything th
smacked of "socialism"—which was how some of Araujo's policies were perceived. F
a fuller discussion of this point, see Anderson, *Matanza*, pp. 55–56.

29. February 1931 letter to the Uruguayan poet Blanca Luz Brum, quoted in A(
derson, *Matanza*, pp. 38–39.

30. Ibid., pp. 40–41; Arias Gómez, "Farabundo Martí," pp. 202–203.

31. Arias Gómez, "Farabundo Martí," p. 230.

32. Interview, San Salvador, January 17, 1980.

33. Zamora suggested that *compadrazgo* might be likened to the first Mayor Richard Daley's Chicago political machine with its system of rewards for the faithful and exclusion (or worse) for the rebellious.

34. Interview with Rubén Zamora, August 1980, Mexico City.

35. Elam, "Appeal to Arms," pp. 45–47. Individuals from the economic elite continued to serve in various government posts, in particular agriculture and economy. This was inevitable, as the oligarchy contained most of the educated elite of the country. In addition, coffee was not even under the Ministry of Agriculture. White, *El Salvador*, 103.

36. Wilson, "Crisis of National Integration," p. 258.

37. Elam, "Appeal to Arms," p. 48; interview, Miguel Mármol, October 1981.

38. Indeed, this is what ultimately happened. Prior to the arrival in the 1950s of the ADOC shoe factory, which was jointly owned by six oligarchic families, there were several thousand shoemakers and assistants in El Salvador. ADOC created several hundred industrial jobs, but it put most of the shoemakers out of business. The families are Palomo, Simán, Dueñas, Hill, Alvarez Meza, and Meza Ayau. Colindres, *Fundamentos Económicos*, pp. 131, 400–428.

39. Wilson, "Crisis of National Integration," pp. 250–254; Elam, "Appeal to Arms," pp. 56–57.

40. *Anuario Estadístico de El Salvador, 1935* [Statistical annual of El Salvador, 1935] (San Salvador: Imprenta Nacional, 1936), p. 58; Elam, "Appeal to Arms," p. 54.

41. Elam, "Appeal to Arms," pp. 48–49; *New York Times*, June 15, 1940.

42. Elam, "Appeal to Arms," p. 50. Martínez's flirtation with the Axis, the presence of Nazi officers in El Salvador during the 1930s, and the training of Salvadorean officers in Germany and Italy raise the question of the extent to which fascist ideology permeated the officer corps and continued long after Martínez switched sides.

43. Ibid., pp. 50–51.

44. Ibid., pp. 60–67; White, *El Salvador*, p. 103. Mariano Castro Morán, *Función política del ejército salvadoreño en el presente siglo* [Political function of the Salvadorean army in the present century] (San Salvador: UCA Editores, 1984), p. 175. An excellent contemporary study of this period is Patricia Parkman's *Nonviolent Insurrection in El Salvador: The Fall of Maximiliano Hernández Martínez* (Tucson: University of Arizona Press, 1988).

45. Martínez was encouraged in his course of action by, among others, the U.S. ambassador to El Salvador, Walter Thurston. See White, *El Salvador*, p. 103. See also Castro Morán, *Función política*, p. 176. Common wisdom has it that the rebels of April 2 assumed that the diplomatic corps, including the U.S. ambassador, would encourage Martínez to go quietly. But David Luna, in a detailed account of the revolt, related that after Thurston exchanged coded cables with Washington early in the morning of April from a telegraph office controlled by the *golpistas*, his attitude toward them chilled. Later that day, as the revolt collapsed, one of its leaders sought asylum in the U.S. Embassy and was turned away by the ambassador. Colonel Tito Tomás Calvo was subsequently shot during Martínez's "reign of terror." See Luna, "Análisis de una dictadura fascista latinoamericana, Maximiliano Hernández Martínez 1931–44" [Analysis of a Latin American fascist dictatorship, Maximiliano Hernández Martínez 1931–44], *La Universidad* 94, no. 5 (September-October 1969):106–126. Patricia Parkman concluded that "Washington policymakers had no interest in the removal of Martínez—indeed, they would probably have preferred to maintain the status quo in Central America for the duration of the war." *Nonviolent Insurrection*, p. 99.

46. For a firsthand account of this period with a focus on political mobilizatic see Francisco Morán, *Las jornadas cívicas de abril y mayo de 1944* [The civic marches April and May 1944] (San Salvador: Editorial Universitaria, 1979).

47. Elam, "Appeal to Arms," pp. 95–105. A final attempt by the liberals to sei. power took the form of an invasion planned by several hundred army officers ar armed civilians and launched from Guatemala through Ahuachapán. White, *El Salv dor*, p. 104. One of the leaders of the invasion was Julio Adalberto Rivera, who wou lead a countercoup from the right in 1961 (discussed in Chapter 2). See also Cast Morán, *Función política*, p. 197.

48. "Sin comentarios a la conciencia ciudadana" [To the citizen's conscienc without commentary], circulated by the Social Democratic Party in September 1948; " Ministerio de Defensa: ¿comité político?" [The Ministry of Defense: Political comm: tee?], unsigned and circulated October 1948; "Hoja suelta de la Directiva Suprema d partido Democrática Republicano" [Leaflet from the Supreme Directorate of the R publican Democratic Party], circulated November 1948; Elam, "Appeal to Arms," 127.

49. Castro Morán, *Función política*, pp. 203–206. Elam, "Appeal to Arms," p 129–130.

50. Elam, "Appeal to Arms," pp. 131–132; White, *El Salvador*, p. 105.

51. William Vogt, *Road to Survival* (New York: William Sloane Associates, 1948 pp. 177–178.

52. Elam, "Appeal to Arms," p. 144.

53. Ibid., p. 147. Castro Moran discussed the Osorio government: "Many progre sive Salvadoreans accuse Osorio of having handed the country back to the oligarchy t the end of his term. The truth of the matter is that Osorio laid the foundation for the a celerated development of capitalism in El Salvador." *Función política*, p. 209.

54. José María Lemus, *Entrevistas y opiniones* [Interviews and opinions] (San Sa vador: Imprenta Nacional, 1955), p. 29.

55. White, *El Salvador*, p. 105.

56. Coffee production grew from 57.7 million short tons in 1945 to 65.9 million 1951, a 14 percent increase. The value of the total crop, however, increased 406 percer from $18.7 million to $76 million. Héctor Dada Hirezi, *La economía de El Salvador y integración centroamericana 1945–1960* [The economy of El Salvador and Central Amer can integration 1945–1960] (San Salvador: UCA Editores, 1978), p. 29.

57. Salvadorean cotton production reached its apogee in 1964. By 1969 overuse fertilizer and insecticides and rising costs forced out speculators and dramatically r duced the area planted to half that in 1965. Browning, *El Salvador*, pp. 232, 234–235, 24 By the mid-1970s cotton production had rebounded to levels exceeding those of 1960

58. White, *El Salvador*, p. 131.

59. William Durham, *Scarcity and Survival in Central America: Ecological Origins the Soccer War* (Stanford: Stanford University Press, 1979), p. 36. Another cost, whic was not studied until the 1980s, is the effect on the health of the Salvadoreans who liv and work in the cotton-growing area. Between 1971 and 1976, 8,917 cases of pestici poisoning were *reported* to health officials; in 1987 over fifty children died of such pc soning in *one* hospital in the capital. These data are found in "El Salvador: Ecology Conflict," Green Paper no. 4, (San Francisco: Environmental Project on Central Ame ica, 1989), p. 4. They are originally taken from H. Jeffrey Leonard, *Natural Resources ar Economic Development in Central America* (New Brunswick, N.J.: Transaction Book 1987), p. 149.

On January 22, 1980, I was in a section of the largest demonstration in Salvadc ean history with people from Usulután, the heart of the cotton-growing region. Lov flying planes passed directly overhead and sprayed the crowd. I was not affected, but dozens of people around me were. Their eyes turned red and began tearing heavily, a reaction that lasted at least thirty minutes. Clearly, these people had developed an allergy to the material with which we had been sprayed. They had undoubtedly been caught many times before in the spray from a crop-dusting plane, although perhaps not deliberately as on this day.

60. Elam, "Appeal to Arms," p. 149.

61. Thorsten V. Kalijarvi, *Central America: Land of Lords and Lizards* (Princeton, N.J.: Van Nostrand Co., 1962), p. 84. Kalijarvi served as U.S. ambassador in El Salvador during the late 1950s and left after the 1960 U.S. election.

62. Ibid., pp. 151–153.

63. *New York Times,* December 19, 1959.

64. The repression and the methods of torture were recounted in painful detail by Salvador Cayetano Carpio, *Secuestro y capucha en un país del "mundo libre"* [Kidnapping and hooding in a country of the "free world"] (San José, Costa Rica: EDUCA, 1979). This book was originally written in 1954. See also Elam, "Appeal to Arms," pp. 153–155.

65. Stephen Webre, *José Napoleón Duarte and the Christian Democratic Party in Salvadoran Politics 1960–1972* (Baton Rouge: Louisiana State University Press, 1979), pp. 28–29.

CHAPTER 2

1. U.S. Congress, House, "Human Rights in Nicaragua, Guatemala and El Salvador: Implications for U.S. Policy," Hearings before the Subcommittee on International Organizations of the Committee on International Relations, 94th Congress, 2d session, June 8 and 9, 1976, p. 47.

2. Robert Varney Elam, "Appeal to Arms: The Army and Politics in El Salvador 1931–1964" (Ph.D. dissertation, University of New Mexico, 1968), pp. 146–147; Stephen Webre, *José Napoleón Duarte and the Christian Democratic Party in Salvadoran Politics 1960–1972* (Baton Rouge: Louisiana State University Press, 1979), p. 35.

3. Webre, *Duarte,* p. 37.

4. U.S. Congress, House, "Human Rights," pp. 47–48.

5. Elam, "Appeal to Arms," pp. 162–163. Alastair White, in *El Salvador* (London: Ernest Benn; Boulder: Westview, 1973), p. 193, reported that Rivera and other leaders of the 1961 coup approached the recently formed Christian Democratic Party and offered to make it the official party, a fact confirmed by Hugo Carillo, the PCN secretary general in the late 1980s. The price was that a military officer would continue to occupy the presidency. According to Rubén Zamora, who was a member of the PDC until March 1980, there was a conservative faction within the party that wanted to accept Rivera's offer. When the PDC decided not to, that faction left and joined the PCN. Interview, June 28, 1981. Carillo said that the main founders of the PCN were old PRUDistas, not from the PDC, as reported in the first edition. Interview, Washington, D.C., April 12, 1989.

6. Webre, *Duarte,* p. 47. AGEUS said it was "the only candidate worthy to compete against officialism." AGEUS, "El pueblo tiene una cita" [The people have an appointment], *Diario de Hoy* (San Salvador), April 16, 1962.

7. In the late 1940s Murat Williams was a young political officer in the embassy in San Salvador. President John F. Kennedy named Williams ambassador to El Salvador in early 1961. In the first edition I wrote that the United States, through Williams, pressured President Rivera to open the electoral process to opposition parties. Ambassador Williams wrote me that although his memory "is far from perfect ... I cannot remember

exerting any such pressure on the Salvadorean Government. It was against my personal convictions. I believe that the USA has no right to interfere in the internal affairs of another republic. ... There were many well-informed and intelligent people in the [Salvadorean] government who needed no prodding from me. They should get the credit for whatever progress Rivera's presidency made." Letter from Williams to Montgomery, June 1, 1988.

8. Interview with Murat Williams, Washington, D.C., May 30, 1988. Williams opened the interview by saying "The worst mistake we've made since World War II [in El Salvador] was not supporting Fabio Castillo. It is comparable to the overthrow of [Jacobo] Arbenz [in Guatemala]."

9. Ibid.

10. The information in this section, unless otherwise noted, is derived from four interviews with members of the PDC and with Dr. Edgar Jiménez Cabrera of the Ibero-American University in Mexico City.

11. See Webre, *Duarte*, pp. 49–68, for a full discussion of the ideology and progress of the Salvadorean PDC.

12. Allan Nairn, "Behind the Death Squads," *The Progressive*, May 1984, p. 21. Much of the information in this section comes from Nairn's article, pp. 20–29. See also Craig Pyes, "A Dirty War in the Name of Freedom," *Albuquerque Sunday Journal*, December 12, 1983; and Christopher Dickey, "Behind the Death Squads," *New Republic*, December 26, 1983, pp. 16–21.

13. Medrano quoted in Nairn, "Behind the Death Squads," p. 21.

14. Ibid., p. 23.

15. Ibid. See also Pyes, "A Dirty War." The name "Mano Blanca" was borrowed from a Guatemalan death squad.

16. Nairn, "Behind the Death Squads."

17. First Meeting of the Committee of Economic Cooperation of the Central American Isthmus (CCE), Resolution 2, August 27, 1952, cited in Héctor Dada Hirezi, *La economía de El Salvador y la integración centroamericana 1945–1960* [The economy of El Salvador and Central American integration 1945–1960] (San Salvador: UCA Editores, 1978), pp. 88, 96; *NACLA Report on the Americas* (hereafter *NACLA Report*), p. 11.

18. "Central American Patterns of Regional Economic Integration," *Bank of London and South American Review*, June 1979, pp. 340–342; *NACLA Report*, p. 11.

19. Carmen Sermeño Zelidon, "Las nuevas formas de dominación política en El Salvador 1972–1977," [New forms of political domination in El Salvador] (thesis for the *licenciatura* in sociology, University of Costa Rica, 1979), p. 65.

20. Francisco Chavarría Kleinhenm, "Fundamentos políticos, económicos, y sociales de la evolución y desarrollo del movimiento sindical en El Salvador" [Political economic, and social fundamentals of the evolution and development of the union movement in El Salvador] (thesis for the *licenciatura* in sociology, University of Costa Rica, 1977), p. 451.

21. Rafael Menjívar, *Crisis del desarrollismo: Caso El Salvador* [Crisis of development: The El Salvador case] (San José, Costa Rica: EDUCA, 1977), pp. 70–71.

22. White, *El Salvador*, pp. 227–228, 249.

23. Melvin Burke, "El sistema de plantación, y la proletarización del trabajo agrícola en El Salvador" [The plantation system and the proletarianization of agricultural work in El Salvador]. *Estudios Centroamericanos (ECA)* 31, no. 335–336 (September October 1976):476. A fraction of this increase was due to the influx of thousands of Salvadoreans expelled from Honduras in 1969. If we assume an average rural family of six children, then by 1975 more than 1 million people, or 25 percent of the population, had no means of regular income.

24. For a fuller discussion of the war and its causes, see William Durham, *Scarcity
d Survival in Central America* (Stanford: Stanford University Press, 1979); Thomas An-
rson, *The War of the Dispossessed: Honduras and El Salvador, 1969* (Lincoln: University
Nebraska Press, 1981).

25. Frank T. Bachmura, "Toward Economic Reconciliation in Central America,"
orld Affairs 133, no. 4 (1971):286.

26. Webre, *Duarte,* pp. 93, 97.

27. *Diario de Hoy,* January 15, 1967.

28. In fact the Catholic Church had moved away from that position during the
cond Vatican Council, which ended in 1965, but the Salvadorean bishops had not yet
tten the message.

29. White, *El Salvador,* p. 203. Immediately after the election the PAR was out-
wed.

30. Webre, *Duarte,* p. 106.

31. Ibid., p. 119.

32. Casa Presidencial press release, in *Prensa Gráfica,* August 15, 1969.

33. Alvarez was the first and only member of the Salvadorean oligarchy to give
s *hacienda* to the *colonos* who worked it as a cooperative—an act that earned him the
ntempt of his fellow oligarchs. He began the process in 1972, but the workers did not
ceive title for five years because there was no Salvadorean law under which such
ansfer could occur. Meanwhile, Alvarez drew a salary as farm administrator and
ained the workers to run the farm themselves.

34. "Resoluciones y recomendaciones del Primer Congreso Nacional de Reforma
graria" [Resolutions and recommendations of the first national agrarian reform con-
ess], *Economía salvadoreña* 28 (1969):109.

35. Ibid., p. 114.

36. Webre, *Duarte,* p. 105. For a personal version, see Duarte, *My Story,* chap. 3.

37. The UDN was founded by former vice-president Francisco Roberto Lima, a
rmer PARista, and has always included noncommunists. Interviews with Farid
andal, Mexico City, January 25, 1981; Aronette Díaz, San Salvador, August 1993.

38. "Manifiesto al pueblo salvadoreño" [Public declaration to the Salvadorean
ople], *Prensa Gráfica,* September 3, 1971, quoted (in translation) in Webre, *Duarte,* p.
8.

39. "Programa de gobierno de UNO" [UNO's program of government], *Prensa
ráfica,* January 17, 1972.

40. UNO figures were Duarte, 326,968; Molina, 317,535. The CCE figures on Feb-
ary 21 were Molina, 314,748; Duarte 292,621.

41. Webre, *Duarte,* p. 177; Duarte, *My Story,* pp. 79–80. Mejía was assassinated on
ly 18, 1981.

42. The U.S. Embassy and government remained silent throughout this period.
ll the 1960s rhetoric about finding a democratic "third way" between military dicta-
rship and communism were lost in the realpolitik world of Richard Nixon and Henry
issinger. Ambassador Henry Catto, who would later become President George Bush's
mbassador to Belgium, never publicly condemned the blatant electoral manipula-
ns. The United States did provide Molina, who was in Taiwan, transportation di-
ctly back to El Salvador. Duarte reported that his wife called U.S. Ambassador Henry
atto, who said he would see what he could do. Duarte's brother, Rodrigo, called Fa-
er Theodore Hesburg, the president of Notre Dame and Napoleón Duarte's old pro-
ssor, for help. Hesburg could not reach Kissinger, but he did reach the presidents of
anama and Venezuela—and the pope—all of whom pressured Sánchez Hernández to

ensure Duarte's safety. José Napoleón Duarte, *My Story* (New York: G. P. Putnam's Sons), p. 82.

43. Webre, *Duarte*, p. 181.

44. Mariano Castro Morán, *Función política del ejército salvadoreño en el presente siglo* [Political function of the Salvadorean army in the present century] (San Salvador: UCA Editores, 1984), p. 242. Castro Morán graduated from El Salvador's military academy in 1939. He participated in the April 2, 1944, rebellion against Hernández Martínez, then fled into exile in Guatemala and Mexico after being condemned to death by a military tribunal. After returning to El Salvador he studied engineering at the UES, then rejoined the army in 1949. He was a member of the Civilian-Military Directorate that was installed following the countercoup of January 25, 1961. Castro Morán retired as a lieutenant colonel in January 1962.

45. Interview, Peter Dumas, January 1980. This assertion was indirectly confirmed when I asked then junta member Colonel Adolfo Majano about corruption in the officer corps. Majano, who was widely regarded as incorruptible, said he did not have any firsthand knowledge. He may well have been telling the truth, because he had always been a barracks officer. René Guerra added further credence to this in an interview with Dermot Keogh: "The Myth of the Liberal Coup: The United States and the 15 October 1979 Coup in El Salvador," *Journal of International Studies* (London School of Economics) 13 (Summer 1984):159.

46. Interview, René Guerra, January 1980.

47. White, *El Salvador*, p. 95.

48. Latin American universities, unless they are private, by tradition are completely autonomous institutions, although much of their funding comes from government sources. This was true of the UES.

49. Webre, *Duarte*, p. 185; Mario Flores Macal, "Historia de la Universidad El Salvador" [History of the University of El Salvador], *Anuario de Estudios Centroamericanos* vol. 2 (1976):13–35.

50. The actual amount expended was kept secret, but the figure of $30 million is generally agreed upon by knowledgeable sources. The pageant itself was strictly for the elite. Tickets were sold by invitation only.

51. The director of the National Guard, Colonel Mario Rosales, had been ordered not to let the march leave the UES campus. But Rosales had his own game plan. According to sources within the officer corps, he was trying to set up the conditions for a coup from the right, so he let the demonstrators leave the university and set a trap.

52. U.S. Congress, House, "Human Rights," pp. 40–41; Webre, *Duarte*, p. 188.

53. Other groups were the White Warriors Union; the White Hand; the Anticommunist Front of Central American Liberation (FALCA), which made its appearance claiming responsibility for bombing on at least two occasions the radio transmitter of the archdiocesan radio station, YSAX, in San Salvador in 1980; and the Death Squad (EM). Later, other names would appear.

54. The sources for this information are both civilian and military. The first official admission of record that security forces moonlighted as death squads came from junta president Duarte following the rape and murder by National Guardsmen of four U.S. nuns and a Catholic lay worker in December 1980. In 1983–1984 a number of articles on the death squads, some written after months of investigation, appeared in the U.S. press. See, for example, Nairn, "Behind the Death Squads"; Pyes, "A Dirty War in the Name of Freedom" (the first of a five-day series); and Dickey, "Behind the Death Squads."

55. "Pronunciamientos de ANEP," nos. 1, 2, and 3, reprinted in *ECA* 31, no. 335-336 (September-October 1976):611–615. This issue of *ECA* is devoted to the question of agrarian transformation.

56. Webre, *Duarte*, pp. 193–195; interview with Luís de Sebastian, December 13, 1979; Castro Morán, *Función política*, pp. 238–239.

57. Data here and in the following paragraph are from Sermeño Zelidon, "Nuevas formas."

58. Eduardo Colindres, *Fundamentos económicos de la burguesia salvadoreña* [Economic fundamentals of the Salvadorean bourgeoisie] (San Salvador: UCA Editores, 1977), p. 140; White, *El Salvador*, p. 173.

59. Manuel Sevilla, "Visión global sobre la concentración económica en El Salvador" [Overview of the concentration of wealth in El Salvador], *Boletín de Ciencias Económicos y Sociales*, May–June 1984, pp. 179, 188–189.

60. Ibid., pp. 181–182.

61. Castro Morán, *Función política*, p. 244.

62. Ibid.; Webre, *Duarte*, p. 197.

63. *Central American Report* (Guatemala City), March 7, 1977; Webre, *Duarte*, pp. 197–198; Castro Morán, *Función política*, p. 245.

64. There was heavy cable traffic between the embassy and the Department of State during April about the Richardson case. See, for example, "Milgp [military group] Reduction and Richardson Case," confidential cable from Ambassador Ignacio Lozano to Secretary of State, April 12, 1977; "Milgroup Reduction," confidential cable from Ambassador Lozano to Assistant Secretary of State Terence Todman, April 20, 1977; "Relations with the GOES [Government of El Salvador]: Next Phase," secret cable from the Secretary of State to U.S. Embassy, San Salvador, April 30, 1977. These cables were released under FOIA.

65. Frank Devine, *El Salvador: Embassy Under Attack* (New York: Vantage Press, 1981), p. 194.

66. Ibid., p. 5.

67. Text, Law for the Defense of … Public Order (mimeo), November 25, 1977.

68. Raymond Bonner, *Weakness and Deceit: U.S. Policy and El Salvador* (New York: Times Books, 1984), p. 42.

69. All information on the coup d'etat of October 15, 1979, unless otherwise noted, comes from interviews with eight individuals who had firsthand knowledge of this event, including René and Rodrigo Guerra y Guerra. More complete stories of the coup are told in Bonner, *Weakness and Deceit*, chap. 7; and in Dermot Keogh, "The Myth of the Liberal Coup," pp. 152–183.

70. Alan Riding, "Militants in El Salvador Undeterred by the Death of 22," *New York Times*, May 10, 1979; "Salvador: Murder at the Cathedral," *Newsweek*, May 21, 1979, pp. 47–49; "Salvadoran Police Fire into Crowds; 8 Reported Killed," *Washington Post*, May 9, 1979.

71. For a study of the Nicaraguan National Guard, see Richard Millett, *Guardians of the Dynasty* (Maryknoll, N.Y.: Orbis Books, 1978).

72. Laurie Becklund, "Death Squads: Deadly 'Other War,'" *Los Angeles Times*, December 18, 1983.

73. Ibid.

74. Gutiérrez was in close contact with Colonels José Guillermo García, Nicolás Carranza, and Eduardo Vides Casanova, a fact that would have profound implications for the coup. All of them had worked together from 1974 to 1977 in ANTEL, the government-owned National Telecommunications Company. This group became known as the "ANTEL Mafia." See Keogh, "The Myth of the Liberal Coup," p. 162. See also "New Government of El Salvador," confidential cable from Ambassador Devine to Secretary of State, October 16, 1979. Released under FOIA.

75. See also Bonner, *Weakness and Deceit*, pp. 154–155; Devine, *Embassy Under Attack*, pp. 133–142; Keogh, "The Myth of the Liberal Coup," pp. 163–165.

76. General Fred F. Woerner got it right when he summarized the coup as "when General Romero was overthrown and General García came to power." Max G. Manwaring and Court Prisk, eds., *El Salvador at War: An Oral History* (Washington, D.C.: National Defense University Press, 1988), p. 33.

Carranza's CIA connection was reported by Walter Cronkite on CBS, March 21, 1984, and by Philip Taubman in the *New York Times* the next day. Ray Bonner, in *Weakness and Deceit*, p. 166, reported that García may have received $50,000 from the CIA. See also Nairn, "Behind the Death Squads," p. 28; Dennis Volman, "Salvador Death Squads, a CIA Connection?" *Christian Science Monitor*, May 8, 1984; "Short Circuit: Inside the Death Squads," film transcript of interview with Colonel Roberto Santivañez, released March 21, 1985, p. 8.

77. Interview with René Guerra, June 21, 1981. Guerra also said that García was already calling back some of former president Romero's closest aides. Guerra, García, Gutiérrez, and Majano met with Archbishop Romero on October 17. During that meeting Romero accused García of human rights violations in San Vicente during his tenure as commander of the local garrison.

78. Nairn, "Behind the Death Squads," p. 28; Dickey, "Behind the Death Squads," p. 18; Becklund, "Deadly 'Other War.'"

79. Volman, "Salvador Death Squads"; Nairn, "Behind the Death Squads"; Becklund, "Deadly 'Other War.'"

80. Becklund, "Deadly 'Other War'"; Craig Pyes, "Right Built Itself in Mirror Image of Left for Civil War," *Albuquerque Journal*, December 18, 1983.

81. Becklund, "Deadly 'Other War.'"

82. Román Mayorga Quiroz, *La universidad para el cambio social* [The university for social change] (San Salvador: UCA Editores, 1978).

83. "Disappeared" has come to be used as a noun in Latin America to refer to people who simply vanish without a trace, often while in official custody.

84. See "Informe de la Comisión Especial Investigadora de Reos y Desaparecidos Políticos" [Report of the special investigative commission on political prisoners and disappeared], *ECA*, no. 375-376 (January-February 1980):136–139.

85. In 1980 El Salvador's four security forces numbered 9,000: National Guard (4,000); National Police (2,500); Treasury Police (2,000); Customs Police (500). According to both the CIA and the Democratic Revolutionary Front (FDR), army strength in 1980 was about 8,000 soldiers and 500 officers. See Becklund, "Deadly 'Other War.'"

Between January 1 and October 15, 1979, 475 people died at the hands of security forces and ORDEN. Between October 15 and November 3, 105 died under similar circumstances. Figures are from the Commission on Human Rights of El Salvador. It should be noted that according to both human rights and church organizations, 80 percent of the more than 10,000 deaths in the country during 1980 were caused by government forces, ORDEN, or death squads.

86. Devine, *Embassy Under Siege*, p. 171; confidential cable (no title) from Ambassador Devine to Secretary of State, October 24, 1979. Released under FOIA.

87. Interview, December 1979.

88. The Young Military's statement appeared in all newspapers in San Salvador on January 3, 1980.

89. Accounts of the crisis may be found in *Prensa Gráfica, El Independiente, Diario de Hoy, El Mundo*, and *La Crónica*, January 3–6, 1980. Archbishop Romero, in his homily on January 6, called on Minister of Defense García to resign. García declined, explaining that because he was a military officer his orders could be changed only by the military. "Ministro de Defensa explica razones para no renunciar" [Minister of defense explains reasons for not resigning], *El Mundo*, January 10, 1980. Andino was encouraged to re

sign by the U.S. Embassy, which delivered the message that the Christian Democrats did not want anyone from the private sector on the junta. Bonner, *Weakness and Deceit,* p. 167; Duarte, *My Story,* pp. 109–110.

CHAPTER 3

1. This account is taken from interviews with Arturo Rivera Damas, Ricardo Urioste, and José Alas. For an extended discussion of the agrarian reform congress, see Stephen Webre, *José Napoleón Duarte and the Christian Democratic Party in Salvadoran Politics 1960–1972* (Baton Rouge: Louisiana State University Press, 1979), pp. 126–130. Webre erred when he said, "The abduction of a young priest in San Salvador during the congress may have been entirely unrelated to this issue [of the church's support for agrarian reform]." On the contrary, Alas's abduction was directly related to the church's position and to the fact that he presented it.

2. The social doctrine of the church is dated generally from Pope Leo XIII's encyclical, *Rerum Novarum,* in 1891. In it he recognized exploitation of workers by callous employers through unrestrained competition, and although he rejected socialism, he criticized capitalism. *Quadragesimo Anno,* issued by Pope Pius XI in 1930, reiterated the themes of *Rerum* in a new social situation; it was more critical of the right of private property and distinguished between "communism," which it rejected, and "mitigated socialism," which, Pius affirmed, had some affinity with Christian principles. Pius also asserted that sin is collectivized in modern life, an idea that prefigured the contemporary notion of "institutionalized sin." In *Mater et Magistra,* John XXIII brought a global perspective, announced the need for economic assistance to the Third World to help surmount inequality, and reminded the well nourished to provide for the malnourished without "imperialistic aggrandizement."

3. Penny Lernoux, *Cry of the People* (New York: Doubleday, 1980), pp. 36–41.

4. *The Church in the Present-Day Transformation of Latin America in the Light of the Council* (Washington, D.C.: U.S. Catholic Conference, 1970), pp. 80–82.

5. Michael Dodson discussed the concept of a prophetic church at length in "Prophetic Politics and Political Theory," *Polity* 12, no. 3 (Spring 1980):388–408. T. S. Montgomery reviewed contemporary ferment in Latin American Protestantism in "Latin American Evangelicals: Oaxtepec and Beyond," in Daniel Levine, ed., *Churches and Politics in Latin America* (Beverly Hills, Calif.: Sage Publications, 1980), pp. 87–107. The nexus between theology and political action was explored in Montgomery, "Liberation and Revolution: Christianity as a Subversive Activity in Central America," in Martin Diskin, ed., *Trouble in Our Backyard: Central America and the United States in the Eighties* (New York: Pantheon, 1984), pp. 76–99.

6. Thomas Quigley of the U.S. Catholic Conference's Office of Justice and Peace coined this phrase.

7. The four were the bishops of Santa Ana (Marco René Revelo), San Vicente (Pedro Aparicio), and San Miguel (José Eduardo Alvarez) and the president of the Episcopal Conference, Freddy Delgado. The previous bishop of Santa Ana, Benjamin Barrera, was also among this group. He retired in early 1981.

8. Interview, December 14, 1979.

9. This phrase, which came out of CELAM III, appeared in El Salvador on posters with pictures of the six priests who were assassinated between March 1977 and August 1979.

10. This chapter deals only with the Catholic Church because with only one exception (until the mid-1980s), the Protestant churches in El Salvador were either politi-

cally conservative or simply apolitical. One Baptist church, the Iglesia Emanuel in Sa
Salvador, went through a process similar to that described in this chapter with the de
velopment of Christian Base Communities. This one church produced at least a ha
dozen leaders of the revolutionary organizations, the best known of whom wa
Augusto Cotto, its minister for several years. At the time of his death in an accidenta
plane crash off the coast of Panama in September 1980, Cotto was one of the top leader
of the National Resistance.

On the other side, an alliance of sorts was struck between the Salvadorean gov
ernment and several Protestant leaders (most of whom were from the United States). I
August 1980, for example, photos appeared in the newspapers of San Salvador showin
two visiting U.S. ministers holding hands with the members of the junta. The captio
said that they were "praying for justice and peace in El Salvador."

In the countryside, the National Guard found yet another means of intimidatin
the peasantry. A refugee from the Department of Cabañas told me in Nicaragua in Feb
ruary 1980 that the commander of the local garrison went around to all the Catholics i
her village and told them that the "true Christians" were going to the Protestant churc
and that anyone who went to the Catholic church was a "communist" or a "subver
sive."

11. As a result, much of the discussion in this chapter about the "church" is abou
the archdiocese.

12. Interview, Arturo Rivera Damas, January 25, 1980, Santiago de María
Usulután.

13. *Rutilio Grande: Mártir de la evangelización rural en El Salvador* [Rutilio Grande
Martyr of rural evangelization in El Salvador] (San Salvador: UCA Editores, 1978), p
38. See also Phillip Berryman, *The Religious Roots of Rebellion: Christians in Central Ameri
can Revolutions* (Maryknoll, N.Y.: Orbis, 1984), pp. 104–106.

14. By 1981 that ratio had leapt to about 1:17,000, after the assassination of
dozen priests and the exile or expulsion of another sixty.

15. For a fuller discussion, see Montgomery, "Christianity as a Subversive Activi
ty."

16. Charles Clements, *Witness to War: An American Doctor in El Salvador* (Nev
York: Bantam, 1984), p. 101; conversations with Clements, Ithaca, N.Y., March an
April 1983.

17. Interview, Mexico City, February 7, 1981.

18. Interview, Maryknoll, N.Y., February 22, 1981.

19. Pablo Galdámez, *Faith of a People: The Life of a Basic Christian Community in E
Salvador* (Maryknoll, N.Y.: Orbis, 1986), pp. xvii–xviii. This book was first published i
El Salvador under the title *La fe de un pueblo: Historia de una comunidad cristiana en El Sal
vador 1970–1980* [Story of a Christian community in El Salvador] (San Salvador: UC
Editores, 1983).

20. Ibid., pp. 3–17.

21. Ibid., p. 24.

22. Ibid., pp. 27–28.

23. One priest took responsibility for the CEBs in the town while the other
worked in the countryside, but they were all assisted by twenty "collaborators," wh
included Jesuits and university and seminary students. Additional discussion of th
Aguilares experience may be found in Berryman, *The Religious Roots of Rebellion*, pp
106–107, 114–115, 119–121, passim; and in Rodolfo Cardenal, *Historia de una esperanz
vida de Rutilio Grande* [Story of a hope: The life of Rutilio Grande] (San Salvador: UC
Editores, 1985), Chaps. 6–9.

24. *Rutilio Grande*, pp. 68–75. There were other indicators of success: In the first nine months there were 700 baptisms, each after approximately four preparatory sessions; the Men's Association of the Holy Sacrament developed and had more than 300 members; novenas were celebrated for the feast days of the patron saints of Aguilares and El Paisnal, the other major town in the parish, and audiovisual presentations of the Word of God were given in the various neighborhoods; and Holy Week was celebrated in eight different locations in the parish. *Rutilio Grande*, p. 72. These details are important because they reveal the extent of the emphasis on religious education and training and on the sacraments.

25. See also, for example, "The Rich Man and Lazarus" (Luke 16:19–31), "The Last Judgment" (Matt. 25:31–46), and "The Rich Fool" (Luke 12:13–21).

26. *Rutilio Grande*, p. 72. *Conciencia mágica* is a state of mind that attributes to human events a "superior power that dominates them from outside and to which it is necessary to submit docilely. This type of consciousness is dominated by fatalism." *Rutilio Grande*, p. 72.

27. Ibid., pp. 83–85. For more on the discussion about FECCAS that follows, see Cardenal, *Historia de una esperanza*, chap. 10.

28. *Grupos fantasmos* are phantom organizations created by individuals or groups on the political right that take responsibility for paid political advertisements, fliers, and the like and that attack proposed reforms or individuals whom their sponsors consider "subversive" or "communist."

29. This and the quotations in the remainder of the paragraph are from Lernoux, *Cry of the People*, p. 68. In the late 1970s, Aparicio became more concerned with the threat of international communism than with the problems of poverty and injustice in his diocese. He was owner of a large *hacienda*, a gift from President Molina, and his sympathies tended more and more toward his fellow proprietors. On at least three occasions he suspended a diocesan priest, Father David Rodríguez, who was trying to carry out pastoral work similar to that of Rutilio Grande. Suspended in the fall of 1979, Rodríguez was forbidden to say Mass or conduct courses in his own parishes; further, Aparicio threatened to suspend any priest who invited Rodríguez into his parish. Because a bishop's authority extends only to the boundaries of his diocese, Rodríguez at the invitation of Archbishop Romero spent a great deal of time in the archdiocese doing all the things he was forbidden to do in San Vicente. But he continued to live in his parish to be near his people, commuting to San Salvador when necessary. By 1979 Rodríguez was one of many priests on right-wing death lists; by 1981 he was in the mountains with the FMLN. Aparicio retired in 1985.

30. Interview with Luís de Sebastián, then vice-rector of the UCA, fall 1979; Alastair White, *El Salvador* (London: Ernest Benn; Boulder, Colo.: Westview Press, 1973), pp. 238-239.

31. Galdámez, *Faith of a People*, p. 59.

32. See *Estudios Centroamericanos (ECA)* 31, no. 335–336 (September-October 1976). The entire issue is devoted to a political and economic analysis of the proposed reform and includes various manifestos of interested groups such as ANEP, political parties, and the popular organizations.

33. *ECA* 31, no. 337 (November 1976):637–643. The title is a play on words. The Spanish equivalent of "Aye, aye, sir" is "A sus ordenes, mi capitan"—idiomatically, "At your service, my captain."

34. Lernoux, *Cry of the People*, pp. 73–76; *Rutilio Grande*, pp. 106–118. In a homily a month earlier, Grande anticipated his own martyrdom: "In Christianity it is necessary to be willing to give one's life in service for a just order, to save the rest, for the values of the Gospel." "Homilia de Apopa," February 13, 1977.

The campaign against the church included widespread attacks in the newspa
pers. Between November 29, 1976, and May 31, 1977, for example, sixty-three *campo*
pagados appeared in Salvadorean newspapers. In the same period, there were thirty-
two editorials against the church and only two in favor. In May 1977 alone, there ap
peared a series of fourteen articles under the same name. See *Persecución de la iglesia er*
El Salvador [Persecution of the church in El Salvador] (San Salvador: Secretariado Socia
Interdiocesano, 1977), passim. A similar, although slightly less intense, campaign en
sued in December 1979. Ibid., pp. 19–20.

35. This anecdote was recounted to me by Jorge Lara-Braud who had heard i
from Romero.

36. Interview, December 14, 1979. Phillip Berryman suggested that Romero'$
"conversion" dated to the mid-1970s when he was bishop of Santiago de María. Fathe
David Rodríguez came to speak to some members of the diocesan clergy. Rodríguez'$
bishop, Aparicio, warned Romero that Rodríguez was a communist, so Romero de
cided to listen secretly to him. Later Romero told Aparicio that Rodríguez was only ap
plying the gospel to El Salvador. Romero said later, "David opened my eyes and evan
gelized me from behind that door." Berryman, *Religious Roots of Rebellion*, p. 124.

37. James Brockman, *The Word Remains: A Life of Oscar Romero* (Maryknoll, N.Y.
Orbis Books, 1983); Galdámez, *Faith of a People*, p. 69.

38. Many of these commentaries are gathered in *El Salvador entre el terror y l(*
esperanza: Los sucesos de 1979 y su impacto en el drama salvadoreña de los años siguentes [E
Salvador between hope and terror: The events of 1979 and their impact on the Salvador
ean drama in the following years] (San Salvador: UCA Editores, 1982).

39. Philip Land, "Military Aid to El Salvador," *America*, March 22, 1980, p. 245.

40. See any homily reprinted (in part before December 16, 1979, and in full there
after) in *Orientación*, the archdiocesan newspaper.

41. Lernoux, *Cry of the People*, p. 79. It should also be added that right-wing terror
ist groups always took responsibility for these attacks. When the transmitter was blow
up in January 1980, the archdiocese asked other stations in San Salvador to broadcas
the Mass, but all declined. Then a 50,000-watt station in Costa Rica volunteered ai
time, and the homily was transmitted live via telephone every Sunday morning for sev
eral weeks. Subsequently, it was reported that the Costa Rican station was bombed fo
its efforts.

42. Galdámez, *Faith of a People*, p. 19.

43. Personal statements from Sister Nicolasa Ramírez Contreras, San Salvador
January 17, 1980; *Orientación*, July 27, 1980, p. 7.

44. Ana Carrigan, *Salvador Witness: The Life and Calling of Jean Donovan* (New
York: Simon and Schuster, 1984).

45. Jack Anderson, "Of Arabs, Weapons, and Peanuts," *Washington Post*, July 1(
1980, p. D.C. 9. The documents that came into Anderson's possession were found in &
suitcase of Roberto D'Aubuisson at the time he was arrested for attempting a right
wing coup in early May 1980. In 1993 D'Aubuisson would be named organizer of the as
sassination by the Truth Commission set up under the peace accords. See Chapter 8.

José Napoleón Duarte made some remarkable assertions in *My Story* (New York
G. P. Putnam's Sons, 1986) that must be addressed. On page 117 he stated that "Th
church would not allow even the nuns who were with Archbishop Romero at the tim
[he was shot] to be questioned." Monseñor Ricardo Urioste, who as vicar general wa
the church's principal representative from the first moment they received word of th
deed, described this assertion as "absolutely false. In fact, they [the government] didn'
try to do anything until later, years later. Four years later [Urioste and the nuns were in
terrogated]."

Duarte also asserted that "no autopsy was permitted by the church so the fatal bullet could not be obtained for analysis." When I read this to Urioste, he put his head in his hands and said "Oh, my God." He then continued: "We tried to look for a pathologist. Ambassador White was looking for one. But we couldn't find one because of fear. At the end we found Dr. Cuéllar, a forensic doctor and a surgeon for the military hospital, so he was not [as personally fearful as a civilian doctor]." Urioste was "personally there" for the autopsy. Interview, San Salvador, January 3, 1989.

46. All information in this section, unless otherwise noted, comes from interviews with José Inocencio Alas in April and July 1980 in Washington, D.C.

47. Interview with Miguel Angel Salaverría, San Salvador, July 21, 1988. "Parcelaciones rurales de desarrollo, S.A." [Rural development parcels, S.A. (sociedad anónima = incorporated)], April 30, 1971 (mimeo), p. 2.

48. These data are taken from "Realizaciones de 'Parcelaciones Rurales de Desarrollo, S.A.'" [Accomplishments of "Rural Development Parcels"], September 20, 1976 (mimeo), a financial summary of the company's first five years, provided to me by Miguel Angel Salaverría. There is a discrepancy in the financial statement. It says that 12,403 *manzanas* were purchased for $2,415,194. Expenditures associated with the purchase ("gastos de compra"), investment in the company and improvements, taxes, and financial and operating costs added another $1,944,238 to the investment, for a grand total invested of $4,359,433.

Then, the statement says, the "average cost" per *manzana* was $397.98. But if $4.36 million is divided by 12,403, the average cost per *manzana* is $351.48—for a difference of $46.50. Next the statement asserts that the total value of properties sold, 10,626 *manzanas*, was $4,673,274, or an average cost per *manzana* of $439.80. These figures are internally consistent.

If the average cost per *manzana* was $46.50 *less* than that stated on the summary, then Parcelaciones Rurales earned $494,109 *more* between 1971 and 1976 than declared on the statement. This figure is arrived at by multiplying 10,626 by $46.50. This represents a profit margin of 9.5 percent or 20.1 percent depending on real cost per *manzana*.

49. *Persecución de la iglesia,* p. 20. José Alas and his brother Higinio were slandered, threatened, and forced into exile three years later during the right-wing campaign against all activist priests. In May 1977 Monseñor Chávez went to Suchitoto the day after the Alas brothers departed to prevent a massacre by the government's security forces, as had happened in Aguilares following the assassination of Rutilio Grande. Chávez reasoned (correctly) that the government would not chance injuring or killing the recently retired archbishop.

CHAPTER 4

1. Charles Clements, *Witness to War: An American Doctor in El Salvador* (New York: Bantam, 1984), p. 123.

2. Comandante Fermán Cienfuegos interviewed by Chris Norton, "Salvador Rebels Pitch for Political Deal," *Christian Science Monitor,* December 8, 1988.

3. "Declaración del CC del PCS in ocasión del 50 aniversario del levantamiento armado de 1932" [Declaration of the Central Committee of the Salvadorean Communist Party on the 50th anniversary of the 1932 armed uprising], El Salvador, January 1982.

4. Salvador Cayetano Carpio, *Secuestro y capucha en un país del "mundo libre"* [Kidnapping and hooding in a country of the "free world"] (San José, Costa Rica: EDUCA, 1979).

5. Mario Menéndez, "Salvador Cayetano Carpio: Top Leader of the Farabundo Martí FPL" (written for *Prensa Latina*), February 1980 (mimeo.)

6. "Declaración del CC."

7. Menéndez, "Salvador Cayetano Carpio."

8. Agusto Cotto, one of the top twenty leaders of the RN until his death in September 1980, confirmed in an interview in August 1980 that this work had been going on. Cotto said Alas did not know the leftists were working with the *campesinos*. The following month I asked Alas if he had known, and he said that he had not until that moment.

9. In a September 1989 interview, Joaquin Villalobos acknowledged that "We have made some errors, we are aware to that," among which was the murder of Dalton. Larry Rohter, "Salvador Rebel Chief Offers Truce If U.S. Halts Aid," *New York Times*, September 18, 1989. In February 1992 Villalobos publicly apologized for Dalton's death and offered to help look for his grave in Morazán.

10. "Schafik Handal," *NACLA Report*, p. 38.

11. Interview, Miguel Sáenz, Managua, 1981.

12. Interview, Mario López, Comandante Venancio, Managua, 1982.

13. ORDEN is discussed in Chapter 2.

14. About 60 percent of the UCS was in the first group, 40 percent in the second.

15. Charles Clements told of a two-day congress in the Guazapa front of civilians and guerrillas to resolve a crisis precipitated by the spreading of rumors about the zone's top commander. The congress also dealt with issues like the educational system, then ended with a watermelon party and singing the Salvadorean national anthem: "The music, taken from Giacomo Meyerbeer's opera, 'The Prophet,' is much admired by Salvadoreans. I thought it sounded like a dirge." "Why can't you people think up something a little more stirring?" Clements asked a guerrilla at the end. "We do not sing the song for you, gringo," he responded. *Witness to War*, p. 160.

16. Democratic centralism is the procedural principle of binding all members of an organization to a decision that has been approved by a majority. The procedure assumes that until the vote is taken all opinons may be freely expressed and debated; thereafter, all members are expected to adhere to the decision taken by the majority, whether or not they agree.

17. "Comunicado de las Fuerzas Armadas de la Resistencia National (FARN)" (Communique of the FARN), September 15, 1980, in *Estudios Centroamericanos (ECA)* 35, no. 383 (September 1980):921–922.

18. This information comes from interviews I conducted with several dozen refugees on March 15, 1980, at the Arzobispado. The people came from the archdiocese of San Salvador and the diocese of San Vicente. As time passed, they began coming in from as far away as Morazán and San Miguel.

19. Interviews with Héctor Dada, Rubén Zamora, and Juan José Martel, who were present at the convention. See Duarte's version in José Napoleón Duarte, *My Story* (New York: G. P. Putnam's Sons, 1986), pp. 115–116.

20. Adolfo Gilly, "Experiencias y conquistas de una huelga límite" [Experiences and conquests of a limited strike], *Uno más Uno*, August 21, 1980.

21. "En los Cerros de San Pedro el FMLN construye el poder popular" [In the Hills of St. Peter the FMLN constructs popular power], *Venceremos*, vol. 1, no. 2 (January 1982):8. *Venceremos* was the official newspaper of the FMLN.

22. Press release, SALPRESS, Mexico City, January 12, 1981.

23. "Entrevista con el Comandante Fermán Cienfuegos," [Interview with Commander Fermán Cienfuegos], *Pensamiento Revolucionario* [Revolutionary Thought] (Centro de Documentación e Información [CDI] of the FMLN), no. 11 (1981):10; Joaquin

Villalobos, "Acerca de la situación militar en El Salvador" [About the military situation in El Salvador] (n.p.: July 1981), passim.

24. Raymond Bonner, *Weakness and Deceit: U.S. Policy and El Salvador* (New York: Times Books, 1984), p. 97.

25. Cynthia Arnson, "Background Information on El Salvador and U.S. Military Assistance to Central America," Update no. 4, Institute for Policy Studies, Washington, D.C., April 1981 (mimeo).

26. Alex Drehsler, "Revolution or Death!" *San Diego Union*, March 1, 1981. Journalist Drehsler accompanied a contingent of eighty-five guerrillas in a midnight attack on the village of San Antonio de la Cruz, Chalatenango, on the night of February 19–20, 1981. There were, according to the FMLN, between fifty and seventy soldiers in the hamlet. When it was over, four hours later, there were eighteen dead soldiers, five prisoners of war, and one wounded guerrilla. A similar ratio was reflected in many reports of similar attacks by guerrillas throughout the country.

27. Reports from various journalists who visited FMLN-controlled areas tended to confirm this.

28. Miguel Angel Guardado Rivas, "Así fue la voladura del Puente de Oro" [That's how the Bridge of Gold was blown up], *Barricada* (Managua), November 23, 1981; privileged interview, 1982.

29. I got a sense of this during my three days in Jucuarán in January 1984. On the most remote and isolated roads there were houses every few hundred meters.

30. The soldiers told him they would spare him if he gave them $200. He offered them a cow; they took it and let him live. My informant said the army returned the next day, and a man who had come back was killed. This woman was interviewed in a refugee camp in Chinandega, Nicaragua. She said she and her family had been members of a CEB for two years. One son was a guerrilla, but eight other children, her husband, and she had fled to Nicaragua on December 28, 1980.

31. A growing number of journalistic reports in 1981 and 1982 confirmed Martel's analysis: Alex Drehsler, "Guerrillas Use Guns to Forge Marxist Society," *San Diego Union*, March 2, 1981; Bob Rivard, "A Journey into the 'Liberated Zone,'" *Dallas Times Herald*, January 18, 1981; Raymond Bonner, "With Salvador's Rebels in Combat Zone," *New York Times*, January 26, 1982, and "In a Salvador Classroom, Rebels Study Marx," *New York Times*, January 28, 1982; and John Dinges, "Salvadorean Rebels Hold Base," *Washington Post*, January 22, 1982.

Martel, born in 1955, was a founding member of the MPSC. During the 1970s he was secretary general of Christian Democratic Youth for the Department of Santa Ana and a member of the departmental directorate. He, along with other Christian Democrats, resigned from the party in March 1980. At the time Martel was a member of the PDC national Executive Committee, among other party posts.

On November 27, 1980, security forces surrounded the Externado San José, a Jesuit high school three blocks south of the U.S. Embassy, where the FDR Executive Committee was to hold a press conference. Men in civilian clothes entered the school and forced the six committee members who were there to go with them. Hours later the bodies of the six, including FDR president Enrique Alvarez Córdova, BPR secretary general Juan Chacón, and UDN secretary general Manuel Franco, were found along roads near San Salvador. At a press conference commemorating the first anniversary of the assassinations, Martel related that he had avoided being a seventh victim by sheer luck; he was late and as he neared the school he could see the troops. He immediately went to a safe house where he remained for some time.

32. Clements, *Witness to War*, p. 59.

33. Interview, February 20, 1982. See also Clements, *Witness to War*, pp. 59, 181.

34. In interviews with Salvadorean refugees who were fleeing government repression following promulgation of the agrarian reform in March 1980 and with refugees in Mexico and Nicaragua in August 1980 and January–February 1981 and in Honduras in 1982, every person supported the FDR-FMLN. Many others have had the same experience. Alex Drehsler related in a conversation an identical experience in the refugee camps of Honduras; U.S. Representatives Gerry Studds and (later Senator) Barbara Mikulski reported the same following their trip to Central America. See Barbara Mikulski, "An American Tragedy," *Baltimore Sun*, February 24, 1981.

On the other side, peasants knew who their enemies were. *Campesinos* reported armed men in civilian dress coming into their villages, indiscriminately or selectively killing people, all the while screaming that they were from the BPR or FPL. But, the people later said, "That's crazy, the Bloc [BPR] doesn't act like that." See T. S. Montgomery, "The Refugees from El Salvador," *Florida Times-Union*, February 23, 1981; letter from the Christian community of Villa Dolores, Cabañas ("A la conciencia de todas las personal de buena voluntad" [To the conscience of all people of good will]), *CRIE* (Centro Regional de Información Ecuménica), no. 52 (June 9, 1980):10–11.

35. "Entrevista con Cienfuegos," p. 11.

36. Sáenz quotation from author's interview, February 20, 1982; Raul Hercules was interviewed in Mexico City, January 14, 1992.

37. Quoted in Bonner, *Weakness and Deceit*, p. 121. Krauss's series of four articles appeared in the *Atlanta Constitution*, February 7–10, 1982.

38. Wayne Smith, *The Closest of Enemies: A Personal and Diplomatic History of the Castro Years* (New York: W. W. Norton, 1987), p. 241; Robert Pastor, *Condemned to Repetition: The United States and Nicaragua* (Princeton: Princeton University Press, 1987), pp. 217–219, 225–227; Roy Gutman, *Banana Diplomacy: The Making of American Policy in Nicaragua 1981–1987* (New York: Simon and Schuster, 1988), pp. 22, 35–37.

39. Smith, *The Closest of Enemies*, pp. 242–243; Pastor, *Condemned to Repetition*, pp. 232–234; Anne Marie O'Connor and Nancy Nusser, "Salvadoran Rebel Plane Goes Down," *Atlanta Journal and Constitution*, November 26, 1989.

40. Bonner, *Weakness and Deceit*, p. 126. The FMLN's *talleres de armas* (arms workshops) were located in all the areas under guerrilla control and became increasingly important by the late 1980s. I was present for a review of the troops in Guazapa, four days after the cease-fire, where the guerrillas displayed a large number of homemade weapons.

41. Drehsler, "Revolution or Death!" A similar story can be found in Bonner, *Weakness and Deceit*, pp. 125–126.

42. Cañas was interviewed in San Salvador, January 1980.

43. "Plataforma Programatica del Gobierno Democrático Revolucionario" [Programmatic platform of the Democratic Revolutionary Government], *Diario de Hoy*, February 28, 1980.

44. "Avanza la guerra popular revolucionario y se agrava la crisis de poder de la dictadura" [The popular revolutionary war advances and the crisis of power of the dictatorship is aggravated], Declaration of the FMLN General Command, *Boletin de Prensa* [Press bulletin] no. 38, August 12, 1981.

45. Jenny Pearce, *Promised Land: Peasant Rebellion in Chalatenango, El Salvador* (London: Latin American Bureau, 1986), p. 242. See also Iosu Perales, *Chalatenango: Un viaje por la guerrilla salvadoreña* [A trip with the Salvadorean guerrillas] (Madrid: Editorial Revolución, 1986).

46. Drehsler, "Guerrillas Use Guns."

47. Pearce, *Promised Land*, pp. 243–244.

48. Interview with Juan Ramón Medrano, January 11, 1984.

49. "En los Cerros de San Pedro."

50. Interview, February 1982. Charles Clements discussed his efforts to get the *campesinos* to use native medicines in *Witness to War*, pp. 98–99, 103.

51. Clements, *Witness to War*, p. 47.

52. Ibid., p. 156.

53. Ibid., p. 239.

54. "Cartilla de alfabetización revolucionaria" [Workbook of revolutionary literacy] (El Salvador: Colectivo de Comunicación Humberto Mendoza [Communication Collective–COLCOM-HM], n.d.); "Cuaderno de orientaciones para la alfabetización revolucionaria" [Teacher's guide for revolutionary literacy] (El Salvador: COLCOM-HM, n.d.). See also Pearce, *Promised Land*, pp. 261–267.

55. Drehsler, "Guerrillas Use Guns."

56. Ibid.

57. Clements, *Witness to War*, p. 189.

58. Pearce, *Promised Land*, p. 274.

59. In 1989 María cut her hair. In 1988 she became a political officer-combatant in the FMLN. Women combatants knew that if they were captured and had long hair, the army would drag them off by their hair. "María's Story." Pilot films 1 and 2 for documentary by Camino Film Project, Pamela Cohen, producer.

60. Clements, *Witness to War*, pp. 188–189.

61. Ibid., p. 157. Interviews with Marisol Galindo, Norma Guevara, 1981-1982.

62. "El Salvador: The Women's Struggle," in *No Pasarán* (London: Third World First, June 1986), p. 21; Brenda Carter et al., *A Dream Compels Us: Voices of Salvadorean Women* (Boston: South End Press, 1989).

63. Interview with María Caminos. These and other comments are from a February 11, 1982, interview.

64. Interview with Norma Guevara and Marisol Galindo, Managua, Nicaragua, February 1, 1981. All subsequent quotations are from this interview.

65. Interview, January 18, 1982. Zamora was probably thinking of Nicaragua, where he and his family lived in exile from 1980 to 1987.

66. Interview, October 22, 1981. Later in the 1980s the FMLN would carry out actions without prior consultation. There were, for example, the collection of *cedulas* in eastern El Salvador before the 1984 election; the commando attack in San Salvador's "Zona Rosa" in 1985 in which four U.S. Marines and several civilians died; and the transportation stoppage in the days before and during election day 1989. On the whole, however, consultation continued, as discussed in later chapters.

Martel's characterization of the Christian Democrats was borne out after 1984 when the government of José Napoleón Duarte proved itself to be as corrupt as any in Salvadorean history. However, Martel's assertion regarding the broad base of popular support for the MPSC was not reflected in the electoral results in 1989 (see Chapter 8).

CHAPTER 5

1. Emphasis in original. The original letters, with signatures, were shown to me in mid-March by an officer who had been closely connected with the impeachment effort. He allowed me to hand-copy the letter.

2. Interview, Héctor Dada Hirezi, Cuernavaca, Mexico, March 22, 1980.

3. José Napoleón Duarte, *My Story* (New York: G. P. Putnam's Sons, 1986), p. 108.

4. Shirley Christian, "Final Members Prove Snag for New Salvadorean Junta," *Miami Herald*, January 10, 1980; Raymond Bonner, *Weakness and Deceit: U.S. Policy and El Salvador* (New York: Times Books, 1984), p. 167; Duarte, *My Story*, pp. 108–110.

5. "Morales Erlich y Dada Hirezi candidatos a junta" [Morales Erlich and Dada Hirezi candidates for junta], *Prensa Gráfica,* January 7, 1980. For Duarte's account, see *My Story,* pp. 108–111.

6. Interview with Héctor Dada, March 22, 1980. García had the power and authority because all security forces were part of the Armed Forces and therefore under the minister of defense. Staben's name would become closely linked to the death squads by 1981, a fact acknowledged in subsequent U.S. government documents, including an October 27, 1983, "Briefing Paper on Right-Wing Terrorism in El Salvador," which identifies Staben as a probable member of the White Warriors Union. Joint CIA-Department of State document released by U.S. government, November 9, 1993.

7. "LP-28 tómanse PDC" [LP-28 occupies PDC], *El Mundo,* January 29, 1980. An anonymous, detailed account by one of the LP-28 members who escaped appears in *Pensamiento Revolucionario,* no. 11 (1981):19–21. The same officers who had announced their intentions of attacking the national university on January 23 were the two "officers of the day" when the PDC headquarters was attacked. Also, the U.S. chargé d'affaires, James Cheek, was in the Ministry of Defense Communications Center at the time of the attack.†

8. Duarte, *My Story,* p. 112.

9. Interview, Juan Vicente Maldonado, January 29, 1980.

10. Information in this section comes from three interviews: Héctor Dada, Cuernavaca, Mexico, March 22, 1980; Rubén Zamora, Mexico City, August 18, 1980; and James Cheek, Washington, D.C., April 29, 1980. In 1993, Cheek, after enduring diplomatic exile for twelve years, was named U.S. ambassador to Argentina.

11. The measure that Cheek proposed would be unconstitutional in the United States, for it meant the suspension of habeas corpus.

12. In 1986 the United States provided $454.7 million in military and economic assistance. Mark Hatfield, Jim Leach, and George Miller, "Bankrolling Failure: United States Policy in El Salvador and the Urgent Need for Reform" report to the Arms Control and Foreign Policy Caucus, November 1987 (hereafter "Caucus Report 1987"), p. 33.

13. Mimeo copy of letter read during mass February 17, 1980.

14. "ANEP retirase de instituciones oficiales" [ANEP to retire from official institutions], *El Mundo,* January 18, 1980.

15. After the meeting Duarte said he considered the four-hour session a "good beginning." Confidential cable from U.S. Embassy in Guatemala City to Secretary of State, Washington, D.C., February 8, 1980. Released under Freedom of Information Act (FOIA).

16. Laurie Becklund, "Death Squads: Deadly 'Other War,'" *Los Angeles Times,* December 18, 1983. A February 15, 1980, CIA document, "Rightist Terrorism in El Salvador," identifies two death squads: the White Warriors Union and the Organization for Liberation from Communism. It asserts that hard-liners in the economic elite were financing the squads and that they were soliciting support from the right wing in Guatemala. A March 18, 1981, CIA assessment, "El Salvador: The Right Wing," identified Roberto D'Aubuisson and Alfredo Mesa Lagos as the FAN's leaders. Documents released by U.S. government, November 9, 1993.

17. The information in this section, unless otherwise noted, comes from Craig Pyes, "D'Aubuisson's Fledgling Party Finds a Mentor in Guatemala" and "Right Built Itself in Mirror Image of Left for Civil War," *Albuquerque Journal,* December 18, 1983; Pyes, "A Chilling Plan Maps a Terror Road to Rule," *Albuquerque Journal,* December 19, 1983; Christopher Dickey, *With the Contras* (New York: Simon and Schuster, 1985), p. 87; Becklund, "Deadly 'Other War.'"

The MLN was created by the CIA in 1953 as a paramilitary force under Carlos Castillo Armas to overthrow the democratically elected president of Guatemala, Jacobo Arbenz Guzman. Afterward the MLN transformed itself into a political party and established links with the World Anticommunist League, based in Taiwan and dominated by neofascist, anti-Semitic groups.

18. Dickey wrote that the pilots were Salvadorean. *With the Contras*, p. 87; Roberto Santivañez, transcript of filmed interview, "Short Circuit: Inside the Death Squads," March 21, 1985. The French OAS fought against Algerian nationalists in the late 1950s during their struggle for independence.

19. The plan never succeeded because the United States foiled every attempt.

20. Pyes, "Right Built Itself in Mirror Image"; Becklund, "Deadly 'Other War' "; and Santivañez, "Short Circuit," p. 7.

21. "Millionaires' Murder, Inc," secret cable from Mark Dion, U.S. Embassy, San Salvador, to Secretary of State, January 5, 1981. The information in the second paragraph is corroborated in a November 21, 1983, *New York Times* article by James LeMoyne, "Death Squads in Salvador: Centrists Become Targets."

Mark Dion, the deputy chief of mission, urged the State Department to investigate immediately. "It is unacceptable," he wrote, "that such an operation is guided from a major American city and that nothing can be done to stop it before another American official or contract employee is murdered here." There were several news reports that investigations were conducted but that nothing conclusive was learned: Joel Brinkley, "Ex-Envoy Accuses 6 Salvador Exiles," *New York Times*, February 3, 1984, and "U.S. Denies Concealing Data on 6 Salvadorans," *New York Times*, February 4, 1984. After the Sheraton case (discussed later in this chapter) and Dion's cable, no more U.S. citizens were killed by death squads. The U.S. Government was aware as early as February 1980 that Salvadoran businessmen willing to work with the civilian-military junta were being threatened with kidnapping. "Rightist Terrorism in El Salvador," February 15, 1980.

22. Allan Nairn, "Behind the Death Squads," *The Progressive*, May 1984, p. 28.

23. Interview with Héctor Dada, March 20, 1980.

24. Santivañez, "Short Circuit," p. 6.

25. Information from a church official who had talked with the sexton and other principals. See also Americas Watch and American Civil Liberties Union (AW-ACLU), *Report on Human Rights in El Salvador* (Washington, D.C.: Center for National Security Studies, 1982), p. 127.

26. The information in this paragraph comes from Craig Pyes, "Who Killed Archbishop Romero?" *The Nation*, October 14, 1984, p. 337 and passim; Bonner, *Weakness and Deceit*, pp. 178–179, 330–332; Dickey, *With the Contras*, p. 88; "Former U.S. Envoy to Salvador Accuses Administration of Cover-Up in Slaying," *Washington Post*, February 3, 1984; Pyes, "U.S. Cables Reveal Salvador Archbishop Assassination Plan," *Albuquerque Journal*, April 15, 1983; Santivañez, "Short Circuit," p. 6.

27. AW-ACLU, *Report on Human Rights*, p. 137. A facsimile of the army's list is in Amnesty International, *El Salvador: 'Death Squads'—A Government Strategy* (London: Amnesty International Publications, October 1988), p. 11.

28. Dickey, *With the Contras*, p. 87. The weakness of Amnesty International's 1988 report is that it ignores the civilian death squads. See p. 9.

29. The information in this section comes from Becklund, "Deadly 'Other War' "; Dennis Volman, "Salvador Death Squads, a CIA Connection?" *Christian Science Monitor*, May 8, 1984; Nairn, "Behind the Death Squads," pp. 22, 24–25, 28; Christopher Dickey, "Behind the Death Squads," *The New Republic*, December 26, 1983, p. 18; Pyes,

"Right Built Itself in Mirror Image"; Bonner, *Weakness and Deceit*, pp. 328-329, 333; Pyes, "A Dirty War in the Name of Freedom," *Albuquerque Sunday Journal*, December 12, 1983.

30. Personal interviews with political prisoners in Mariona and Ilopango prisons, 1983 and 1984, who had been held in CAIN; Craig Pyes, "A Policeman's Initiation: 'We Put Two Bullets in His Head,'" *Albuquerque Journal*, December 19, 1983. An untitled March 19, 1983, CIA document released by the U.S. government on November 9, 1993, reports that CAIN leadership was trained in Venezuela between mid-1982 and February 1983 and that CAIN maintained a secret prison in La Libertad or San Salvador.

31. Pyes, "'A Regular Americano' Joins the Kidnappers," *Albuquerque Journal*, December 21, 1983.

32. Craig Pyes, "'The Doctor' Prescribes Torture for the Hesitant," *Albuquerque Journal*, December 20, 1983; Laurie Becklund, "Death Squad Members Tell Their Stories," *Los Angeles Times*, December 19, 1983. A January 5, 1981, Department of State "memo of conversation" also deals with the subject: "El Salvador and Rightists Allegedly Receive Assistance of Argentine Right-Wing Civilians." That there were multiple houses was confirmed in a February 1985 CIA document, "Controlling Right-Wing Terrorism," released by U.S. government, November 9, 1993.

33. "It's that simple," a U.S. Embassy officer told Allan Nairn. "Behind the Death Squads," p. 25.

34. Pyes, "Right Built Itself in Mirror Image."

35. Nairn, "Behind the Death Squads," p. 20.

36. Héctor Dada confirmed the intent to carry out a coup in his letter of resignation to the junta, March 3, 1980. See also Duarte, *My Story*, p. 112.

37. "Rightist Coup Imminent in El Salvador," secret cable from U.S. Embassy to Secretary of State, February 22, 1980; "The Rightest Coup That Was, and Yet May Be," secret cable from U.S. Embassy, San Salvador, to U.S. Embassy, Panama, and Secretary of State, February 24, 1980. Released under FOIA.

38. Guillermo Manuel Ungo related that in December 1979 an army colonel said that it would be better to go ahead and kill 100,000 people then; it would prevent having to kill 200,000 later. A Salvadorean businessman made a similar statement in a conversation in March 1980.

39. FOIA cable, "The Rightest Coup That Was, and Yet May Be." Also "Draft Manifesto of Major D'Aubuisson for Use in Aborted Right-Wing Coup," confidential cable from U.S. Embassy, San Salvador, to Secretary of State, May 8, 1980. Released under FOIA.

40. Dada's letter of resignation appeared in *Orientación*, March 16, 1980. Archbishop Romero also read Dada's letter during his homily on March 9. All quotations by Duarte are from Duarte, *My Story*, pp. 113–115, unless otherwise noted.

41. "Carta de renuncia al Partido Democrática Cristiana" [Letter of resignation to the Christian Democratic Party], March 10, 1980 (mimeo).

42. Interviews with Rubén Zamora and Juan José Martel, San Salvador, January 1989. In August 1981 Duarte ordered the preparation of a list of MPSC sympathizers still in the party, supposedly to exclude them from being candidates in the elections scheduled for March 1982. See "PDC National Assembly," confidential cable from U.S. Embassy to Secretary of State, March 4, 1980. Released under FOIA.

43. Between January 1 and March 3, 1980, the OP-Ms killed 75 people; 527 were killed by security forces, ORDEN, or death squads. Between March 8 and May 25, 1,317 more people were killed by the latter groups. Information from the Archdiocese of San Salvador and the Salvadorean Commission on Human Rights. "JRG Suspends Certain Individual Rights," limited official use cable from U.S. Embassy to Secretary of State, March 7, 1980. Released under FOIA.

44. Telephone interview with Diskin, 1990.

45. Interview with Jorge Villacorta, Atlanta, Georgia, June 13, 1990.

46. "Analysis of El Salvador's Land Reform Law," confidential cable from U.S. Embassy to Secretary of State, March 3, 1980. Released under FOIA.

47. "Historia del M.P.S.C. 1980–1988 [History of the MPSC]" (San Salvador: MPSC Commission on Press and Information, 1988), p. 14; Peter Shiras, "The False Promise and Real Violence of Land Reform," *Food Monitor,* January-February 1981, p. 17. In 1991 Villacorta was elected deputy to the Legislative Assembly on the MPSC ticket.

48. "Land Reform Expert Assesses Implementation," confidential cable from U.S. Embassy, San Salvador, to Secretary of State, March 15, 1980. Released under FOIA.

49. Memorandum from Michael Hammer and Roy Prosterman to William C. Doherty (executive director of AIFLD), "The Latin Reform in El Salvador," March 25, 1980. From National Security Archive, Washington, D.C.

50. Letter to John Pino, director of the Rockefeller Foundation, March 12, 1980. Copy from National Security Archive.

51. I had the opportunity to talk with several dozen *campesinos* between March 10 and March 18, 1980. See also "El Salvador: Brighter Prospects for Land Reform," Department of State Bureau of Intelligence and Research unclassified report 579-CA, March 17, 1983. Copy from National Security Archive.

52. Norman Chapin, "A Few Comments on Land Tenure and the Course of Agrarian Reform in El Salvador," Agency for International Development, June 1980; "Difficulties with the Implementation of Decree 207," memorandum from Norman Chapin to Jack Vaughn, head, Latin American Bureau, AID, August 1980; Bonner, *Weakness and Deceit,* pp. 200–202.

AIFLD is an agency of the AFL-CIO with known ties to the CIA. See Jonathan Kwitney, *Endless Enemies* (New York: Congdon & Weed, 1984), pp. 341–344 and 347–349. It was created to train peasant leaders under the Alliance for Progress and came to El Salvador in 1965 with an AID contract. It held training seminars through the 1960s, set up cooperatives in the Salvdorean countryside, and founded the Salvadorean Communal Union (UCS) in 1968. AIFLD was expelled from El Salvador in 1973 but returned in June 1979 under stringent limitations. After the October coup, AIFLD brought a large number of personnel into the country, installed them on two floors of San Salvador's Hotel Sheraton, and acquired a direct telephone line to the Salvadorean High Command. See "Press Statement on the Role of AIFLD Agrarian Reform Process in El Salvador," EPICA, Washington, D.C., May 1980; Bonner, *Weakness and Deceit,* pp. 190–194.

53. Memorandum to Tom Mehen, Development Support, Rural and Administrative Development, U.S. AID, July 18, 1980.

54. According to an AIFLD investigation and the gunmen's public statements, they received their instructions and weapons from Lieutenant Isidro López Sibrian and Captain Eduardo Alfonso Avila after Hans Crist, a civilian with close ties to D'Aubuisson, had spotted Viera, Michael Hammer, and Mark Perlman walking into the Sheraton and commented, "I wish he [Viera] were dead." Craig Pyes, "Two Dinner Parties Meet and Two Americans Die," *Albuquerque Journal,* December 19, 1983. Strenuous efforts by the U.S. government to bring those responsible for ordering the deaths to trial failed. Two men, including Crist, were arrested in April 1981, one in Miami and one in San Salvador, but were released. "Two Suspects Arrested in Salvadorean Killings," *Tampa Tribune,* April 16, 1981. The problem, according to a well-placed U.S. source, was that if the case were pushed, "you will destroy the Salvadorean government as it exists today. If you pressed it—the investigation—you would destroy the in-

stitution of the military." Pyes, "Two Dinner Parties Meet." See also Dion's cable, "Millionaires' Murder, Inc."

55. An AID audit completed about the same time and official U.S. reaction to the UCS report were reported in Karen DeYoung, "Salvadoran Land Reform Imperiled, Report Says," *Washington Post,* January 25, 1982. End-of-year data from *Proceso,* no. 94 (December 1982). *Proceso* is a weekly news and analysis bulletin published since 1980 by the UCA.

56. The information in this section comes from numerous conversations with UES faculty in Mexico and the United States between 1980 and 1984 and with the former rector, Miguel Angel Parada, and from the Faculty for Human Rights in El Salvador and Central America (FACHRES-CA) document, "Education and Human Rights in El Salvador," Report of a National Faculty Delegation to El Salvador January 3–10, 1983 (mimeo).

57. Inter-American Development Bank (IDB), *Economic and Social Progress in Latin America, 1979 Report* (Washington, D.C.: IDB, 1980), p. 250. The 1980 CPI figure is from INFORPRESS, *Central American Economic Report* (Guatemala City, 1981), p. ES-10.

58. IDB, *Economic and Social Progress,* p. 255; "Mas de 1000 milliones de dólares se han fugado del país: Banco Central de Reserva" [More than $1 billion has left the country: Central Reserve Bank], *El Independiente,* January 15, 1980; "2 millones diarios retiran de asociaciones de ahorro" [2 million (colones) withdrawn daily from savings associations], *Prensa Gráfica,* January 28, 1980.

59. In the 1960s the Zona Franca was created on the eastern side of San Salvador. Industries that located in this zone were exempt from Salvadorean taxes. In addition, the land was owned by members of the oligarchy, who made a sizable profit on the sale of land to companies like Texas Instruments.

60. "Millares sin empleo por cierre empresas" [Thousands without employment with business closings], *Prensa Gráfica,* January 12, 1980; "Que se evite colapso económico pide la ASI" [ASI asks that economic collapse be avoided], *Prensa Gráfica,* January 21, 1980; "Balance Económico: 1982," *Proceso,* no. 94, p. 8.

61. "Balance Económico: 1982," p. 9.

62. Productive Alliance of El Salvador, "Position Paper," no date (mimeo); press release, Productive Alliance of El Salvador, June 26, 1980.

63. Craig Pyes, "America's Right Sympathizes and Serves up a Hot Potato," *Albuquerque Journal,* December 22, 1983; Margot Hornblower, "The Exiles," *Washington Post,* March 22, 1981.

64. Oscar A. Romero and Arturo Rivera Damas, "La iglesia y las organizaciones políticas populares" [The church and the popular political organizations], third pastoral letter of Oscar Romero and first of Arturo Rivera Damas, El Salvador, October 1978, pp. 43–49.

65. "Reacciones nacionales" [National reactions], *Proceso,* no. 33 (August 31–September 6, 1981):5.

66. "El arzobispo de San Salvador afirma que debe haber diálogo entre las partes en conflicto antes de las elecciones" [The archbishop of San Salvador affirms that there must be dialogue betweeen the parties in conflict before elections], Agencia Independiente de Prensa (AIP) telex news release, San José, Costa Rica, November 3, 1981; "El Salvador: Elecciones no pueden esperar normalización del país" [El Salvador: Elections cannot await normalization of the country], ACAN-EFE telex news release, San Salvador, November 20, 1981.

67. "Statement from the Bishop, Apostolic Administrator, Priests, and Women Religious of the Archdiocese of San Salvador," December 5, 1980 (mimeo).

68. Interview with Father Walter Guerra, Mexico City, February 7, 1981. CONIP's leaders were closely allied with the FPL faction headed by Cayetano Carpio and were extremely sectarian.

69. "Arrest of D'Aubuisson and Cohorts; Some Observations and Comments," confidential cable from Ambassador Robert White to Secretary of State, May 9, 1980. Released under FOIA.

70. "Former Salvadoran Official Captured," *Washington Post,* February 21, 1981; "Ex-Junta Member Majano Said to Be Bound for Exile," *Miami Herald,* March 22, 1981.

71. Bonner, *Weakness and Deceit,* p. 219.

72. Ibid.; Duarte, *My Story,* pp. 130–134.

73. "El Salvador, One Year After the Coup," confidential cable from U.S. Embassy to Secretary of State, November 4, 1980. Released under FOIA.

74. "Fireworks Celebrate Alleged Dismissal of Ambassador White," limited official use cable from Mark Dion to Secretary of State, December 20, 1980. Released under FOIA.

75. The distinction between "lethal" and "nonlethal" weapons may be clear on paper but blurs in the field. The aid package included fifty PVS-2B night-vision devices, electro-optic machines that are used for observation and nighttime weapon targeting. There were also private arms transactions. In January 1980 the Commerce Department licensed export of $8,000 worth of "nonmilitary" shotguns and spare parts to El Salvador. During 1980 the State Department Office of Munitions Control expected to issue as much as $250,000 worth of licenses, "mostly for carbines, handguns, and rifles." See Thomas Conrad and Cynthia Arnson, "The Aid for El Salvador is Called Nonlethal," *New York Times,* June 15, 1980; U.S. Department of State, Press Statement, January 17, 1981.

76. "U.S. Policy and El Salvador," confidential cable from Secretary of State Edmund Muskie to all American Republic Diplomatic Posts, December 20, 1980. Released under FOIA.

77. Alexander Haig, *Caveat: Realism, Reagan and Foreign Policy* (New York: Macmillan, 1984), pp. 118, 126.

78. Letter of Apostolic Administrator of San Salvador Arturo Rivera Damas to Vice-President George Bush, April 6, 1981, mimeo.

79. Emphasis added. "Annual Integrated Assessment of Security Assistance for El Salvador," confidential cable from Ambassador Deane Hinton to Secretary of State, June 12, 1981, pp. 7, 17. Released under FOIA.

80. Emphasis in original. John D. Waghelstein, "Post-Vietnam Counterinsurgency Doctrine," *Military Review* 65 (May 1985):42.

81. Interview by Max Manwaring with General Fred F. Woerner, San Francisco, California, November 7, 1987, in *Oral History of the Conflict in El Salvador 1979–Present* (Carlisle, Pa.: Military History Institute, 1988) (mimeo), pp. 16, 38. The Woerner Report, which was finally declassified in 1993, "did not go far enough," according to four lieutenant colonels who wrote a critical study in 1988 of the U.S. role in El Salvador. They quoted a senior member of the Woerner team: "Our original purpose was to design a national strategy; (but) that mission proved too broad. Our purpose got reduced to assisting GOES (government of El Salvador) to draft and design a national military strategy." A. J. Bacevich, James D. Hallums, Richard H. White, and Thomas F. Young, "American Military Policy in Small Wars: The Case of El Salvador," paper presented March 22, 1988, John F. Kennedy School of Government, Harvard University (mimeo). The four lieutenant colonels were studying for a year at the Kennedy School.

82. Bacevich et al., "American Military Policy," p. 44.

83. Michael Shafer, *Deadly Paradigms: The Failure of U.S. Counterinsurgency Polic* (Princeton: Princeton University Press, 1988), pp. 118–127.

84. Hinton's remarks appear in Max G. Manwaring and Court E. Prisk, eds., *E Salvador at War: An Oral History* (Washington, D.C.: National Defense University Press 1988), p. 234.

85. In fiscal year 1981, direct and indirect military aid totaled (in millions $103.88; in fiscal year 1982, $222.33; in fiscal year 1984, $412.59. In each of the next fou fiscal years, this aid averaged $312.2 million. "U.S. Aid to El Salvador: An Evaluation o the Past, a Proposal for the Future," report to the Arms Control and Foreign Policy Cau cus of the U.S. Congress from Congressmen Jim Leach and George Miller and Senato Mark O. Hatfield, February 1985 (hereafter "Caucus Report 1985"); and "Caucus Re port 1987." Not until fiscal year 1991 did Congress, outraged by El Salvador's failure t prosecute military officers implicated in the murder of six Jesuit priests, their house keeper, and her daughter during the November 1989 offensive, significantly reduc military aid.

86. Manwaring and Prisk, *El Salvador at War,* pp. 196–197.

87. "Annual Integrated Assessment of Security Assistance for El Salvador," con fidential cable from U.S. Embassy, San Salvador, to Secretary of State, May 26, 1982, p. 5 Released under FOIA.

88. "Communist Interference in El Salvador," Special Report no. 80, U.S. Depart ment of State, February 23, 1981 (the White Paper). See also Haig, *Caveat,* p. 130.

89. For extended analyses of the White Paper, see John Dinges, "White Paper o Blank Paper?" *Los Angeles Times,* March 17, 1981; James Petras, "White Paper on th White Paper," *Nation,* March 28, 1981, p. 1; Kwitney, *Endless Enemies,* chap. 21. Alexan der Haig rejected these analyses, charging a "will to disbelieve" on the part of the au thors. *Caveat,* pp. 139–140.

90. "Is El Salvador 'Another Vietnam'?" *Tampa Tribune,* March 26, 1981; "*A Newsweek* Poll: 'Stay Out,'" *Newsweek,* March 8, 1982.

91. "Confounding Calculations," *NACLA Report* 16 (March-April 1982):4.

92. John M. Goshko, "Panel Rejects Reagan Cuts," *Washington Post,* April 30 1981; Bonner, *Weakness and Deceit,* pp. 343–346.

93. U.S. Department of State, Press Statement, March 2, 1981.

94. *Oral History,* interview with Colonel John Waghelstein, pp. 7–8.

95. "Annual Integrated Assessment," June 12, 1981.

96. Reports of Radio Venceremos, August 11–20, 1981; "Mientras 'F.M.L.N. respeta prisioneros junta duartista asesina a la población" [While the FMLN respect prisoners, the Duarte junta kills the population], *El Nuevo Diario* (Managua), August 19 1981.

97. Interview with Commander Raul Hercules (Fidel Recinos), Mexico City, Janu ary 14, 1992. For a description of the bombing, see Charles Clements, *Witness to War: A American Doctor in El Salvador* (New York: Bantam, 1984), pp. 3–6; 223, 251–252 passim.

98. Interview with FMLN official, Dr. Miguel Sáenz, January 1982; "Annual Inte grated Assessment," June 12, 1981, pp. 3–6; "Annual Integrated Assessment," May 26 1982.

99. Alma Guillermoprieto, "Salvadoran Peasants Describe Mass Killing," *Wash ington Post,* January 27, 1982; Raymond Bonner, "Massacre of Hundreds Is Reported ir El Salvador," *New York Times,* January 28, 1982. See also Bonner, *Weakness and Deceit* pp. 112–113, 337–344. Mark Dannen, "The Truth of El Mozote," *The New Yorker* 69 (De cember 6, 1993):50–133.

100. Mary Jo McConahay, "Little-Known Air War Terrorized Population in Rura El Salvador," *National Catholic Reporter,* April 20, 1984; Carlos Ramos, "Puedc

ombardear zonas donde hay subversivos" [I can bomb zones where subversives are], *a Jornada* (Mexico), January 19, 1985.

101. "Annual Integrated Assessment," May 26, 1982, p. 7.

102. Interview, Managua, December 1981.

103. "A la expectativa" [Waiting], *Proceso*, no. 72 (July 5–11, 1982):1–2.

104. *NACLA Report* 18 (March-April 1984):43.

CHAPTER 6

1. Max G. Manwaring and Court Prisk, eds., *El Salvador at War: An Oral History* (Washington, D.C.: National Defense University Press, 1988), p. 240.

2. Raymond Bonner, *Weakness and Deceit: U.S. Policy and El Salvador* (New York: Times Books, 1984), pp. 290–292.

3. Frank Brodhead, "Demonstration Elections in El Salvador," in Marvin E. Gettleman et al., *El Salvador: Central America in the New Cold War*, rev. ed. (New York: Grove Press, 1986), p. 175. See also Edward S. Herman and Frank Brodhead, *Demonstration Elections: U.S.-Staged Elections in the Dominican Republic, Vietnam, and El Salvador* (Boston: South End Press, 1984).

4. Herman and Brodhead, *Demonstration Elections*, pp. 11–15.

5. Ibid., chap. 4; Bonner, *Weakness and Deceit*, chap. 15; Americas Watch and American Civil Liberties Union (AW-ACLU), *Report on Human Rights in El Salvador* (Washington, D.C.: Center for National Security Studies, 1982), chap. 5; CUDI, "Las elecciones de 1982: Realidades detrás de las apariencias" [The 1982 elections: Realities behind the appearances], *Estudios Centroamericanos (ECA)*, no. 403-404 (May-June 1982):574–581.

6. "Arena Celebrates Its First Anniversary," October 5, 1982, confidential cable. Released under FOIA.

7. Craig Pyes, "The New American Right Picks up a Hot Potato," *Albuquerque Journal*, December 22, 1983, pp. A1, A6–10.

8. The three parties were the Salvadorean Popular Party (PPS), the Renovating Action Party (PAR), and the Businessmen, Peasants and Workers Party (ECO), which registered as a party at the end of January 1982. Yan Verbeek, "Radiografía de unas elecciones con tiros y sin nacatamales" [X-ray of some elections with gunfire and without nacatamales (a Central American version of tamales)], *Barricada* (Nicaragua), February 1, 1982.

9. "Reconocen representatividad política al FDR en El Salvador" [Political representativity of FDR in El Salvador recognized], Agence France Presse release, *La Prensa*, September 22, 1981.

10. Letter of FMLN General Command to President Ronald Reagan, January 18, 1982, reprinted in *Barricada*, February 1, 1982.

11. A "finding" is a formal order, signed by the president, authorizing a covert action by the Central Intelligence Agency.

12. Bob Woodward, *Veil: The Secret Wars of the CIA 1981–1987* (New York: Simon and Schuster, 1987), p. 117.

13. Bonner, *Weakness and Deceit*, pp. 292–293. See also Lynda Schuster, "Having a Free Election in Midst of a Civil War Challenges El Salvador," *Wall Street Journal*, March 17, 1982.

14. John Dinges, "Bad Guys," *Toronto Globe and Mail*, July 1983. Dinges's article provoked a heated denial from AID director Peter McPherson to Pacific News Service editor Sandy Close that AID had provided "about $240,000 of the $400,000 spent by the electoral commission on the … campaign." Dinges wrote Close in a July 30, 1983, letter

that his two main sources were the head of the CCE, Jorge Bustamante, who was named in the article, and Kenneth Bleakley, the deputy chief of mission (number two in the embassy), who spoke on condition that he not be named. Both men, Dinges wrote, "talked openly about the [comic book] project and there was no implication that they had ever tried to hide it." Photocopy of letter in my possession.

15. "Las elecciones de 1982," p. 578. All information in this section, unless otherwise noted, is from this article.

16. *La Prensa Gráfica*, January 23, 1982.

17. Paco led his troops into an ambush; thirteen were killed, twelve wounded. Charles Clements, *Witness to War: An American Doctor in El Salvador* (New York: Bantam, 1984), pp. 81–84, 87–90, 121, 158.

18. Bonner, *Weakness and Deceit*, p. 304, 305.

19. Bonner, "U.S. Visitors Warn Salvador Rightists on Centrist Role," *New York Times*, April 10, 1982.

20. José Napoleón Duarte, *My Story* (New York: G. P. Putnam's Sons, 1986), p. 185.

21. LeoGrande, a professor of government at The American University in Washington, D.C., made this comment in a private conversation in 1982.

22. Jack Cobb, "Survey of Illegal Evictions of Beneficiaries of the Decree 207 Agrarian Reform Program: 1980–1983," manuscript (San Salvador, September 1983). Martin Diskin showed how different methods of counting the number of evictees and reinstallations varied wildly among FINATA, AIFLD, and AID. Diskin, "Agrarian Reform in El Salvador: An Evaluation" (San Francisco: Institute for Food and Development Policy, 1985):17–18. See also AIFLD, "Status of Land Reform," May 19, 1982. Declassified document released by Department of State.

23. Diskin, "Agrarian Reform in El Salvador," p. 13. For other assessments of the agrarian reform, see AIFLD, "El Salvador Agrarian Reform Update: Second Anniversary of Decree 207," April 28, 1982; "Agrarian Reform in El Salvador" (Washington, D.C.: Checchi and Company, January 1983).

24. The information in this paragraph is based on firsthand information from an individual who still lives in El Salvador and shared these and other details on condition of absolute anonymity. The individual said that when the storeroom was emptied, "three days before D'Aubuisson left to become a presidential candidate," the security men were farmed out to various other government agencies, including ISTA and the Ministry of the Economy, and to ARENA headquarters. The individual also said that "at least fifteen of the forty men had been prisoners in Mariona, eight of them for kidnapping," and that in spring 1989 "at least six were prisoners again for assault and murder." The U.S. government knew all about Regalado. See "Briefing Paper on Right-Wing Terrorism in El Salvador," October 27, 1983.

25. The reference to "ARENA death squads" is in October 27, 1983, "Briefing Paper on Right-Wing Terrorism." Revision of biography is in Bonner, *Weakness and Deceit*, p. 309.

26. Interview with Deane Hinton, San Salvador, March 9, 1983.

27. The document was leaked in San Salvador and reprinted in its entirety, in Spanish, in *Proceso*, no. 72 (July 5-11, 1982):6–9.

28. "Crisis," *Proceso*, no. 75 (July 26–August 8, 1982):3.

29. Emphasis added. "Political Pact Signed," confidential cable from U.S. Embassy to Secretary of State, August 4, 1982. Released under FOIA.

30. "Proliferación de crisis" [Crisis spreads], *Proceso*, no. 77 (August 16-22, 1982):1–2.

31. "Pacto de la desunión" [Pact of disunion], *Proceso*, no. 79 (August 30–September 5, 1982):3; "Reparto con calendario" [Delivering on schedule], *Proceso*, no. 83 (September 27–October 3, 1982):3.

32. "La política de la guerra" [The politics of war], *Proceso*, no. 94 (December 1982):7.

33. The massacre was first denounced by a group of priests and nuns in the diocese of Santa Rosa de Copán, Honduras, denied by the Honduran government, then denounced by the Honduran Episcopal Conference. By July 1980 over 5,000 Salvadorean refugees were in Honduras. For accounts of the first Sumpul massacre, see AW-ACLU, *Report on Human Rights in El Salvador* (New York: AW and ACLU, January 1982), pp. 177–178; Renato Camarda, *Forced to Move: Salvadorean Refugees in Honduras* (San Francisco: Solidarity Publications, 1985), p. 81.

34. A chilling eyewitness account is provided by Yvonne Dilling in *In Search of Refuge* (Scottdale, Pa.: Herald Press, 1984), pp. 39–49. Dilling and other international workers swam across the Lempa ferrying children on their backs for hours that day.

35. A. J. Bacevich, James D. Hallums, Richard H. White, and Thomas F. Young, "American Military Policy in Small Wars: The Case of El Salvador," paper presented March 22, 1988, John F. Kennedy School of Government, Harvard University (mimeo), p. 43.

36. Ibid., pp. 47–48.

37. Message from Colonel Francisco Adolfo Castillo, broadcast on Radio Venceremos, March 1983 (mimeo). Castillo was captured by the FMLN in June 1982 when his helicopter was shot down while returning from a trip to Honduras. He was a prisoner of war until May 10, 1984, when he was exchanged for nine FMLN political prisoners.

38. Raymond Bonner, "Green Berets Step Up Honduras Role," *New York Times*, August 9, 1981.

39. Bonner, *Weakness and Deceit*, p. 282.

40. "US Military Trainers in El Salvador," confidential memo, September 23, 1983. Released under FOIA.

41. Rod Nordland, "How U.S. Advisers Run the War in El Salvador," *Philadelphia Inquirer*, May 29, 1983.

42. Bonner, *Weakness and Deceit*, p. 284. *Soldier of Fortune* helped; see, for example, the following articles in that publication: Peter G. Kokalis, "Arms and the Atlacatls," vol. 9 (January 1984):50–55; Dale Dye, "Showdown at Cerron Grande" and "Los Morteros: SOF Schools Salvo Tube Crews," vol. 9 (November 1984):51–59 and 60–69; Alex McColl, "SOF in El Salvador," vol. 14 (December 1989):56–57.

43. AW-ACLU, July 1982 *Report on Human Rights*, pp. 215–216; Michael McClintock, *The American Connection: State Terror and Public Resistance in El Salvador*, vol. 1 (London: Zed Books, 1985), pp. 347–348.

44. Clements, *Witness to War*, p. 231. Clements had been a U.S. Air Force pilot in Vietnam.

45. Frank Smyth, "Secret Warriors," *Village Voice*, August 11, 1987, pp. 21–22.

46. Smyth, "Caught with Their Pants Down," *Village Voice*, December 2, 1989, p. 17.

47. Colonel James Steele in Manwaring and Prisk, *El Salvador at War*, pp. 363–364.

48. James LeMoyne, "Rebels Kill 43 Salvador Troops and U.S. Adviser," *New York Times*, April 1, 1987; LeMoyne, "Salvador Rebel Infiltrators Called Key in Raid on Base," April 2, 1987; John Borrell, "Bloody Setback at El Paraíso," *Time*, April 11, 1987.

49. Milton Jamail and Margo Gutierrez, *It's No Secret: Israel's Military Involvement in Central America* (Belmont, Mass.: AAUG Press, 1986), pp. 43–45.

50. Doyle McManus, "U.S. Pilots in Salvador Missions," *Chicago Sun-Times* March 12, 1984; Lydia Chavez, "U.S. Steps Up Use of Spying Planes in Salvador War," *New York Times*, March 30, 1984.

51. Colonel Robert H. Herrick, interview, in *Oral History of the Conflict in El Salvador 1979–Present* (Carlisle: Pa.: Military History Institute, 1988) (mimeo), p. 20.

52. Bacevich et al., "American Military Policy in Small Wars," p. 39.

53. Secret memorandum from Deputy Chief of Mission Kenneth Bleakley to Ambassador Deane Hinton, "Integrated Plan—Status Report No. 2," February 18, 1983. Released under FOIA.

54. Colonel John Waghelstein in Manwaring and Prisk, *El Salvador at War*, p. 224. The antecedent of the NCP was the "rural pacification" program that the United States attempted to implement in Vietnam.

55. Bacevich et al., "American Military Policy in Small Wars," p. 81.

56. "El Salvador: The National Plan," assessment memorandum from U.S. AID San Salvador, July 1985 (mimeo).

57. Manwaring and Prisk, *El Salvador at War*, p. 273. Colonel (later General) Adolfo Blandón was then commander of the First Brigade in San Salvador. He was later army chief of staff from November 1983 to early 1989.

58. "Rebelión en Cabañas," *Proceso*, no. 95 (January 3-15, 1983):4–5; Sam Dillon, "Garcia Quits, Averting a Mutiny in Salvador," *Miami Herald*, April 19, 1983.

59. "Comunicado de las FPL" [FPL communiqué] and "Comunicado de la Comandancia General sobre el caso Comandante Ana María" [Communiqué from the General Command about the Comandante Ana María case], *Venceremos*, no. 19, December 1983, pp. 14–16, 19–20.

60. Manwaring and Prisk, *El Salvador at War*, p. 233. Clark was a special assistant and a close personal friend of Ronald Reagan.

61. "El Salvador Willing, Mrs. Kirkpatrick Says," *New York Times*, February 10, 1983; Bernard Weinraub, "Reagan Is Seeking $60 Million More in Aid to Salvador," *New York Times*, February 27, 1983.

62. John Waghelstein on the Belloso, quoted in Bonner, *Weakness and Deceit*, p. 277. The Belloso's rout in Morazán came just two weeks after its "successful" inaugural offensive in Chalatenango.

63. Stringham in Manwaring and Prisk, *El Salvador at War*, p. 148.

64. "U.S. Aid to El Salvador: An Evaluation of the Past, a Proposal for the Future," report to the Arms Control and Foreign Policy Caucus of the U.S. Congress, February 1985 (hereafter "Caucus Report 1985"), p. 26.

65. *Proceso*, no. 135 (December 1983):12, 14.

66. *Free Fire: A Report on Human Rights in El Salvador*, 5th supp. (New York: Americas Watch and Lawyers Committee for International Human Rights, August 1984), p. 54; "Previendo ofensiva" [Foreseeing the offensive], *Proceso*, no. 152 (July 23–August 12, 1984):5–6.

Comandante Roberto Roca (Francisco Jovel) acknowledged that "in 1983 and 1984 we committed errors. Often [*compañeros*] who had only joined recently, including some who were forcibly recruited, were sent into combat right off the bat. And as a consequence we had desertions, unnecessary deaths, people who had a very negative psychological response to combat. ... We learned that the only powerful guerrilla force is a voluntary one. We have to involve people gradually, and never, never take a guerrilla fighter away from his people." Quoted in Bob Ostertag and Sara Miles, "Rethinking War," *NACLA Report* 33 (September 1989):18.

67. "Testimony of Dr. Charles Clements, M.D., M.P.H.," submitted to the House Subcommittees on Western Hemisphere and Human Rights, March 23, 1983, (mimeo), p. 2.

68. "Caucus Report 1985," pp. 27, 28.

69. Rubén Zamora on MacNeil-Lehrer News Hour, February 9, 1984. The FMLN estimated in the early and mid-1980s that 10 to 20 percent of POWs chose to remain with the FMLN. Villalobos interview in Marlene Dixon and Susanne Jonas, *Revolution and Intervention in Central America* (San Francisco: Solidarity Press, 1983), p. 102. Charles Clements, who was liaison between the FMLN and the ICRC for the return of POWs, reported in 1983 that a majority of prisoners in Guazapa chose to stay with the guerrillas. "Testimony of Dr. Charles Clements," p. 3.

70. Manwaring and Prisk, *El Salvador at War*, pp. 324–326.

71. "Contadora," *Proceso*, no. 126 (September 26–October 9, 1983):15.

72. "Latin Peace Unit Gains Few Results," *New York Times*, October 2, 1983; "Bernardo Sepúlveda Amor se reunió con G. Shultz" [B. Sepúlveda Amor meets with G. Schultz], *Uno más Uno*, September 29, 1983; "Mexico Asks U.S. to Change Policies," *New York Times*, February 13, 1984. See transcript of President Reagan's May 22, 1984, press conference in *Washington Post*, May 23, 1984, p. A27.

73. *Report of the National Bi-Partisan Commission on Central America*, January 1984 (mimeo). For a brief but incisive review of the politics and process of the Kissinger commission and its report, see Bonner, *Weakness and Deceit*, pp. 361–364. See also "Costa Rica," *Proceso*, no. 137 (January 30–February 12, 1984):16.

74. *Contadora: A Text for Peace*, Center for International Policy report (Washington, D.C.: Center for International Policy, November 1984); Philip Taubman, "Latin Peace Plan: Why the U.S. Balks," *New York Times*, October 2, 1984; "Objectando Contadora" [Objecting to Contadora], *Proceso*, no. 160 (October 8, 1984):8–9.

75. I was in El Salvador for the pope's visit, was present at the mass, and attended the memorial masses for Romero in 1984 and 1985.

76. "Elections," confidential cable from U.S. Embassy, San Salvador, to Secretary of State, June 11, 1983. Released under FOIA.

77. William Bollinger, "El Salvador," in Gerald Michael Greenfield and Sheldon L. Maram, eds., *Latin American Labor Organizations* (New York: Greenwood Press, 1987), pp. 338–341.

78. "Sintesis anual" [Annual synthesis], *Proceso*, no. 135 (December 1983):18.

79. Ibid., pp. 14–15; "Contacto en Miami" [Contact in Miami], *Proceso*, no. 132 (November 14-20, 1983):6; "Declaración del Comité de Prensa de la Fuerza Armada" [Declaration of the Armed Forces Press Committee], reprinted in *ECA*, no. 423-424 (January-February 1984):110–111; "El Salvador: Dealing with Death Squads," CIA cable, January 20, 1984, released by U.S. government, November 9, 1993.

80. "Marcha atras" [Going backwards], *Proceso*, no. 132 (November 14-20, 1983):1; "Paliativos" [Palliatives], *Proceso*, no. 133 (November 21-28, 1983):3.

81. The information in this section, unless otherwise noted, comes from an unpublished manuscript by Martin Diskin and Tommie Sue Montgomery, "The Electronic *Tamale*: Elections and Democracy in El Salvador." Diskin and I were in El Salvador for the general election and the runoff.

82. Thomas R. Pickering, "Elections in El Salvador," address before the corporate Round Table of the World Affairs Council, Washington, D.C., March 1, 1984 (Washington, D.C.: Department of State, Bureau of Public Affairs, Current Policy no. 554, 1984), p. 3.

83. *Excelsior*, May 3, 1984, p. 21.

84. "El río no se revuelve" [The river does not return] and "Pactos y coaliciónes" [Pacts and coalitions], *Proceso*, no. 139 (February 20-26, 1984):1, 3.

85. Richard J. Meislen, "Salvadoran Rebels Won't Try to Disrupt Election," *New York Times*, February 10, 1984.

86. Interview, January 12, 1984.

87. "Municipalities Where Voting Did Not Take Place," confidential cable from U.S. Embassy, San Salvador, to Secretary of State, April 9, 1984; "Post-Mortem Look at Guerrilla Efforts to Disrupt Election," limited official use cable from U.S. Embassy to Secretary of State, May 12, 1984. Released under FOIA.

88. "A Little Help from Friends," *Time*, May 21, 1984, p. 57; "Mr. Reagan Has It His Way," *Newsweek*, May 21, 1984, p. 41.

89. In the oral histories, several Salvadorean officers acknowledged that pressure from U.S. advisers brought the army to identify itself as the defender of the new constitutional order and "democracy." Manwaring and Prisk, *El Salvador at War*, Colonel René Emilio Ponce, p. 215; General Vides Casanova, p. 218; Colonel Oscar Campos Anaya, p. 221.

90. Margaret Shapiro and T. R. Reid, "Reagan Wins Narrowly on Aid to El Salvador," *Washington Post*, May 11, 1984.

91. "Nuevo gobierno" [New government], *Proceso*, no. 155 (September 3, 1984):3–4. Inaugural speech printed and released by the Secretary of Information of the Presidency, June 1, 1984. An early indication of Duarte's lack of independence in foreign policy came in July when the government first announced, then rescinded under pressure, its decision to send a representative to the fifth anniversary celebration of the Sandinista revolution in Nicaragua. Lydia Chavez, "Salvador, in Shift, Rebuffs Sandinistas," *New York Times*, July 18, 1984.

92. "Hacia donde vamos?" [Where are we going?], *Proceso*, no. 155 (September 3, 1984):1. In a June 1985 interview, UCA vice-rector Ignacio Martín-Baró, who had reviewed all of Duarte's speeches and public pronouncements since his inauguration, said "there is no substance, no program of any kind, nothing."

CHAPTER 7

1. A. J. Bacevich, James D. Hallums, Richard H. White, and Thomas F. Young, "American Military Policy in Small Wars: The Case of El Salvador," paper presented March 22, 1988, John F. Kennedy School of Government, Harvard University (mimeo), p. 79.

2. The term "electoral authoritarianism" is borrowed, with permission, from William Stanley and Frank Smyth.

3. Cynthia Brown, ed., *With Friends Like These: The Americas Watch Report on Human Rights and U.S. Policy in Latin America* (New York: Pantheon, 1985), p. 138.

4. Robert J. McCartney, "Duarte Tries Again in El Salvador," *Washington Post*, March 15, 1984.

5. Lydia Chavez, "Salvador to Restructure Security Forces," *New York Times*, June 14, 1984; Dennis Volman, "Salvador Death Squads, a CIA Connection?" *Christian Science Monitor*, May 8, 1984.

6. "Baja" [Cashiered], *Proceso*, no. 168 (December 3, 1984):8; Edward Cody, "Duarte: Limited Power over the Military," *Washington Post*, September 17, 1984; Clifford Krauss, "Solving a Murder Case in El Salvador Is Hard If Suspects Are VIPs," *Wall Street Journal*, December 10, 1984.

7. Allan Nairn, "Behind the Death Squads," *The Progressive*, May 1984, pp. 20ff. Dennis Volman, "Salvador Death Squads"; Edward Cody, "Duarte: Limited Power."

8. "Darkness Before Dawn," *Time*, September 10, 1984, p. 23; also interviews with Christian Democrats and Salvadorean political analysts, November 1984, March and August 1985.

9. "Crónica del mes" [Monthly chronicle], *Estudios Centroamericanos (ECA)*, no. 32-433 (October-November 1984):823, and no. 434 (December 1984):930; Pickering ited in *Proceso*, no. 159 (October 1, 1984):6–7.

10. "Recortes" [Clippings], *Proceso*, no. 170 (January 15, 1985):3.

11. This account is based on personal observation in La Palma and Miramundo n October 15 and 16. See also James LeMoyne, "2 Sides Draw Up Salvadoran Plan to eek War's End," *New York Times*, October 16, 1984; Alma Guillermoprieto, "Salvaoran Left Says Fighting to Continue," *Washington Post*, October 17, 1984.

President Duarte, acting on intelligence that the FMLN was moving "large roups of guerrilla forces into the area around La Palma that was supposed to be demilarized," sent Colonel Sigfrido Ochoa, who had returned from Washington to become ommander of the garrison at El Paraiso, to take the town on October 8. José Napoleón uarte, *My Story* (New York: G. P. Putnam's Sons, 1986), p. 332. Ochoa states that "we aptured many guerrillas, many documents." See Max G. Manwaring and Court Prisk, ds., *El Salvador at War: An Oral History* (Washington, D.C.: National Defense University ress, 1988), p. 332. The *Miami Herald*'s Sam Dillon reported that "As a battalion of govrnment troops stalked up the cobbled streets [of La Palma] last week, a platoon of eavily armed guerrillas across the square ambled out of town and into the pine-forsted mountains. Both sides were close enough to see the whites of each others' eyes— ut neither side fired a shot." "Mood of Peace Sweeps El Salvador for Talks," October 4, 1984.

12. See José Napoleón Duarte, *My Story* (New York: G. P. Putnam's Sons, 1986), hap. 9. Duarte's description of what went on inside the church (pp. 217–221) is, accordng to Rubén Zamora, a mixture of fact and fantasy. For example, Duarte wrote that Zaiora was "all for eliminating the rightist sectors, but I told him that his theory was toilitarian" (p. 218). Zamora maintained he never said that (interview, Washington,).C., April 12, 1989). In fact, in interviews going back to 1980, Zamora consistently arued the necessity for building bridges to moderate conservatives in the private sector. uarte also charged that FPL Comandante Facundo Guardado was "wearing the uniorm of a dead army lieutenant" and that "at the peace table [he] should not have aunted the fact that they killed one of our men" (p. 219). Guardado acknowledged that e was wearing the jacket of a member of the Armed Forces who had died in battle; inrview, October 25, 1993. Venezuelan ambassador Luís Rodríguez Malaspina credited uarte in an interview, January 21, 1994.

13. James LeMoyne, "Duarte Will Not Attend Peace Talks Next Week," *New York imes*, November 24, 1984.

14. For a fuller discussion of events in La Palma and Ayagualo, see *Proceso*, nos. 61 and 162 (October 15 and 22, 1984); Tommie Sue Montgomery, "El Salvador," in Jack V. Hopkins, ed., *Latin American and Caribbean Contemporary Record*, vol. 4 (1984–1985) Vew York: Holmes & Meier, 1985), pp. 484–486.

15. Fidel Chávez Mena, "El Salvador: Crisis, estabilidad y proceso democrático" Crisis, stability, and democratic process], *ECA*, no. 432-433 (October-November 984):72.

16. "Balance" [Assessment], *Proceso*, no. 190 (June 10, 1985):4.

17. Economic Commission for Latin America (CEPAL), "Notas para el estudio conómico de América Latin y el Caribe 1984: El Salvador" [Notes for the economic udy of Latin America and the Caribbean], U.N., L.C./Mex/L.3 (April 8, 1985):1–2, 8, 3, 45–50; "Economic Trends Report—El Salvador," U.S. Embassy, San Salvador, July 1, 1985 (mimeo); "Central America Report" (Guatemala), vol. 12 (May 31, 1985):156.

18. CEPAL, "Notas para el estudio."

19. Central de Información y Acción Social (CINAS), "El Salvador: Crónica mensuales" [Monthly chronicle], no. 130 (April-June 1984):53; "Crónica del mes," *ECA* no. 431 (September 1984):824.

20. CEPAL, "Estudio económico de América Latina y el Caribe 1987: El Salva dor" [Economic study of Latin America and the Caribbean 1987], U.N. L.C./L.463, add.12, September 1988.

21. Kenneth Sharpe, "El Salvador," in Jack W. Hopkins, ed., *Latin American an Caribbean Contemporary Record*, vol. 5 (1985–1986) (New York: Holmes & Meier, 1986) pp. B275–B298. FUSADES was founded in 1984 as a "private sector foundation .. staffed and managed by private sector leaders." It is a combination think tank and agency for promoting new agribusiness and nontraditional exports (description from U.S. Embassy official, January 1988). It receives considerable funding from AID.

22. "Marcha por la supervivencia de los trabajadores" [March for workers' sur vival], *Proceso*, no. 226 (February 24, 1986):4.

23. William Bollinger, "El Salvador," in Gerald Michael Greenfield and Sheldo L. Maram, eds., *Latin American Labor Organizations* (New York: Greenwood Press, 1987) p. 321. This monograph provides an excellent labor history and detailed description o Salvadorean unions and federations, past and present.

24. Ibid., pp. 321, 366, 381–383. It should be noted that center-right and right wing unions also fared badly. The National Workers Central (CNT) was founded i 1982 as a union base for ARENA but was able to control only two unions. The Genera Confederation of Labor (CGT) was founded in 1983 to provide union support fo Duarte but fell on hard times as conditions deteriorated in 1984. Unless otherwis noted, the information in this section comes from Bollinger, "El Salvador."

25. "Malestar laboral" [Labor unrest], *ECA*, no. 445 (November 1985):835. For a extended analysis of labor developments and the government's response, see *Labo Rights in El Salvador* (New York: Americas Watch, March 1988).

26. "Contradicciones laborales" [Labor contradictions], *Proceso*, no. 186 (May 1 1985):3–4; *Proceso*, no. 191 (June 17, 1985):3–4, 7–9; documents relating to these events i *ECA*, no. 441-442 (July-August 1986):598–607; Sharpe, "El Salvador," pp. B287–B288 "Comunicado público de la UPD" [Public communiqué of UPD], carbon copy, Jun 1985.

27. "Surge la Unidad Nacional de Trabajadores Salvadoreños" [The UNT emerges], *Proceso*, no. 224 (February 10, 1986):10–11.

28. "Guerrillas Infiltrate Salvadorean Unions," *AFL-CIO News*, May 3, 198 quoted in Bollinger, "El Salvador," p. 324.

29. "Marcha de la UNOC" [UNOC's march], *Proceso*, no. 229 (March 17, 1986): Frank Smyth, "AFL-CIO Is Spanish for Union Busting," *Washington Monthly*, Septem ber 1987, pp. 24–27; interview, July 22, 1988.

30. Interview, U.S. Embassy, July 22, 1988.

31. Robert J. McCartney, "U.S. Cools Support for Duarte," *Washington Pos* March 20, 1985, p. Al.

32. Sam Dillon, "Win by Duarte Party Could Spur Backlash, U.S. Officials Pr dict," *Miami Herald*, February 9, 1985; James LeMoyne, "Duarte's Power Eroded as Sa vador Vote Nears," *New York Times*, February 17, 1985.

33. Chris Norton, "Duarte Election Win Thwarts Right Wing," *In These Time* April 17–23, 1985, p. 3; George Russell et al., "New Strength and Hope," *Time*, April 1 1985, pp. 74–75.

34. Nancy Cooper and Joseph Contreras, "A Major Win for Duarte," *Newswee* April 15, 1985, p. 75; Robert J. McCartney, "Salvadoran Armed Forces Back Election R

sults," *Washington Post,* April 4, 1985; telephone interview with Mary Jo McConahay in San Salvador, April 3, 1985.

35. Part of the analysis in this paragraph is from the April 3 conversation with McConahay.

36. "Resumen anual: Balance militar" [Annual summary: Military assessment], *Proceso,* no. 269 (December 1986):12; Manwaring and Prisk, *El Salvador at War,* pp. 335–336.

37. Duryea interview in Manwaring and Prisk, *El Salvador at War,* p. 471.

38. Juan Orlando Zepeda, "Estrategia global revolucionaria y su aplicación en El Salvador" [Revolutionary global strategy and its application in El Salvador], June 1988, pp. 21–22. This is a confidential, twenty-two-page analysis of the antecedents and evolution of the conflict, and of the FMLN's global strategy, written for the Salvadorean General Staff.

39. The information in this section comes from two articles by and a conversation with Joel Millman, a freelance writer who spent fourteen months in El Salvador in 1988 and 1989 studying the impact of arms aid. The first is in the form of a letter, dated December 3, 1988, to the Institute of Current World Affairs in Hanover, N.H. Second is "A Force unto Itself," *New York Times Magazine,* December 10, 1989, pp. 47, 95–97. Our conversation took place in San Salvador January 5, 1989.

40. Walker is quoted in Millman, "A Force unto Itself," p. 95. Millman does not identify Walker by name, but he was the only U.S. diplomat in El Salvador in 1989 who also served in 1977.

41. Colonel Robert M. Herrick, quoted in ibid., p. 97.

42. Chris Norton, "Charges of Widespread Corruption Rock Salvadoran Government," computer printout of draft manuscript, August 4, 1987.

43. Clifford Krauss and Robert S. Greenberger, "Corruption Threatens Political Gains Made by U.S. in El Salvador," *Wall Street Journal,* September 14, 1987.

44. The following information comes from Norton, draft manuscript, "Charges of Widespread Corruption"; Krauss and Greenberger, "Corruption Threatens"; memo from journalist Sandra Smith to Dan Noyes of the Center for Investigative Reporting, San Francisco, fall 1987; and "El iceberg de la corrupción" [The iceberg of corruption], *Proceso,* no. 345 (July 20, 1988):5–6.

45. Photocopies of some of these documents are in my possession.

46. Quoted in *Underwriting Injustice: AID and El Salvador's Judicial Reform Program* (New York: Lawyers Committee for Human Rights, April 1989), frontispiece. Unless otherwise noted, the information in this section on efforts to reform the judicial system comes from this study.

47. *From the Ashes: A Report on Justice in El Salvador* (New York: Lawyers Committee for Human Rights, 1987), p. 5.

48. *Underwriting Injustice,* pp. 10–11. Emphasis in original.

49. Ibid., p. 4. The interview was conducted by the Lawyers Committee in San Salvador, September 1988.

50. Quoted in ibid., p. 9; "Crónica del mes," *ECA,* no. 483-484 (January-February 1989):107. García Alvarado was assassinated by the FAL on April 19, 1989.

51. Quoted in report prepared by retired U.S. district judge Harold Tyler for U.S. State Department; publicly released May 1984.

52. Rod Nordland, "Trial Leaves Suspicions Unresolved," *Philadelphia Inquirer,* May 27, 1984; Lydia Chavez, "5 Salvadorans Are Found Guilty in Slaying of U.S. Churchwomen," *New York Times,* May 25, 1984. El Salvador has no death penalty in its legal code.

53. *Underwriting Injustice,* p. 5.

54. Ibid., pp. 28–29; *Condoning the Killing: Ten Years of Massacres in El Salvador* (Washington, D.C.: EPICA, 1990), pp. 20–21; interview, U.S. Embassy, July 21, 1988.

55. Douglas Farah, "Death Squad Began as Scout Troop," *Washington Post*, August 29, 1988; "Briefing Paper on Right-Wing Terrorism in El Salvador," October 27, 1983.

56. In addition to the previous article, much of the story about resurgence of the death squads appeared in articles in the *Washington Post* and *Miami Herald*: Douglas Farah, "Salvadoran Death Squads Threaten Resurgence," *Washington Post*, August 28, 1988; Tom Gibb, "Killings Tied to Salvador Official" and "Informant: Re-Arming Precedes Elections," *Miami Herald*, August 28, 1988. Farah and Gibb also wrote a six-part magazine article with many more details than appeared in the newspapers: draft manuscript, "Magazine Story on Death Squads in El Salvador"; this quotation from copy of computer printout in my possession.

57. Gibb and Farah, draft manuscript, "Magazine Story"; Farah, "Death Squad Began as Scout Troop."

58. William Branigin, "Leftists Kill Officials, Civilians, Lifting Salvadoran Toll," *Washington Post*, August 29, 1988.

59. This research was done under a Fulbright grant. A "well-founded fear" is the international standard for granting political-refugee status.

60. Much of the information that follows comes from Americas Watch, *El Salvador's Decade of Terror: Human Rights Since the Assassination of Archbishop Romero* (New Haven: Yale University Press, 1991), chap. 4.

61. *Condoning the Killing* summarizes thirty-two cases of mass killings by government forces between 1980 and 1990. Thirteen cases involved 20 to 100 killed; five cases involved over 100.

62. *Violations of Fair Trial Guarantees by the FMLN's Ad Hoc Courts* (New York: Americas Watch, May 1990), p. 3.

63. "FDR-FMLN Pacto Político" [Political pact], *ECA*, no. 461 (March 1987):281–282.

64. "Plataforma Programática" [Programmatic platform], the Democratic Convergence, September 1988, reprinted in *ECA*, no. 481-482 (November-December 1988):1130–1134.

65. Douglas Farah, "Duarte to Be Treated in U.S. for Bleeding Ulcer," *Washington Post*, May 29, 1988; "Duarte Has Stomach Cancer and Liver Problems," *New York Times*, June 3, 1988.

66. Chris Norton, "Salvador Rebel-Government Peace Talks End with Some Gain," *Christian Science Monitor*, October 7, 1987.

67. The Truth Commission, which was formed as a part of the 1991 peace accords to investigate all major human rights cases, concluded that a young member of the ERP may have been Anaya's assassin. See *De la locura a al esperanza: La guerra de doce años en El Salvador* [From insanity to hope: The twelve-year war in El Salvador], report of the Truth Commission for El Salvador (New York: United Nations, 1993), pp. 167–172.

68. *ECA* devoted an entire issue to the National Debate: See *ECA*, no. 478-479 (August-September 1988).

CHAPTER 8

1. David Escobar Galindo, "Filtraciones de pacificador" [Reflections of a peace maker], *Ejercicios Matinales* [Morning exercise], San Salvador, 1993, p. 40. Escobar Galindo, lawyer, poet, and writer, was President Alfredo Cristiani's personal representative on the government's team during the peace negotiations.

2. On one occasion, D'Aubuisson handed a journalist accompanying Cristiani two clay pistols that had barrels in the shape of oversized penises. When asked if he had killed many "*subversivos*" with them, D'Aubuisson said no, but he had killed "*subversivas*" (women). Then he writhed and groaned as an audience of *campesinos* laughed and Cristiani turned crimson. Sara Miles and Bob Ostertag, "Absolute, Diabolical Terror," *Mother Jones* 14 (April 1989): 27, 46.

3. Miles and Ostertag, "D'Aubuisson's New ARENA," *NACLA Report* 23 (July 1989):20–22.

4. "FMLN Proposal to Convert the Elections to a Contribution Toward Peace," issued by the FMLN General Command, January 23, 1989 (mimeo); "A New Reality: Peace Is on the Agenda," *Venceremos*, February-March 1989, pp. 1–12; "Obispo distribuye la propuesta de los subversivos al gobierno" [(Auxiliary) bishop distributes the subversives' proposal to the government], *La Prensa Gráfica*, January 24, 1989; interview with Miguel Sáenz, January 13, 1989.

5. Douglas Farah, "Salvadorans Divided on Rebel Plan," *Washington Post*, January 25, 1989; "Propuesta de FMLN es positivo, dice Perdomo" [The FMLN proposal is positive, Perdomo says], *La Noticia*, January 24, 1989; "Gobierno rechaza la propuesta del FMLN" [Government rejects FMLN proposal], *El Diario de Hoy*, January 26, 1989; "Descártase versión sobre división: EU–El Salvador" [Discard version that there is a U.S.–El Salvador split], *La Prensa Gráfica*, January 28, 1989.

6. Julia Preston, "Salvadoran Peace Diplomacy Fails but Leaves Lasting Effects," *Washington Post*, March 5, 1989; "Focus on El Salvador: Commentaries by the FDR-FMLN Political-Diplomatic Commission," April 18, 1989 (mimeo).

7. Interview, San Salvador, July 27, 1992.

8. Lindsey Gruson, "Gun Battles Flare As Salvadorans Vote for a Leader," *New York Times*, March 20, 1989. Twenty-five journalists were killed in El Salvador between 1980 and 1989.

9. Douglas Farah and Tom Gibb, draft manuscript, "Magazine Story on Death Squads in El Salvador"; Frank Smyth, "In a Season of Frustration, Fear, and Warfare, El Salvador Goes to the Polls: Fighting, Relations with America Are Factors," *Fort Worth Star-Telegram*, March 19, 1989, p. 8.

10. Lindsey Gruson, "New Latin Leader Urges Peace Talks," *New York Times*, March 22, 1989; Kenneth Freed, "Cristiani Vows to 'Rescue' El Salvador, Will 'Seek Contact' with Rebels," *Los Angeles Times*, June 2, 1989.

11. "Poll Says Salvadorans Want Talks with Rebels," UPI wire story, May 30, 1989.

12. "Communiqué" from the FMLN General Command, September 7, 1989 (mimeo).

13. Larry Rohter, "Salvador Rebels Reduce Demands," *New York Times*, September 15, 1989.

14. "El diálogo entre gobierno y FMLN en Costa Rica" [The dialogue between government and FMLN in Costa Rica], *Proceso*, no. 405 (October 18, 1989):2–5.

15. Andres Oppenheimer, "Salvador Battles Flare Despite Talks," *Miami Herald*, November 2, 1989; Chris Norton, "Upstairs at the Bombing: The FENASTRAS Attack," *In These Times*, November 8–14, 1989. Norton escaped serious injury because he was on the second floor interviewing a union leader.

16. Douglas Farah, "Salvadoran Rebels Vow Vengeance for Killings," *Washington Post*, November 2, 1989.

17. "Estrategia global revolucionaria," June 1988, pp. 21–22.

18. All quotations by Francisco Jovel from an interview in San Salvador, July 27, 1992.

19. Interview, San Salvador, July 27, 1992.

20. David Brand, "The Sheraton Siege," *Time*, December 4, 1989, p. 51.

21. "U.S., Salvadoran Government Contend Rebels Losing Punch in War," *Atlanta Journal and Constitution*, July 30, 1989. The FMLN was cognizant of these views: "The government believed," said Francisco Jovel, that "the situation was developing in which we would have to accept military defeat; they never understood the context in which we were making our proposal [to postpone and participate in the elections]." Interview, July 27, 1992. And see Chris Norton, "U.S. Self-Delusion Exacts Brutal Price in El Salvador," *In these Times*, December 6–12, 1989.

22. Douglas Farah, "War Confronts El Salvador's Wealthy," *Washington Post*, December 1, 1989, p. A50.

23. Frank Smyth, "Caught with Their Pants Down," *The Village Voice*, December 5, 1989, p. 16.

24. "Violations of the Laws of War by Both Sides," New York Americas Watch, November 25, 1989, p. 84; Mark A. Uhlig, "Rights Group Accuses U.S. over El Salvador," *New York Times*, November 27, 1989.

25. "Radio Farabundo Martí Notices," *New York Times*, November 27, 1989.

26. Many of the details in this discussion of the peace talks may be found in K. Larry Storrs, "El Salvador: Status of U.N.-mediated Government-Guerrilla Peace Talks," *CRS Report for Congress* (Washington, D.C.: Congressional Research Service, March 26, 1991).

27. The information in this section comes from off-the-record interviews in San Salvador with U.N. officials who were close to the negotiating process, and from "Highlights of El Salvador Negotiations—Chronology, April 1990–August 1991," U.S.–El Salvador Institute for Democratic Development (San Francisco), September 1991.

28. *Proceso*, no. 402 (September 26, 1989):3.

29. Al Kamen, "Senate Votes to Slash Salvadoran Aid," *Washington Post*, October 20, 1990; Lindsay Gruson, "Salvador Arms Aid: Will Congress's Tactic Work?" *New York Times*, October 22, 1989.

30. Lindsay Gruson, "Missiles Give Salvador Rebels a New Advantage," *New York Times*, December 10, 1990; Associated Press, "Salvadoran Unit's Defeat Sparks Furor," *Atlanta Constitution*, December 14, 1990. The FMLN had missiles in the 1989 offensive but was not prepared to use them.

31. Conversation with Joy Hackel in San Salvador, November 19, 1990, who reported on Ponce's appearance on Salvadorean television.

32. Interview, July 24, 1992.

33. I arrived in El Salvador three days after the election and spent the next three days talking to the embassy, members of political parties, election observers, the UCA and the army.

34. Telephone conversations with Rubén Zamora and Chris Norton in San Salvador, May 1 and 2, 1991; interview with Zamora, Washington, D.C., April 6, 1991.

35. Chris Norton, "Rightist Intimidation Wins in El Salvador," *In These Times*, April 3–9, 1991, p. 9.

36. Interview in Miami, Florida, June 13, 1991.

37. Lee Hockstader, "U.S. Envoy, Colonel Meet Salvadorean Rebels," *Washington Post*, September 13, 1991, p. A33; interview with Ambassador William Walker, San Salvador, October 1, 1991.

38. Telephone interview, Mexico City, December 13, 1991.

39. I was in El Salvador for the week of the cease-fire, January 31–February 5. On February 1 rumors were flying that D'Aubuisson had died the night before, which would have been a supreme historic irony—February 1 was the sixtieth anniversary of Farabundo Martí's death by firing squad. The ARENA founder died on February 20.

40. Much of this section originally appeared, in a different version, as "El Salvador from Civil War to Negotiated Revolution," *North-South* 2 (April-May 1993):22–25.

41. A useful overview of developments in 1992 is George Vickers et al., *Endgame: A Progress Report on Implementation of the Salvadorean Peace Accords* (Cambridge, Mass.: Hemisphere Initiatives, December 3, 1992).

42. Press conference of FMLN commanders, San Salvador, August 3, 1992.

43. "Informe del secretario general sobre la Misión de Observadores de las Naciones Unidas en El Salvador" [Report of the secretary general on the United Nations Observer Mission in El Salvador], S/25006, December 23, 1992, p. 7; "Statement of Dr. Augusto Ramírez Ocampo on the Occasion of the Report on the Destruction of Arms Acknowledged by the FMLN and the Registry of Arms for Private Use of the Armed Forces," ONUSAL Press Bulletin, August 18, 1993, p. 6.

44. The Bush administration's choice to succeed Ambassador William Walker was held up for months in the U.S. Senate by a bizarre coalition of Christopher Dodd (D.–Conn.) and Jesse Helms (R.–N.C.). Walker was extended for several months but left soon after the cease-fire. The senior embassy official was the political officer who was naturally perceived as having far less authority than an ambassador or DCM.

45. The information in this section, unless otherwise noted, comes from Peter Sollis, *Reluctant Reforms: The Cristiani Government and the International Community in the Process of Salvadorean Post-War Reconstruction* (Washington, D.C.: Washington Office on Latin America, June 1993), quotation on p. iv.

46. Interview with senior AID official, San Salvador, November 19, 1991. The fact is, the NGOs were organized by people who also belonged to the FMLN, but their operation and leadership were separate from the FMLN. They had their own programs and sought their own funding. By 1993, in some cases, rifts and even outright divorces occurred between some NGOs and the FMLN because of policy and/or administrative differences.

47. Statement of General George Joulwan, commander-in-chief, U.S. Southern Command, before the Armed Services Committee, U.S. Senate, April 21, 1993, p. 19.

48. Sollis, *Reluctant Reforms*, p. 42.

49. "Programa para la restablecimiento de la administración pública en zonas conflictivas" (version final) [Program for the reestablishment of public administration in conflict zones (final version)], September 16, 1992 (mimeo), provided by ONUSAL; "Informe del secretario general sobre la Misión de Observadores de las Naciones Unidas en El Salvador" [Report of the secretary general on the United Nations Observer Mission in El Salvador], S/25812, May 21, 1993, pp. 19–20; interview with Henry Morris, San Salvador, December 1993.

50. Interviews with ONUSAL officials Henry Morris and Vladimiro Huaroc, November and December 1993.

51. The opposition in the Legislative Assembly attempted, through COPAZ, to change the winner-take-all system to proportional representation. ARENA opposed this idea, arguing that it would make "governing" (*gobernabilidad*) more difficult. The opposition responded with a compromise proposal that the winning party receive one-half of the council seats, which with the mayor's vote would give the party a working majority. ARENA opposed this as well. An interesting question was whether ARENA would adhere to this position if the FMLN and CD won a significant number of mayoralties in 1994.

52. "Nuevo informe del secretario general sobre la Misión de Observadores de las Naciones Unidas en El Salvador" [New report of the secretary general on the United Nations Observer Mission in El Salvador], S/26790, November 23, 1993, pp. 15–16.

53. Interview with ONUSAL political officer, San Miguel, February 11, 1994.

54. Television news report, Pedro Martínez, spokesman, Channel 12, 9:00 P.M. news, February 23, 1994. It is interesting to note that El Salvador's largest circulation

daily, *La Prensa Gráfica*, did not run one story on this issue, but television channels 6 and 12 covered it for several days.

55. "Report of the Secretary-General on the United Nations Observer Mission in El Salvador," Addendum, S/25812/Add.2, May 25, 1993.

56. "Informe del secretario general," May 21, 1993, p. 15; "Nuevo informe del secretario general," November 23, 1993, pp. 12–14.

57. Interview, San Salvador, February 2, 1994.

58. "Balance laboral" [Labor assessment], *Proceso*, no. 593 (December 30, 1993):23. See also "Nuevo informe del secretario general," November 23, 1993, p. 15.

59. Telephone interview, San Salvador, February 28, 1994.

60. "Tardía y sintomática resolución de la Corte Suprema" [Tardy and symptomatic resolution by the Supreme Court], *Proceso*, no. 567 (June 16, 1993):13–15.

61. "Corte Suprema de Justicia bloquea evaluación de magistrados y jueces" [Supreme Court of Justice blocks evaluation of magistrates and judges], *campo pagado* published by the National Judicial Council, *La Prensa Gráfica*, February 25, 1994, p. 14; "Actitud del CNJ es de tipo política: Gutiérrez Castro" [CNJ attitude is political], *La Prensa Gráfica*, February 26, 1994, p. 7.

62. Interviews with Vladimiro Huaroc, coordinator of ONUSAL's San Miguel office, November 25, 1993, and an ONUSAL human rights officer, San Miguel, March 2, 1994; "Ahora en Santa Ana: 9 muertos en penal" [Now in Santa Ana: 9 dead in prison], *La Prensa Gráfica*, February 25, 1994, p. 5.

63. "Propuesta de Justicia para evitar riñas en penales" [Justice (Ministry's) proposal to avoid arguments in prisons], *La Prensa Gráfica*, February 26, 1994, p. 6.

64. *El Salvador Agreements: The Path to Peace* (San Salvador: United Nations, May 1992), pp. 59–61.

65. "Report of the Secretary-General on the United Nations Observer Mission in El Salvador," S/24833, November 23, 1992, pp. 8–9; S/25812, May 21, 1993, pp. 9–10.

66. Material in this section comes from interviews with PNC officers and agents in five departments between August 1993 and February 1994. An excellent assessment of the PNC can be found in William Stanley, *Risking Failure: The Problems and Promise o the New Civilian Police in El Salvador* (Cambridge, Mass.: Hemisphere Initiatives, Sep tember 1993).

67. "Letter dated 7 January 1993 from the Secretary-General Addressed to th President of the Security Council," S/25078, January 9, 1993. Not all officers retired a announced. General Juan Orlando Zepeda revealed that he was still *"disponible,"* in ef fect, in the reserves as late as mid-October, by way of explaining that he could not join political party while still a member of the Armed Forces. "General Zepeda dismient ingresa al partido ARENA" [General Zepeda denies joining the ARENA party], *l Diario de Hoy*, October 14, 1993.

68. *De la locura a la esperanza: La guerra de 12 años en El Salvador*, Informe de l Comisión de la Verdad para El Salvador [From madness to hope: The 12-year war in E Salvador, report of the Truth Commission for El Salvador] (New York: United Nation March 15, 1993). The Commission members were former Colombian president Belisar Betancur, Venezuelan congressman Reinaldo Figueredo Planchart, and Thom Buergenthal, a U.S. professor of international law and former president of the Inter American Court of Human Rights.

69. Interview published in *Excelsior*, March 11, 1993, cited in "Crónica del mes [Monthly chronicle], *Estudios Centroamericanos (ECA)*, no. 534-535 (April-May 1993):44

70. "Crónica del mes," pp. 448–449. In a move that defied belief, given the Tru Commission's report, Gutiérrez Castro was elected by the OAS in June 1993 to the I ter-American Judicial Committee for a term of four years.

71. Interviews with Nguyen Dong, coordinator of ONUSAL's San Miguel office, November 16, 1991; San Salvador, March 14, 1992. Nguyen was regional director until February 1992 when he was replaced by Henry Morris.

72. "Report of the Secretary-General on the United Nations Observer Mission in El Salvador," S/25812, May 21, 1993, pp. 9–10.

73. Telephone interview with ONUSAL official, May 21, 1993.

74. Security Council Resolution S/Res/832, May 27, 1993 (mimeo).

75. Interview, February 3, 1994.

76. Why was Solórzano selected? According to several CD members, who did not want to be quoted, there were two reasons. The most important was the need within the CD to share political plums among its constituent members. Solórzano was proposed by the PSD, which needed a plum. The second reason is that few realized how important the magistrate would be in the registration process.

77. Madalene O'Donnell, Jack Spence, and George Vickers, *El Salvador Elections 1994: The Voter Registration Tangle* (Cambridge, Mass.: Hemisphere Initiatives, July 1993), p. 3.

78. "Incorporación de actividades de observación electoral a ONUSAL" [Incorporation of electoral observation activities of ONUSAL], report of the Preparatory Mission, May 6, 1993, p. 13.

79. The information in these two paragraphs comes from two trips to El Salvador in August 1993, the first for personal research and the second as a member of an electoral observation delegation sponsored by the El Salvador Free and Fair Election Project in Washington, D.C.

80. "II Informe de la División Electoral de ONUSAL" [Second report of the ONUSAL Electoral Division], January 31, 1994, p. 6.

81. This anecdote was related to me by the person who asked the question and heard the response.

82. Interview with Armando Calderon Sol, San Salvador, August 31, 1993.

83. In the mid-1980s the FMLN slaughtered a herd of cattle belonging to one of the most reactionary ranchers in eastern El Salvador. The next day newspaper headlines screamed, "Terrorists murder (*asesinan*) cows."

84. All data in this paragraph are from "II Informe de la División Electoral de ONUSAL," p. 9.

85. The discussion in this section is based on personal viewing of Salvadorean television channels 6 and 12, largely during prime-time hours of 8 to 11 P.M., from January 13 to March 2, 1994.

EPILOGUE

1. Interviews with Hector Dada Hirezi, April 1994; ONUSAL electoral observer, March 29, 1994; Cabañas voter, March 20, 1994. All information in this section, unless otherwise noted, is from personal observation and conversations between March 20 and May 1, 1994.

2. The figures on abstentions are problematic because the TSE figure of 2.4 million voters is unreliable.

3. I have used "coalition" in its generic sense as well as in reference to the three leftist parties that joined together for the presidential race. In the latter case I have capitalized the word, as the Salvadoreans did during the campaign. The three parties formally called themselves La Coalicion, and their campaign propaganda usually ended with "Vote Coalition!"

4. Conversation with Tom Gibb, April 14, 1994

5. Interviews with Oscar Ortiz, Salvador Sánchez Ceren, and Salvador Cortez, April 1994.

6. Gutiérrez recorded on floor of Assembly, May 1, 1994; Ana Guadalupe interview on Channel 6, May 2, 1994.

7. "División entre ex-guerrilleros de El Salvador" [Division among Salvadorean ex-guerillas], *Nuevo Herald* (Miami), May 11, 1994, p. 1A.

8. "Amenazan a ex-guerrilleros por 'traición'" [Ex-guerrillas threatened for being 'traitors'], *Nuevo Herald*, May 7, 1994, p. 3A

Glossary

Aparcero. A person who rents a plot of land for cash and/or for a portion of the harvest.

Arzobispado. The administrative offices of the archdiocese.

Audiencia. Court or governing body of a subregion of a viceroyalty; the subregion itself. The Audiencia of Guatemala was part of the viceroyalty of New Spain (Mexico).

Cacique. An indigenous chief.

Campo pagado. A Salvadorean term for a printed paid political advertisement; includes manifestos, ads, commentaries.

Colono. A person who works on a *hacienda* in exchange for shelter and (usually) a small plot of land on which to grow subsistence crops. The relationship of a *colono* to his *patrón* is similar to that of serf to lord of the manor.

Communal lands. Tierras comunales was an institution in America for centuries before the Spanish conquest. An area of land was held in common by a group related by blood or totemic bonds but was cultivated in the Aztec world individually. This institution existed in Central America but in a less developed and less rigid form than in Mexico.

Compañero. Literally, "companion, friend"; like the English "companion," the term has the Latin root *"cum pani"* (with bread), someone with whom one shares one's bread. This etymological meaning is much closer to the Spanish connotation than "companion," a person who accompanies one. *"Compañero"* is the traditional title used among revolutionaries, replacing *"Señor"* and *"Señora"*; however, it is commonly heard in popular organizations of all kinds.

Creole. A Spanish immigrant during the colonial period.

Derechizacíon. The process of moving to the right; in political terms it signifies a swing toward right-wing policies, including repression.

Encomendero. One who held an *encomienda* grant.

Encomienda. A royal grant of authority over a defined territory; it did not include title to the land, merely control over it and all who lived on it.

Finca. A cash-crop farm of less than 100 hectares; a coffee plantation of any size.

Golpe. Coup d'etat; the sudden overthrow of a government, usually by one faction within the army.

Golpista. A military officer who participated in the planning and execution of a coup d'etat.

Guerra popular prolongada. Literally, "prolonged popular war"—a concept of revolutionary struggle that emphasizes wearing down the existing regime through tactics such as hit-and-run attacks on military installations and sabotage of power and water sources, transportation, and strategic industries.

315

Hacienda. In the colonial era, a large, self-sufficient plantation; in modern times, a large farm or ranch.

Hectare. 2.47 acres.

Ladino. A *mestizo* or an indigenous, Spanish-speaking person who has adopted Western culture and dress. The term is common in Guatemala and Chiapas, Mexico, but rare elsewhere in the region.

Machismo. The attitude that males are superior to females by virtue of their sex; also a "tough guy" image cultivated by males in an effort to impress other males or females.

Manzana. 0.7 hectare, or 1.73 acres.

Mestizo. A person of mixed indigenous and European parentage.

Milpa. A small plot of land, usually one hectare or less, which a peasant is given or rents from a *patrón* to grow subsistence crops like corn and beans.

Oreja. Literally, "ear"; a government informer.

Patrón. The owner of a farm or *hacienca*; the term is used in relation to the *colono* or *aparcero*; the boss.

Tribute. A forced contribution by Indians to the Spanish colonists. Tribute ranged from forced labor to a portion of one's crop.

Acronyms

AD	Democratic Action Party
AGEUS	General Association of Salvadorean University Students
AID	U.S. Agency for International Development
AIFLD	American Institute for Free Labor Development
AMES	Association of Women of El Salvador
AMPES	Association of Progressive Women of El Salvador
AMS	Association of Salvadorean Women
ANDA	Government water works agency
ANDES-21	National Association of Salvadorean Educators
ANEP	National Association of Private Enterprise
ANIS	National Association of Indigenous Salvadoreans
ANSESAL	Salvadorean National Security Agency
ANTEL	National Telecommunications Company
ARENA	Nationalist Republican Alliance
ASMUSA	Association of Salvadorean Women
ASTIRA	Regulatory Institute for Basic Goods Workers Union
BIRI	Rapid-response battalion
BPR	Popular Revolutionary Bloc
BRAZ	Rafael Arce Zablah battalion of FMLN
CACM	Central American Common Market
CAIN	National Center for Analysis and Investigations
CAMFA	Armed Forces Mutual Savings Bank
CCE	Central Elections Council
CCTEM	State and Municipal Workers Coordinating Council
CD	Democratic Convergence
CEB	Christian Base Community
CEDES	Salvadorean Episcopal Conference
CELAM	Conference of Latin American Bishops
CEMFA	Armed Forces Military Training Center
CEPAL	U.N. Economic Commission for Latin America
CIA	Central Intelligence Agency
CINAS	Research and Social Action Center
COACES	Cooperative Associations of El Salvador
COES	Great Confederation of Workers of El Salvador

317

CONARA	National Commission on Reconstruction of Areas
CONIP	National Conference of the Popular Church
COPAZ	National Commissions for Consolidation of Peace
COPEFA	Permanent Council of the Armed Forces
COPREFA	Press Office of the Armed Forces
CPD	Political-Diplomatic Commission of the FDR-FMLN
CRM	Revolutionary Coordination of the Masses
CST	Workers Solidarity Coordinating Committee
CTD	Democratic Workers Central
CUDI	University (UCA) Center for Documentation and Information
DCM	Deputy chief of mission
DRU	Unified Revolutionary Directorate
ECO	Businessmen, Campesinos, and Workers Party
EPR	Revolutionary Popular Army
ERP	Revolutionary Army of the People
ESA	Secret Anticommunist Army
FAL	Armed Forces of Liberation
FALANGE	Anticommunist Wars of Elimination Liberation Armed Forces
FAN	Broad Nationalist Front
FAPU	United Popular Action Front
FARN	Armed Forces of National Resistance
FD	Democratic Front
FDR	Democratic Revolutionary Front
FECCAS	Christian Federation of Salvadorean Campesinos
FENASTRAS	National Union Federation of Salvadorean Workers
FINATA	National Financial Institution for Agricultural Lands
FMLN	Farabundo Martí Front for National Liberation
FOIA	Freedom of Information Act
FPL	Popular Forces of Liberation
FRS	Salvadorean Revolutionary Front
FSLN	Sandinista National Liberation Front
FUERSA	Salvador Allende University Front of Revolutionary Students
FUSADES	Salvadorean Foundation for Economic and Social Development
FUSS	Unitary Union Federation of El Salvador
GDR	Revolutionary Democratic Government
GPP	Prolonged popular war
ICRC	International Committee of the Red Cross
INCAE	Central American Business Institute
IPSFA	Armed Forces Institute of Social Foresight
IRA	Regulatory Institute for Basic Goods
ISTA	Salvadorean Institute of Agrarian Transformation
JED	Junta Electoral Departmental
LP-28	February 28 Popular Leagues
MAC	Authentic Christian Movement
MilGroup	U.S. Military Group
MIPTES	Independent Movement of Professionals and Technicians of El Salvador

MLP	Popular Liberation Movement
MNR	Revolutionary National Movement
MOR	Revolutionary Workers' Movement
MPSC	Popular Social Christian Movement
MSN	Movement of National Solidarity
MU	Unity Movement
MUSYGES	Unitary Trade Union and Guild Movement
NCP	National Campaign Plan
NGO	Nongovernmental organization
NRP	National Reconstruction Plan
ONUSAL	United Nations Observer Mission in El Salvador
OP	Popular organization
OP-M	Political-military organization
ORDEN	Nationalist Democratic Organization
PAD	Democratic Action Party
PAISA	Salvadorean Institutional Authentic Party
PAR	Renovating Action Party
PCN	National Conciliation Party
PCS	Salvadorean Communist Party
PDC	Christian Democratic Party
PNC	National Civilian Police
POP	Popular Orientation Party
PPL	Local popular power
PPS	Salvadorean Popular Party
PRS	Party of the Salvadorean Revolution
PRTC	Revolutionary Party of Central American Workers
PRUD	Revolutionary Party of Democratic Unification
PSD	Social Democrat Party
PUN	National Union Party
RN	National Resistance
SIRE	application for voter registration card
SOUTHCOM	U.S. Southern Command
SRN	Secretariat for National Reconstruction
STISSS	Workers Union of the Salvadorean Social Security Institute
TSE	Supreme Electoral Tribunal
UCA	José Simeón Cañas Central American University
UCS	Salvadorean Communal Union
UDN	Nationalist Democratic Union
UES	University of El Salvador
UNDP	United Nations Development Program
UNO	National Opposition Union
UNOC	National Union of Workers and Campesinos
UNTS	National Unity of Salvadorean Workers
UPD	Popular Democratic Union
UPR	United to Reconstruct Plan

Bibliography

BOOKS

Alegría, Claribel. *They Won't Take Me Alive: Salvadorean Women in Struggle for National Liberation.* London: The Women's Press, 1987.

Americas Watch. *El Salvador's Decade of Terror: Human Rights Since the Assassination of Archbishop Romero.* New Haven: Yale University Press, 1991.

Anderson, Thomas P. *Matanza* [Massacre]: *El Salvador's Communist Revolt of 1932.* Lincoln: University of Nebraska Press, 1971.

_____. *The War of the Dispossessed: Honduras and El Salvador, 1969.* Lincoln: University of Nebraska Press, 1981.

Argueta, Manlio. *Cuzcatlán: Donde bate la mar del sur* [Cuzcatlán: Where the southern ocean was defeated]. Tegucigalpa: Editorial Guaymuras, 1986.

Armstrong, Robert, and Janet Shenk. *El Salvador: The Face of Revolution.* Boston: South End Press, 1982.

Arnson, Cynthia. *El Salvador: A Revolution Confronts the United States.* Washington D.C.: Institute for Policy Studies, 1982.

_____. *Crossroads: Congress, the Reagan Administration, and Central America.* New York: Pantheon, 1989.

Baily, John, et al. *El Salvador de 1840 a 1935* [El Salvador from 1840 to 1935]. San Salvador: UCA Editores, 1978.

Baloyra, Enrique A. *El Salvador in Transition.* Chapel Hill: University of North Carolina Press, 1982.

Barón Castro, Rodolfo. *La población de El Salvador* [The population of El Salvador]. San Salvador: UCA Editores, 1978.

Barry, Tom. *El Salvador: A Country Guide.* Albuquerque, N.M.: The Inter-Hemispheric Education Resource Center, 1990.

Benítez Manaut, Raúl. *La teoría militar y la guerra civil en El Salvador* [Military theory and civil war in El Salvador]. San Salvador: UCA Editores, 1989.

Bermudez, Alejandro. *Salvador al vuelo* [El Salvador: An overview]. San Salvador: n.p., 1917.

Bonner, Raymond. *Weakness and Deceit: U.S. Policy and El Salvador.* New York: Times Books, 1984.

Brannon, Max P. *El Salvador: Esquema estadística de la vida nacional* [El Salvador: Statistical outline of national life]. San Salvador: n.p., 1936.

Brodhead, Frank, and Edward S. Herman. *Demonstration Elections: U.S.-Staged Elections in the Dominican Republic, Vietnam, and El Salvador.* Boston: South End Press, 1984.

Browning, David. *El Salvador: Landscape and Society.* Oxford: Clarendon Press, 1971.

321

Cagan, Beth, and Steven Cagan. *This Promised Land, El Salvador: The Refugee Community of Colomoncagua and Their Return to Morazán.* New Brunswick, N.J.: Rutgers University Press, 1991.

Cardenal, Rodolfo. *Historia de una esperanza: Vida de Rutilio Grande* [Story of a hope: The life of Rutilio Grande]. San Salvador: UCA Editores, 1985.

Carnage Again: Preliminary Report on Violations of the Laws of War by Both Sides in the November 1989 Offensive in El Salvador. New York and Washington, D.C.: The Americas Watch Committee, 1989.

Carpio, Salvador Cayetano. *Secuestro y capucha en un país del "mundo libre"* [Kidnapped and hooded in a country of the "free world"]. San Salvador: UCA Editores, 1979.

Carranza, Salvador. *Mártires de la UCA: 16 de noviembre de 1989* [Martyrs of the UCA: November 16, 1989]. San Salvador: UCA Editores, 1990.

Carrigan, Ana. *Salvador Witness: The Life and Calling of Jean Donovan.* New York: Ballantine Books, 1984.

Castro Morán, Mariano. *Función política del ejército salvadoreño en el presente siglo* [The political function of the Salvadorean military in this century]. San Salvador: UCA Editores, 1984.

Clariond, Jean-Louis. *El Salvador arde: La verdad sobre la tragedia salvadoreña* [El Salvador in flames: The truth about the Salvadorean tragedy]. San José, Costa Rica: n.p., 1981.

Clements, Charles. *Witness to War: An American Doctor in El Salvador.* New York: Bantam Books, 1984.

Colindres, Eduardo. *Fundamentos económicos de la burguesia salvadoreña* [Economic fundamentals of the Salvadorean bourgeoisie]. San Salvador: UCA Editores, 1978.

Condoning the Killing: Ten Years of Massacres in El Salvador. Washington, D.C.: EPICA, 1990.

Dada Hirezi, Héctor. *La economía de El Salvador y la integración centroamericana 1945–1960* [The economy of El Salvador and Central American integration 1945–1960]. San Salvador: UCA Editores, 1978.

Dalton, Roque. *El Salvador* (Monografía) [El Salvador (monograph)]. San Salvador: Editorial Universitaria, 1979.

_____. *Miguel Mármol.* San José, Costa Rica: EDUCA, 1982.

Devine, Frank J. *El Salvador: Embassy Under Attack.* New York: Vantage Press, 1981.

Díaz, Nidia. *I Was Never Alone.* Melbourne, Australia: Ocean Press, 1992.

Dilling, Yvonne, with Ingrid Rogers. *In Search of Refuge.* Scottdale, Pa.: Herald Press, 1984.

A Dream Compels Us: Voices of Salvadorean Women. New Americas Press, ed. Boston: South End Press, 1989.

Duarte, José Napoleón. *My Story.* New York: G. P. Putnam's Sons, 1986.

Dunkerly, James. *The Long War: Dictatorship and Revolution in El Salvador.* London: Junction Books, 1982.

El "Cipitío" en El Salvador Sheraton: Un round de 11 días de 10 años de guerra [The "leprechaun" of the El Salvador Sheraton: A round of 11 days in 10 years of war]. San Salvador: Editorial Universitaria, 1990.

El Salvador Agreements: The Path to Peace. New York: United Nations, 1992.

El Salvador: Concertación y nuevo modelo económico [Concertation and the new economic model]. Mexico City: CINAS [Centro de Investigación y Acción Social], no. 12, June 1990.

El Salvador: Guerra, política y paz (1979–1988) [El Salvador: War, politics, and peace (1979–1988)]. El Salvador: CINAS, 1988.

El Salvador: Human Rights Dismissed: A Report on 16 Unresolved Cases. New York: Lawyers Committee for Human Rights, 1986.

El Salvador: War and Health. San Salvador: Committee of Professional Health Workers, 1983.

Galdámez, Pablo. *The Faith of a People: The Life of a Basic Christian Community in El Salvador, 1970–1980.* Maryknoll, N.Y.: Orbis Books, 1986.

Gelber, George, and Anjali Sundaram. *A Decade of War: El Salvador Confronts the Future.* New York: Monthly Review Press, 1991.

Gettleman, Marvin E., et al. *El Salvador: Central America in the New Cold War.* 2d ed. New York: Grove Press, 1981.

Guerra, Tomás. *El Salvador en la hora de la liberación* [El Salvador in the hour of liberation]. San José, Costa Rica: n.p., 1980.

Guidos Vejar, Rafael. *El ascenso del militarismo en El Salvador* [The rise of militarism in El Salvador]. San Salvador: UCA Editores, 1980.

LaFeber, Walter. *Inevitable Revolutions: The United States and Central America.* 2d ed. New York: W. W. Norton and Company, 1993.

Land Mines in El Salvador and Nicaragua: The Civilian Victims. New York and Washington, D.C.: The Americas Watch Committee, 1986.

Lernoux, Penny. *Cry of the People.* New York: Doubleday, 1980.

Lindo-Fuentes, Héctor. *Weak Foundations: The Economy of El Salvador in the Nineteenth Century 1821–1898.* Berkeley: University of California Press, 1990.

López, Carlos Roberto. *Industrialización y urbanización en El Salvador 1969–1979* [Industrialization and urbanization in El Salvador 1969–1979]. San Salvador: UCA Editores, 1983.

López Vigil, Mario. *Don Lito de El Salvador: Habla un campesino* [Don Lito of El Salvador: A peasant speaks]. San Salvador: UCA Editores, 1987.

_____. *Muerte y vida en Morazán: Testimonio de un sacerdote* [Death and life in Morazán: Testimony of a priest]. San Salvador: UCA Editores, 1987.

Lungo Uclés, Mario. *La lucha de las masas en El Salvador* [Mass struggle in El Salvador]. San Salvador: UCA Editores, 1987.

_____. *El Salvador en los 80: Contra-insurgencia y revolución* [El Salvador in the 80s: Counterinsurgency and revolution]. San José, Costa Rica: Editorial Universitaria Centroamericana, 1990.

MacLean, John. *Prolonging the Agony: The Human Cost of Low-Intensity Warfare in El Salvador.* London: El Salvador Committee for Human Rights, 1987.

MacLeod, Murdo J. *Spanish Central America: A Socioeconomic History 1520–1720.* Berkeley: University of California Press, 1973.

Manwaring, Max G., and Court Prisk, eds. *El Salvador at War: An Oral History.* Washington, D.C.: National Defense University Press, 1988.

Martínez, Ana Guadalupe. *Las cárceles clandestinas de El Salvador.* [The clandestine prisons of El Salvador]. San Salvador: UCA Editores, 1992.

Mayorga Quiroz, Román. *La universidad para el cambio social* [The university for social change]. San Salvador: UCA Editores, 1978.

McClintock, Michael. *The American Connection: State Terror and Public Resistance in El Salvador.* Vol. 1. London: Zed Books, 1985.

Menjívar, Rafael. *Crisis del desarrollismo: Caso El Salvador* [Crisis of development: The case of El Salvador]. San José, Costa Rica: EDUCA, 1977.

Metzi, Francisco. *The People's Remedy: The Struggle for Health Care in El Salvador's War of Liberation.* New York: Monthly Review Press, 1988.

Montes, Segundo. *Estudio sobre estraficación social en El Salvador* [Study of social stratification in El Salvador]. San Salvador: UCA Editores, 1979.

324 BIBLIOGRAPHY

_____. *El agro salvadoreño (1973–1980)* [Salvadorean agriculture (1973–1980)]. San Salvador: UCA Department of Sociology and Political Science, 1980.

_____. *El Salvador: Las fuerzas sociales en la presente coyuntura (Enero 1980 a Diciembre 1983)* [Social forces in the present juncture (January 1980 to December 1983)]. San Salvador: UCA Department of Sociology, 1984.

Morán, Francisco. *Las jornados cívicas de abril y mayo de 1944* [The civic marches of April and May 1944]. San Salvador: Editorial Universitaria, 1979.

North, Liisa. *Bitter Grounds: Roots of Revolt in El Salvador*. Toronto: Between the Lines, 1981.

Parkman, Patricia. *Nonviolent Insurrection in El Salvador: The Fall of Maximiliano Hernández Martínez*. Tucson: University of Arizona Press, 1988.

Pinto, Jorge. *El grito del más pequeño* [The cry of the smallest]. Mexico: Editorial Comete y Licenciada, 1985.

Ruhl, Arthur. *The Central Americans*. New York: n.p., 1927.

Rutilio Grande: Mártir de la evangelización rural en El Salvador [Rutilio Grande: Martyr of rural evangelization in El Salvador]. San Salvador: UCA Editores, 1978.

Shaull, Wendy. *Tortillas, Beans, and M-16s: A Year with the Guerrillas in El Salvador*. London: Pluto Press, 1990.

Smyth, Frank, and Riordan Roett. *Dialogue and Armed Conflict: Negotiating the Civil War in El Salvador*. Washington, D.C.: Johns Hopkins Foreign Policy Institute, 1988.

Thompson, Marilyn. *Women of El Salvador: The Price of Freedom*. Philadelphia: Institute for the Study of Human Issues, 1986.

Underwriting Injustice: AID and El Salvador's Judicial Reform Program. New York: Lawyers Committee for Human Rights, 1989.

Urrutia Glamenco, Carlos. *La ciudad de San Salvador* [The city of San Salvador]. San Salvador: n.p., 1924.

Villacorta, Emilio. *Por la patria y su gobierno* [For the homeland and its government]. San Salvador: n.p., 1919.

Villalobos, Joaquin, and Claudio Armijo. *El Salvador: Balance y perspectivas de la guerra* [El Salvador: Assessment and perspectives on the war]. Buenos Aires: Editorial Antarca, 1986.

Webre, Stephen. *José Napoleón Duarte and the Christian Democratic Party in Salvadoran Politics 1960–1972*. Baton Rouge: Louisiana State University Press, 1979.

White, Alastair. *El Salvador*. London: Ernest Benn; Boulder, Colo.: Westview Press, 1973.

Williams, Robert G. *Export Agriculture and the Crisis in Central America*. Chapel Hill: University of North Carolina Press, 1986.

THESES

Chavarría Kleinhenm, Francisco. "Fundamentos políticos, económicos y sociales de la evolución y desarrollo del movimiento sindical en El Salvador" [Political, economic, and social fundamentals of the evolution and development of the union movement in El Salvador]. Thesis for the *Licenciatura* in sociology, University of Costa Rica, 1977.

Cruz, Octavio. "Conciencia y cambio social en la hacienda Tres Ceibas (El Salvador)" [Consciousness and social change in the Tres Ceibas *hacienda*]. Thesis for the *licenciatura* in sociology, University of Costa Rica, 1978.

Elam, Robert Varney. "Appeal to Arms: Army and Politics in El Salvador 1931–1964." Ph.D. dissertation, University of New Mexico, 1968.

Sermeño Zelidon, Carmen. "Las nuevas formas de dominación política en El Salvador 1972–1977" [New forms of political domination in El Salvador 1972–1977]. Thesis for the *licenciatura* in sociology, University of Costa Rica, 1979.

Wilson, Everett Alan. "The Crisis of National Integration in El Salvador 1919–1935." Ph.D. dissertation, Stanford University, 1968.

ARTICLES

Arias Gómez, Jorge. "Augustín Farabundo Martí (Esbozo biográfico)" [Augustín Farabundo Martí (biographical sketch)]. *La Universidad* (University of El Salvador, San Salvador), no. 4 (July–August 1971):181–240.

"A sus ordenes, mi capital" [Aye, aye, sir]. *Estudios Centroamericanos (ECA)*, 31, no. 337 (November 1976):637–643.

Burke, Melvin. "El sistema de plantación y la proletarización del trabajo agrícola en El Salvador" [The plantation system and the proletarization of agricultural work in El Salvador]. *ECA* 31, no. 335–336 (September–October 1976):473–486.

"Central America: Patterns of Regional Economic Integration." *Bank of London and South American Review*, June 1979.

Colindres, Eduardo. "La tenencia de la tierra en El Salvador" [Land tenancy in El Salvador]. *ECA* 31, no. 335–336 (September–October 1976):463–472.

Cuellar Zaavedra, Oscar. "Las tendencias de cambio en Centro América y el caso de El Salvador: El periodo 1960–1975" [Tendencies for change in Central America and the case of El Salvador: The 1960–1975 period]. UCA,1977 (mimeo).

Flores Macal, Mario. "Historia de la Universidad de El Salvador" [History of the University of El Salvador]. *Anuario de Estudios Centroamericanos* 2 (1976):107–140.

Forché, Carolyn, and Philip Wheaton. "History and Motivations of U.S. Involvement in the Control of the Peasant Movement in El Salvador: The Role of AIFLD in the Agrarian Reform Process 1970–1980." EPICA, Washington, D.C., 1980 (mimeo).

Grande, Rutilio. "Aguilares: Una experiencia de evangelización rural parroquial" [Aguilares: An experience of rural parish evangelization]. *Búsqueda* 3, no. 8 (March 1975):21–45.

"H.O." "La iglesia y los acontecimientos de mayo en El Salvador" [The church and the events of May in El Salvador]. *ECA* 34, no. 368 (June 1979):436–439.

Larín, Arístides Augusto. "Historia del movimiento sindical de El Salvador" [History of the union movement in El Salvador]. *La Universidad*, no. 4 (July–August 1971):135–179.

Mena, David. "Estado y grupos dominates en El Salvador" [State and dominant groups in El Salvador]. Paper presented at the Third Central American Sociology Conference, Tegucigalpa, Honduras, April 24–29, 1979 (mimeo).

Montgomery, Tommie Sue. "Fighting Guerrillas: The United States and Low-Intensity Conflict in El Salvador." *New Political Science* 18/19 (Fall/Winter 1990):21–54.

———. "El Salvador." In Charles Ameringer, ed., *Political Parties of the Americas, 1980s to 1990s*. Westport, Conn.: Greenwood Press, 1992.

———. "Armed Struggle and Popular Resistance in El Salvador: The Struggle for Peace." In Barry Carr and Steve Ellner, eds., *The Latin American Left from the Fall of Allende to Perestroika*. Boulder: Westview Press, 1993.

Paredes, Ivan D. "La situación de la Iglesia Católica en El Salvador y su influjo social" [The situation of the Catholic Church in El Salvador and its social influence]. *ECA* 34, no. 369–370 (July–August 1979):601–614.

Sobrino, Jon. "La iglesia en el actual proceso del país" [The church in the current process of the country]. *ECA* 34, no. 372–373 (October–November 1979):905–922.

Villalobos, Joaquin. "A Democratic Revolution for El Salvador." *Foreign Policy* 74 (Spring 1989):103–122.

_____. "Popular Insurrection: Desire or Reality?" *Latin American Perspectives* 62 (Summer 1989):5–37.

Zamora, Rubén. "¿Segura de vida o despojo? Análisis político de la transformación agraria" [Life insurance or plunder? Political analysis of the agrarian transformation]. *ECA* 31, no. 335-336 (September-October 1976):511–534.

DOCUMENTS

Arnson, Cynthia. "Background Information on El Salvador and US Military Assistance to Central America." Update no. 4. Institute for Policy Studies, Washington, D.C., April 1981 (mimeo).

"Como nacemos y que hacemos" [How we were formed and what we do]. San Salvador: Asociacion de Mujeres de El Salvador [Women's Association of El Salvador], August 1982.

De la locura a la esperanza: La guerra de doce años en El Salvador [From madness to hope: The twelve-year war in El Salvador]. Report of the Truth Commission for El Salvador. New York: United Nations, 1993.

Diskin, Martin, et al. *El Salvador Land Reform 1980–1981: Impact Audit.* Boston: Oxfam America, 1982.

El Salvador Is Your Best Buy. San Salvador: Salvadorean Foundation for Economic and Social Development (FUSADES), 1989.

Indicadores económicos y sociales Enero–Junio 1979 [Economic and social indicators January–June 1979]. San Salvador: Ministry of Planning, 1979.

"Mensajes y discurso del presidente Alvaro Magaña" [Messages and speeches of President Alvaro Magaña], May–December 1982. San Salvador: Secretariat of Information of the President of the Republic, 1983.

"Paying to Lose Our Jobs." Special report prepared for the National Labor Committee in Support of Worker and Human Rights in Central America. New York: National Labor Committee, 1992.

"¡Por que lucha el FMLN?" [Why is the FMLN fighting?]. El Salvador: Ediciones Sistema Radio Venceremos, January 1984.

Romero y Galdámez, Oscar A., and Arturo Rivera Damas. "La iglesia y las organizaciones políticas populares" [The church and the popular political organizations]. Pastoral letter of Monseñor Romero and third pastoral letter of Monseñor Rivera Damas, with Annexes. El Salvador, October 1978.

U.S. Congress, House. "Human Rights in Nicaragua, Guatemala, and El Salvador: Implications for U.S. Policy." Hearings before the Subcommittee on International Organizations of the Committee on International Relations, 94th Congress, 2d session, June 8 and 9, 1976.

About the Book and Author

Since the first edition of this book appeared in 1982, El Salvador has experienced the most radical social change in its history. Ten years of civil war, in which a tenacious and creative revolutionary movement battled a larger, better-equipped, U.S.-supported army to a standstill, have ended with twenty months of negotiations and a peace accord that promises to change the course of Salvadorean society and politics.

This book traces the history of El Salvador, focusing on the two actors—the oligarchy and the armed forces—that shaped the Salvadorean economy and political system. Concentrating on the period since 1960, the author sheds new light on the U.S. role in the increasing militarization of the country and the origins of the oligarchy-army rupture in 1979. Separate chapters deal with the Catholic church and the revolutionary organizations, which challenged the status quo after 1968. In the new edition, Dr. Montgomery continues the story from 1982 to the present, offering a detailed account of the evolution of the war. She examines why Duarte's two inaugural promises, peace and economic prosperity, could not be fulfilled and analyzes the electoral victory of the oligarchy in 1989. The final chapters closely follow the peace negotiations, ending with an assessment of the peace accords and an evaluation of the future prospects for El Salvador. An Epilogue analyzes the 1994 elections. Dr. Montgomery's prognosis in the first edition—that no lasting, viable political solution was possible without the participation of the revolutionary organizations—has been borne out by events: Today the FMLN is a legal political party.

Ignacio Martín-Baró, who began the Introduction to the book, held a Ph.D. in social psychology from the University of Chicago and was vice rector of the UCA at the time of his death. Rodolfo Cardenal, who finished the Introduction, is currently UCA vice rector for social outreach.

Tommie Sue Montgomery has taught at Dickinson College, Agnes Scott College, and Emory University. She is currently a senior research associate with the North-South Center at the University of Miami.

327

Index

329

National Association of Private
  Enterprise (ANEP), 68, 130, 131
National Association of Salvadorean
  Educators. *See* ANDES-21
National Campaign Plan, 167, 168
National Center for Analysis and
  Investigations. *See* CAIN
National Civilian Police (PNC), 6, 224,
  237–241
  government efforts to undermine, 239–
    241
  lack of resources, 240
  ONUSAL and, 237–238
  recruitment, training, and deployment,
    237–239
National Commission for the
  Consolidation of Peace. *See* COPAZ
National Commission for the Restoration
  of Areas. *See* CONARA
National Conciliation Party (PCN), 53,
  54, 62, 67, 157, 179, 196, 197, 208, 256
  origins, 277(n5)
  splits, 163
National Conference of the Popular
  Church (CONIP), 144–145
National Financial Institution for
  Agricultural Lands. *See* FINATA
National Guard, 64
  efforts to convert into Frontier Police,
    246
  and extortion, 16
  origins, 30–32
  and repression, 40, 48, 56, 67, 73, 91, 97,
    106, 108, 129, 182
National Intelligence Agency (ANI), 76
Nationalist Democratic Organization. *See*
  ORDEN
Nationalist Democratic Union (UDN), 62,
  105, 108, 253
  merges with MPSC and PSD to found
  Democratic Convergence Party, 254
Nationalist Feminine League, 77
Nationalist Liberation Movement (MLN)
  (Guatemala), 132
Nationalist Republican Alliance. *See*
  ARENA
National Judicial Council, 235
National Opposition Union (UNO), 62–
  64, 67
National Police, 43, 67, 129
  origins, 30

in PNC, 239
and repression, 72, 74, 108, 134
National Reconstruction Plan, 228, 229.
  See also Peace process
National Resistance (RN), 104, 105, 107
National Telephone Company. *See*
  ANTEL
National Union Party (PUN), 43
National Unity of Salvadorean Workers.
  See UNTS
National University. *See* University of El
  Salvador
National Worker-Peasant Union. *See*
  UNOC
Navarro, Alfonso, 93, 98
NGOs. *See* Nongovernmental
  organizations
Nguyen, Dong, 245
Nicaragua, 3, 5, 21, 36, 74, 115, 117, 175
1989 offensive, 217–220
1932 peasant uprising, 36–37
Nixon, Richard, 52
Nongovermental organizations (NGOs),
  228, 229, 230, 232, 241
  FMLN related, 217, 311(n46)
  and 1994 elections, 251
  See also Popular organizations
Norland, Rod, 166
Nutting, Wallace, 169

Ochoa, Sigfrido, 152, 168–169
Official party, 38, 53. *See also* National
  Conciliation Party; National Union
  Party, *Pro-Patria;* Revolutionary
  Party of Democratic Unification
Oligarchy, 2, 9, 35, 39, 40, 51, 74, 77
  and coup attempt, 1980, 135
  and death squads, 127, 132–133
  economic attitudes, 29, 30, 32, 33, 34
  "Fourteen Families," 2
  and industrialization, 47
  kidnapping of, 205–206
  opposition to reform, 29, 68
  origins, 26–32
  rupture with army, 74
  and UCA, 92
ONUCA (U.N. observer mission in
  Central America), 209
ONUSAL (United Nations Observer
  Mission in El Salvador), 7, 19, 230–
  231, 232, 237, 243–248